The Handbook
of MIS Application
Software Testing

ANDREWS AND LEVENTHAL   Fusion: Integrating IE, CASE, and JAD
AUGUST   Joint Application Design
BAUDIN   Manufacturing Systems Analysis with Application to Production Scheduling
BELLIN AND SUCHMAN   Structured Systems Development Manual
BLOCK   The Politics of Projects
BODDIE   Crunch Mode: Building Effective Systems on a Tight Schedule
BOULDIN   Agents of Change: Managing the Introduction of Automated Tools
BRILL   Building Controls into Structured Systems
BRILL   Techniques of EDP Project Management: A Book of Readings
CHANG   Principles of Visual Programming Systems
COAD AND YOURDON   Object-Oriented Analysis, 2/E
COAD AND YOURDON   Object-Oriented Design
CONNELL AND SHAFER   Structured Rapid Prototyping
CONSTANTINE AND YOURDON   Structured Design
DeGRACE AND STAHL   Wicked Problems, Righteous Solutions
DeMARCO   Controlling Software Projects
DeMARCO   Structured Analysis and System Specification
EMBLEY, KURTZ, AND WOODFIELD   Object-Oriented Systems Analysis
FLAVIN   Fundamental Concepts in Information Modeling
FOLLMAN   Business Applications with Microcomputers
FOURNIER   Practical Guide to Structured System Development and Maintenance
GLASS   Software Conflict
GROCHOW SAA: A Guide to Implementing IBM's Systems Application Architecture
KING   Current Practices in Software Development: A Guide to Successful Systems
KING   Project Management Made Simple
LARSON   Interactive Software: Tools for Building Interactive User Interfaces
MARTIN   Transaction Processing Facility: A Guide for Application Programmers
McMENAMIN AND PALMER   Essential System Design
MOSLEY   The Handbook of MIS Application Software Testing
PAGE-JONES   Practical Guide to Structured Systems Design, 2/E
PINSON   Designing Screen Interfaces in C
PUTNAM AND MYERS   Measures for Excellence: Reliable Software on Time, within
   Budget
RIPPS   An Implementation Guide to Real-Time Programming
RODGERS   ORACLE®: A Database Developer's Guide
RODGERS   UNIX®: Database Management Systems
SERBANATI   Integrating Tools for Software Development
SHLAER AND MELLOR   Object Lifecycles: Modeling the World in States
SHLAER AND MELLOR   Object-Oriented Systems Analysis: Modeling the World in
   Data
SHILLER   Software Excellence
TOIGO   Disaster Recovery Planning: Managing Risk and Catastrophe in Information
   Systems
VESELY   Strategic Data Management: The Key to Corporate Competitiveness
WARD   System Development Without Pain
WARD AND MELLOR   Structured Development for Real-Time Systems
YOURDON   Decline and Fall of the American Programmer
YOURDON   Managing the Structured Techniques, 4/E
YOURDON   Managing the System Life Cycle, 2/E
YOURDON   Modern Structured Analysis
YOURDON   Structured Walkthroughs, 4/E
YOURDON   Techniques of Program Structure and Design

The Handbook of MIS Application Software Testing

Methods, Techniques, and Tools for Assuring Quality Through Testing

Daniel J. Mosley

YOURDON PRESS
P T R PRENTICE HALL BUILDING
Englewood Cliffs, New Jersey 07632

Library of Congress Cataloging-in-Publication Data

Mosley, Daniel J.
    The handbook of MIS application software testing : methods,
techniques, and tools for assuring quality through testing / Daniel
J. Mosley.
        p.   cm.—(Yourdon Press computing series)
    Includes bibliogrpahical references and index.
    ISBN 0-13-907007-9
    1. Application software—Testing.   2. Management information
systems.   I. Title.   II. Series.
QA76.76.A65M68   1993
005.1'4—dc20   92-4352
                                                                    CIP

Editorial/production supervision: Mary P. Rottino
Cover design: Joe Di Domenico
Prepress buyer: Mary McCartney
Manufacturing buyer: Susan Brunke
Acquisitions editor: Paul Becker

 © 1993 by P T R Prentice Hall
Prentice-Hall, Inc.
A Paramount Communications Company
Englewood Cliffs, New Jersey 07632

The publisher offers discounts on this book when ordered
in bulk quantities. For more information, write:

    Special Sales/Professional Marketing
    P T R Prentice-Hall, Inc.
    Englewood Cliffs, New Jersey 07632

Printed in the United States of America

10 9 8 7 6 5 4 3 2

ISBN 0-13-907007-9

Prentice-Hall International (UK) Limited, *London*
Prentice-Hall of Australia Pty. Limited, *Sydney*
Prentice-Hall Canada Inc., *Toronto*
Prentice-Hall Hispanoamericana, S.A., *Mexico*
Prentice-Hall of India Private Limited, *New Delhi*
Prentice-Hall of Japan, Inc., *Tokyo*
Simon & Schuster Asia Pte. Ltd., *Singapore*
Editora Prentice-Hall do Brasil, Ltda., *Rio de Janeiro*

Dedication

This book is dedicated to my partner in life, Elizabeth, to my daughter Paige, to my sister Sue for the day two believers moved the mountain, and in particular, to my great grandfather, the late Thomas A. Williams, whose advice and counsel have directed me even in his absence, and foremost, to the father, the son, and the holy spirit.

Contents

Foreword

Testing has been part of the culture of programmers and software engineers since the first binary-code machine-language program was written—but only recently has it begun to enter the consciousness of the general public, which depends on properly functioning software more and more each day. An article in the June 14, 1992 *New York Sunday Times* magazine section described the year-long battle by popular author James Gleick to persuade Microsoft to adequately test, and then correct, numerous errors in the Word-for-Windows word processing program. As millions of ordinary citizens begin to read that respectable software companies have a category of bug called "Will Not Fix," and that the most egregious bugs can take more than a year to track down, perhaps they will begin to clamor more loudly for adequate testing of the software we write. After 45 years of shoddy testing in the software industry, it should not surprise us if the general public comes to the conclusion that we cannot or will not do an adequate testing job voluntarily—and the next generation of software engineers may find itself working under far stricter standards of behavior than my generation would have dreamed possible.

If this should happen, it is quite likely that Dan Mosley's new handbook will become standard equipment for professional software engineers who want to be licensed, certified, and generally respected for the work they do. As Mosley points out in his preface, the problem is not so much a lack of adequate methods, techniques, or tools in the testing trade—but rather a lack of *practice* of those methods. Certainly, there is a great deal more to be accomplished by computer scientists and by the gurus of software testing; but the first order of business is to raise the "state of the practice" up to the current state of the art. A solid, comprehensive handbook like Mosley's should prove to be of immeasurable value in that effort.

Comprehensiveness is a mandatory feature in anything that purports to be a "handbook"—such a tome must cater to a wide variety of needs, and must cover the spectrum from "preventive" techniques for minimizing the likelihood that bugs will exist in the first place, to "discovery" techniques for finding them once they exist. It should come as no surprise, in this context, that Mosley places a great deal of emphasis on software quality and the software *process*—for ultimately, it is the visible, repeatable, measurable process of software development that will minimize the creation of software defects.

For those who want to plunge into the "practical" aspects of testing, all of the obvious topics are covered: test plans; black-box/white box strategies; control flow graphs; equivalence partitioning and boundary analysis; cause-effect graphs; decision logic tables; top-down testing, bottom-up testing, integration testing, and system testing; walkthroughs and inspections; and testing tools. And for those who want to get their hands on everything *else* that has ever been written on software testing, Mosley provides a thorough bibliography of some 300 books and papers.

There are only a few classics in the field of software testing—notably the books by Myers, Beizer, and Hetzel—and I think there is a good chance that Mosley's compendium will join that modest collection. The fact that Glenford Myers' 1979 book is still referred to as a "bible" more than a decade after it was written suggests that many of the principles of software testing are timeless. Still, some things *do* change: Myers wrote his book before the PC revolution, before 4GLs, and before the creation of numerous other hardware and software technologies with which the complex systems of the 90s are being built. Even if Mosley's work becomes an instant classic, it too will eventually show its age; in this regard, the book's most valuable component may be an appendix listing some 38 journals and magazines which will hopefully continue to publish up-to-date testing methods and techniques long after the current generation of software engineers has retired to a noncomputerized old-age home.

Perhaps the problem that North American software engineers have with testing is that it isn't sexy. Perhaps the only way Dan Mosley could get his book on a best-seller list would be to retitle it "Sex and the Computer: A Lover's Guide to Better Testing," complete with suggestive centerfold pictures. But it's also possible that we have developed this pervasive opinion that testing is boring because we have only focused on finding defects *after* they have been introduced into the software; and perhaps we have considered it boring because we have had the luxury of selling our software to a marketplace hungry for products regardless of their high price and low quality.

If the experience of other industries (steel, autos, televisions, etc) during the past 20 years is any guideline, this situation will not continue: software suppliers around the world will begin offering higher-quality products to the marketplace, and will do so at substantially lower cost. These software suppliers are already beginning to emerge, not only in North America and Europe, but in numerous Third World countries hungry to build competitive export industries.

They will *not* accomplish this in the manner practiced by many of the PC-software companies that are currently creating products with "Will Not Fix" bugs—namely, by employing an average of one software tester for every programmer (reminiscent of the apocryphal stories of Depression-era government policies of hiring one person to dig a hole in the ground, and another person to shovel the dirt back into the hole). Nor will they employ the tactics of sponsoring beer-and-pizza parties in a dozen cities around the country to exercise their new software products, hoping that software hackers will emerge from the woodwork and find bugs that the software development team couldn't find on their own. Instead, they will concentrate on *smart* testing, using the best tools, techniques, and methods available. And while this new breed of software supplier will probably invent a few new testing methods of its own, chances are that it will depend primarily on commercially available testing tools and proven testing practices— practices documented in comprehensive books like Dan Mosley's *The Handbook of MIS Application Software Testing*.

Thus, maybe we should be excited about Mosley's book for a very simple reason: it could help save our jobs.

Edward Yourdon

Preface

If you are familiar with the discipline of Software Testing, as you open this book you are probably thinking to yourself, why another software testing text covering well-worn and time-honored testing principles? The answer is because: (1) this writing is aimed at a new audience (Management Information Systems—MIS—professionals and their partners the end users), the majority of whom are not versed in software testing concepts; (2) it offers as a foundation a subset of proven testing approaches which until now could not be found in a single text because they were scattered piecemeal about the testing literature; (3) it discusses software testing from a practical perspective which does not require the reader to have a technical background to grasp its content, even though the content is to a great extent technical in nature.

Thus, the purpose of this book is to give its readers practical knowledge in the establishment of software testing standards and the planning of software testing activities; for organizing the testing function within MIS and determining the associated job descriptions; in the construction of a software testing methodology which includes methods, tools, and techniques for test planning, test execution, and test analysis and reporting. It contains a useful mixture of "strategic" and "tactical" knowledge for testing managers and testing specialists (these roles are described in Chapter Two).

The need for this book is well established. In 1983, Beck and Perkins surveyed software method, technique, and tool usage in MIS organizations. Their results confirmed what most of us in the information systems development industry suspected. Methods, techniques, and tools for testing application software represent one of the least understood and applied aspects of systems development. The sad commentary is that even though major testing texts were written over the 25 or so years prior to and have been revised subsequent to this survey (circa 1988), the state of testing in the MIS field has changed very little. This position is supported by the skyrocketing enrollments in software testing seminars and the reported sales of existing software testing reference/textbooks. This is ample evidence of an accelerated attempt by the MIS public to educate itself in this area.

William Hetzel and David Gelperin, the co-founders of Software Quality Engineering, recently (April 1991 in *American Programmer*) listed a number of unresolved issues concerning software testing practice (see the discussion in Chapter Two). Prominent among those issues is the fact that information systems industry testing practices are lagging far behind accepted "best" testing practices. This further corroborates the need for a practical MIS-oriented testing book.

These statistics do not indicate that adequate software testing methods, techniques, and tools are not available, but rather, that practicing information systems professionals are not aware of them or are adverse to implementing them. What they convey is that software testing activities are undefined and are implemented either haphazardly or not at all. The term ad hoc has been applied to describe this improvised approach to testing. While some authorities may argue that an improvisational approach is both necessary and sufficient because software testing must be directed toward a particular end (which as was gruffly pointed out to me is another meaning of ad hoc), I strongly disagree. Flexibility of methods, techniques, and tools is required, but within predetermined bounds.

It is gradually being realized that providing the enterprise with information requires software systems that are "engineered" as opposed to "crafted." To many people, the term engineered means inflexible, but this is a major misconception. Engineers are forced to make many environmentally related compromises when implementing their system designs. The same is true of information systems professionals. The flexibility requirement comes because of the need to make trade-offs when converting a logical model into a physical reality. Methodology (methods, techniques, and tools) gives us guidelines for establishing a process of designing and constructing software systems, but translation of these abstractions into a physical process while implementing them offers a lot of opportunity for flexibility within prespecified standards. This is what James Martin and others have identified as the discipline of *Information Engineering*.

Software testing activities must be based in established software development standards, and those standards must be used to develop and implement a plan for testing. In essence, systems development including testing must be an engineered process. The urgent need for a standardized/engineered approach to software testing is magnified by the fact that the most respected and referenced text in the industry today was published 12 years ago, and is entitled, *The Art of Software Testing*, not *Software Testing for Information Engineers*. An engineering approach to software testing should be a compromise of the latter meaning of ad hoc within a defined methodological framework which rigorously guides the process. Some individuals and organizations have defined formal testing methodologies, but many are too inflexible, and thus, useless.

For example, I recently did a series of in-house testing seminars for a very large telecommunications company. They decided to use the educational resources of the Center for the Study of Data Processing, instead of those of a much larger, well-known consulting firm because that firm was unwilling to customize their testing methods to the company's needs. The consultant/trainers believed in only one way to do software testing and urged the client company to conform to their approach. The consulting firm's methodology was focused on testing as a component of new system development; however, the client organization was primarily doing maintenance of legacy (also known as "embedded" systems in some circles) systems and very little new development. The consulting firm's tunnel vision with respect to testing cost them business.

With respect to this book, I hope I have avoided this kind of software testing myopia by offering a variety of testing methods, techniques, and tools which can be used for both development and maintenance, and leaving the choice of testing activities and their combined implementation as a testing process that is a component of your system development methodology up to you, the reader.

Although defined testing practices must be an essential part of an IS organization's development standards, the coup de grace is that the majority of IS departments have not yet defined and standardized their overall systems development process. The advent of Computer-Aided Software Engineering (CASE) has been succeeded by an awareness that technology to support software development can only effectively support a defined development process. So, the search for the "ideal" development methodology is under way. Thus, this is the appropriate time to lobby for the inclusion of software testing methods, techniques, and tools in the new automated and defined development process.

It is absolutely necessary that software testing procedures are included in this optimal development environment because a separate "testing methodology" would only add additional overhead to the development cycle. Testing methods, techniques, and tools should instead be integrated into the chosen development methodology. Furthermore, given the uniqueness of each IS organization, and its development needs, the choice of and implementation of a methodology will vary almost infinitely, as will the desired testing activities embedded in that methodology. There are already software products on the market which automate the selection of a unique set of methods, techniques, and tools for specific development project needs. The software tools that do this, and the methodological guidelines that serve as standards, are "meta-methodologies."

With these thoughts in mind, I decided that a comprehensive software testing reference work describing the available methods, techniques, and tools which includes clearly illustrated examples of their usage was the appropriate direction to proceed. As I have indicated, the majority of the methods, techniques, and tools are not new, and are recorded elsewhere, but obviously the majority of IS professionals are not aware of the topics and their importance to the software development process, much less the classical sources of their conception.

Consequently, my goal is to convey to you a sense of existing software testing principles in an easily understandable format, and in a single reference. I surveyed the available works on software testing and chose what I consider to be the best information available to date. I have done so to eliminate the need for you to assimilate several different books and read many journal/trade press articles in order to gain a full understanding of testing; however, for those of you who are interested, there is a semi-exhaustive software testing bibliography in Appendix A, and a list of publications that print testing articles in Appendix B.

In addition, I have attempted to include some original thoughts about software testing (e.g., A New Approach to Basic Testing in Chapter Six; Structured Tableau in Chapter Nine). I hope these will tease your minds, cause you to question the way you work with and think of systems development and testing. The methods, techniques, and tools in this book will definitely improve your testing skills, but independent and creative thought when using them will separate the ordinary from the exceptional tester.

I organized this book in a manner that provides a frame of reference for understanding and using software testing methods, tools, and techniques. The first three chapters create this basic framework via discussions of software quality and how it should really be defined in Chapter One; of the software testing organization's structure; of a classification scheme for software testing methods, techniques, and tools, of the software testing process and the software process maturity model in Chapter Two; of the psychology of software testing in Chapter Three.

Chapter Four is devoted to standardizing and planning the testing process, and is one of the most important topics. Furthermore, its contents are reinforced through a comprehensive example of a real test plan (The Hardware Tracking System—HTS—Test Plan) in Appendix C, which was developed following the test plan guidelines described in Chapter Four. This example provides a model that can be absorbed as an aid to understanding the test plan table of contents provided in the chapter. The table of contents, in turn, can be modified and extended for the reader's own test planning needs.

Chapter Five serves as an introduction to test case design concepts and sets the stage for the next four chapters, which discuss the various formal test case design methods, techniques, and tools. Chapters Six, Seven, Eight, and Nine cover Basis Testing; Equivalence Partitioning, Boundary Analysis, and Error Guessing; Cause-Effect Graphing; Decision Logic Tables, and Structured Tableau, respectively. The four chapters are synthesized through the application of the Rolling Rock Polytechnic University College Boards example, which is described in Chapter Six, but which is expanded for each of the formal approaches described in the subsequent chapters. In this manner the reader can follow the creation of a comprehensive set of test cases through intelligent combination of the design methods, and can compare the strengths and weaknesses of the different design strategies. Although this example is presented in COBOL terms, the testing techniques and tools that are discussed are programming language independent, which means they are applicable to any third generation language.

Chapter Eleven discusses integration testing with an emphasis on the importance of testing both internal and external system interfaces. Chapter Twelve stresses the importance of the external (business-oriented) nature of system testing, and its effect on test case design.

Chapter Thirteen presents a basic discussion of software tools that aid the software development process, and focuses on those that are used for testing. A general software tool classification framework (The National Bureau of Standards scheme) is presented as a foundation. It is followed by a discussion of the software testing tools classifications offered by Software Quality Engineering (William Hetzel and David Gelperin) and Programming Environments, Inc. (Robert Poston). The chapter concludes with some discussion of IBM's AD/Cycle and its effects on software testing.

Chapter Fourteen covers software metrics and their use in software testing. It takes a statistical process control tact because project-level productivity can only be increased by monitoring and controlling activities at the process level. A software metrics classification scheme based on type and usage is described, and Pareto analysis, Ishikawa diagramming, and Shewhard control charting are discussed as they can be applied to the testing process.

This book is suitable for use in an established curriculum in software development methods, techniques, and tools such as the information management program leading to a Bachelor's degree which is offered by the School of Technology and Information Management (STIM) under the auspices of the School of Engineering and Applied Sciences at Washington University in Saint Louis, Missouri.

In addition to formal education, it is also appropriate for continuing professional education programs which keep information professionals abreast of current software testing technologies and trends, such as the Professional Development and Technical Training Programs in The Center for the Study of Data Processing. The Center is a consortium of Washington University (under the auspices of STIM) and forty-plus Fortune 500 companies, financial institutions, and governmental organizations in St. Louis, the continental United States, and Canada. Much of the contents in this book have come as a result of seminar and consulting work with the Center's affiliated base of corporations.

Daniel J. Mosley

Acknowledgments

Many individuals in the Management Information Systems community have contributed to this book. First and foremost is Edward Yourdon without whom this work would not have been published, and to Toni Nash. Ed and Toni's faith in my skills and experience prompted their on-going support. Next, of course, are the people who guided the evolution of Software Testing methods, techniques, and tools: Glenford Myers, William Hetzel, Boris Beizer, William Perry, Thomas McCabe, and countless others who are not named here. I offer my thanks to Gene Lauver, my co-instructor in Software Testing Methods, whose ideas contributed to this book; to Thomas Browdy and Curt Hartog for their guidance and support; and to Daryl Youngman, director of the CSDP library, for all of his hard work. In addition I want to thank Robert Poston and David Gelperin for their work on software testing and for allowing the inclusion of the Poston and Software Quality Engineering software testing tool classification schemes. Thanks to Richard Bender and William Elmendorf for their expertise in Cause Effecting graphing and Requirements Based Testing. Special thanks to Dr. Eldon Li who generously allowed the use of his unpublished test plan outline. Thanks to Gerald Weinberg for his insights on the Psychology of Programming which directly reflect upon the Software Testing Process. Thanks to Ken Orr for his DSSD work. Thanks to David Sharon for his CASE Locator Series on Software Testing Tools. I also want to express my appreciation to David King for his work on Structured Methods and in particular the Data Structured approach, and his useful technique for Walk-throughs and Inspections. Another special thanks to Capers Jones and Howard Rubin for their advice and consultation on software metrics.

Thanks to The Association of Computing Machinery (ACM) and the Data Processing Management Association (DPMA) for their cooperation. Thanks to SouthWestern Bell Yellow Pages for their employees' insights on maintenance and Regression Testing. A special thanks to all of the members of the St. Louis Quality Assurance Association for their ideas and support. Thanks to the many professionals who have attended my Software Testing seminars over the past seven years, and to the students in my academic Software Testing course. Many of the ideas expressed herein are yours.

I want to thank Mary Shapiro, my editor Paul Becker, and my production editor Mary Rottino for their patience while we worked on the book. I also want to say thanks to Dr. Dennis Wright and Dr. Lee Becker whose constructive criticisms of my early writing inspired me to greater accomplishments. Thanks to god for his guidance.

1

Software Quality: The Elusive Butterfly

*Although good quality may be difficult to define
and measure, poor quality is glaringly apparent.*

Adrian, Branstad, and Cherniavisky, 1982 [1]

Quality in information systems has been defined, redefined, and redefined again much to no one's satisfaction; however, some kind of
definition must be established before a meaningful discussion of software quality can occur. As elusive as a formal definition of quality is
in our industry, we can usually come to some level of agreement among
ourselves (as professionals) as to what abstract characteristics demonstrate quality in a given set of circumstances.

The aspects of quality in software systems have been discussed
at length [1,8,9,10]. As an example, Figure 1.1 presents the software
quality attributes identified by Adrian, Branstad, and Cherniavisky [1].
The framework presented in the figure is by no means the only classification of attributes that could be identified for software, but it is
one that can be used as a starting point. It is, however, flawed in that
it treats software as the end product of systems development. In manufacturing operations product definition is the key to defining quality
[2] and software may not be the place to look for a product definition.
Quality and product definition as they relate to manufacturing are
thoroughly covered in two classical works on the subject by Crosby [6]
and Deming [7].

Quality is in great measure based on our perceptions and expec-

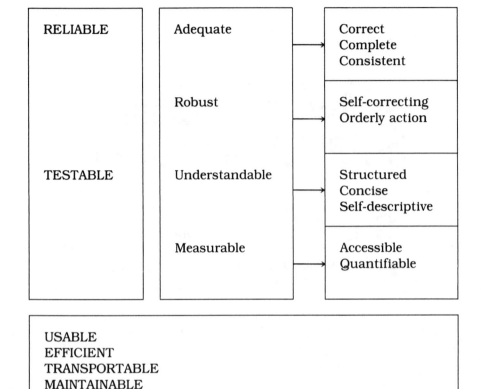

Figure 1.1 Software Quality Attributes: A Classification Framework [1]

tations. Consequently, there is a psychological dimension to quality which represents properties that are to a large extent intangible, as implied in Webster's definition of quality.

A particular and essential character: An inherent feature: Degree of excellence

Webster's Ninth New Collegiate Dictionary

Our perception of quality is through preconceived ideas of what quality is. If the "particular and essential" characteristics of an information system agree with our perceptions of quality, then the system possesses a "degree of excellence." The question is are those particular and essential characteristics tied to the software itself?

How do we quantify something as abstract, yet as concrete as, quality? Psychologists have for years tried to develop scales for measuring abstract properties of human attitudes and behavior. They have made progress but have constantly been forced to accept and use less than adequate definitions for the phenomena they have sought to study. They have reached one inexhaustible conclusion: *behavior does not necessarily reflect attitude*. Hence, the difficulty of measuring attitude is that we measure behavior as being representative of attitude. Attitude cannot be measured directly.

The same dilemma appears before those of us who would define information systems quality. We are attempting to measure something we cannot really describe. Furthermore, we are attempting to measure something that each of us may perceive very differently. Finally, we are attempting to measure something that may not be directly measurable. Thus, quality really is *in the eye of the beholder*. Therefore:

The definition of quality is external to the object being appraised.

The word "external" is the clue indicating where we might look to formulate a definition of quality in information systems. Information system professionals have an "internal" perspective (the quality attributes represented in Figure 1.1 represent an internal view of quality based on the acceptance of software as the end product), while other nontechnical business professionals have an external perception of the system that does not accept the software as the end product. These individuals see the system through an interface of screens and dialogs, reports, and the procedures required to interact with the system. But what is even more important is that they view the system primarily from the perspective of the *information* it provides that can be used to conduct business.

So, quality depends on perspective as much as any other property or dimension we might use for our analysis. This leads to a lot of conjecture as to which perspective provides a useful definition of quality in information systems. In essence, both the internal and external perspectives can be used to generate definitions and to assess quality. The conclusion that I have formed concerning quality in information systems is that the place to begin is with an external view of quality, and then to use its associated definitions to establish and drive the internal view.

Perhaps the most common external definitions of quality are: quality is meeting user requirements, or quality is best determined by measuring user satisfaction. Both of these definitions have problems.

1.1 QUALITY AND REQUIREMENTS

Assessing quality as "meeting requirements" has some very inherent difficulties. Requirements specification tends to be a dynamic process. The requirements change as the development cycle progresses. Ken

Orr of the Ken Orr Institute and The Center for the Study of Data Processing at Washington University in St. Louis dubbed this phenomenon "maintenance during development." He was one of the first to realize that "human nature" is driving the dynamics of requirements gathering and that we must allow for this variable.

Psychology has shown that humans tend to "think a little" then "work a little." What this means is that the classical processes of analysis, design, and construction are complementary. Even though the Systems Development Life Cycle (SDLC) approach is monolithic, humans do not work that way. We don't complete analysis before we begin design, and we frequently do not complete design before building and testing partially finished products.

Why do we work in this manner? We proceed this way because analysis and design are very "abstract" processes. Thus, we begin analysis without a clear understanding of what we want or need in the final product. The technique we use when proceeding from the abstraction of the product to its concrete form is to cycle forward in the development process until we feel comfortable that we have a better picture of what we want to build, and then, cycle backward and modify our abstract model to reflect our new understanding. Gradually, the product requirements become more distinct. So, defining quality in terms of systems requirements is to link quality to a moving target. The associated dangers are very prominent in large-scale systems development projects.

John Morrison, former director of System Engineering and Development at the "Star Wars" National Test Bed Joint Program Office, wrote of the requirements specification:

> **Textbook approaches to programming in the small largely assume that the starting point for system development is a well-defined specification. In the world of large-scale systems, this is not a valid assumption. That is one of the reasons such systems are "wicked."** [13, p. 4]

The term "wicked" as used in the quote refers to systems that are intrinsically hard to engineer (hard to define, plan, construct, test, and implement). They are wicked because their high levels of structural complexity negatively impact the natural way human beings work. The formal SDLC approach to Project Management and Structuring of the development process offer little to help the situation. Currently Rapid Prototyping, Joint Application Design (JAD), and Rapid Application Development (RAD) are being combined with the traditional SDLC to address this problem.

From a requirements testing point of view, virtually all medium to large information systems are wicked. Morrison continued:

> **Consistency of requirements may become a significant problem in the large-scale system. The impact on software testing is that the testers must test something. From the tester's point of view, something isn't a requirement *unless* it is testable. If requirements were vague or inconsistent to begin with, then testers will have to make assumptions about what was really meant. (p. 5)**

The essence of this quote is that changing requirements cause testing to be performed against the wrong set of requirements. Thus, requirements testing does not assure quality in an information system, and from a tester's point of view it does not make sense to define quality as meeting requirements.

1.2 QUALITY AND USER SATISFACTION

Measuring quality is not as easy as measuring "user satisfaction" because user satisfaction is not easy to measure (How's that for circular reasoning?). What do we consider as an appropriate measure of user satisfaction, attitude or behavior? Since attitudes and behavior can be and frequently are discrepant, which really measures user satisfaction? We must determine whether we should observe the way users behave toward an information system or rely on the choices they indicate on an attitudinal survey or some combination of these approaches.

Besides, the more fundamental question is what is the product with which the user is satisfied? Is it the system screens and reports or is it the *information* they contain? If it is the former, then colorful screens with lots of bells and whistles, and reports that are easy to read, should elicit kudos from users. If the latter, the content of the screens and reports and its effect on business behaviors should be questioned. To really determine the effectiveness of an information system, measures of "information content" must be developed and applied. They can be behavioral assessments of which items of information are used in business processes and how they are used, and attitudinal assessments of how effective they are in particular business contexts including suggestions for improvement.

There are many dimensions on which users assess quality. The means to an accurate assessment of satisfaction is (1) product definition and (2) identification of the relevant product attributes that are key effectiveness indicators as quality is synonymous with effectiveness. So, what we are really discussing is not user satisfaction but rather product effectiveness as an indication of both satisfaction and quality.

1.3 THE EXTERNAL VIEW AND PRODUCT DEFINITION

From an external (business user) perspective, the closest to an *operational definition* of quality comes from Appleton [2] and is based on the previous work of Levitt [12]. It begins with Levitt's definition of a *product*.

> **A product, to the potential buyer, is a complex cluster of value satisfactions. . . . Customers attach value to products in proportion to the perceived ability of those products to help solve their problems.**

From this definition, it can be inferred that quality (a perception) is directly proportional to the product's effectiveness. Appleton used Levitt's notion of a product to establish an information systems product definition. He said, "In the final analysis, what the IS customer wants is *information*." As he explains:

> **Information is a message that resolves a user's uncertainty. All other messages are noise.**

The information signal consists of "messages" used by knowledge workers in a specific business context to solve specific business problems. The *signal to noise ratio* reflects the information's effectiveness [14].

> **The higher the signal and the lower the noise, the more effective or useful the information.**

So, quality in information systems can be operationally defined as effective information! Defining quality in this way makes it measurable. The information's signal to noise ratio is an external system quality metric that represents an absolute index reflecting both end-user attitude and end-user behavior toward that information. Thus, effective information is information that has high perceived value by the knowledge workers using the system, and is actually used by those workers to guide business conduct. To completely assess system quality, satisfaction, and usage must be inventoried with respect to specific information components. This is also consistant with an Enterprise-level Information Engineering approach.

History in the manufacturing industries has shown us that the key to producing a better product is a clear understanding of the nature of the product. Since information, and not the information system, is the real product of the system development process, it stands to reason that the quest for a high signal to noise ratio has to begin during the process that is used to develop the information system which is the factory that manufactures information. The better that process, the better the product. The better the product the more useful it is. The more useful the product, the more valuable it is to the customer and the more the customer will use it.

Software testing should be oriented toward achieving quality in information. The purpose of testing, therefore, should be to assure a high signal to noise ratio in the output of the finished system. Thus, testing must be both *preventive* and *corrective* in scope. Testing activities must monitor both the development *process* providing data that are used to improve the process (this is accomplished through process monitoring and reviewing procedures), and the *product* providing data which are used to correct defects (this is accomplished through the planned preparation, execution, and analysis of test data).

The primary strategy of the testing function should be to prevent defects in the final product, a defect in this sense being anything that affects the information signal. Second, defect identification and removal should be layered on top of this prevention stratagem. Traditionally, the domain of software testing has been the latter. The following discussion of the software status quo is an indication of how effective software testing has been when used in the traditional manner.

1.4 THE SOFTWARE STATUS QUO

Although we have come a long way toward improving the quality of software systems in the last decade or two, we still have further to go. The trade journals are filled with stories of software malfunctions that have caused monetary losses, have spawned law suits, and have caused injury and even death to human beings.

For instance, a software error, "MALFUNCTION 54," in the system that controls the operation of the Therac 25, an accelerator machine used for administering radiation treatments to cancer patients, caused at least two deaths in patients treated with the machine. The software malfunction in question caused the machine to generate 25,000 rads, more than 100 times the therapeutic dose that was supposed to be given. The sad part of this incident is that a simple sequence of key strokes caused the malfunction.

It has since been determined that "MALFUNCTION 54" occurs only when the up-arrow key is used to edit certain parameters on the system display screen. This caused the machine not to lower the dosage from the level used for X-ray radiation therapy to the level required for electron radiation therapy. The Therac 25 is capable of both kinds of therapy.

In an article that discussed this incident, Ed Joyce wrote:

In short, the case epitomizes the software reliability crisis at its worst and brings into question the responsibilities—both moral and legal—of software programmers, designers, and engineers in a society that increasingly entrusts to computers everything from routine bank transactions to matters of national defense. [11]

In a world where countries and their economies are becoming dependent on information, it is absolutely essential that we in the information industry understand the significance of the product we provide. Ed Yourdon [16] says in an "information economy" we must realize that "every product and every service provided by society depends on productive, high-quality information systems."

Furthermore, in a three part series [16,17,18] entitled "The Decline and Fall of the American Programmer," Yourdon foresees the loss of information industry related jobs because of foreign competition in much the same way as Japanese competition in the automobile industry put many U.S. workers in the ranks of the unemployed.

One factor that Yourdon points out is the wage differential. American information systems workers are commanding wages many times higher than those in off-shore software houses. But the cost factor alone is not what devastated the American automobile industry. The Japanese paid strict attention to building quality (product effectiveness) into their products and American, auto makers focused on productivity (process efficiency).

I will not purchase the products of one U.S. auto maker because of their historical lack of reliability. This is true in spite of the fact that I know the company has substantially improved the quality of its cars and trucks. A negative reputation that grew out of the lack of quality in those products still lingers in my mind.

The question is one of confidence. Confidence in a particular product is not established through product testing, but rather, through product use. Product use determines product reliability and we develop confidence in reliable products. And so it must be with consumers of American manufactured information systems. The customers, traditionally called "users," have long been subjected to unreliable information systems (IS). These systems were, through automation of the user's job tasks, supposed to increase the efficiency and effectiveness of the organization's business functions, but instead, have at times actually inhibited the carrying out of business as usual.

If an information system is reliable, it is available when we need it and it provides us with useful messages, not a lot of noise. So, availability and signal to noise ratio (effectiveness) are direct determinants of confidence in an information system. These considerations are key to improved IS consumer confidence.

Why is the IS status quo one of unreliability and low confidence? It is the status quo because IS organizations have, as did the U.S. auto industry, concentrated on productivity. Productivity is generally considered as *output divided by input over a specified unit of time*. But why is productivity so important? It is important because the labor costs associated with software have risen steadily over the last 40 years. Unfortunately, this emphasis on producing the most product at the lowest cost in the shortest time has caused our industry to lose sight of what the product really is.

Productivity as it is viewed and measured in IS organizations is linked to an internal view of an information system. This focus causes IS professionals to mistakenly believe that the product is the software system itself and not the information it delivers. So, we worry about budget and schedule constraints, and think of code as the product. What has happened in many instances is that we have become very good at delivering "ineffective" information systems on time and within budget. In other instances, we have failed miserably to do even this much.

1.5 THE IMPACT

With the increasing proportion of the U.S. gross national product representing software [15], information systems will touch the daily lives of every person in America and the world. In a recent personal experience, I was affected by an error in the Department of Revenue information systems in the state of Missouri where I reside.

One Sunday morning in 1988 I was presented with a traffic citation by a Richmond Heights, Missouri policeman. The ticket was for failing to renew my vehicle license plates. Well now, the state normally sends a renewal notice approximately 30 days before the renewal date; however, I did not receive one. I am sure you can guess how they are generated—by computer of course.

Upon attempting to renew my plates at a Department of Revenue satellite office, I was informed there was a problem. I had purchased my automobile in 1987 and had registered it with the state at this same location. The clerk who originally entered the registration and license information into the state's computer had made a mistake. She entered a date of expiration for my plates that was the same as the date of purchase! I bought the plates in August 1987, and according to the state's data base they expired in August 1987. I drove my car for a solid year on expired plates.

MISSOURI DEPARTMENT OF REVENUE
POST OFFICE BOX 629
JEFFERSON CITY
65105

PAUL S. McNEILL, JR.
DIRECTOR OF REVENUE

DEBORAH L. ROBISON
DIRECTOR
DIVISION OF MOTOR VEHIC
AND DRIVERS LICENSING

November 18, 1988

Mr. Daniel J. Mosley
10431 Savannah
Frontenac, Missouri 63131

Dear Mr. Mosley:

Paul S. McNeill, Jr., the Director of Revenue, has requested that
I respond to your letter of November 1, 1988 in which you stated
you did not receive a motor vehicle license renewal notice for
your 1987 Pontiac, vehicle identification number
1G2FS21H4HL224049. You also addressed the issue of lack of
proper data verification procedures to eliminate computer errors.

As a result of your letter, I have checked our computer records
to verify the expiration month and year shown on your title
application. Our records show you applied for title and license
at the Clayton Fee Agent Office on July 31, 1987. At that time
you were issued license plate number RNS-530 which expired
August, 1988. As you stated in your letter, personnel of the
Clayton Fee Agent Office mistakenly entered the expiration year
of your license plate as 1987 instead of 1988. Because of this
error, you did not receive a license renewal notice for 1989
as they are generated from the license records of the previous
year. Please contact my office at your earliest convenience if
the registration receipt you currently have in your possession
does not reflect an expiration date of 1989 for license plate
RNS-530.

I am forwarding the article "Acceptable Legal Standards for
Software" to the Information Systems Division for review since
the mainframe computer utilized by the Department of Revenue is
maintained by that division.

The Department of Revenue's Motor Vehicle Bureau currently has
numerous data verification procedures to guard against incorrect
information being entered into the computer. It is not
practical, however, for the department to have an edit for the
year a registration is due to expire because of the many varied
situations that can arise which would require different
expiration years.

I sincerely regret the problems you have experienced due to our
error and hope that your future motor vehicle registration
experiences will be more positive. If I may be of assistance in
the future, please feel free to contact my office.

Respectfully,

Deborah L. Robison, Director
Division of Motor Vehicle
and Drivers Licensing

Exhibit 1

The reason I did not receive the usual computer-generated notice was because they are only created for plates about to expire, not for expired vehicle plates. I wrote a terse letter to the Director of the Department of Revenue pointing out the error and suggesting why it might have occurred. The department's assistant director responded (see Exhibit 1), and her admission of the problem saved me from a subsequent fine for improper vehicle licensing.

The moral here is that this albeit minor data integrity problem should not have been able to occur in the first place. The state specifically includes a warning on the renewal notice that says that it is not responsible for notifying a vehicle owner of an impending plate expiration; however, the residents of the state of Missouri have come to depend on the timeliness of such notices. So, there is no excuse. It is my contention that the state, by using computer-generated notices, has encouraged dependence on their timeliness to remind its residents to renew their automobile plates, and failure to generate such notice *is the state's responsibility.*

More and more, customers of information are assuming the attitude I already have. There is no reason why we cannot construct reliable information systems that produce quality information. To paraphrase a well-known movie line, "I'm mad as hell and I am not going to take it any more!"

1.6 WHEN QUALITY IS LACKING, WHO IS RESPONSIBLE?

In an enlightening May 1988 article in IEEE Software magazine entitled "Acceptable Legal Standards for Software" [5], Doris Carver attempted to answer this question. What she found was that legal interpretations concerning software developers and their responsibilities are inconsistent. Accordingly, legal recourse for those who purchase and use the software against those who develop and sell software systems falls under the areas of breach-of-contract and tort actions (negligence actions). This may change as the legal definition of software is more clearly formulated.

The important point here is that we as software developers are responsible for what we create. As Carver notes, software litigation is among the fastest growing areas of law. And because this is so, she wrote:

Delivered software typically contains errors. . . . This is not new: Unreliable software has been a persistent problem for many years. And it is likely that problems will increase as software demands and

TABLE 1.1 DPMA Standards of Conduct*

These standards expand on the Code of Ethics by providing specific statements of behavior in support of each element of the Code. They are not objectives to be strived for, they are rules that no true professional will violate. It is first of all expected that an information processing professional will abide by the appropriate laws of their country and community. The following standards address tenets that apply to the profession.

IN RECOGNITION OF MY OBLIGATION TO MANAGEMENT I SHALL:

- Keep my personal knowledge up to date and insure that proper expertise is available when needed.
- Share my knowledge with others and present factual and objective information to management to the best of my ability.
- Accept full responsibility for the work that I perform.
- Not to misuse the authority entrusted to me.
- Not misrepresent or withhold information concerning the capabilities of equipment, software or systems.
- Not take advantage of the lack of knowledge or inexperience on the part of others.

IN RECOGNITION OF MY OBLIGATION TO MY FELLOW MEMBERS AND THE PROFESSION I SHALL:

- Be honest in all my professional relationships.
- Take appropriate action in regard to any illegal or unethical practices that come to my attention.
- However, I will bring charges against any person only when I have reasonable basis for believing in the truth of the allegations and without regard to personal interests.
- Endeavor to share my special knowledge.
- Cooperate with others in achieving understanding and in identifying problems.
- Not to use or take credit for the work of others without specific acknowledgment and authorization.
- Not to take advantage of the lack of knowledge or inexperience on the part of others.

IN RECOGNITION TO MY OBLIGATION TO SOCIETY I SHALL:

- Protect the privacy and confidentiality of all information entrusted to me.
- Use my skill and knowledge to inform the public in all areas of my expertise.
- To the best of my ability, insure that the products of my work are used in a socially responsible way.

- Support, respect and abide by the appropriate local, state, provincial and Federal laws.
- Never misrepresent or withhold information that is germane to a problem or situation of public concern nor will I allow any such known information to remain unchallenged.
- Not use knowledge of a confidential or personal nature in any unauthorized manner or to achieve personal gain.

IN RECOGNITION OF MY OBLIGATION TO MY EMPLOYER I SHALL:

- Make every effort to insure that I have the most current knowledge and that the proper expertise is available when needed.
- Avoid conflict of interest and insure that my employer is aware of any potential conflicts.
- Present a fair, honest and objective viewpoint.
- Protect the proper interests of my employer at all times.
- Protect the privacy and confidentiality of all information entrusted to me.
- Not misrepresent or withhold information that is germane to the situation.
- Not attempt to use the resources of my employer for personal gain or for any purpose without proper approval.
- Not exploit the weakness of a computer system for personal gain or personal satisfaction.

* Reprinted by permission of Data Processing Management Association.

the resulting software complexity continue to increase. Furthermore, as the legal duty of developers becomes more important, evaluating these errors becomes critical.

"Evaluating these errors becomes critical." That phrase is worth repeating. If we are to produce software that is reliable, trustworthy, meets the user's requirements (provides the messages the user requested), in other words, *quality software*, we must take this responsibility seriously. This means establishing an enterprisewide Total Quality Management Program [15]. A portion of the program should be devoted to Continuous Process Improvement through Statistical Process Control techniques applied to the MIS systems development process. This will assure productivity (efficiency) in the software development and testing processes, and quality (effectiveness) in the final product, the information.

1.7 PROFESSIONALISM

It is important that we view ourselves as professionals because when we do so, we accept responsibility for our actions [3]. Professional codes of ethics are published by the Data Processing Management Association (DPMA) (see Table 1.1), and the Association for Computing Machinery (ACM). They are, however, nonbinding on IS professionals and an official industrywide certification program does not yet exist. So, it is currently up to us to police our own ranks, but that may soon change.

Recently, precedents have been established in landmark legal decisions concerning the responsibilities of "professionals." Even though the DPMA and ACM codes of conduct may be nonbinding, IS professionals who are members of these organizations can be held legally responsible if they fail to adhere to these professional guidelines. If it can be proved in court that members of these and other professional groups did not reasonably uphold the group's guidelines while executing their profession damages, criminal prosecution can and will result [3].

1.8 CONCLUSION

Software quality has two dimensions, an external dimension and an internal dimension. The definition of the product of systems development should be based on an external view of software quality. Software testers who view information as the product of systems development and who spend time understanding the business the system must support will be more rigorous testers because their objectives will be to test for faulty and omitted information signals.

Effective information is complete, correct, and consistent information that is used by business workers to conduct business activities intelligently. Effective information must have a high content of useful detail compared to useless detail (a high signal to noise ratio). A quality information system is one that outputs a strong information signal. Furthermore, a strong signal ensures that the system will be used and it will not become "shelfware." This coupled with reliability ensures that it will be used and trusted.

Producing quality software is important because the United States currently holds 57 percent of the world software market [4]. This tremendous lead is not because we produce quality software systems, but because of the sheer momentum of software industry growth and because the software industry began in the late 1960s in the United States. The question many experts are asking [4,16,17,18] is can we maintain this vanguard position. A recent article in Business Week [4] suggests that our advanced position is in jeopardy.

Quality could be the Achilles' heel of the United States software industry. . . . and industry executives know it.

A lack of quality in commercially produced software from U.S. software companies will eventually reduce our place in world software markets. It is important that we, as an industry, and as professionals, attack this problem immediately. A software quality control program as part of companywide quality efforts will go a long way toward alleviating this danger.

REFERENCES

1. Adrian, W. R., M. A. Branstad, and J. C. Cherniavisky, "Validation, Verification, And Testing Of Computer Software," *ACM Computing Surveys,* 14, no. 2 (June 1982), 159–92.

2. Appleton, Daniel, "Applying Lessons from the Industrial Revolution to the Information Revolution," *CIO Journal* (Winter 1990), 10–16.

3. Bloombecker, J. J., "Malpractice In IS?" *Datamation* (October 1989), 85–86.

4. Brandt, Richard, Evan Schwartz, and Neil Gross, "Can the U.S. Stay Ahead In Software," *Business Week* (March 1991), 98–105.

5. Carver, Doris, "Acceptable Legal Standards for Software." *IEEE Software,* 5, no. 3 (May 1988), 87–93.

6. Crosby, Philip, *Quality is Free: The Art of Making Quality Certain.* New York: McGraw-Hill, 1979.

7. Deming, Edward, *Out of the Crisis.* Cambridge, MA: MIT Center for Advanced Engineering Study, 1982.

8. Evans, Michael, *Productive Software Test Management.* New York: Wiley-Interscience, 1984.

9. Grady, Robert, and Deborah Caswell, *SOFTWARE METRICS: Establishing A Company-Wide Program.* Englewood Cliffs, N.J.: Prentice Hall, 1987.

10. Hetzel, Bill, *The Complete Guide to Software Testing* (2d ed.). Wellesley, MA: QED Information Sciences, 1988.

11. Joyce, Edward, "Software Bugs: A Matter of Life and Liability," *Datamation*, 33, no. 10 (May 1987), 88–92.

12. Levitt, T, *The Marketing Imagination.* New York: Free Press, 1983.

13. Morrison, John, "A Wicked Problem—Software Testing In Large-Scale Systems," *American Programmer*, 4, no. 4 (April 1991), 3–10.

14. Mosley, Daniel, "Software Testing: A Process Metrics Approach," *System Development*, 11, no. 3 (March 1991), 5–9.

15. Pfau, Loren, "Total Quality Management Gives Companies a Way to Enhance Position in a Global Marketplace," *Industrial Engineering* (April 1989), 17–18, 20–21.

16. Yourdon, Edward, "The Decline and Fall of the American Programmer," *American Programmer*, 1, no. 1 (March 1988), 1–8.

17. Yourdon, Edward, "The Decline and Fall of the American Programmer, part 3," *American Programmer*, 1, no. 3 (May 1988), 1–2.

18. Yourdon, Edward, "The Decline and Fall Continues," *American Programmer* 1, no. 6 (August 1988), 1–3.

2

Software Testing: An Overview

Getting the basics right and ensuring that the industry understands them are critical to real progress toward more effective testing in the 1990s.

William Hetzel and David Gelperin, 1991 [5]

Software development is labor intensive. Of all the phases of systems development, testing by far consumes the majority of the development team's resources (see Table 2.1). It exceeds the combined total for analysis and design by as much as 15 percent. The important question is why does testing require so much effort? The answer is, first, that testing traditionally occurs so late in software development that errors are costly and time consuming to locate and correct (see Figure 2.1), and second, that the test procedures used are informal. This means that the procedures are not defined and documented, and thus, cannot be repeated with consistency across development projects.

IS professionals tend to visualize software testing as a Quality Control (QC) process. They think of testing as a point in time at which they can correct the errors they introduced because they rushed through analysis and design. Conversely, the view of testing that has evolved in IS organizations today is that it is a series of related activities that occur after coding, before implementation with the intent of finding as many errors as possible [10,13]. This is reflected in many System Development Life Cycle (SDLC) packages where testing is confined to a single stage in the life cycle, and a formal testing phase may or may not exist. If not, testing is usually included as part of the coding phase.

TABLE 2.1   Systems Development Life Cycle Cost
Which Stages Are Labor-Intensive?

	Lifetime Cost (%)	Development (%)
Development	20	
Analysis and design		35
Coding		15
Testing		50
Operations	Insignificant!	
Maintenance	80	

Notes:

Development productivity is 10–15 lines of code per person-day.

Maintenance estimates vary from 40% to 80%.

Sources: Brooks [2], Boehm [1].

Because of the IS profession's tunnel vision with respect to testing, developers falsely believe that they can catch and correct the majority of their errors by executing the software using test data. This invalid assumption has caused developers not to spend enough of their resources verifying that requirements (to the extent that they can be defined) are completely specified, that the system specification is correctly translated from the requirements, and that the system design is complete, consistent, and correct with respect to the design specifications.

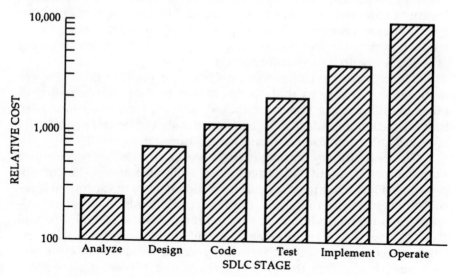

Figure 2.1   Relative Cost to Remove Error as a Function of Development Stage (Source: Boehm [1])

This limited approach to Software Testing stems from the idea that the only development deliverables to be tested are computer programs. Nothing could be further from the truth. Review and inspection of the intermediate partially completed and completed deliverables is required at every level of development. The most error-prone activities of system development are associated with the earlier life cycle stages.

Errors in information systems can grossly be classified into two kinds of errors [9]. Of the two, analysis/design errors and coding errors, the former occur the most frequently, are the hardest to detect, and the most costly to repair. To our embarrassment, they account for fully two thirds of the errors found by end users after Acceptance Testing. The review processes (walkthroughs, inspections, desk checking, etc.), which are effective in preventing analysis/design errors, must be considered legitimate software testing techniques, and testing itself must be thought of not only as *corrective* in nature but also as *preventative* if software development cost reductions are ever going to be realized.

We must review existing testing processes with an eye toward preventing errors and improve them to that end. In addition, we must track errors to determine where they occurred so that they may be avoided the next time. We must evaluate the products of all stages of systems development, and finally, we must test with the intention of finding any remaining errors prior to implementation.

Software testing is more than a QC process. The purpose of effective software testing is to guarantee a minimum level of quality in the finished product (testing cannot demonstrate quality). This makes testing a Quality Assurance (QA) process. Though some might disagree, software systems are not the products of development (see Chapter 1); however, the software development process is a manufacturing process. It manufactures information.

The System Development Life Cycle is a product life cycle. QA management strategies that are analogous to those implemented in other manufacturing processes should, and do, have analogous uses in information manufacture. Thus, testing should be considered part of an organization's overall commitment to assuring quality.

The best strategy for developing a disciplined testing process and manufacturing quality information is really a combination of approaches. First, training programmers and analysts in the formal techniques of Structured Analysis and Structured Design, and standardizing the implementation of the structured methods, techniques, and tools, is an absolute requirement. Second, enlightenment of the practitioner that testing should begin early in the development cycle and continue throughout the entire development process is essential. Third, developing and applying a formal testing program via a SDLC framework is crucial.

The extent to which the "methodology" of a specific SDLC implementation is *defined* and *controlled* will impact the extent to which software testing is defined and controlled. A methodology consists of a set a *methods*, each composed of one or more *techniques*, and each technique employing one or more *tools* (see Chapter Thirteen for comprehensive definitions of these terms). Furthermore, a methodology is only a methodology on paper. When applied it becomes a process. What is really relevant is the amount of discipline and control that exists in the implemented development process steps through the *operational definitions* of individual activities occurring within each step.

The fullness to which development activities (including testing) are operationally defined determines the extent to which they can be controlled and improved. The magnitude of operational definition ultimately determines the equivalent process maturity.

2.1 SOFTWARE DEVELOPMENT PROCESS MATURITY

Watts Humphrey of the Software Engineering Institute at Carnegie Mellon University says an effective software development process is predictable and measurable [6]. An effective process must account for all of the required development tasks (including testing activities) and inter-task relationships, the methods, techniques, and tools used by the process. Humphrey believes that IS professionals, and others involved in the development process, should have the proper training, the necessary skills, and the appropriate motivational levels. The degree to which these dimensions are defined depends on the maturity of the software development process.

Process maturity is an index of the information systems organization's abilities to measure and control the development process.

Humphrey identified five maturity levels for the software development process. Each level is briefly described in the following sections. Be aware that Humphrey's maturity categories do not imply a mathematical scale for rating process maturity. Each class is a subjective entity, and magnitude of maturity difference among the classes is not constant and does represent not an interval scale measure.

2.1.1 Initial Process Maturity

Initial Process Maturity is present when the development process can be described as "chaotic." The process has little or no formal structure. Methods and tools are not integrated. Cost and schedule estimates are crude at best. Development standards may exist, but are not enforced by management. The development team is loosely cohesive, and tool use is inconsistent among the team members. Team members may proceed to low-level (physical) activities such as coding and testing at the expense of high-level (logical) analysis and design procedures. When schedule slippage occurs, the solution is to throw more bodies at the project.

Testing as it occurs in IS organizations at this maturity level is far from being a formalized procedure, and testing may not be distinguished from debugging, which is a separate process. It usually consists of off-loading production data that is then used to test the software. Disciplined testing techniques are either not used or used indiscriminately, and developers (who are not trained in formal testing methods) test their own programs. The testing process at this level is highly ineffective. Consequently, many errors are not detected until after the software is in general use.

2.1.2 Repeatable Process Maturity

Repeatable process maturity is similar to initial process maturity except that the collective "psyche" of the IS organization has changed. The same "Mongolian Hoard" approach is still in place, but the development teams believe they have the process under control. Humphrey says this false sense of security stems from experience, and as King [7] said in his book, the courage with which IS professionals face systems development tasks comes from having done the "thing" before.

To use Yourdon's characterization of this level, information systems are developed using "Tribal Folklore." There is some rhyme and some reason, but the methodological guidelines are stored in the brains of the longer-term individuals who hand it down to new hires by word of mouth during on-the-job training sessions. The dominant design here is to have new programmers and the like learn the rules through a stint in a production support role with periodic advice from the long-timers.

The problem with this approach is that previous experience turns out to be inadequate when the development team must construct a new type of system. When novelty is encountered, the concepts learned from prior projects may not be generalizable to the new and unfamiliar development circumstances. New methods and tools may be required. Consequently, the development team's chances of successfully completing the system are substantially reduced, and the chances of completing the project on time and within budget are practically nonexistent.

At this level, testing is still a hit or miss proposition. Testing procedures are not documented and testing deliverables are frequently discarded at the end of the project. The approach used to test the last system is known only to the person who tested that system, and even if it were common knowledge, it might not be adequate for testing the present system. What testing techniques there are are not sufficient and may break down when used in different development situations.

The choice of testing techniques should be based on the characteristics of the system under development and not on historical usage.

2.1.3 Defined Process Maturity

Defined process maturity is several orders of magnitude better than the preceding levels because software engineering methods, techniques, and tools have been researched and successfully implemented. The process can be described as successful only with caution. Software metrics for assessing the quality and productivity of the process are not yet in place. Success at this level is qualitative as opposed to quantitative; however, the process is formally defined and documented.

The problem at this level is that the formal SDLC/Structured Methodology packages provide support for only a portion of the systems development process. The most well known methods are aimed at the analysis and design phases and many do not properly define review procedures for these stages. The latter stages of development are included in the life cycle, but effective methods, techniques, and tools that support coding, testing, and implementation are neither mature nor plentiful. Many IS organizations at this level of maturity are still unaware of existing software testing methods. Consequently, when testing is addressed on this plane it is viewed as a single stage of activities late in the cycle, and it represents a QC action not a QA maneuver.

2.1.4 Managed Process Maturity

Managed process maturity is present when the development deliverables are regularly scrutinized. Management collects data and views it with an eye toward improvement. Software metrics, as imperfect as they are, are applied to the development process. Standards for developing information systems and ensuring their quality have been firmly established and are being radiated throughout the MIS organization.

Testing activities may have evolved into an independent QC/QA function. For the most part, software testing is better managed and much more organized with a definite formal structure. Testing career paths mays have been established based on formal testing job descriptions. Ad hoc test teams are a frequent occurrence (refer to Chapter 4 for an explanation of this term as it has special meaning here which is reflected in that chapter). Finally, testing is being integrated with other development activities in the SDLC.

2.1.5 Optimized Process Maturity

Optimized process maturity is when the organization recognizes the need to improve the development process (this included software testing). Management support for an independent QA group is apparent. Humphrey points out that management tries to identify and repair the weakest steps in the development process. This includes improvements in software testing techniques and their use. Testing has blossomed into an effective program of defect prevention and defect correction.

Several paths to improved process maturity are possible. Humphrey [6] suggested five steps that can significantly improve the development process; however, a more disciplined approach may be preferable. Pressman [14] suggests that a Software Engineering Transition plan is strategic, and he presents a detailed plan outline in *Making Software Engineering Happen: A Guide to Instituting the Technology.*

2.2 SOFTWARE TESTING AND THE SYSTEM DEVELOPMENT LIFE CYCLE

The SDLC is grossly composed of three general sets of activities: analysis, design, and implementation (see Figure 2.2). Each series of tasks produces well-defined end products, commonly termed "deliverables." Analysis may produce a cost benefit analysis, a requirements definition document, and other deliverables. Design can produce system flow diagrams, data base schema, flow charts, Warnier/Orr process structure diagrams, and so on. Implementation can result in source listings, object modules, Module Test results, Integration and System Test results, as well as other documentation. Refer to King [7] for a complete description of each life cycle stage and its deliverables (see also Table 2.2).

All of the SDLC deliverables are subject to errors. A beautifully implemented software system is not worth very much if it is not the system the users requested. The way information systems are validated is that the end user actually uses and checks the system against its requirements (Acceptance Testing). But, what if the requirements were

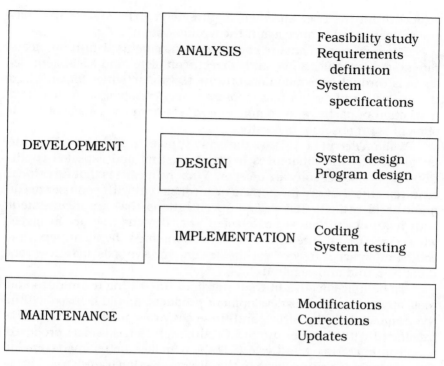

Figure 2.2   The Systems Development Process

documented incompletely? Chances are that the system will not survive user validation procedures. Why? Because it is the wrong system.

Let's take this line of reasoning one step further. What if the requirements are correct, but the design is inconsistent with the requirements. Once again the completed product will probably fail the system validation procedures. It will fail because it does not adhere to the design specifications.The original design specifications were de-

TABLE 2.2   Systems Development Life Cycle

SDLC
Feasibility study
Requirements definition
System specifications
System design
Program design and development
Testing
Production support

Source: King [7].

veloped from the user specified requirements. The system that has been constructed is once again the wrong system.

The only way to ensure complete requirements definition, accurate system specifications, and correct, complete, and consistent designs is through expansion of software testing activities forward into the analysis and design phases of systems development. Review and inspection of partial and complete products from each stage of development is an absolute necessity.

William Perry [11,12] says the primary objective of software testing is "to identify the differences between existing and expected conditions. . . . to detect software defects." What he means is that functional requirements that are incomplete or inconsistent with end-user needs must be identified, that design specifications that are inconsistent with requirements must be detected, that designs that are incorrect when compared to the design specifications must be identified, that coding must accurately reflect the design, and syntax/semantic errors must be found and removed.

To be fully effective in their mission, the testing techniques and tools applied to systems development products should be used within the framework of the SDLC, and these activities must parallel and be integrated with those of the SDLC. Although Hetzel [4] has proposed a Software Testing Life Cycle (STLC), it makes better management sense to include testing tasks in the already existing framework. Variations in how testing functions are incorporated are possible, and in certain development environments and for specific projects may be strongly recommended; however, the basic idea of specific testing activities as complementary to specific development activities in each and every one of the development process phases should be maintained when modifying the SDLC.

Perry [11] set 30 percent as the maximum percentage of the development effort which should be devoted to testing. The resources allocated to testing should be spread throughout the development proc-

TABLE 2.3   Testing Effort Allocation

Systems Development Phase	Percentage of Testing Effort
Analysis	2.5
Design	5.0
Construction	7.5
Testing	12.5
Implementation	2.5
Total	30.0

Source: Adapted from Li [8].

ess. Li [8] has suggested a breakdown for each phase of development (see Table 2.3) with the greatest percentage of effort during the phase where System Testing occurs.

2.3 A SOFTWARE TESTING TECHNIQUES CLASSIFICATION FRAMEWORK

There are many different classification schemes for software testing procedures. The problem with the present framework is that some kinds of tests do not fit exactly into one or another of the categories. They seem to be representative of more than one approach to testing. Consequently, the contrived classes of kinds of tests are not mutually exclusive but rather overlap one another.

Software Testing techniques can be categorized as being Dynamic as opposed to Static, or Manual versus Automated. In addition, a broad classification of levels of testing as "Testing in the Small" and "Testing in the Large" is possible [4]. The terms "White Box" and "Black Box" have been applied to these two levels of testing; however, these terms are more appropriate for classifying test case generation techniques than the testing process itself, and will not be discussed until Chapter Five, which contains an in-depth discussion of the two concepts.

Static testing techniques include Syntax Checking and Inspections. The reason these kinds of test procedures are included in this class is because they do not involve either manual or automated execution of the product being tested. For example, an Inspection of a program source code listing involves reading the code line by line and discussing each line, but not walking paper test cases through the program. In addition, an Inspection should check the program against a list of historically prevalent software errors. Li [8] says Static Testing techniques are time independent, whereas Dynamic techniques are time dependent.

Dynamic Testing techniques, on the other hand, do involve execution on paper or by machine. Walk-through, desk checking, module testing (sometimes termed Unit Testing; discussed in Chapter 6), Integration Testing (covered in Chapter 10), and System Testing (see Chapter 11) all require the execution of test cases. Walkthroughs and desk checking involve "paper and pencil" execution, while Module Testing, Integration Testing, and System Testing require machine time for execution.

Manual Testing techniques are reviews which include walk-throughs, inspections, and desk checking. The basis of categorization here is that manual techniques are carried out by people and automated techniques are implemented by the computer [8]. Chapter 12 discusses these techniques in great detail.

Automated Testing techniques are Module Testing, Integration Testing, System Testing, and Syntax Checking. Syntax Checking is classified as Automated because it is done by the language compiler and the compiler is a program that executes on a computer. Refer to Figure 2.3 for a summary of the testing techniques and their classifications.

Many authors and probably many practicing professionals may disagree with this framework for classifying types of software tests. It is based on my interpretation of a very muddled classification scheme. The terms describing the differing testing approaches have been consistently misused because of the lack of clarity as to how the types of tests relate to each other, and when each should be applied during development. Figure 2.4 illustrates in which stage of systems development each test is best applicable and when each test planning document should begin development.

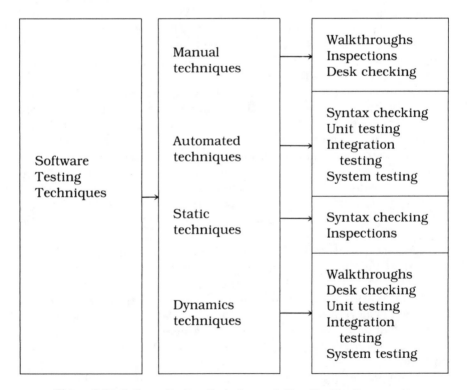

Figure 2.3 Software Testing Techniques: A Classification Framework

DEVELOPMENT	ANALYSIS	Feasibility study Requirements definition System specifications *Master test plan*
	DESIGN	System design *System test plan* Program design *Integration test plan* *Unit test plan*
	IMPLEMENTATION	Coding *Implement unit test* *Implement integration test* *Implement system test*
MAINTENANCE		Modifications Corrections Updates *Regression testing*

Figure 2.4 The Systems Development Life Cycle with Integrated Testing Functions

2.4 STATISTICAL QUALITY CONTROL

Testing is not just executing a program using a test data file of randomly selected test cases just prior to implementation. It is an on going process using techniques based in Statistical Process Control (SPC) principles and product quality concepts implemented as components as a Statistical Quality Control (SQC) program. The framework presented above does not include techniques that can be classified as SQC techniques. Thus, software testing as it is commonly practiced does not use *statistical inference* to ensure product reliability, and the software testing procedures discussed previously do not incorporate SQC concepts, but conceivably could be modified to do so.

If we view the software system itself as a factory that produces the desired output products, then *statistical sampling procedures* and *statistical inference* can also be used to predict the reliability of the products (the products sampled here are the system's outputs). Cho [3] compares the system development process to that of planning for construction of the factory. It is not possible to design and build the factory until the product is well defined. Yet, Cho says that is exactly what we are doing in the software industry because we treat the software instead of the information it produces as the end product.The important point in Cho's work is that we are not paying enough attention to proper definition of the raw materials (data) which our software factory will convert to product (information) and to the quality (signal strength) of the product.

For testing purposes we must strictly define the input and output domains. The problem is twofold. The questions that must be answered are: What sampling techniques will ensure an adequate subset of the possible input values which will provide as complete a test of the software as possible? What product sampling procedures will allow the developers to predict product reliability?

Cho describes a complete testing methodology based on Statistical Quality Control procedures. Although he uses widely accepted standard statistical sampling techniques to observe the product population (the output domain), Cho suggests that White Box and Black Box test case design strategies be used to sample the raw materials (input domain). (Chapters Six through Nine describe the input domain sampling procedures of Basis Set; Equivalence Partitioning, Boundary Analysis, and Error Guessing; Cause Effect Graphing; Structured Tableau, respectively.)

Chapter Fourteen of this book offers an introduction to Software Metrics and Statistical Process Control, and you are encouraged to follow this text with Cho's book, however, it is important that the basics of Software Testing be understood before the more abstract principles of statistical inference are tackled.

2.5 SOFTWARE TESTING ORGANIZATIONAL STRUCTURE

Perry [12] suggests that there are two major areas of responsibility during software systems testing. What he terms as "application" testing is the responsibility of the Test Team and involves actually carrying out the tests. Testing management is a much broader set of responsibilities requiring a diverse set of skills. An ideal test organization [4] should include a competent *Test Manager*, as well as members of the software development team, one or more *Testing Specialists*, and knowledgeable members of the end-user community that will eventually use the system. Other interested individuals may be invited to attend as observers as long as the total number present during testing does not interfere with the testing process. They may represent EDP Auditing or Quality Assurance (QA) functions.

There are problems with this ideal team. First, it will absolutely flop if it is not supported by management. It must be strongly endorsed by the Data Processing Steering Committee members if such a committee exists. It should receive multi-level support from the senior executives through the MIS director down to the applications managers, and the team participants. If any portion of the support is not in place, an attempt to create an effective testing program will most likely fail.

A lot of political groundwork must be laid before any testing effort begins. It is important to use and report the results of whatever metrics are available (refer to Chapter Fourteen) to support the use of a specific process or tool because managerial support is gained only if the data corroborate their effectiveness. This is especially important when both proving the successful implementation of new procedures or demonstrating the success of on-going processes.

Measurement is extremely important but not necessarily easy to achieve. The purpose of testing is to instill quality in software, but to date we do not have a standard measure of software quality. The reason is that we have not had an operational definition of quality. Operationally defining a property is to state it in such a way that it can be measured (refer back to Chapter One for our operational definition of quality).

Most software productivity/quality metrics tend to look at direct costs as they are related to concepts such as Lines of Code and Function Points. Software quality, however, should be viewed differently. Simple things that occur during development and that are easily recorded may be much better indicators of quality. In addition, quality seems more apparent when we look at quantities that represent indirect costs for software development. Keeping track of rework cycles, defect rates, and so on yields more valuable data concerning software quality.

Psychologists commonly develop operational definitions of behavior for measurement purposes. Any measure of quality an MIS organization tries to implement will be inherently imperfect, but an approximate metric is better than no metric. For example, Mean Time Between Failures (MTBF) is a somewhat indirect, and difficult, measure of software quality, because it can only be used after system implementation or during prolonged testing such as Volume Testing. An Information Signal To Noise Ratio (ISNR), as defined in Chapter One, is much better because it is a direct measure of software quality and it is easier to implement.

A second problem is that end users generally are not very enthusiastic about participating in the software development process. For years advocates of the structured methodologies have argued that user participation is lacking in the development process. They blame MIS organizations for not including end users. The real story comes out when practicing analysts are asked about user involvement.

End users have their own job-related responsibilities and are not interested in taking on new responsibilities. They are frequently irritated because over-zealous analysts try to coerce participation. The answer is once again management support. It involves lobbying end-user department managers to require that their employees become involved with the IS development functions as part of their jobs. It may be tough to win the managers over to your side, but it is very necessary. System development is a partnership. It must be cooperative, not antagonistic. As a process that parallels system development, testing also draws heavily on user participation for successful implementation.

A third problem is that very few MIS organizations have individuals who are trained Testing Managers and Testing Specialists. In addition, most of the organizations do not have an independent testing group. An independent QC group is ideal, but not completely necessary in order to implement proper testing procedures. However, adequate training in the software testing techniques and tools is a must! The Testing Manager is the local testing expert, and should be able to impart his or her knowledge to other team members, and be current in what new methods and tools are available. The Testing Manager and the Testing Specialist have differing responsibilities, but have similar skill requirements. They differ in their experience levels. Hetzel [4] does an excellent job of summarizing their responsibilities (see Tables 2.4 and 2.5).

TABLE 2.4   The Testing Manager's Role

Testing Management Responsibilities

- Establishment of testing standards
- Integration of testing and development activities
- Development of the test plan
- Establishment of a review process for test plans and test activity deliverables
- Acquisition of the necessary hardware and software resources
- Testing configuration management
- Testing progress tracking
- Ensuring completion of test documentation
- Change management

Source: Adapted from Hetzel [4].

TABLE 2.5   The Testing Specialist

Testing Specialist Responsibilities

- Aid construct of the test plans
- Create test cases
- Implement pretest activities
- Execute tests
- Analyze and report test results
- Follow up on required corrections

Source: Adapted from Hetzel [4].

2.6 UNFINISHED ISSUES

Hetzel and Gelperin [5] identified the main issues that software testing professionals are attempting to resolve.

- What are the inputs and outputs of testing?
- Which comes first, code or test?
- Why are industry practices so far behind recognized best practices?
- Why are testing cost and effectiveness not measured?
- What is good testing and how should it be measured?

We are much closer to answering some of these questions than others. Each has its own hidden agenda of relevant problems to be solved. In many ways it is up to the practitioner to supply the solutions, as testing theory can go only so far. I have tried to address as many of these considerations as possible in this text, but the ideas will remain just that unless they are accepted and implemented by you.

2.7 CONCLUSION

For far too many years information consumers have been brainwashed to believe that information systems cannot be improved because it is not possible to build the same level of quality in software as has been achieved in hardware. While it is true that software is more difficult to handle than hardware, we as software developers know that this point of view is a lot of nonsense. The things we do are esoteric in nature only because they are not documented and saved for later generations.

The lack of documentation allows us to function in an amorphous development environment. Documenting what we do forces us to define the activities and describe how they are managed. It is only after defining what we do that we can control and improve it. This is why Humphrey's process maturity model of the software development process is so important. [The fact that it models stages of process maturity is not the critical ingredient], but rather that it gives us pause to stop and think about what we are doing. In essence, it focuses our attention on the right things to ponder.

From a testing perspective, we have loosely defined a partially documented process we call software testing. This process does not have all of the necessary integration it needs. Testing activities are not integrated with one another, the classification of testing components and activities is confusing, but most important, testing activities and deliverables are not built into the SDLC framework.

Testing proponents [15] frame its importance by saying that testing differentiates science and technology from other intellectual disciplines such as art, philosophy, and religion. Scientists try to disprove their discoveries as a method of assuring that they are valid. Those that withstand the rigors of this "destructive" testing become scientific theories that are released for public consumption. This very basic approach is what experts such as Myers have been advocating for software for some time.

REFERENCES

1. Boehm, B. W. "Software Engineering," *IEEE Transactions on Computers* C-25, no. 12 (December 1976), 1226–41.
2. Brooks, Frederick, *The Mythical Man-Month: Essays on Software Engineering*. Reading, MA: Addison Wesley, 1975.

3. Cho, Chin-Quei, *Quality Programming: Developing and Testing Software Using Statistical Quality Control.* New York: Wiley, 1987.

4. Hetzel, William, *The Complete Guide to Software Testing* (2d ed.). Englewood Cliffs, N.J.: Prentice Hall, 1988.

5. Hetzel, William, and David Gelperin, "Software Testing: Some Troubling Issues," *American Programmer,* 4, no. 4 (April 1991), 22–27.

6. Humphrey, Watts, "Characterizing the Software Process: A Maturity Framework," *IEEE Software,* 5, no. 2 (March 1988), 73–79.

7. King, David, *Current Practices In Software Development: A Guide to Successful Systems.* Englewood Cliffs, N.J.: Prentice Hall, 1984.

8. Li, Eldon, *Structured Software Testing: An Introduction.* San Luis Obispo, CA: The Working Paper and Reprint Series, Center for Business and Economic Research, School of Business, California Polytechnic State University.

9. Myers, Glenford, *Composite/Structured Design.* New York: Van Nostrand Reinhold, 1979.

10. Myers, Glenford, *The Art of Software Testing.* New York: Wiley-Interscience, 1979.

11. Perry, William, *A Structured Approach to System Testing* (2d ed.). Wellesley, MA: QED Information Sciences, 1988.

12. Perry, William, *A Standard for Testing Application Software 1992.* Boston, MA: Auerbach, 1992.

13. Philips, Roger, "No-Test Software Is 'Unobtainable,' " *Software Magazine,* 34, no. 24 (December 1988) 33–44.

14. Pressman, Roger, *Making Software Engineering Happen: A Guide to Instituting the Technology.* Englewood Cliffs, N.J.: Prentice Hall, 1988.

15. Ryan, Hugh, "Why CASE Is Not a Cure for Testing," *Journal of Information Systems Management* (Summer 1990), 63–66.

3

The Psychology of
Software Testing

Testing is first and foremost a psychological problem.

Gerald Weinberg, 1971 [14]

In the quote above, taken from *The Psychology of Computer Programming*, Weinberg [14] established a basis for software testing that is still valid today. The definition of testing, the design of test cases, the execution of test procedures, and the confidence we have in the correctness of our software systems are all psychological in nature. Our approach to testing, and ultimately, how the Management Information Systems (MIS) organization structures its testing program, is dependent on these as well as other psychological considerations. As Weinberg rightfully points out, the psychology of testing computer programs has been overlooked in the development of testing tools, and more importantly, has been ignored in the establishment of testing guidelines (with the exception of Myers's work [8]: see Figure 3.1).

3.1 SOFTWARE TESTING'S FALSE BELIEFS

The foundation of present psychological attitudes toward software testing can be traced back to false beliefs about the nature of testing. Hetzel [2] and Ryan [13] described several beliefs about software testing which it is necessary to dispel. Let's briefly discuss each one.

1. An important and necessary part of a test case is a definition of the expected output.
2. A programmer should not destructively test one's own programs.
3. A programmer should test his/her own programs to prove that they do what they were intended to do.
4. A programming organization should not destructively test its own programs.
5. Thoroughly inspect the results of each test.
6. Test cases must be written for invalid and unexpected, as well as valid and expected, input conditions.
7. Examine a program not only to see if it does what it is supposed to do, but to see if it does what it is not supposed to do.
8. Avoid throw-away test cases.
9. Do not plan a testing effort under the naive assumption that no errors will be found.
10. The probability of the existence of more errors in a section of a program is proportional to the number of errors already found in that section.
11. Testing is an extremely creative, intellectually challenging task.

Figure 3.1   Testing Guidelines (*Source:* Adapted from Myers [8])

3.1.1 Degrees of Difficulty

Testing is easy.

This is contrary to the very nature of testing. Computer programs are in themselves extremely complex entities and when they are linked together in an information system, they form even more complex wholes. A relationship that can be used as a rule of thumb for testing is "even small programs are difficult to test and the difficulty increases as program size increases." In an individual program (or program module), the structural complexity is a result of the program's internal decision structure (the number of times in the program when control is transferred from one segment to another), the number of information processing functions the program implements, and the number of inputs to the program and the number of outputs from the program [3]. When programs are interconnected, the inter-program interfaces add a new dimension to the overall complexity of the information system. Consequently, Myers [8] says the design and execution of program tests represent activities that require far more creativity than analyzing and designing software.

Miller's Magical Number.

With respect to complexity, testing initiatives frequently ignore a very important psychological concept that was reported by Miller [9] in the article *The Magical Number Seven, Plus or Minus Two: Some Limits on Our Capacity for Processing Information*. What he described is a limitation on our short-term memory which affects the way we function in our daily work. Miller said that the human short-term memory is capable of dealing with only seven pieces of data simultaneously.

In a situation where two equally likely alternatives are being considered, we must discriminate between two data points such as in the IF/THEN/ELSE statement frequently used in COBOL programs, the THEN clause representing one alternative and the ELSE clause representing the second alternative. If we were to nest one IF/THEN/ELSE statement within another, the number of alternatives being considered becomes four (the alternatives increase geometrically [by the power of the exponent, e.g., 2^1 is 2, 2^2 is 4]). If we nest a third IF/THEN/ELSE statement, we have eight alternatives (2^3 is 8) from which we can choose. According to Miller's principle, eight items approaches the absolute limit of our short-term memory which is nine alternates. Adding a fourth level of IF/THEN/ELSE nesting exceeds this limit (increasing the number of alternatives we must handle simultaneously to sixteen, 2^4) making the logic of the module very difficult to understand. Hence, the rule of thumb that many applications development managers, analysts, and programmers know but few implement is *IF/THEN/ELSE statements should not be nested more than three levels deep.*

How does Miller's work affect software testing? Every human differs with respect to his or her short-term memory capabilities and every human differs in how he or she perceives complexity [9]. Software that is complex from Miller's point of view can be several orders of magnitude more difficult to test. This situation could exaggerate the individual differences among testers with respect to short-term memory. From a Unit Testing perspective, any program module that has more than ten alternative logical pathways is too complex. McCabe's Cyclomatic Complexity [5,6], which is discussed in Chapter Six, appears to represent structural complexity of software modules in a manner that parallels the way Miller says humans perceive complexity. This means that the Cyclomatic Complexity of a program can be taken as an indication of the module's understandability when studied by humans, and this in turn is an index of future difficulty of maintenance activities.

McCabe's metric is really an indication of the number of independent (control) paths through a module. From a path perspective, a complexity value greater than 10 indicates that the module is too complicated because there are too many paths to be stored and simultaneously processed in the tester's short-term memory. Consequently, testing the module will be unnecessarily difficult, and it may even be impossible to design test cases that will constitute an effective test of the module.

It is frequently said that we must design software with ease of testing in mind. Designing software system components that have low structural complexity will certainly do a lot toward simplifying testing. Structural complexity and its effect on test case design are discussed in more detail in Chapter Six on Basis Testing.

Figure 3.2 contains a set of testing guidelines based on our discussion of Miller's work. You will probably be able to create additional guidelines after referring to the figure. For a complete discussion of how Miller's principle applies to information systems development, read Poole and Prokop [12].

3.1.2 Nature versus Nurture

Anyone can do testing.

Not everyone seems to be born to test. Some MIS professionals are better testers than others. These individuals seem to posses a natural instinct which makes them quite good at what some of my students and peers have termed "Monkey Testing." This kind of testing involves generating test input using a process that has absolutely no intelligence behind it. For on-line systems it means sitting at the keyboard and "randomly" punching keys, occasionally hitting an appropriate command to enter the input. This form of testing is very inefficient

1. A tester's ability to handle structural complexity is limited by his/ her short-term memory capabilities.
2. The difficulty of test case generation is dependent on structural complexity.
3. Program modules should be designed with less than 10 independent logical paths.
4. For testing purposes, decompose existing complex modules to modules with 10 or less logical paths.
5. Decompose each stage of testing into 10 or less tasks.
6. Decompose testing tasks into groups of 10 or less activities.
7. Decompose testing activities into 10 or less steps.

Source: Based on Miller [9].

Figure 3.2   Testing Guidelines

and could be done blindfolded. It is a bad approach because its lack of intelligence means that the test cases generated will not uniformly represent all of the possible situations that must be tested. One rule we must follow is that at least one test case must be created for each type of situation (see Chapter Seven).

Thus, the essence of this statement is not that software testing belongs to a select few, but rather, that all of us need to be trained in formal testing techniques, a premise that also disputes the last belief concerning testing.

3.1.3 No Skills Required

No training or prior expertise is required.

Effective software testing requires training. Training should not be limited to an introductory set of seminars or classes. It should be an ongoing supportive activity because constant retraining is absolutely necessary. The Testing Specialist (as defined in Chapter Two) is an IS staff member who must be completely up to date in testing methods and tools. The Testing Specialist must not be forced into stagnation because of lack of training.

Two levels of experience are required for effective testing.

First, the Testing Specialist must have experience with specific testing methods and procedures, and experience with specific testing tools. To have confidence that we have tested the software to the best of our ability, we must be sure that the testing methods and testing tools are not mis-applied. Experienced testing personnel are less likely to inappropriately implement a test procedure, misuse a testing tool, or misinterpret test results.

Second, the tester must be familiar with the application domain for which the software is being constructed. If an accounting system is being tested, the Testing Specialist must become an "expert" in accounting functions. The more diversity the Testing Specialist has with respect to application areas, the better. Application knowledge is particularly important in test planning when establishing the objectives for System Testing where an understanding of the business functions is required.

The differing system tests execute test cases which are developed from the requirements definition documentation or from the draft of the system users manual. The system tests evaluate whether or not the business functions of the system are implemented according to the end user's view of the business area. System Testing is the last point at which the user requirements can be verified and validated before production begins. This type of testing represents an external or Black Box view that requires a working knowledge of the business application area being automated.

3.1.4 Just a Matter of Luck

Errors are just bad luck.

Ryan [13] identified a widespread covert belief in the MIS community that the errors in a current system are just "bad luck" and they will not happen in later system development projects. He recounts interactions with development personnel who appeared surprised when advised of errors. The corollary to this belief is that testing is only necessary because of bad luck, which leads to the notion that with a little luck errors will not occur in future development projects and testing will not be needed.

This belief is false because errors tend to cluster [8]. If errors were just due to bad luck, their distribution would be strictly random. Clustering in specific system components might occur occasionally, but not at the frequency that has been observed. The systematic clustering is a function of the component's structural complexity (discussed previously and in Chapter Six).

3.1.5 The Automation Panacea

Development automation will eliminate the need to test.

Many MIS professionals have been lulled into believing that software testing will no longer be necessary because Computer-Aided Software Engineering (CASE) will eradicate those pesky errors. Software will be built right the first time and there won't be any need to test. *This is the most dangerous falsehood in the industry today!* CASE will not make testing unnecessary. There are several reasons why.

First, the present generation of CASE workbench products are reasonably unintelligent. They do not do analysis, design, and coding for you. They merely assist you when you are in the process of executing these activities. Ultimate responsibility for the correctness of the products these activities produce is in your hands. CASE tools are extensions of your mind that aid your thinking. The end result is that you will probably think in a more organized (structured) way and you may (or may not) produce fewer errors, but you will still make errors—this is simply human nature.

To date there isn't a substantive body of work available on the effects of CASE implementation; however, a five-year field study [4] conducted in Europe suggests that CASE can reduce the number of postimplementation analysis and design errors that are found by system users. As Myers [7] has previously indicated, these errors account for two thirds of all the postimplementation errors found. The study noted a 69 percent decrease in maintenance costs over the five-year period. This is impressive reduction, and is obviously due in great measure to the lower number of analysis and design errors in the systems examined. Furthermore, the reason there is a reduced number of errors of this type is because CASE use forces software developers to complete the analysis and design phases [10]. Previously, developers could short cut to implementation activities if there were budget or schedule slippages.

Second, CASE workbench components, with a few notable exceptions, are not integrated. Their lack of integration requires them to *import* and *export* data to and from one another. At this juncture no common data interchange format exists in the CASE world. Granted, there are several disjointed standardization efforts under way, but it will be several years before an industry standard arises. This immaturity in CASE technology itself represents a grand opportunity for introducing errors into the systems developed with CASE products. Furthermore, if these data conversion activities are completed manually (by humans) the potential for error is magnified by several orders of magnitude.

Third, CASE vendors themselves are acknowledging the need for testing because they are now beginning to build software testing capabilities into their products. The first generation CASE products vary in their components, but is is generally accepted that a complete suite of CASE tools should include a Planning Workbench, an Analysis Workbench, a Design Workbench, and an Implementation Workbench. Testing activities are being automated as improvements in existing Implementation workbench components. Testing , however, is a staple (Ryan [13] says it is the one "constant" in development) of software development, and is important enough to deserve implementation as an independent CASE workbench product.

A Software Testing Workbench that is integrated into a complete suite of CASE tools is needed because testing activities intensify tremendously at the level of System Testing which occurs as the last bastion of error detection before the system goes into production. Thus, the ideal CASE tool suite from a Software Testing point of view is one that includes automated testing activities in all of its workbench segments for the verification of products at every level, and that also includes a System Testing Workbench as the last component which does both system *verification* and *validation*.

Verification activities are those tests intended to compare the development product that has been completed or partially completed to the envisioned product. Essentially, it is a mapping of the product characteristics back to specific requirements or specifications. For example, requirements are translated into specifications and in order to be sure the specifications adequately reflect the requirements, a review process must take place which checks each of the specifications for completeness, correctness, and consistency with its corresponding requirement. Any discrepancies are noted and corrected. This kind of verification process should occur at all levels of development.

Additionally, executing a set of test cases against a program (Unit Testing) is a verification process because a definition of the test cases includes a description of the expected outputs. After the test run the observed outputs are verified against the expected outputs.

Validation is a different process. System validation simply means that you use it in a controlled production environment with live data and it works or it doesn't work. If it works it is valid, if not it is invalid. User Acceptance Testing (that is a form of System Testing, see Chapter Twelve) is a validation process when done correctly, while what is traditionally termed System Testing (as are all other forms of testing prior to System Testing) is a verification process ocurring in a controlled nonproduction environment.

3.2 A DEFINITION

Myers [8] argues that the most important consideration in software testing is what we mean when we speak of of testing. Our definition will frame the purpose of testing. Weinberg [14] said, " . . . the only real problem in programming is getting the program to work correctly and proving it." A noble point of view toward an impossible task. Hetzel [2] similarly defined testing as " . . . the process of establishing confidence that a program or system does what it is supposed to do." Myers, however, pointed out that programs may do exactly what they were intended to do, and at the same time, do some things they were not intended to do. So, Myers formally defined testing as "the process of executing a program with the intent of finding errors."

From Myers's perspective, testing becomes a value-added process. His definition is more realistic than earlier definitions because testing to find errors is feasible, while testing to demonstrate the absence of errors is not. The only errors that we can say beyond a shadow of a doubt are not in the program are the ones we have discovered and removed. The program may still contain errors of which we are not

aware. Thus, we must assume that all programs contain some unde-
termined number of errors that we must identify and remove.

Programming is often thought of as an art form and not an engineering discipline. In objects of art the presence of small mistakes
(a slip of the painter's brush or the wood carver's blade) make the final
product unique, and hence, more valuable. The same is not true for
software programs. Errors in programs make the programs less valuable because they are not reliable. Information systems must be reliable. From a software engineering point of view, the more errors we
remove, the more valuable the program.

Myers summarized his ideas in three main points.

1. The purpose of software testing is to find errors.
2. Every effort must be made to ensure that each test case has a high
   probability of finding a new error.
3. A successful test case is one that detects a previously unknown
   error (implied in this statement is the definition of a successful
   test run).

As implied in Myers's definition, testing must be approached with a
destructive frame of mind. This is an idea that has strong implications
about who should test a program. In order to test effectively, a program's author must switch from a constructive attitude toward the
program to a destructive attitude. This is a difficult task. Some individuals may not be able to adjust their mental frame of reference, and
as a result, will approach testing with the wrong definition of a successful test run—one that does not identify any new errors. The obvious conclusion is that the programmer who built the program is not
the best candidate for destructively testing it.

Another reason this is so is program testing is a lot like proof-
reading [8]. The author is too close to his or her work to find a significant number of errors. When an author sees a plausible result, there
is a tendency to mentally shift the incorrect result over to the correct
side of the spectrum. For instance, the word "case" in a document may,
in reality, be a misspelling of the word "cause." A hasty reading of the
manuscript by the author might result in case being read as cause.
Consequently, a substantially larger amount of effort is required for
the author to find the errors than for an uninvolved proofreader. This
is why the publishing industry employs editors instead of relying on
authors to find errors.

The idea that programmers should not test their programs, however, presents problems at the Unit Testing level. In COBOL, a program
module is defined as a COBOL paragraph or section. COBOL programmers usually complete an entire PROCEDURE DIVISION before Unit

Testing begins, and it is the programmer who usually does the testing on his or her own program. Programmers frequently argue that at this level the author of the program is the only person qualified to design the test cases and execute the tests. Not so; if properly documented, another programmer, or analyst with previous programming experience, could complete the unit tests.

This does not imply that the program's author should not do any testing of the program. A minimum level of quality should exist before any program is subjected to independent testing. This base level of quality is the author's responsibility and it does require at least testing of the valid conditions the program will encounter (i.e., prove that it does what it was intended to do). Independent testers must subject the program to both valid and invalid conditions.

Perhaps a friendly rivalry among programmers could be developed and used for testing purposes. Implementing this approach, however, requires strong management initiative. Programmers polled (my personal poll) thus far appear to be resistant to the idea that someone else might assess their work. They will need reassurance that the results of any scrutiny will not result in black marks on individual work records.

Debugging, on the other hand, must be carried out by the program's author. Programmers and analysts other than the author can sometimes provide insights into possible locations for the error, but their limited familiarity with the program makes them less than favorable candidates for the task of debugging the program.

Since Myers first formulated his definition of testing, the discipline has evolved to a broader interpretation of what software testing entails. In the 1970s, software testing was used synonymously with program testing and debugging. Although Myers was correct in the way he defined testing, his definition has to be broadened in scope.

3.3 THE PSYCHOLOGICAL EVOLUTION OF SOFTWARE TESTING

Many MIS managers and professionals today still think of testing as a set of activities that occur only after coding during the Testing stage of the System Development Life Cycle (SDLC). Fortunately the numbers of these individuals are shrinking because the truth is (refer back to Chapter Two) testing activities should be allocated for every stage of the SDLC.

In a recent software magazine article [1], David Gelperin of Software Quality Engineering was quoted as saying, " . . . the testing process must find as many faults as early in the development cycle and as quickly as possible." This allows testing to become a "verification" process which when implemented across the SDLC strengthens the validity of the final product.

The perception of what is meant by software testing has changed several times in the young history of software development. Gelperin identified five accepted historical paradigms for software testing.

1. **Debugging Oriented.** Hardware concerns take priority over software problems and testing is not distinguished from debugging.
2. **Demonstration Oriented.** Prove that the software works.
3. **Destruction Oriented.** Find errors after construction during implementation. This is currently the dominant view.
4. **Evaluation Oriented.** Find errors in requirement specifications, designs, and code.
5. **Prevention Oriented.** Prevent errors in requirement specifications, designs, and code.

The optimal approach to software testing is one that combines the destruction-oriented, evaluation-oriented, and prevention-oriented paradigms.

As we discussed in Chapter Two, software testing falls under the guise of Quality Control (QC) which represents a subset of the Quality Assurance (QA) domain. QA in manufacturing deals specifically with the raw materials input to the manufacturing process and the process itself. QA attempts to enhance the quality of the final product through efforts to improve the raw materials and the manufacturing process. QA is preventive in its psyche. QC seeks to detect and repair problems with the product as a last line of defense before it is given to the customer. Correspondingly, QA dictates finding and eliminating potential defects before they become defects in the final product, while QC dictates repairing the defects as a means of improving the quality of the final product.

3.4 A NEW DEFINITION

From a quality standpoint, the only acceptable definition of testing is one that views software testing as:

> **a planned process based on previously established standards which begins before software development and continues throughout the development process including implementation and maintenance,**

and which includes both preventive and corrective activities at all levels; the major objective of these activities being to assure the effectiveness of the information produced by the system in question.

Ultimately, software testing should be part of a Total Quality Management (TQM) program which is implemented companywide. TQM is an approach to improving product quality that is a management philosophy. It sets the overall psychological tone for the company and should be accepted by the MIS department. Pfau [11] says, "The basic premise of TQM is that any product or service can be improved upon, and that a successful organization is one that consciously seeks out and exploits improvement opportunities." Improving the quality of information is the "key" to increased user satisfaction, increased productivity of the software development process, and reduced development and maintenance costs.

3.5 CONCLUSION

The right psychological environment for software testing is one in which both management and professionals understand the real purpose of testing activities—*to prevent and correct errors.* Acceptance of testing as having these two objectives tremendously broadens the scope of what can be included as testing activities. This opens testing to review techniques as testing techniques. There are individuals who will vehemently argue against this, but they are only demonstrating their shortsightedness.

Another important characteristic of the proper environment is a commitment to education and training in software testing methods, techniques, and tools. This is important because effective testing when completed by more than one individual must achieve some level of uniformity across individuals. Individuals with different knowledge and skill levels will test differently. This leaves no chance of comparing test results across projects and for that matter even across the same project.

Software has evolved rapidly over the last three decades, but it is not finished yet. The advent of two significant software technology guideposts will greatly impact the future of software testing. Computer-Aided Software Engineering is providing the platform for integrated and automated testing, and Information Engineering is providing the conceptual framework and guidelines that will determine how testing is integrated in the system development process.

REFERENCES

1. Gelperin, David, "Defining the Five Types of Testing Tools," *Software News*, 7, no. 9 (August 1987), 42–47.

2. Hetzel, William, *The Complete Guide To Software Testing*, (2d ed.). Wellsely, MA: QED Information Sciences, 1988.

3. King, David, *Current Practices In Systems Development: A Guide to Successful Systems*. Englewood Cliffs, N.J.: Prentice Hall, 1984.

4. Lempp, P., and R. Lauber, "What Productivity Increases to Expect from a CASE Environment: Results of a User Survey," *Productivity: Progress, Prospects, and Payoff* (June 1988), 13–19.

5. McCabe, Thomas, "A Complexity Measure," *IEEE Transactions on Software Engineering*, SE-2, no. 4 (1975), 308–320.

6. McCabe, Thomas, *Structured Testing*. Silver Springs, MD: IEEE Computer Society Press, 1983.

7. Myers, Glenford, *Composite/Structured Design*. New York: Van Nostrand Reinhold, 1979.

8. Myers, Glenford, *The Art of Software Testing*. New York: Wiley-Interscience, 1979.

9. Miller, George, "The Magical Number, Seven Plus Or Minus Two: Some Limits on Our Capacity for Processing Information," *The Psychological Review*, 63, no. 2 (March 1956), 81–97.

10. Necco, Charles, R., Nancy W. Tsai, and Kreg W. Holgeson, "Current Usage of CASE Software," *Journal of Systems Management*, 40, no. 5 (May 1989), 6–10.

11. Pfau, Loren, "Total Quality Management Gives Companies a Way to Enhance Position in Global Marketplace," *Industrial Engineering* (April 1989), 17–18, 20–21.

12. Poole, Bernard, and Noreen Prokop, "Miller's Magical Number: A Heuristic Applied to Software Engineering," *Information Executive* (1989), 12–13, 16, 68.

13. Ryan, Hugh B., "Why CASE Is Not a Cure for Testing," *Journal of Information Systems Management* (Summer 1990), 63–66.

14. Weinberg, Gerald, *The Psychology of Computer Programming*. New York: Van Nostrand Reinhold, 1971.

4

The Test Plan

As is the case for most undertakings, the plan is the crucial part of the management of the testing process.

Glenford Myers, 1979 [6]

4.1 TEST PLANNING

Myers [6] has said that many application development managers believe that data processing professionals "instinctively" know how to test, and the formality of a written test plan is not necessary. Managers who presuppose such knowledge are making a colossal mistake: a written test plan is necessary. It is beneficial because it specifies what activities are to be part of the testing process, and it delegates the responsibility for particular testing activities to specific members of the test team. It is a yardstick that can be used to measure the progress of testing activities by tracking actual performance against expected performance.

The most important reason for requiring a written test plan is it improves communication among the individuals involved in testing applications software. A major problem in systems development is one of communication. Each member of the project team must constantly make other team members aware of his or her progress, summarize what has been accomplished and what methods have been used to complete the task. As the number of team members increases, so does the number of communication channels, but team size increases arithmetically while communication channels increase geometrically. A written test plan can overcome this problem and significantly decrease the amount of time team members spend communicating with each other.

Test planning really begins before an applications project is started. Work on the test plan can begin as soon as the project's requirements are defined, but before the test plan can be formulated testing standards must have been established. Testing standards should be developed independently of any specific project, but should be such that they can be modified to suit the needs of individual development efforts.

Standards for software testing should be rigid enough to ensure that testing is uniformly executed across different projects and systems. Those same standards should also be malleable enough to create a structured yet ad hoc testing procedure. Ad hoc as it is used here means designed to achieve a specific set of testing objectives, not a disorganized attempt at testing. Traditionally, in the domain of Management Information Systems (MIS) the Latin phrase ad hoc has had negative connotations when applied to systems development processes. Ad hoc methods have been construed as informal (not documented) and somewhat anarchical (undefined and unrepeatable) approaches. Because ad hoc really refers to a process designed to achieve a specific end and because one general testing process will not work for all MIS development projects, project-specific test plans constitute and will be implemented as ad hoc procedures. Such procedures are not bad unless they are defined and implemented without specific limits on the kinds of behaviors and activities they can generate.

So, standards for testing applications software are important because they impose needed discipline on testing activities independent of project boundaries. They outline a set of uniform procedures for testing applications software; procedures that can be customized on a project by project basis, and this assures a certain level of testing competence, yet allows flexibility.

The standards also serve as a checklist which can be used to verify that the finished test plan is complete, and is appropriate content-wise for the project at hand. More importantly, standards provide the Testing Manager with control of testing activities. Milestones are established which later become indexes of testing progress. This allows the Testing Manager to be sure that things happen when they should and that needed human, hardware, and software resources are available in a timely fashion.

Meredith [5] defines a standard as "a consistent uniform procedure or pattern to be followed." With the variety of test case design methods, test execution procedures, and test analysis techniques from which to choose, an ad hoc (in this instance ad hoc is being used in the vernacular to mean disorganized) approach to testing can result in software testing chaos. It is easy to determine when an MIS organization is using an undefined testing process because a commonly heard statement among project team members is "We just don't have the time to do an adequate job of testing."

Thorough testing does require extra time and effort, but the exclamation above is an exaggeration of resource requirements which are directly related to the implementation of an undisciplined testing process. Most of the costs associated with testing are incurred because we enter testing without a clear idea of what is to be accomplished, and how it is to be accomplished. A lot of effort is wasted on unimportant activities. This approach to testing can be one blind alley after another. If testing standards are instituted and the testing process is properly planned, the required time and resources can be substantially reduced.

4.2 AUTOMATED SUPPORT FOR TEST PLANNING

Because a planned testing process is intrinsically an expensive process, test planning should include a strategy for automating the testing process. Automating as many of the testing activities as possible will increase the reliability of the test results, and in the long run save time and money. Automation will also remove a good portion of the "drudgery" of testing.

Software tools that automate testing can be an expensive proposition, but they return their cost because they tremendously ease the Regression Testing burden. An automated testing environment will increase reusability of test cases and ease implementation of testing execution, analysis, and reporting activities. A test plan that is stored on-line and used for one project can become the skeleton of a test plan for another project. For too long now, we have had a "build from scratch" mentality when starting new projects.

Computer-Aided Software Engineering (CASE) represents the automation of the systems development process, and in spite of vendor claims, not enough attention has been given to testing considerations. It is understandable that the majority of CASE vendors have marketed analysis and design workbench products (attending to the front end of the life cycle) as these areas are the most troublesome phases of development [1]. Some CASE vendors have addressed testing in their tool suites, but usually in construction/implementation workbench components that attend to the back end of the life cycle. Thus, the first generation of CASE workbench software products has not gone far enough to include capabilities that would substantially lessen the testing burden. Second or third generation CASE products will almost certainly have to integrate testing activities which support the entire life cycle across toolset products.

There are, outside of CASE, many software products available to aid in the testing process. While some are integrated into software testing workbench-like products, most are not. They represent isolated utilities that can be used to improve specific areas of testing. They are not considered integrated because they do not communicate with one another. The term integration, as it is used in the CASE arena, means that through a common data interchange standard the products can export and import data to and from one another. This ideal arrangement is still in its formulative stages for CASE technology and will not be realized for some time. Testing packages are even further behind in the race to integrate. Consequently, human intervention is required in order to use more than a single testing aide. The tester must convert the data into the necessary format for each product.

Even so, whatever tools are available can still be quite useful. Even software productivity packages that are not aimed specifically at testing can impact test team productivity. For example, desktop publishing software can reduce the drudgery associated with planning testing, and documenting testing activities and test results. Such packages can organize the materials into chapters, create the table of contents, index important terms, and combine illustrations and text.

One consulting firm with which I am familiar uses spreadsheet software to organize and create their test case and testing process folios. The use of tools in software testing is so important that an entire chapter in this book is dedicated to describing manual and automated testing tools.

4.3 ESTABLISHING TESTING OBJECTIVES

The test plan must specify a *general* set of objectives for the overall testing process and a set of *specific* objectives for each phase of the testing process. Because software testing activities are not limited to the formal Testing phase of software development but span the entire development process, specific objectives should be formulated for each testing activity in each and every phase of systems development.

The first step in establishing objectives for software testing is to consider what the testing process is to accomplish. The primary objective may be to assess whether or not the system in question meets the user's needs, or it may be to determine the correctness and accuracy of system outputs. Another objective might be to verify that system restart and data recovery capabilities are present. Other objectives could be testing the system interfaces with humans and other information systems. The latter involves testing the system user and operator manuals and clerical procedures, as well as the system training manuals. If a system modification is being tested, the overall objective might be to ensure that the modification does not impact existing portions of the system.

One objective that frequently is not included in this set of overall objectives is to determine, and thereby assure, the effectiveness of the information the system provides the user. Such an objective is consistent with the externally based definition of quality developed in Chapter One and would be implemented during System Testing.

Of all the tasks required to produce a test plan, stating the objectives is by far the most difficult. In some instances, establishing quantitative objectives is extremely taxing. The key to providing good objectives is to ask yourself how you can demonstrate that the objective has been met. In many cases this may be the result of a qualitative judgment. Because an objective is qualitative as opposed to quantitative does not mean that it is impossible to measure, but rather, that more creative ways of demonstrating that the objective has been fulfilled are necessary.

Meredith [5] suggests that checklists be developed for each testing activity and that objectives for each testing phase be developed from the list(s) applicable to that phase. The objectives are simply checklist items stated more formally. An example demonstrating the development of objectives from testing activities is contained in the discussion of the Generic Test Plan XXXXX (section V of Li's test plan outline), which is presented in Section 4.6.

The advantage of checklists is that it is easier to develop objectives that are directly measurable. The activities in life cycle phase checklists produce tangible results (deliverables) which can be compared with the expected results. The measures obtained may not be interval-scale measures, but they can be considered a demonstration of proof that an objective has been achieved. Of course, whenever possible, interval-scale measures of testing results are highly desirable because an interval scale is one in which the magnitude of difference between points along the scale is constant; interval-scale measurement is a requirement if we want to do mathematical (statistical) computations. Because measurement of test results is the best way to determine if an objective has been met, Chapter Fourteen describes a complete software metrics framework (with an emphasis on Statistical Process Control and Statistical Quality Control Charts) and discusses which aspects can be applied to software testing.

4.4 TEST PLAN PURPOSE

Software testing is inherently a project management problem [7]. It involves managing the complexity associated with designing, writing, executing, and verifying test cases. Hetzel [2] says a test plan is a plan for testing, a plan for verifying test results, and a vehicle for documenting test results. The test plan must plan, monitor, and control all of the activities of the testing process.

The test plan provides the framework within which testing will be implemented. It is a document detailing the standards, objectives, activities, schedules, and products of software testing. Perry [7] formally defines the test plan as "a document describing the intended scope, approach, resources, and schedule of testing activities."

4.5 TEST PLAN DESCRIPTION

A written test plan is not a single document, but rather, a set of documents [4]. It consists of a master test plan which is an overview of the entire testing process, and several mini-test plans that detail with specific types of tests. Mini-test plans should be created for Unit Testing, Integration Testing, System Testing, and Regression Testing.

Myers [6] has described the specific attributes of a "good" test plan. A revised set of attributes which incorporate some of Myers's ideas follows.

A comprehensive test plan:

1. Defines the overall testing objectives in the master test plan, plans and defines specific objectives in each mini-test plan while in all instances providing objectives that are measurable.
2. Provides a complete description of the function and structure of the software system to be tested.
3. Addresses testing from the standpoint of testing activities which are integrated into traditional systems development life cycle, thus ensuring that testing begins early in development and continues through the entire process and specific review points are established.

4. Specifies specific tasks to be completed during each phase of the life cycle with accompanying resource expenditure estimates.

5. Identifies entry criteria and completion criteria for each testing activity.

6. Identifies all individuals who will be involved in the testing process, assigns responsibilities for testing activities to specific test team members, and establishes work schedules.

7. Identifies resources necessary for designing, storing, and executing test cases and scenarios, and capturing, analyzing, and reporting test results (both hardware and software resources).

8. Identifies expected results for all tests and arbitration procedures for disputed results.

9. Identifies contingency procedures for fall-back to the previous system in case of catastrophic failure of the new system or version.

10. Identifies manual and automated testing tools, and details when and how each will be used.

11. Defines procedures for locating, removing, and tracking errors (debugging procedures).

12. Outlines training procedures for test team personnel.

13. Includes an index to sources of information concerning the testing methods and procedures that are implemented.

4.6 TEST PLAN CREATION

The first step in developing a formal test plan is to complete an outline. The outline should be based on previously established testing standards. If your organization does not have a set of established standards, several very good sources are available which provide a test plan outline. In *A Standard for Testing Application Software, 1992*, Perry [7] provides both suggestions for testing standards and a test plan outline that could be adapted to specific testing needs. In addition, Federal Information Processing Standards (FIPS) publication No. 39 has a simple but straightforward test plan outline. A basic test plan Table of Contents is given in Figure 4.1. It is based on the work of Eldon Li [4].

Why re-invent the wheel. One way in which humans learn is through modelling the behavior of other humans. If it is possible to acquire a sample of a test plan some one else has created, use it as a place to start. The plan can be adapted to your organization's needs. Be careful to model your test plan after one which has been proven through prior testing campaigns. A test plan is not a test plan is not a test plan!

Table of Contents

I. INTRODUCTION

A. Brief description of the system to be tested

    1. System components—DFD chart, Structure charts, etc.
    2. Other components relevant to the tests
    3. General characteristics of the environment in which the system will be used

B. Objectives of the test plan

    1. Levels of tests—module, integration, system, etc.
    2. Types of tests—functions, performance, documentation, stress, etc.
    3. Things that will not be tested as part of this plan—installation, readiness, unique user characteristics, etc.

C. Method of Testing

    1. Integration and regression strategy
    2. Test case development, inspection, and verification
    3. Job stream and scenario control that isolates problems to specific test case
    4. Problem reporting and resolution
    5. Test tools—inspection, review, walk-through, machine test, etc.
    6. Test aids—profilers, file comparers, simulators, test harnesses, etc.

D. Supporting Documents

    1. References
    2. Attachments

II. OVERALL PLAN

A. Milestone—test network, schedule, and locations

B. Test Materials

    1. Test Plans
    2. Test Cases Summary

Figure 4.1 Project Test Plan

3. Test Case/Data Specifications
4. Test Scenarios/Scripts
5. Test Case/Function Matrix
6. Calling/Called Modules Matrix
7. Program Test Cases Checklist
8. Screen Test Cases Checklist
9. Test Results Summary
10. Test Log
11. Discrepancy Reports
12. Discrepancy Summary
13. Operator Procedures and Training Outlines
14. Test Run Binder
15. Improvement Suggestion Forms
16. Test Summary Report
17. Other desirable documents

C. Criteria

1. Entry criteria—Clean compiled, desk checked, etc.
2. Exit criteria—error-to-statement ratio, logic path

III. TESTING REQUIREMENTS

A. Hardware

1. Configuration required for developing test cases
2. Configuration required for simulating test environments: host, terminals, communication links, load generator
3. Configuration required for user acceptance tests
4. Usage schedule: batch, interactive, dedicated

B. Software

1. Software system to be tested (in various configurations)
2. Operating System
3. Communication subsystems
4. Network load simulation software
5. Environment simulation software
6. Measurement software
7. Test-aid software
8. Schedule for availability of each software system generation

Figure 4.1   (continued)

C. Personnel

    1. Skill types and number of personnel
    2. Available schedule
    3. Other special requirements

IV. PROCEDURE CONTROL

A. Test initiation

B. Test execution

C. Test failure

D. Access/change control

E. Document control

V. XXXXX TEST PLAN

A. Objectives

B. Software description

C. Method

    1. List functions to be tested
    2. Test case design methods to be used
    3. Test tools to be used

D. Milestone—test network, schedule, progression, and locations

E. Requirements

    1. Hardware
    2. Software
    3. Data/Files
    4. Personnel

F. Criteria

    1. Entry criteria
    2. Exit criteria

Figure 4.1   (*continued*)

G. Resulting Test Materials (including post-test documents)

H. Execution Control

 1. Test initiation
 2. How to carry out the scripted activities
 3. What to do when something goes wrong; test failure; test environment failure; safety; recovery
 4. Can problem be fixed without authorization?

I. Attachments

Source: Li [4].

Figure 4.1   (*continued*)

4.6.1 A Discussion of Li's Table of Contents

Li adheres to the basic idea (as previously discussed) of a test plan that is composed of an overview and a series of mini-plans which describe the detail of specific kinds of tests. Thus, his outline for test plan contents reflects this approach. It is divided into five sections. An Introduction is followed by the Overall Plan, which is succeeded by a Testing Requirements section, a Procedure Control section, and finally, by a Generic section which is repeated for each of the different kinds of tests to be planned.

One aspect that all the sections in the outline have in common is a subsection describing references which detail the methods, techniques, and tools cited in the section. This is important because individual experience and knowledge will vary with respect to these things. These subsections should also contain information about software tools that could automate the testing activities described in the various sections.

I. Introduction

The introduction consists of a brief and concise description of the system to be tested including relevant analysis and design diagrams that clarify the narrative. This should also include a description of the system's operating environment.

The section also covers the high-level testing objectives. These objectives should specify what system components (functions) are to be tested and give a general statement about performance expectations. Furthermore, it is important to specify what will NOT be tested. If this is included, there can be no disputes during or after testing about what should have been done because consensus was obtained before hand.

This section should also include an overview discussion of the specific approaches and testing strategies that are suggested and the problems and difficulties that will have to be overcome (perhaps additional hardware must be secured or a new version of the operating system installed).

Another important item that should be included is a description of the documentation and reporting procedures that will be used for planning, executing, and analyzing the test results. Tips on the kinds of documents that should be used can be found in Perry's *A Standard For Testing Application Software 1992*, in Hetzel's *The Complete Guide to Software Testing, 2ed.*, in the FIPS publication NO. 38, *Guidelines for Documentation of Computer Programs and Automated Data Systems*, in ANSI/IEEE Std 829-1983 *Software Test Documentation*, in ANSI/IEEE Std 1012-1986 *Software Verification and Validation Plans*, and in ANSI/IEEE Std 1008-1987 *Software Unit Testing*. (The ANSI/IEEE software engineering standards documents are published in a comprehensive volume entitled *Software Engineering Standards, 3ed.*, that can be ordered from the IEEE Service Center, 445 Hoes Lane, P. O. Box 1331, Piscataway, NJ 08855-1331. The service center's toll-free number is 1-800-678-IEEE.)

II. Overall Plan

This section drafts the overall work plan including specific testing milestones that must be reached during testing in order to continue. Various project management tools such as Critical Path Analysis diagrams, Pert Charts, Gantt Charts, and the like can be used to picture the testing effort.

In addition, this section describes the test materials that will be necessary to support the planned test procedures. It can also contain specific examples of a subset of the documentation generally described in the previous section. Not all of the documents will apply to a particular project, in a particular environment. So, some agreement must be obtained as to which documents will be used in this instance.

This section also describes the "state of things" that must exist in order for each testing activity to begin and the conditions that must be observed before testing can end. It is possible to begin testing too early and to test much more than necessary. For example, Integration Testing must not begin before the detailed design is complete or system components are properly Unit Tested. Testing must not stop until the tester is comfortable with the thoroughness of the procedures.

When should you stop testing? This is a question with many possible answers. Myers [6] suggested several alternatives, for example, predicting the number of errors you expect to find using statistical models and/or industry standards, and applying what is known about the nature of software errors (that one third are coding errors and two thirds are logic errors).

Suppose the industry average for errors in systems implemented in COBOL is 3 errors per 100 lines of code (it has been estimated to be between 3–5 errors per 100 lines). If you were responsible for testing a 10,000 line COBOL program, you could project a total of 300 errors that must be removed. Furthermore, you could predict that approximately 100 of those errors would be coding errors and that the remaining 200 would be logic errors. Given that our testing procedures are good at removing coding errors but not as effective when it comes to logic errors, we could say that we will feel comfortable when we have discovered 99 percent of the code errors and 90 percent of the logic errors. This means that we can stop testing when we have uncovered 99 coding errors and 180 logic errors.

Of course, a time limit must also be established for situations that deviate from the industry norms. What if we found 25 coding errors and 75 logic errors and had been testing for more than a month? We must consider that we may have overestimated the total number of errors and decide whether to discontinue testing.

What if we encounter 200 coding errors and 350 logic errors in the first few days of testing. Should we continue? Yes, because the error estimates were probably too low. In this case, we should revise the estimates upward and allocate more time for testing.

Thus, testing activities should have specifically stated criteria for stopping, but with provisions that allow those criteria to be modified when necessary. (Chapter Fourteen describes statistically based criteria for terminating the testing process that are several orders of magnitude better than the example procedure just discussed.)

III. Testing Requirements

This section describes the hardware, software, and personnel requirements. If new hardware must be purchased or if the software must run on several different hardware platforms, those details are included here. For example, the software must execute in an environment that is diverse in terms of the terminals that will be connected to the system. Suppose the kinds of terminals that will be used are VT100, TeleVideo 950, and the Freedom 110. A sampling of these VDTs must be included during testing.

What if the application system you are testing must be installed under several different versions of an operating system? It should be tested several times using each version with which it will interact.

How many people are going to be needed to conduct the tests?

What background skills and levels of training are necessary before they can participate? These questions must all be answered as the last part of this test plan section.

IV. Procedure Control

This section defines who the decision makers are who will control the testing process. This is particularly important when a failure occurs or a dispute arises. Supreme control is usually given to the Testing Manager, with the Testing Specialist being next in line. Other members of the test team should be ranked by experience and area of expertise as consultants on important decisions.

Many of the required controls, however, can be prespecified in this section of the test plan. Control issues relating to test initiation, test execution, change control crisis resolution, and documentation control should be elaborated. For example, it could be stated that a test log must be kept for each test session or that each session must result in an error discrepancy report. It could also be stated that the Testing Manager must be physically present during Integration and System Testing.

V. Generic Test Plan XXXXX

This section must be completed for each kind of testing that is to be done. This includes Unit Tests, Integration/Function Tests, System Tests (Acceptance Testing should be considered a type of System Test— see Chapter Eleven), and Regression Tests.

For each iteration of this section, very detailed and verifiable objectives must be included. As Meredith pointed out, activities checklists can be a good starting place for crafting objectives. As an example, suppose we are testing a program that updates a master file once a month. We want to be certain that the program properly handles all incoming transactions, can specify a new record to be added, or a record that must be changed, or a record that must be deleted.

Our scope is not as simple as executing a single test case designed to represent each type of transaction. The transaction processing conditions could be stated as follows.

1. The program must properly add a new record to the master file.
2. The program must produce an error message when a duplicate add occurs.
3. The program must ignore the duplicate and continue processing.
4. The program must properly perform a modification to a record when the transaction is a change.

5. The program must produce an error message when a change is requested for a nonexistent record.

6. The program must ignore the change request and continue processing remaining transactions.

7. The program must properly process deleted records.

8. The program must report delete transactions for nonexistent master records.

9. The program must ignore unmatched delete transactions and continue processing.

10. The program must report transaction types that are not add, change, or delete.

11. The program must ignore invalid transaction types.

The unit testing objectives for these situations could be specified as follows.

1. To demonstrate that the program correctly adds a new record to the master file.

2. To demonstrate that the program logs duplicate add transactions to an error report.

3. To demonstrate that the program does not terminate processing when a duplicate add is encountered.

4. To demonstrate that the program correctly modifies the data record/field specified in the transaction record.

5. To demonstrate that the program logs unmatched change requests to an error report.

6. To demonstrate that the program does not terminate processing when an unmatched change request is encountered.

7. To demonstrate that the program correctly removes or flags master records that are deleted.

8. To demonstrate that the program logs the unmatched delete request to an error report.

9. To demonstrate that the program does not terminate when an unmatched delete transaction is encountered.

10. To demonstrate that the program logs transaction types other than add, change, and delete as errors in an error report.

11. To demonstrate that the program does not terminate processing when an invalid transaction type is encountered.

The procedure that would be employed to validate these objectives is to try to DISPROVE each one during the Unit Tests. So, it is also acceptable to word the objectives in a negative fashion. For example, Objective 1 might be worded: to demonstrate that the program *incorrectly* adds a new record to the master file. The reason I have spent so much time on objectives is because of their importance in setting the directions for specific testing activities.

This section also defines the formal procedures for the type of testing being described. It discusses how the procedures are used, how the test cases are to be constructed, how the test cases are executed, and which members of the test team are responsible for which of these aspects of testing. Furthermore, the completed test data including the expected results for each test case should be appended to this section once they are actually created. The test log and discrepancy report related to these data should also be appended after the data have been executed.

It should discuss verification procedures that will ensure that the test case design methods used were properly implemented, and verification processes that review the execution steps to be sure the data were properly processed.

A more detailed mini-version of the work plan should be included. It should assign responsibilities to specific testing milestones that represent the testing goals.

Hardware and software requirements specific to this section should be further defined. For example, Unit Testing may require "scaffolding" software to provide *drivers* and *stubs* when needed.

Finally, comments on execution control should be incorporated in this section.

4.7 THE TEST PLAN AND REGRESSION TESTING

The previous outline is intended to guide your development of a full-blown test plan to be used during application development. It can also be used during system maintenance and enhancement. Thus, when development is completed, DO NOT DISCARD the test plan. It is excellent system documentation and can serve as the basis of Regression Testing during maintenance activities. When a change to the system is required, a mini-version of the Generic Test Plan XXXXX section can be quickly derived.

Regression Testing, as any other type of testing, should be a planned affair. The problem is that maintenance work is frequently done under extreme pressure due to time and monetary constraints. Thus, the poor production support person doesn't have a lot of time to plan for testing the change.

In one very large communications company, with which I am ac-

1. A well-written SEMR
2. An illustration of the SEMR test data consisting of:
   a. a description of the required inputs.
   b. a description of the expected outputs.
3. A selection of test case design methods.
4. A procedure for capturing the actual outputs.
5. A procedure for comparing the expected outputs with the observed outputs.

Figure 4.2   Necessary Ingredients for SEMR Testing

The following is a set of guidelines for the kinds of details that should be included in a SEMR attachment in order to facilitate the development and execution of test data.

1. Use *clear, concise*, and *complete* sentences.
2. Organize the content of the description so related aspects of the problem are together.
3. Completely describe any *unique* characteristics of the problem.
4. Carefully describe any relevant restrictions that must be observed (e.g., conditions that dictate the kinds of inputs that are acceptable).
5. List any other system components that this change could affect. Carefully describe any known component interactions that must be regressed.
6. Separate physical details (e.g., data field location and size) from logic description statements such as:

   "If a work exist that required adv payment of more than $25.00 and the rep reworks the account and the rework requires less than $25.00 Do not require at least $25.00."

7. Give examples of valid inputs for each of the categories identified as part of 4 above.
8. Describe the expected output for each category of input you have identified.
9. When it clarifies the narrative description in the SEMR proper, include diagrams such as Decision Logic Tables, etc.
10. Never assume. Ask questions.

Figure 4.3   Guidelines for Writing SEMR Attachments for Software Testing

quainted, new development accounts for very little work. The MIS employees spend the majority of their time maintaining existing systems. The changes to their production systems are controlled through an on-line configuration management system. In that system, change requests generate single-page documents known as System Enhancement Maintenance Requests (SEMRs). SEMRs contain a verbal description of the change and the reason it has been requested. In addition to the SEMR proper, attachments are also created which supply additional details.

The SEMR is the logical document to serve as a basis for Regression Testing, but it does not contain enough information to do the testing. So, the procedure I recommend to test SEMRs is to generate an attachment that contains the necessary information. The attachment should be an abbreviated Generic Test Plan XXXXX section. Figure 4.2 illustrates the necessary ingredients for Regression testing SEMR's testing, and Figure 4.3 sets forth a battery of guidelines I developed for writing a SEMR attachment that facilitates the Regression Testing process.

4.8 TEST PLAN VERIFICATION

Quality assurance doctrine requires that test plans be submitted for formal review. The review's purpose is to ensure the quality of the test plan itself. Before using a test plan another individual has created, investigate what measures were used to ensure that the plan is of high quality. The plan must undergo one or more quality reviews. When enough partial product is available, an initial review is in order. This should be a short (less than one hour) review with the purpose of verifying that test plan construction is proceeding in the proper directions. Another objective is to verify that testing standards are being incorporated into test planning documents.

For this review, the participants should have a preliminary copy of the plan at least 72 hours ahead of the scheduled review date. Each participant should spend no more than two hours becoming acquainted with the details of the plan. The review itself should last no longer than one hour and should be a formal reading of the test plan. All sections of the test plan should be covered and discrepancies with the original conceptualization should be noted. The Testing Manager and the Testing Specialist are responsible for resolving the discrepancies.

When the final version of the test plan is available, a second and final review is required. Pre-review copies of all relevant materials should be available to participants one week in advance of the review. The actual review should not be longer than two hours. The participants use a formal review checklist, and the test plan is evaluated with respect to each item in the list. Perry [7] provided a comprehensive test plan review checklist that may be modified for specific projects. The attendees for both reviews should be the Testing Manager, the Testing Specialist, the Project Leader, and a user representative.

A complete discussion of the walk-through and the inspection as formal review techniques is available in Chapter Twelve of this book. I suggest that you digest the concepts in that chapter before attempting test plan verification activities.

4.9 TEST PLAN OVERHEAD

Test planning is not free. There are costs. The deciding question is: "Do the benefits of a planned and controlled testing process outweigh the costs?" The answer to this question is a function of the size of the system to be tested. Since it is known that the number of errors increases as the size of the system increases, test planning and proper testing implementation are extremely important for large information systems. Because test planning is very cumbersome for large systems, comprehensive test planning for large system projects must be supported by automation.

Small and medium sized systems can also benefit from organized testing. A rule of thumb King [3] uses to determine when a development project can benefit from an SDLC approach suggests some alternatives for testing. Any project that is greater than six man-months of effort should have a formal test plan. For systems that are smaller than six man-months, a condensed test plan is also possible. The condensed version should be created by considering all of the activities and deliverables of the full-blown test plan, and omitting those that are not applicable. This abbreviated test plan can direct testing activities for small to medium projects. At the very least, test planning for small projects should require use of Section V. of Li's outline as a guide.

4.10 TEST PLAN EXAMPLES

A good test plan skeleton is one that identifies all of the areas that are important to the success of the testing process. When this is the case, each area can be addressed individually and the detailed planning information produced with a minimum of effort. To this end, a complete test plan example is included in Appendix C. The *Hardware Tracking System* (HTS) Test Plan is from a pool of test plans created by students; however, they are not textbook examples. All of the test plans were developed for real information systems, and in several cases, the test plans were later implemented at the students' places of employment. The HTS Test Plan was developed for use at Forrest Ford Corporate Systems. Forrest Ford Consulting, Inc. is a St. Louis-based firm with regional offices in several Midwestern and Southwestern cities.

4.11 CONCLUSION

Test planning is an integral part of software testing. It cannot be omitted. This has been, and is continuing to be, proven by statistics that indicate that far too many critical errors remain undetected until after implementation. This is a consequence of unplanned testing, that is, testing that is not integrated. Each type of testing is being developed in isolation by different individuals for specific but unique purposes. This results in test cases being thrown away, in many sets of test-specific results that are not organized and that are not reported. Ultimately, this creates havoc when Regression Testing is required.

Furthermore, the planning process must be a formal one based in previously established standards. This is necessary to ensure repeatability. Repeatability of the testing process is absolutely necessary for Regression Testing. It is also a requisite for consistent testing across system components and across projects. Repeatability is a must if we plan to control the testing process. A controlled process is an engineered process. Thus, the real goal of planning is to define a repeatable software testing process.

It is interesting to note that Li's Test Plan outline is very similar to the contents of test plans hardware engineers traditionally construct and use. Because any software logic configuration could just as easily be encoded as a circuit in a hardware component as it could be as an algorithm in a software system, it makes sense that we should adopt as much planning procedure from the engineering community as we possibly can.

This is substantiated by students in my software testing class at the university. The ones who understand test planning the quickest almost always have an engineering background. What does this mean for the rest of us? It simply means that we must learn to think about testing with a new, more disciplined perspective.

REFERENCES

1. Herbert, Martin, and Thomas Browdy, *The CASE Studies Consortium Survey Analysis Results.* St. Louis, MO: The Center for the Study of Data Processing, School of Technology and Information Management, School of

Engineering and Applied Science, Washington University in St. Louis, 1989.

2. Hetzel, William, *The Complete Guide to Software Testing, 2ed.* Wellesley, MA: QED Information Sciences, Inc., 1988.

3. King, David, *Current Practices in Systems Development: A Guide to Successful Systems.* Englewood Cliffs, N.J.: Prentice Hall, 1984.

4. Li, Eldon, *STRUCTURED SOFTWARE TESTING: An Introduction,* San Luis Obispo, CA: The Working Paper and Reprint Series; Center for Business and Economic Research, School of Business, California Polytechnic State University.

5. Meredith, Dennis, "Planning Software Testing," in *The Handbook of Systems Management: Development and Support,* ed. Paul C. Tinnirello. Boston, MA: Auerbach, 1990.

6. Myers, Glenford, *The Art of Software Testing.* New York: Wiley-Interscience, 1979.

7. Perry, William, *A Standard for Testing Application Software 1992.* Boston, MA: Auerbach, 1992.

5

A Comparison of Black Box and White Box Test Case Design Strategies

Truly random data remains spread out in an undefined mess. But chaos—deterministic and patterned—pulls the data into visible shapes.

James Gleick, 1987*

The first and most important consideration in software testing is the practitioner's definition of testing [6]. The entire testing process can be affected by the definition. For instance, the criteria for what constitutes a successful test are a direct function of the definition. If the tester's intent is to prove that the software does what it is supposed to do, a successful test run is one that does not find any errors. If the tester's intent is to discover new errors in the software, a successful test run is one in which previously unknown errors are identified.

The definition of testing forms the frame of mind with which the tester approaches software testing. As humans, we establish goals for ourselves and we strive to achieve those goals. If the purpose (goal) of testing is to prove that the software works, the tester may subconsciously create test cases that have a low probability of finding new errors. On the other hand, if the purpose is to find new errors, the test cases that are created will result in a more rigorous test of the software.

Intermingled with the psychological issues involved in testing are issues of economics [6]. A test case requires time and money to develop.

---

* From James Gleick, *Chaos: Making of a New Science*. New York: Penguin, 1987.

Test cases that do not find new errors are a waste of resources. Consequently, the goal of test case design strategy should be to add value to the software through increasing the chances that a given test case will discover a new error. The more errors found and removed, the more valuable the software becomes.

Thus, the second most important consideration for software testing is the design of effective test cases [6]. The intangible nature of software makes this a formidable, but accomplishable task. Because software systems that are discrete state systems have few repeating structures, they cannot be portrayed by a finite set of operating states [7]. Digital computers, that are also discrete state systems, consist mainly of repeated logic structures, and can be represented by a finite number of operating states.

Exhaustive testing of hardware means generating each of its permissible discrete operating states at least once. Exhaustive testing is a reasonable goal for testing hardware systems, but is a virtually impossible goal when testing software systems because of the infinite number of possible discrete states. The infeasibility of exhaustive testing has facilitated development of intelligent methods for testing selected subsets of all possible operating states [6]. The operating states generated are those believed to have the highest potential for error. As implied in the quote that begins this chapter, when designing test cases we are trying to identify the patterns within the chaos. This a problem of reasonable difficulty.

These methods concentrate on generating as many different invalid operating states as possible for each software component within the scope of the allocated testing resources. Of course, all valid operating states are generated at least once. Thus, test cases intended to invoke the invalid states far outnumber those intended to generate valid operating states.

Test case design and construction methods for Dynamic Testing (both manual and automated forms) can be separated into two broad categories based on the perspective used to generate test cases. The techniques are categorized with respect to whether they require knowledge of the internal structure of the software system components (White Box or Logic Driven Testing), or whether they are based on the functional requirements of the system (Black Box or Data Driven Testing, or Input/Output Testing). The former represents an "internal" perspective, and the latter represents an "external" perspective.

The concepts we are discussing have also been termed "White Box Testing" and "Black Box Testing," and have been referenced as "testing in the small" and "testing in the large" respectively. The formal classification is applied to White Box techniques because they address testing with respect to individual program components, and the latter is applied to Black Box techniques because they have broader considerations [4,8].

These categorizations are not completely accurate. While those types of testing (Integration and System Testing) Myers termed "higher order testing" do require test cases that are developed from an external (customer driven) or Black Box perspective, they can and do incorporate test cases designed and constructed using White Box techniques for Module Testing. Furthermore, the White Box and Black Box concepts are taxonomic categories for test case design and construction techniques, and it is stretching the issue to call them "testing" techniques. They do not include, except for McCabe's Basis Testing approach (described in Chapter Six), a defined process for executing the test cases and analyzing the results.

Black Box methods are generally considered to be superior to White Box methods because they can be used very early in the development process. Black Box techniques can be implemented by systems analysts, or even sophisticated end users because they do not require a knowledge of programming skills. On the other hand, White Box methods do require the implementer to possess knowledge of programming semantics and/or syntax. Examples of Black Box approaches are Equivalence Partitioning and Boundary Analysis. White Box methods include Statement Coverage, Decision Coverage, and Decision/Condition Coverage, and Independent Path Coverage (see Figure 5.1).

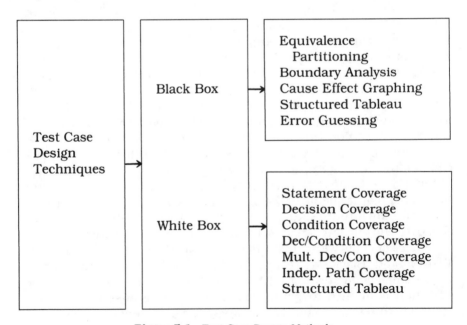

Figure 5.1 Test Case Design Methods

A little known approach to program design, Structured Tableau Design Methodology (STDM) [2,3] is an excellent test case development technique, but it does not fit well as either a Black Box strategy or a White Box strategy. Structured Tableau can be developed from either functional specifications or mini-specs and are detailed representations of program logic which view the structured programming constructs, selection and iteration, as merely sets of conditions and dependent actions. This view reduces all process logic to either sequential actions or conditional actions. Decision Logic Tables (DLT) are the diagrammatic foundation of the Structured Tableau approach. Chapter Nine contains a complete discussion of the DLT/STDM approach.

Although not formally defined as so in the testing literature, the Generally Accepted Testing Practice (GATP) for Unit Testing, Integration Testing, and Function Testing [6] is to develop a comprehensive set of test cases using one or more Black Box methods, and supplement it with additional test cases generated using one or more White Box techniques. Prior to executing the software, the expected output for each test record is predicted. Then, the software is executed with the test data and the output is captured. The observed results are compared with the expected results, and any discrepancies that occur are resolved. If the expected and observed outputs differ in a manner that is unacceptable, the software must be repaired and retested.

5.1 WHITE BOX STRATEGIES

The ideal White Box test data set is one that would exhaustively execute all paths of control flow in a module or program. Exhaustive path testing is impossible because the number of potential paths can be infinitely large. Imagine a COBOL paragraph containing ten alternate pathways. If the paragraph has the potential to be PERFORM ed up to ten times, the total number of possible paths is ten billion. Another way of expressing this is that the module has ten billion potential operating states because for each iteration up to a maximum of ten, there are ten potential paths that can be executed (ten to the tenth power). If one could generate and execute a single test case every minute, it would take over nineteen thousand years to test just this one module. Thus, it is virtually impossible to completely test any program from a White Box perspective, including small ones.

Even if exhaustive path testing were feasible, the tester could not guarantee there are no errors in the program. Edsger Dijkstra [1], the father of Structured Programming, said it best when comparing programs with mathematical theorems (that cannot be absolutely proven correct): "The best one can say is 'I have not yet found any errors.' To say more would be opening ourselves to attack." With direct reference to testing, Pressman [8] said the same thing but much more succinctly: "Testing cannot show the absence of defects; it can only show that software defects are present."

An approach founded in path testing has several problems [6]. Path testing does not test the program against its specifications, and if the program does not match its specifications it is not the right program. Path testing also cannot detect missing paths. If the requirements place specific restrictions on input values, but not all of the restrictions have been documented, the program will be incorrect because it is incomplete. In addition, path testing will not recognize data sensitivity errors. If the comparison operator in a conditional statement is < (less than) but it should really be <= (less than or equal), test cases exercising all paths will not necessarily find this error.

5.2 BLACK BOX STRATEGIES

Black Box test case development is not concerned with the internal structure or behavior of a program or module, but only with instances when the program or module does not behave as indicated in its functional specifications. The test cases are derived from those specifications.

The Black Box corollary to exhaustive path testing is exhaustive input testing. Exhaustive input testing requires that test cases for all possible valid and invalid inputs be developed. Exhaustive input testing is also an impossible task. The range of all possible valid inputs approaches infinity, as does the range of all possible invalid inputs. As pointed out by Myers [6], one must deal with two times infinity to completely test a program or module from a Black Box perspective.

As an example, suppose a small program module accepts a single positive integer value as input. The only way to exhaustively test the module is to input all of the possible positive integer values. The range of possible positive integer values constitutes an infinite set. Realizing this to be an impossible task, the tester might decide that a reasonable approach is to assume that a test of one representative value of the infinite set of all possible positive integers is the same as a test of any other value from the set. Suppose, however, that the integer value is stored internally in a short (one word) integer data field and the maximum value that can be stored in the data item is 32,767. The only way the tester will know that an integer value greater than 32,767 will cause an overflow condition is to actually input an integer value greater than this upper limit. As the tester is unaware of the internal representation, a value greater than 32,767 may not be included. This example does not mean that a Black Box approach is invalid, but merely that there are limitations on any assumptions the tester may make. These limitations should be recognized and offset by supplementing Black Box test cases with White Box test cases.

5.3 A COMPARISON OF THE STRATEGIES

The ineffectiveness of present software testing methods is a consequence of several interacting conditions within the systems development process. First, proven testing approaches have not been fully integrated into any established software development methodology. Most systems development strategies lose their robustness after the detailed design phase. Second, the test case design and development techniques are somewhat difficult to understand and apply, relying on mathematical expertise, experience, and intuition about what system states may be problematic. These abilities will vary from tester to tester (proper education and training can mediate the effect of deficiencies in individual abilities). Third, software structures representing conditional actions and repeated actions have the potential to generate many logical combinations of actions, each resulting in a unique discrete operating state.

Test case design strategies intended to reduce the problems associated with testing have been moderately successful. White Box techniques can produce complex models of discrete operating states, provided the tester has an adequate understanding of the specific test case generation methods being applied. However, White Box techniques are usually implemented after the program's logical design has been translated into the physical design, or into the syntax of the target language. Consequently, correction of analysis and design errors discovered at this point in the process is expensive because the source of the error must be identified (this means traceability backward through SDLC deliverables), and all, or a portion of the software, may possibly require respecification, redesign, and reprogramming.

Because of the problems associated with the White Box approach, one might legitimately ask, why even bother using it? Pressman [8] reasoned that White Box strategies should be employed because: logic paths that have a low probability of being executed are more error prone; logic paths that are thought to have a low probability of execution in reality may be frequently executed; typographical errors are randomly dispersed and have the same chance of existing on an obscure logical path as on a highly executed path. Furthermore, Black Box test cases may miss these kinds of errors. Pressman is really referring to a problem previously pointed out by Myers [6]. Test case developers tend to concentrate on creating valid test inputs while ignoring invalid test inputs. As stated earlier, invalid test cases have a higher probability of uncovering an undiscovered error.

The goal of effective test case design is to reduce the inherent "incompleteness" of program testing. According to Myers [6], the key issue is: "What subset of all possible test cases has the highest probability of detecting the most errors?" Random selection of test cases is by far the poorest method. Random selection means that out of the set of objects that can be selected, each individual object has exactly the same chance of being selected as does any other object in the set. When a programmer speaks of random selection of test cases, he or she generally means that a portion of a production file is being copied into his or her work area and it will be used as a set of test cases. Randomly selected test data records have a very low probability of identifying a new error. If one were to assume that random test data has only a 30 percent chance of discovering an error, in a program containing 100 errors the tester would locate approximately 30 errors.

The flaw is that using segments of production data files as test files does not constitute random selection. It should be more appropriately termed "pseudorandom" selection. The probability of finding an error using this method is almost certainly less than that of randomly selected test cases. In essence, the approach described previously as random test case development is a waste of time for discovering new errors. It, however, can be used to add volume to an already existing test data set which has been constructed from specifications developed by White Box and Black Box techniques. If truly random test cases are desired (at least one author believes that random test cases should be included in the test data set, [6]), special software tools and software utilities exist that can generate test data randomly.

5.4 CONCLUSION

Software testing is one of the most important systems development activities. The proper definition of testing and the implementation of disciplined test case design procedures are the two most important considerations. Test case design approaches can be classified as either Black Box or White Box strategies. Black Box techniques are used throughout development, while White Box methods are used later in the process. The two approaches are complementary and are used in combination to design and construct a comprehensive test data set (this test data set can then be used for Unit Testing, Integration Testing, and even System Testing). A comparison of the two concepts reveals the advantages of each and the reason for combining approaches.

We can view Black Box and White Box approaches as intelligent methods for selecting test cases and not as procedures for executing the test data. The GATP is independent of the approach used to design and develop test cases. Thus, the terms White Box "Testing" and Black Box "Testing" are misleading. More appropriately, they should be termed White Box and Black Box "Test Case Design."

They are intelligent methods because they represent thought processes that, when followed, maximize the error yield for a given set of test records and limit the number of test cases that must be developed. Testing, that accounts for 40–50 percent of the systems development effort [6,8], represents a major investment in time and resources. Thus, a test case that finds a previously undetected error is more valuable than a test case that does not locate a new error [6]. A corollary to this is: every error that is identified and corrected enhances the program's reliability, and thereby increases its value. Of course, it is not possible to know in advance which test cases are the most valuable, but use of standardized and disciplined test case generation techniques will enhance the probability that the test cases are value-added test cases.

Black Box and White Box methods are complementary; however, some redundancy of test case design does exist between certain White Box and other Black Box techniques (Basis Set, Cause Effect Graphing, and Decision Logic Tables produce test cases with a large amount of overlap, and Equivalence Partitioning and Boundary Analysis exhibit a small amount of redundancy). The tester's objective for using these approaches should be to select and use a combination that maximizes yield and minimizes the redundancy. This will ensure that test cases that are not created by a specific White Box technique are included as a result of the Black Box approach used.

Through their sensible combined use, a complete and comprehensive set of test data can be constructed. Thus, a a substantial increase in the rate of return on an organization's testing investment is a certainty. I recommend using both equivalence partitioning and boundary analysis in conjunction with either a basis path approach, or a cause effect graphing approach, or a decision logic table approach.

REFERENCES

1. Dijkstra, Edsger, "Programming Considered as a Human Activity," in *Classics In Software Engineering*, ed. Edward Nash Yourdon. New York: Yourdon Press, 1979.

2. Franz, Don, and D. Gamble, *Structured Tableau Design Methodology*. Specialized Online Systems, Inc., 1981.

3. Franz, Don, *Information Structures and Program Design Student Text Workbook and Problems*. Unpublished.

4. Hetzel, William, *The Complete Guide To Software Testing, 2ed*. Wellesley, MA: QED Information Services, Inc., 1988.

5. Mills, Harland, D., "On the Statistical Validation of Computer Programs," in *Software Productivity*. Boston, MA: Little Brown; 1983, pp.71–81.

6. Myers, Glenford, *The Art Of Software Testing*. New York: Wiley-Interscience, 1979.

7. Parnas, David, "Software Aspects of Strategic Defense Systems," *American Scientist*, 73 (1985).

8. Pressman, Roger, *SOFTWARE ENGINEERING: A Practitioner's Approach, 2nd. ed*. New York: McGraw-Hill, 1987.

6

Basis Testing

Of all the possible pathways of disorder, nature favors just a few.

James Gleick, 1987*

The technique described in this chapter is a White Box test case technique employing control flow graph representations of program module logic. Control Flow Graphs are network diagrams graphically depicting the logical pathways through a module. Test cases are created based on a set of independent paths enumerated from the graph. This method, formally known as Structured Testing, and informally as "Basis" Testing, was developed by Thomas J. McCabe [5,6]. McCabe's approach will be discussed as a White Box test case development strategy and not as a testing methodology. (For a comprehensive discussion of McCabe's methodology see his original work [6].)

The major advantage of McCabe's approach is that it incorporates the Cyclomatic Number as a measure of program/module complexity. The disadvantage is that the control flow charts are generated either from a flow chart before a module is coded or from the source listing after construction is completed. There are two problems with this approach. First, control flow graphs are logical in nature, and flow charts and source listings are inherently physical or implementation dependent. Second, there is not a set of explicit guidelines for systematically

---

* From James Gleick, *Chaos: Making of a New Science.* New York: Penguin, 1987.

converting the physical information contained in flow charts and source listings into the logical detail depicted in control flow graphs.

Another advantage of the Basis Testing approach is that it is supported by automation. McCabe and associates offer two software tools that support its implementation—*Analysis of Complexity Tool (ACT)*, and *BattleMap*. They provide graphing, complexity assessment, and test case construction following McCabe's basis testing methodology.

In the first portion of this chapter, we will discuss the development of control flow graphs and the design of test cases as McCabe proposed. This segment is concluded with a detailed example. In the second portion, we will cover an alternative method for constructing the flow graphs. In this latter section, explicit guidelines are presented for development of control flow graphs based on the structural properties of data structured process logic diagrams.

The second approach has several advantages. Control flow graph construction occurs earlier in the design process, and test case design happens before physical design (via flow charts) and coding. This facilitates design reviews, walk-throughs, and inspections, but more importantly, program and module testing are placed within the framework of a formal structured systems design methodology and incorporated into a life cycle format (refer back to Chapter Two for a discussion of the System Development Life Cycle).

6.1 BASIS TESTING

Basis Testing, as described by McCabe [6], uses source code or flow charts to generate control flow graphs of program modules. The flow graphs are used to enumerate the independent control paths, and calculate the Cyclomatic Number $V(G)$, a measure of procedural complexity. A "basis" set of test cases, covering the independent paths, is then created.

6.1.1 The Control Flow Graph

A *control flow* graph is a network diagram in which *nodes* represent program segments and *edges* are connectors from given segments to other program segments. Edges depict a transfer of control from one node to another and can represent any form of conditional or unconditional transfer. A *decision* is represented by a node with multiple emanating edges. A *loop* is a node with an emanating edge that returns to the node. A *region* is an area within a graph that is completely bounded by nodes and edges. Each graph has an entry and and exit node. A *path* is a route through a graph that traverses edges from node to node beginning with the entry node and ending with the exit node.

A node is a block of sequentially executed (imperative) actions and an edge is a transfer of control from one block to another. In COBOL, statements such as the PERFORM, the GO TO, the GO TO DEPENDING, etc. are all statements that give control to another processing block (paragraph or section). The IF/THEN/ELSE and nested IF/THEN/ELSE are also examples of statements that conditionally transfer control to specific groups of actions.

Structured Programming doctrine advocates that program logic be designed using only the logical constructs Sequence, Selection, and Iteration (e.g., see Bohm and Jacopini [1], King [4], and Orr [9]). Figure 6.1 shows the basic constructs in flow chart notation and compares each to its equivalent control flow graph representation, and can be used to compare the two types of diagrammatic notation. Figure 6.2 is an illustration of a simple control flow graph.

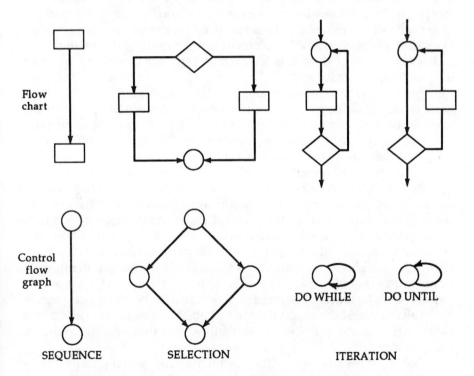

Figure 6.1 Basic Control Flow Graph Symbols Compared with Basic Flow Chart Symbols

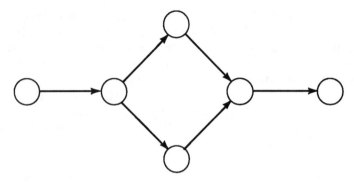

Figure 6.2 A Simple Control Flow Graph

6.1.2 Miller's Magical Number and McCabe's Structural Complexity

Internal structural complexity in program modules is a consequence of the number of functions the module implements, the number of inputs to the module and outputs from the module, and the number of decisions in the module [4]. Structured programming doctrine dictates that a module should implement *one and only one function* [12]. If this basic rule of thumb is followed, complexity due to the number of functions is minimized.

Structured programming dogma also stands on the premise that each module has but a single entry point and a single exit point. If such is the case, complexity due to the number of inputs and outputs can be controlled because the module interface is simplified. This leaves complexity because of the number of decisions as the major structural dimension contributing to module complexity.

McCabe's complexity measure is an indication of a module's decision structure. It measures procedural complexity as a function of the number of decisions in the graph. Cyclomatic Complexity is a useful metric because it is representative of the way humans make discrimination judgments. Miller [7] (refer back to the discussion in Chapter Three) found that the maximum amount of information the human mind can simultaneously process is 3 "bits." He defined a bit as the amount of information required to discriminate between two equally likely alternatives. The total number of alternatives is two raised to a power equal to the number of discriminations that are involved in a complex decision.

Based on his findings, Miller formulated the "seven plus or minus two" rule, which is why your telephone number is seven digits long. Seven numbers is optimal for memorization of phone numbers as each digit is a discrimination alternative. Miller determined that the maximum number of alternatives humans can handle simultaneously is nine.

If this principle is applied to the decision structure of program modules, the number of bits a programmer must process to understand a complex decision is a function of two raised to a power which represents the number of conditions contained in the decision. An IF/THEN/ELSE nested three levels deep has two to the third power (8) alternatives to comprehend, which is below the limit established by Miller. Adding one more nested decision raises the number of alternatives to sixteen, well beyond the inherent limit.

Consequently, a module with a Cyclomatic Complexity greater than eight is too complex for the human mind to understand without placing some of the detail into long-term memory. As a rule, we say that If C is greater than eight, the module must be redesigned and reconstructed. In practice, however, the upper limit has been set as high as fifteen. A compromise of ten has been selected because it is just beyond the short-term memory's upper limit, but is still achievable, and is the base of our numbering system.

King [4] suggests modules exhibiting high structural complexity can be rendered less complex through decomposition into two or more subordinate modules. Decomposition necessitates redesign, and/or recoding depending on whether the control flow graphs were constructed from program listings or flow charts. The earlier structural complexity can be measured, the better from the standpoint of module design.

Calculating C

The Cyclomatic Number can be calculated using any one of three simple equations. The first equation representing the Cyclomatic Number is:

$$C = E - N + 2$$

C is the Cyclomatic Number (C has been substituted for $V(G)$ and 2 is used instead of $2P$ to simplify and make the notation more meaningful), E is the number of edges, and N is the number of nodes. The Cyclomatic Complexity is computed as a function of the relationship of edges to nodes.

Complexity can also be computed as a function of the regions in the control flow graph. Edges can not cross one another, and regions formed by violations of this rule are not "legitimate" regions. Only legitimate regions can be included in the calculation of complexity.

The equation based on the number of regions is:

$$C = R + 1$$

C is again the Cyclomatic Number, and R is the number of legitimate regions.

The Cyclomatic Number can also be computed based on the number of primitive decisions in the graph. A primitive decision is one evaluating the condition states associated with a single condition. Nested conditions, and conditions connected by logical operators (AND, OR, etc.) should be treated as though they were completely separate decisions [8].

The equation is:

$$C = D + 1$$

D is the number of primitive decisions.

The advantage of the latter two equations is that they are easier to understand and use. In fact, the control flow graph does not have to be constructed to use the third equation. The number of decisions in the program flow chart or source listing can be counted and substituted for D in the equation.

The equations discussed above are meant to be applied to individual program modules. A measure of the total program complexity can be derived based on the sum of the individual module complexities with a factor subtracted out for redundant nodes. A redundant node is a node in a high-level module such as the mainline module which would be replaced by a subdiagram if the PERFORMed paragraph were PERFORMed inline as part of the superordinate paragraph.

The equation is:

$$C_t = C_i + 2 - (N - 1)$$

C_t represents the total program complexity, C_i represents the individual module complexities, and N is the number of modules in the program where a module can be defined as a paragraph or section in a COBOL program.

The value of C in each module represents the upper boundary for the maximum number of independent paths through a given program unit. If a set of control paths is constructed equal to C, test cases that exercise those paths will adequately test the module and constitute the "basis" set of test cases. The basis set does not necessarily execute all possible paths through a segment, but rather a subset from which all other paths can be fabricated.

6.1.3 Identifying the Independent Paths

Once the Cyclomatic Number is known, the independent paths can be enumerated. To enumerate the basis set of paths:

1. Identify all nodes with either a unique letter or number.
2. Begin at the entry node and travel the network using the left-

most* path to exit node. List the nodes contained in the path and indicate on the diagram the edges traversed.

3. Follow the previous path backward until a node is encountered that has one or more unmarked emanating edges. Begin at the entry node and follow the preceding path to the node with an unmarked edge. Continue from that point to the exit node using the left-most unmarked edge.

4. If the new path at anytime intersects a previous path, follow the latter path to the exit node.

When no unmarked edges remain, the basis set of paths is complete. The total number of paths must equal C. If a set of paths cannot be created that equals C, then the module is poorly designed and overly complex. It is best to redesign such modules.

It is extremely helpful when constructing the test cases to annotate the decision nodes with the condition being tested and to label the true and false branching edges. One test case is created that will execute each independent path at least once. The basis set of test cases must also exercise each conditional branch at least once. A test case is an input data record containing either a valid or an invalid value for each data field.

6.1.4 The Rolling Rock Polytechnic State
University College Boards Reporting Example

This is a fictitious example that is intended to simply illustrate the development of test data using the approach described in this chapter and will be continued using the techniques described in subsequent chapters. Figure 6.3 represents a simple set of functional requirements that must be met while developing the College Boards reporting procedure in the specification. It is important to note that this specification, albeit an incomplete and simple-minded example, would be available for use during the requirements definition phase of development. Thus, test case development can begin immediately and very early in the development cycle.

After reading the specification in Figure 6.3, review Figure 6.4, that represents a typical COBOL program that might be constructed to do the required processing. In Figure 6.4, focus on paragraph 040-EDIT-DATA as an example.

The first observation you should make is an assessment of the structural complexity of this paragraph. This can be accomplished sim-

---

* Right-most path can be used instead of the left-most, just use one direction or the other consistently.

Data Specifications

The data obtained from high school College Boards are processed to produce two summary reports at Rolling Rock State Polytechnic University. First, a student results summary report includes the student's Identification Number, Name, Sex, Age, and "normalized" test scores for Algebra, Geography, English, Physics, and Chemistry, as well as an overall percentile ranking. This report is used by the admissions committee to assess a potential student's general academic capacity, as well as specific capacity in the subject areas of the test before deciding to admit the student. Second, an error report that is used for internal auditing purposes includes student records which contain invalid data in one or more of the input data fields.

The restrictions on the input data are described as follows. Each record must contain a student Identification Number in the first positions of the record. This datum must contain only numeric values. The Identification Number must be followed by a student Name, which cannot be missing and which must contain only alphabetic values. The student's Sex is next, containing either of the alphabetic characters "M" or "F." The student's Age follows, being numeric and containing values within the range of 15 to 18 years. Algebra Score is found next and contains only numeric values between 000 and 100, inclusive. The same conditions as those specified for Algebra Score apply to the remaining scores Geography, English, Physics, and Chemistry, respectively.

The student Identification Number is four characters in length. The student's Name is 20 characters long. The student's Sex is but a single character. The student's Age is two digits long, and the five test scores are each three digits in length.

Procedure Specifications

Each student data record is input to the system for processing and reporting. Each value in each position in each input record is checked against the conditions specified above for invalid data. The primary output document is the College Boards report containing valid student records which are printed as they were input, which are also summed across the individual test scores to produce a total College Boards score.

The error report is somewhat more complex in that it contains student records printed as they were input except fields containing invalid data are underlined for easy inspection. Because a single input record may have invalid data in several different fields, it is possible for a given output record in the error report to have several underlined fields.

Figure 6.3 College Boards Reporting System Specification

```
     IDENTIFICATION DIVISION.
□    PROGRAM-ID.    SA0905.
□    AUTHOR.        John Q. Cobol.
□    DATE-COMPILED.
□      REMARKS.
□      SKIP3
□    ENVIRONMENT DIVISION.
□    CONFIGURATION SECTION.
□    SOURCE-COMPUTER.      IBM-386.
□    OBJECT-COMPUTER.      IBM-386.
□    SPECIAL-NAMES.   C01 IS TOP-OF-PAGE.
□    INPUT-OUTPUT SECTION.
□    FILE-CONTROL.
□      SELECT CARD-FILE   ASSIGN TO 'INTRO05.DAT'.
□      SELECT PRINT-FILE ASSIGN TO 'INTRO05.RPT'.
□      SELECT ERROR-FILE ASSIGN TO 'INTRO05.ERR'.
□      SKIP3
□    DATA DIVISION.
□    FILE SECTION.
□    FD  CARD-FILE
□      LABEL RECORDS ARE OMITTED
□      BLOCK CONTAINS 0 RECORDS
□      DATA RECORD IS CARD-REC
□      RECORD CONTAINS 80 CHARACTERS.
□    01  CARD-REC          PIC X(80).
□      SKIP1
□    FD  PRINT-FILE
□      LABEL RECORDS ARE OMITTED
□      DATA RECORD IS PRINT-LINE
□      RECORD CONTAINS 133 CHARACTERS.
□    01  PRINT-LINE.
□      05 FILLER          PIC X(01).
□      05 WRITE-LINE      PIC X(132).
□         SKIP1
□    FD  ERROR-FILE
□      LABEL RECORDS ARE OMITTED
□      DATA RECORD IS ERROR-LINE
□      RECORD CONTAINS 133 CHARACTERS.
□    01  ERROR-LINE.
□      05  FILLER           PIC X(01).
□      05  WRITE-ERROR-LINE PIC X(132).
□      EJECT
□    WORKING-STORAGE SECTION.
□    01  WORKING-VARIABLES.
□      05  END-OF-FILE-SWITCH    PIC X(03) VALUE 'NO'.
```

Figure 6.4   A COBOL Source Code Listing for the Rolling Rock Polytechnic
State University College Boards Processing Program

```
☐    05   COUNTER                    PIC 9(02) VALUE 0.
☐    05   E-COUNTER                  PIC 9(02) VALUE 0.
☐    05   LAST-NUM                   PIC 9(04) VALUE 0.
☐    05   LINE-COUNT                 PIC 9(02) VALUE 0.
☐    05   E-LINE-COUNT               PIC 9(02) VALUE 0.
☐    05   REPORT-SELECT              PIC X(01) VALUE 'G'.
☐    05   SCORE-ERROR                PIC X(01) VALUE..SPACE.
☐    05   ERROR-TOTAL                PIC 9(03) VALUE 0.
☐    05   90-PERCENT-COUNT           PIC 9(02) VALUE 0.
☐    05   80-PERCENT-COUNT           PIC 9(02) VALUE 0.
☐    05   70-PERCENT-COUNT           PIC 9(02) VALUE 0.
☐    05   60-PERCENT-COUNT           PIC 9(02) VALUE 0.
☐    05   50-PERCENT-COUNT           PIC 9(02) VALUE 0.
☐    SKIP1
☐ 01  PAGE-LINE.
☐ 05  TODAYS-DATE                    PIC X(08).
☐    05   FILLER                     PIC X(116) VALUE
              SPACES.
☐    05   FILLER                     PIC X(04) VALUE 'PAGE'.
☐    05   FILLER                     PIC X(01) VALUE SPACE.
☐    05   PAGE-NUMBER                PIC 9(03) VALUE 1.
☐    05   E-PAGE-NUMBER              PIC 9(03) VALUE 0.
☐    SKIP2
☐ 01  STUDENT-HEAD.
☐    05   FILLER                     PIC X(59) VALUE SPACES.
☐    05   FILLER                     PIC X(14) VALUE
☐         'STUDENT REPORT'.
☐    05   FILLER                     PIC X(59) VALUE SPACES.
☐    SKIP2
☐ 01  ERROR-HEAD.
☐    05   FILLER                     PIC X(60) VALUE SPACES.
☐    05   FILLER                     PIC X(12) VALUE
☐         'ERROR REPORT'.
☐    05   FILLER                     PIC X(60) VALUE SPACES.
☐    SKIP1
☐ 01  TOTAL-LINE.
☐    05   TL-CARRAGE-CNTRL           PIC X(01).
☐    05   FILLER                     PIC X(17) VALUE
☐         'TOTAL STUDENTS ='.
☐    05   FILLER                     PIC X(01) VALUE SPACE.
☐    05   TOTAL                      PIC 9(02) VALUE 0.
☐    05   FILLER                     PIC X(10) VALUE SPACES.
☐    05   FILLER                     PIC X(04) VALUE '90%='.
☐    05   SUM-NINETY                 PIC 9(02) VALUE 0.
☐    05   FILLER                     PIC X(02) VALUE SPACES.
☐    05   FILLER                     PIC X(04) VALUE '80%='.
```

Figure 6.4   (*continued*)

```
□   05   SUM-EIGHTY              PIC 9(02) VALUE 0.
□   05   FILLER                  PIC X(02) VALUE SPACES.
□   05   FILLER                  PIC X(04) VALUE '70%='.
□   05   SUM-SEVENTY             PIC 9(02) VALUE 0.
□   05   FILLER                  PIC X(02) VALUE SPACES.
□   05   FILLER                  PIC X(04) VALUE '60%='.
□   05   SUM-SIXTY               PIC 9(02) VALUE 0.
□   05   FILLER                  PIC X(02) VALUE SPACES.
□   05   FILLER                  PIC X(04) VALUE '50%='.
□   05   SUM-FIFTY               PIC 9(02) VALUE 0.
□    EJECT
□ 01  E-TOTAL-LINE.
□   05   FILLER                  PIC X(30) VALUE SPACES.
□   05   FILLER                  PIC X(12) VALUE
□     'TOTAL COUNT='.
□   05   FILLER                  PIC X(01) VALUE SPACE.
□   05   TOTAL-ERRORS            PIC 9(02) VALUE 0.
□   05   FILLER                  PIC X(27) VALUE SPACES.
□   05   FILLER                  PIC X(24) VALUE
□     'TOTAL RECORDS PROCESSED='.
□   05   FILLER                  PIC X(01) VALUE SPACE.
□   05   TOTAL-RECORDS           PIC 9(02) VALUE 0.
□    EJECT
□ 01  WS-INPUT-REC.
□   05   I-STU-NUM               PIC 9(04) VALUE ZEROES.
□   05   I-STU-NAME              PIC X(18) VALUE SPACES.
□   05   I-SEX                   PIC X(01).
□        88  VALID-CHARS         VALUES ARE 'F' 'M'.
□   05   I-AGE                   PIC 9(02).
□        88  VALID-RANGE         VALUES 15 THRU 18.
□   05   I-ALG-SCORE             PIC 9(03).
□        88  VALID-ALG           VALUES 000 THRU 100.
□   05   I-GEO-SCORE             PIC 9(03).
□        88  VALID-GEO           VALUES 000 THRU 100.
□   05   I-ENG-SCORE             PIC 9(03).
□        88  VALID-ENG           VALUES 000 THRU 100.
□   05   I-PHY-SCORE             PIC 9(03).
□        88  VALID-PHY           VALUES 000 THRU 100.
□   05   I-CHEM-SCORE            PIC 9(03).
□        88  VALID-CHEM          VALUES 000 THRU 100.
□   05   I-FILLER                PIC X(38).
□   05   I-RECORD-NUMBER         PIC X(02).
□    SKIP2
□ 01  ERROR-UNDERLINE.
□   05      FILLER               PIC X(07) VALUE SPACES.
□   05      EU-ID                PIC X(04) VALUE SPACES.
```

Figure 6.4   (*continued*)

```
□   05     FILLER               PIC X(05) VALUE SPACES.
□   05     EU-NAME              PIC X(18) VALUE SPACES.
□   05     FILLER               PIC X(05) VALUE SPACES.
□   05     EU-SEX               PIC X(01) VALUE SPACES.
□   05     FILLER               PIC X(05) VALUE SPACES.
□   05     EU-AGE               PIC X(02) VALUE SPACES.
□   05     FILLER               PIC X(05) VALUE SPACES.
□   05     EU-ALG               PIC X(03) VALUE SPACES.
□   05     FILLER               PIC X(08) VALUE SPACES.
□   05     EU-GEO               PIC X(03) VALUE SPACES.
□   05     FILLER               PIC X(08) VALUE SPACES.
□   05     EU-ENG               PIC X(03) VALUE SPACES.
□   05     FILLER               PIC X(08) VALUE SPACES.
□   05     EU-PHY               PIC X(03) VALUE SPACES.
□   05     FILLER               PIC X(08) VALUE SPACES.
□   05     EU-CHEM              PIC X(03) VALUE SPACES.
□   05     FILLER               PIC X(20) VALUE SPACES.
□   SKIP2
□ 01 BOARD-PERCENTILE.
□   05  BOARD-RANKING           PIC 999.
□     88  NINETY             VALUE 90 THRU 100.
□     88  EIGHTY             VALUE 80 THRU 89.
□     88  SEVENTY            VALUE 70 THRU 79.
□     88  SIXTY              VALUE 60 THRU 69.
□     88  FIFTY              VALUE 0 THRU 59.
□   SKIP1
□ 01 OUTPUT-RED.
□   05  FILLER               PIC X(05) VALUE SPACES.
□   05  ERROR-CHECK          PIC X(01) VALUE SPACE.
□   05  FILLER               PIC X(01) VALUE SPACE.
□   05  O-STU-NUM            PIC 9(04) VALUE ZERO.
□   05  FILLER               PIC X(05) VALUE SPACES.
□   05  O-STU-NAME           PIC X(18) VALUE SPACES.
□   05  FILLER               PIC X(05) VALUE SPACES.
□   05  O-SEX                PIC X(01) VALUE SPACES.
□   05  FILLER               PIC X(05) VALUE SPACES.
□   05  O-AGE                PIC 9(02)
□   05  FILLER               PIC X(05) VALUE SPACES.
□   05  O-ALG-SCORE          PIC ZZ9  VALUE ZEROES.
□   05  FILLER               PIC X(08) VALUE SPACES.
□   05  O-GEO-SCORE          PIC ZZ9  VALUE ZEROES.
□   05  FILLER               PIC X(08) VALUE SPACES.
□   05  O-ENG-SCORE          PIC ZZ9  VALUE ZEROES.
□   05  FILLER               PIC X(08) VALUE SPACES.
□   05  O-PHY-SCORE          PIC ZZ9  VALUE ZEROES.
□   05  FILLER               PIC X(08) VALUE SPACES.
```

Figure 6.4 (continued)

```
☐   05   O-CHEM-SCORE              PIC ZZ9   VALUE ZEROES.
☐   05   FILLER                    PIC X(09) VALUE SPACES.
☐   05   O-TOTALS                  PIC 9(03) VALUE ZERO.
☐   05   FILLER                    PIC X(04) VALUE SPACES.
☐   05   O-PERCENTILE              PIC ZZ99.9 VALUE
         ZEROES.
☐   05   FILLER                    PIC X(12) VALUE SPACES.
☐   EJECT
☐ 01   ERROR-OUTPUT-REC.
☐   05   FILLER                    PIC X(05) VALUE SPACES.
☐   05   E-ERROR-CHECK             PIC X(01) VALUE SPACE.
☐   05   FILLER                    PIC X(01) VALUE SPACE.
☐   05   E-STU-NUM                 PIC X(04) VALUE SPACES.
☐   05   FILLER                    PIC X(05) VALUE SPACES.
☐   05   E-STU-NAME                PIC X(18) VALUE SPACES.
☐   05   FILLER                    PIC X(05) VALUE SPACES.
☐   05   E-SEX                     PIC X(01) VALUE SPACE.
☐   05   FILLER                    PIC X(05) VALUE SPACES.
☐   05   E-AGE                     PIC X(02) VALUE ZEROES.
☐   05   FILLER                    PIC X(05) VALUE SPACES.
☐   05   E-ALG-SCORE               PIC XXX   VALUE SPACES.
☐   05   FILLER                    PIC X(08) VALUE SPACES.
☐   05   E-GEO-SCORE               PIC XXX   VALUE SPACES.
☐   05   FILLER                    PIC X(08) VALUE SPACES.
☐   05   E-ENG-SCORE               PIC XXX   VALUE SPACES.
☐   05   FILLER                    PIC X(08) VALUE SPACES.
☐   05   E-PHY-SCORE               PIC XXX   VALUE SPACES.
☐   05   FILLER                    PIC X(08) VALUE SPACES.
☐   05   E-CHEM-SCORE              PIC XXX   VALUE SPACES.
☐   05   FILLER                    PIC X(09) VALUE SPACES.
☐   05   E-TOTALS                  PIC ZZZ   VALUE ZEROES.
☐   05   FILLER                    PIC X(04) VALUE SPACES.
☐   05   E-PERCENTILE              PIC ZZZZ.Z VALUE ZEROES.
☐   05   FILLER                    PIC X(08) VALUE SPACES.
☐   EJECT
☐ 01   HEADING-LINE.
☐   05   FILLER                    PIC X(05) VALUE SPACES.
☐   05   FILLER                    PIC X(09) VALUE
☐        'ID-NUMBER'.
☐   05   FILLER                    PIC X(08) VALUE SPACES.
☐   05   FILLER                    PIC X(04) VALUE 'NAME'.
☐   05   FILLER                    PIC X(11) VALUE SPACES.
☐   05   FILLER                    PIC X(03) VALUE 'SEX'.
☐   05   FILLER                    PIC X(03) VALUE SPACES.
☐   05   FILLER                    PIC X(03) VALUE 'AGE'.
☐   05   FILLER                    PIC X(04) VALUE SPACES.
```

Figure 6.4   (*continued*)

```
☐   05  FILLER                        PIC X(07) VALUE
☐     'ALGEBRA'.
☐   05  FILLER                        PIC X(04) VALUE SPACES.
☐   05  FILLER                        PIC X(08) VALUE
☐     'GEOMETRY'.
☐   05  FILLER                        PIC X(04) VALUE SPACES.
☐   05  FILLER                        PIC X(07) VALUE
☐     'ENGLISH'.
☐   05  FILLER                        PIC X(04) VALUE SPACES.
☐   05  FILLER                        PIC X(07) VALUE
☐     'PHYSICS'.
☐   05  FILLER                        PIC X(04) VALUE SPACES.
☐   05  FILLER                        PIC X(09) VALUE
☐     'CHEMISTRY'.
☐   05  FILLER                        PIC X(03) VALUE SPACES.
☐   05  FILLER                        PIC X(05) VALUE
☐     'TOTAL'.
☐   05  FILLER                        PIC X(04) VALUE SPACES.
☐   05  FILLER                        PIC X(07) VALUE
☐     'PERCENTILE'.
☐   05  FILLER                        PIC X(08) VALUE SPACES.
☐   EJECT
☐ PROCEDURE DIVISION.
☐   SKIP2
☐ 000-PREPARE-STUDENT-REPORT.
☐   PERFORM 010-SET-UP THRU 010-EXIT.
☐   PERFORM 020-CHOOSE-REPORT THRU 020-EXIT
☐       UNTIL END-OF-FILE-SWITCH = 'YES'.
☐   PERFORM 030-WRAP-UP THRU 030-EXIT.
☐   STOP RUN.
☐ 000-EXIT.
☐   SKIP2
☐ 010-SET-UP.
☐   OPEN INPUT   CARD-FILE
☐     OUTPUT    PRINT-FILE, ERROR-FILE.
☐   PERFORM 100-WRITE-HEADINGS THRU 100-EXIT.
☐   PERFORM 060-READ-FILE THRU 060-EXIT.
☐ 010-EXIT.
☐   SKIP2
☐ 020-CHOOSE-REPORT.
☐   PERFORM 040-EDIT-DATA THRU 040-EXIT.
☐   SKIP1
☐     IF REPORT-SELECT = 'G'
☐        PERFORM 050-PRINT-REPORT THRU 050-EXIT
☐     ELSE
☐        PERFORM 051-PRINT-ERROR-REPORT THRU
☐          051-EXIT.
```

Figure 6.4   (*continued*)

```
☐    MOVE 'G' TO REPORT-SELECT.
☐    MOVE SPACE TO SCORE-ERROR.
☐    SKIP1
☐    PERFORM 060-READ-FILE THRU 060-EXIT.
☐ 020-EXIT.
☐    SKIP2
☐ 030-WRAP-UP.
☐    PERFORM 160-TOTALS THRU 160-EXIT.
☐    PERFORM 161-ERROR-TOTALS THRU 161-EXIT.
☐    CLOSE CARD-FILE
☐        PRINT-FILE
☐        ERROR-FILE.
☐ 030-EXIT.
☐    EJECT
☐ 040-EDIT-DATA.
☐    MOVE SPACES TO ERROR-UNDERLINE.
☐    IF I-STU-NUM IS NUMERIC
☐        NEXT SENTENCE
☐    ELSE
☐      MOVE ALL '-' TO EU-ID
☐      MOVE 'E' TO REPORT-SELECT.
☐    SKIP2
☐    IF I-STU-NAME EQUAL SPACES
☐      MOVE ALL '-' TO EU-NAME
☐      MOVE 'E' TO REPORT-SELECT
☐    ELSE
☐      IF I-STU-NAME IS ALPHABETIC
☐            NEXT SENTENCE
☐      ELSE
☐          MOVE ALL '-' TO EU-NAME
☐          MOVE 'E' TO REPORT-SELECT.
☐      SKIP2
☐    IF I-SEX IS ALPHABETIC
☐      IF VALID-CHARS
☐            NEXT SENTENCE
☐      ELSE
☐            MOVE ALL '-' TO EU-SEX
☐ MOVE 'E' TO REPORT-SELECT
☐    ELSE
☐      MOVE ALL '-' TO EU-SEX
☐      MOVE 'E' TO REPORT-SELECT.
☐    SKIP2
☐    IF VALID-RANGE
☐      NEXT SENTENCE
☐    ELSE
☐      MOVE ALL '-' TO EU-AGE
☐      MOVE 'E' TO REPORT-SELECT.
```

Figure 6.4   (*continued*)

```
□    SKIP1
□    IF I-ALG-SCORE IS NUMERIC
□       IF VALID-ALG
□            NEXT SENTENCE
□       ELSE
□            MOVE ALL '-' TO EU-ALG
□            MOVE 'E' TO REPORT-SELECT
□            MOVE '*' TO SCORE-ERROR
□    ELSE
□       MOVE ALL '-' TO EU-ALG
□       MOVE 'E' TO REPORT-SELECT
□       MOVE '*' TO SCORE-ERROR.
□    EJECT
□    IF I-GEO-SCORE IS NUMERIC
□         IF VALID-GEO
□              NEXT SENTENCE
□           ELSE
□             MOVE ALL '-' TO EU-GEO
□             MOVE 'E' TO REPORT-SELECT
□             MOVE '*' TO SCORE-ERROR
□    ELSE
□       MOVE ALL '-' TO EU-GEO
□       MOVE 'E' TO REPORT-SELECT
□       MOVE '*' TO SCORE-ERROR.
□    SKIP2
□    IF I-ENG-SCORE IS NUMERIC
□       IF VALID-ENG
□            NEXT SENTENCE
□       ELSE
□            MOVE ALL '-' TO EU-ENG
□            MOVE 'E' TO REPORT-SELECT
□            MOVE '*' TO SCORE-ERROR
□    ELSE
□       MOVE ALL '-' TO EU-ENG
□       MOVE 'E' TO REPORT-SELECT
□       MOVE '*' TO SCORE-ERROR.
□    SKIP2
□    IF I-PHY-SCORE IS NUMERIC
□       IF VALID-PHY
□            NEXT SENTENCE
□       ELSE
□            MOVE ALL '-' TO EU-PHY
□            MOVE 'E' TO REPORT-SELECT
□            MOVE '*' TO SCORE-ERROR
□    ELSE
□       MOVE ALL '-' TO EU-PHY
```

Figure 6.4   (*continued*)

```
□      MOVE 'E' TO REPORT-SELECT
□      MOVE '*' TO SCORE-ERROR.
□    SKIP2
□    IF I-CHEM-SCORE IS NUMERIC
□      IF VALID-CHEM
□          NEXT SENTENCE
□      ELSE
□          MOVE ALL '-' TO EU-CHEM
□          MOVE 'E' TO REPORT-SELECT
□          MOVE '*' TO SCORE-ERROR
□    ELSE
□      MOVE ALL '-' TO EU-CHEM
□      MOVE 'E' TO REPORT-SELECT
□      MOVE '*' TO SCORE-ERROR.
□ 040-EXIT.
□    EJECT
□ 050-PRINT-REPORT.
□    IF LINE-COUNT = 15
□      PERFORM 100-WRITE-HEADINGS THRU 100-EXIT.
□    PERFORM 110-COMPUTE-PERCENT THRU 110-EXIT.
□    PERFORM 120-PRINT-STUDENTS THRU   120-EXIT.
□ 050-EXIT.
□    SKIP2
□ 051-PRINT-ERROR-REPORT.
□    IF E-LINE-COUNT = 0
□      PERFORM 101-ERROR-HEADINGS THRU 101-EXIT.
□    IF E-LINE-COUNT = 7
□      PERFORM 101-ERROR-HEADINGS THRU 101-EXIT.
□    IF SCORE-ERROR = SPACE
□      PERFORM 130-COMPUTE-PERCENT THRU 130-EXIT.
□    PERFORM 131-E-OUTPUT-FORMAT THRU 131 EXIT.
□    MOVE ERROR-OUTPUT-REC TO WRITE-ERROR-LINE.
□    WRITE ERROR-LINE
□      AFTER ADVANCING 1 LINES.
□    MOVE ERROR-UNDERLINE TO WRITE-ERROR-LINE.
□    WRITE ERROR-LINE
□      AFTER ADVANCING 2 LINES.
□    ADD 1 TO E-LINE-COUNT.
□ 051-EXIT.
□    SKIP2
□ 060-READ-FILE.
□    READ CARD-FILE INTO WS-INPUT-REC
□      AT END MOVE 'YES' TO END-OF-FILE-SWITCH.
□ 060-EXIT.
□    EJECT
□ 100-WRITE-HEADINGS.
```

Figure 6.4   (*continued*)

```
□    MOVE SPACES TO PRINT-LINE.
□    WRITE PRINT-LINE FROM STUDENT-HEAD
□       AFTER TOP-OF-PAGE.
□    MOVE CURRENT-DATE TO TODAYS-DATE.
□    MOVE PAGE-LINE TO WRITE-LINE.
□    WRITE PRINT-LINE
□       AFTER ADVANCING 1 LINES.
□    ADD 1 TO PAGE-NUMBER.
□    MOVE HEADING-LINE TO WRITE-LINE.
□    WRITE PRINT-LINE
□       AFTER ADVANCING 1 LINES.
□    MOVE 0 TO LINE-COUNT.
□ 100-EXIT.
□       SKIP2
□ 101-ERROR-HEADINGS.
□ 101-ERROR-HEADINGS.
□    MOVE SPACES TO ERROR-LINE.
□    MOVE ERROR-HEAD TO WRITE-ERROR-LINE.
□    WRITE ERROR-LINE
□       AFTER TOP-OF-PAGE.
□    MOVE CURRENT-DATE TO TODAYS-DATE.
□    ADD 1 TO E-PAGE-NUMBER.
□    MOVE PAGE-LINE TO WRITE-ERROR-LINE.
□    WRITE ERROR-LINE
□       AFTER ADVANCING 1 LINES.
□    MOVE HEADING-LINE TO WRITE-ERROR-LINE.
□    WRITE ERROR-LINE
□       AFTER ADVANCING 1 LINES.
□    101-EXIT.
□       SKIP2
□ 110-COMPUTE-PERCENT.
□       COMPUTE O-TOTALS = I-ALG-SCORE + I-GEO-SCORE +
□       I-ENG-SCORE + I-PHY-SCORE + I-CHEM-SCORE.
□    DIVIDE O-TOTALS BY 5 GIVING
□       BOARD-PERCENTILE ROUNDED.
□    PERFORM 140-ASSIGN-PERCENTILE THRU 140-EXIT.
□ 110-EXIT.
□    EJECT
□ 120-PRINT-STUDENTS.
□    MOVE SPACES TO PRINT-LINE
□    PERFORM 121-OUTPUT-FORMAT THRU 121-EXIT.
□    WRITE PRINT-LINE FROM OUTPUT-REC
□       AFTER ADVANCING 2 LINES.
□    ADD 1 TO COUNTER.
□    ADD 1 TO LINE-COUNT.
□ 120-EXIT.
```

Figure 6.4   (*continued*)

```
☐    SKIP2
☐  121-OUTPUT-FORMAT.
☐    MOVE I-STU-NUM TO O-STU-NUM.
☐    MOVE I-STU-NAME TO O-STU-NAME.
☐    MOVE I-SEX TO O-SEX.
☐    MOVE I-AGE TO O-AGE.
☐    MOVE I-ALG-SCORE TO O-ALG-SCORE.
☐    MOVE I-GEO-SCORE TO O-GEO-SCORE.
☐    MOVE I-ENG-SCORE TO O-ENG-SCORE.
☐    MOVE I-PHY-SCORE TO O-PHY-SCORE.
☐    MOVE I-CHEM-SCORE TO O-CHEM-SCORE.
☐    MOVE BOARD-PERCENTILE TO O-PERCENTILE.
☐  121-EXIT.
☐    SKIP2
☐  130-COMPUTE-PERCENT.
☐    COMPUTE ERROR-TOTAL = I-ALG-SCORE + I-GEO-SCORE +
☐       I-ENG-SCORE + I-PHY-SCORE + I-CHEM-SCORE.
☐    DIVIDE ERROR-TOTAL BY 5 GIVING
☐       BOARD-PERCENTILE ROUNDED.
☐    PERFORM 150-ASSIGN-PERCENTILE THRU 150-EXIT.
☐  130-EXIT.
☐    SKIP2
☐  131-E-OUTPUT-FORMAT.
☐    MOVE I-STU-NUM TO E-STU-NUM.
☐    MOVE I-STU-NAME TO E-STU-NAME.
☐    MOVE I-SEX TO E-SEX.
☐    MOVE I-AGE TO E-AGE.
☐    MOVE I-ALG-SCORE TO E-ALG-SCORE.
☐    MOVE I-GEO-SCORE TO E-GEO-SCORE.
☐    MOVE I-ENG-SCORE TO E-ENG-SCORE.
☐    MOVE I-PHY-SCORE TO E-PHY-SCORE.
☐    MOVE I-CHEM-SCORE TO E-CHEM-SCORE.
☐    IF SCORE-ERROR = SPACE
☐      MOVE ERROR-TOTAL TO E-TOTALS
☐      MOVE BOARD-PERCENTILE TO E-PERCENTILE
☐    ELSE
☐      MOVE ZEROES TO E-TOTALS
☐                      E-PERCENTILE.
☐  131-EXIT.
☐    EJECT
☐  140-ASSIGN-PERCENTILE.
☐    IF NINETY
☐      ADD 1 TO 90-PERCENT-COUNT
☐    IF EIGHTY
☐      ADD 1 TO 80-PERCENT-COUNT
☐    IF SEVENTY
```

Figure 6.4   (*continued*)

```
☐       ADD 1 TO 70-PERCENT-COUNT
☐    IF SIXTY
☐       ADD 1 TO 60-PERCENT-COUNT
☐    IF FIFTY
☐       ADD 1 TO 50-PERCENT-COUNT
☐ 140-EXIT.
☐    SKIP2
☐ 150-ASSIGN-PERCENTILE.
☐    IF NINETY
            ADD 1 TO 90-PERCENT-COUNT
☐    IF EIGHTY
☐       ADD 1 TO 80-PERCENT-COUNT
☐    IF SEVENTY
☐       ADD 1 TO 70-PERCENT-COUNT
☐    IF SIXTY
☐       ADD 1 TO 60-PERCENT-COUNT
☐    IF FIFTY
☐       ADD 1 TO 50-PERCENT-COUNT
☐ 150-EXIT.
☐    EJECT
☐ 160-TOTALS.
☐    MOVE SPACES TO PRINT-LINE.
☐    MOVE COUNTER TO TOTAL.
☐    MOVE 90-COUNT TO SUM-NINETY.
☐    MOVE 80-COUNT TO SUM-EIGHTY.
☐    MOVE 70-COUNT TO SUM-SEVENTY.
☐    MOVE 60-COUNT TO SUM-SIXTY.
☐    MOVE 50-COUNT TO SUM-FIFTY.
☐    MOVE TOTAL-LINE TO WRITE-LINE.
☐    WRITE PRINT-LINE
☐       AFTER ADVANCING 2 LINES.
☐ 160-EXIT.
☐    SKIP2
☐ 161-ERROR-TOTALS.
☐    COMPUTE TOTAL-RECORDS = E-LINE-COUNT + COUNTER.
☐     MOVE E-LINE-COUNT TO TOTAL-ERRORS.
☐     MOVE E-TOTAL-LINE TO WRITE-ERROR-LINE.
☐     WRITE ERROR-LINE
☐       AFTER ADVANCING 1 LINES.
☐ 161-EXIT.
☐☐
☐
```

Figure 6.4   (*continued*)

ply by counting the decisions (IF THEN ELSE constructs) in the paragraph. There are no loops or GOTO's which would complicate matters further, but the Cyclomatic Complexity value is still too large. You should have counted 16 decisions (don't forget to count primitive decisions). Using the $C = D + 1$ equation, $C = 17$. To understand this paragraph's logic requires an ability to comprehend greater than 2^4 unique pathways (or unique processing situations).

You should immediately see why creating a basis set of paths is prudent. But even a basis set of paths > 10 is more than we want to understand. According to our previous discussion of Miller's work, The human mind is only capable of processing approximately three bits of information (or 2^3 paths). This paragraph requires us to process over four bits of information. Although, it can be done, life is simpler if you do not have to construct or maintain this paragraph.

The alternative is to redesign this program segment through functional decomposition (using the rule that each paragraph contains only a single processing function). The paragraph actually contains nine functions that could be put into nine independent paragraphs, one for Student Number with a C of 2; one for Student Name with a C of 3; one for Student Sex with a C of 3; one for Student Age with a C of 2; one for Student Algebra Score with a C of 3; one for Student Geography Score with a C of 3; one for Student English Score with a C of 3; one for Student Physics Score with a C of 3; and one for Student Chemistry Score with a C of 3.

The result of decomposition is that we are in every instance handling less that two bits of information, which is acceptable. For our purposes, however, we are not going to decompose the paragraph, but will work with it as is to demonstrate how to develop test cases for a reasonably complicated example because decomposition will not always be a reasonable option.

Figure 6.5 represents the control flow graph that could be constructed for the paragraph. This is by no means the only version of a graph that could be built. So, other control flow graph interpretations are possible. Notice that I have annotated the graph with (1) the conditions represented in each decision, and (2) which edges represent the "true" and "false" branches. With these annotations and the field lengths specified in the requirements document (see Figure 6.3), we now have enough information to build test cases.

The first step is to enumerate the pathways following the rules discussed earlier. The 17 independent paths are shown in Figure 6.6. The second step is completed on a path by path basis. It is to determine the set of values, one for each field, in the student College Boards record which will result in the path being exercised during test execution.

Cyclomatic number = 17

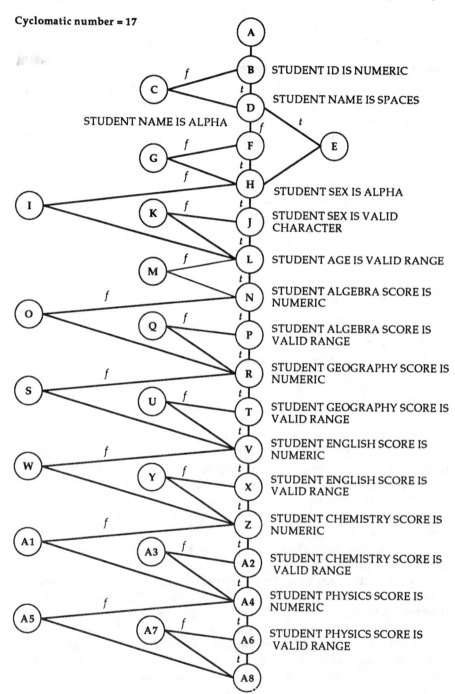

Figure 6.5 Control Flow Graph for Paragraph 040-EDIT-DATA

1. ABCD	FGHI	LMNO	RS	VW	ZA1 A4A5	A8
2. ABCD	FGHI	LMNO	RS	VW	ZA1 A4A6	A7A8
3. ABCD	FGHI	LMNO	RS	VW	ZA1 A4A6	A8
4. ABCD	FGHI	LMNO	RS	VW	ZA2 A3A4	A6A8
5. ABCD	FGHI	LMNO	RS	VW	ZA2 A4A6	A8
6. ABCD	FGHI	LMNO	RS	VXY	ZA2 A4A6	A8
7. ABCD	FGHI	LMNO	RS	VX	ZA2 A4A6	A8
8. ABCD	FGHI	LMNO	RTU	VX	ZA2 A4A6	A8
9. ABCD	FGHI	LMNO	RTV	X	ZA2 A4A6	A8
10. ABCD	FGHI	LMNPQ	RTV	X	ZA2 A4A6	A8
11. ABCD	FGHI	LMNP	RTV	X	ZA2 A4A6	A8
12. ABCD	FGHI	LNP	RTV	X	ZA2 A4A6	A8
13. ABCD	FGHJK	LNP	RTV	X	ZA2 A4A6	A8
14. ABCD	FGHJ	LNP	RTV	X	ZA2 A4A6	A8
15. ABCD	FHJ	LNP	RTV	X	ZA2 A4A6	A8
16. ABCDE	HJ	LNP	RTV	X	ZA2 A4A6	A8
17. AB DE	HJ	LNP	RTV	X	ZA2 A4A6	A8

Figure 6.6   The Basis Paths for Paragraph 040-EDIT-DATA

Figure 6.7 is a set of test data records that will result in each of the 17 independent paths be executed.

One thing you may notice is that the test data do not contain a record that possesses valid values in every field. This data set, if executed as is, would not generate a single detail line on the valid report of student Collage Boards scores. Do not despair. The techniques discussed in later chapters would force us to generate at least one valid student record. Remember, your intention is to construct a file of test data records that is the combination of the test data developed using both the White box and Black Box approaches.

Wouldn't it be easier to develop the control flow graph if the logic in the sample paragraph were represented in a Warnier/Orr diagram? If so, we could follow the rules described earlier for this type of transition. I did not tell you how I developed the graph in Figure 6.5 because I followed my intuition and used my experience designing systems to structure the graph. This is the kind of esoteric approach we must avoid! Avoiding this type of procedure is important because following explicit (documented) rules results in consistent control flow graph interpretations of the same program structure. This in turn results in more effective Regression Testing.

As a final note, the Warnier/Orr diagrams, which are based in classical set theory, automatically generate a functionally decomposed

	ID	NAME	SEX	AGE	ALG	GEO	ENG	CHE	PHY
1.	WXYZ	99999999 . . . 9	1	19	X94	X94	X94	X94	X94
2.	WXYZ	99999999 . . . 9	1	19	X94	X94	X94	X94	150
3.	WXYZ	99999999 . . . 9	1	19	X94	X94	X94	X94	094
4.	WXYZ	99999999 . . . 9	1	19	X94	X94	X94	150	094
5.	WXYZ	99999999 . . . 9	1	19	X94	X94	X94	094	094
6.	WXYZ	99999999 . . . 9	1	19	X94	X94	150	094	094
7.	WXYZ	99999999 . . . 9	1	19	X94	X94	094	094	094
8.	WXYZ	99999999 . . . 9	1	19	X94	150	094	094	094
9.	WXYZ	99999999 . . . 9	1	19	X94	094	094	094	094
10.	WXYZ	99999999 . . . 9	1	19	150	094	094	094	094
11.	WXYZ	99999999 . . . 9	1	19	094	094	094	094	094
12.	WXYZ	99999999 . . . 9	1	17	094	094	094	094	094
13.	WXYZ	99999999 . . . 9	X	17	094	094	094	094	094
14.	WXYZ	99999999 . . . 9	M	17	094	094	094	094	094
15.	WXYZ	DAN MOSLEY	M	17	094	094	094	094	094
16.	WXYZ		M	17	094	094	094	094	094
17.	0001		M	17	094	094	094	094	094

Figure 6.7   The Basis Set of Test Cases for Paragraph 040-EDIT-DATA

process logic diagram when properly used. Thus, we would not be dealing with program modules of high structural complexity.

6.2 BASIS TESTING: A NEW APPROACH

Constructing the control flow graph from program statements or program flow charts is problematic. There are no specific guidelines (see Hetzel [3] for a limited set) for moving from one level of representation to the other, and physical detail present in both source listings and flow charts obscures the logical structure that must be brought out by the translation. Consequently, the ability to create the control flow graph from a logical program design diagram using a set of concise transformation rules would facilitate test case development. It would also allow paper and pencil execution of the test cases during review of the detailed design. A further advantage is that the systems development life cycle becomes more economical because module complexity can assessed earlier in the cycle. Thus, redesign of complex modules can precede physical design and coding.

Combining McCabe's testing technique with an already formalized and integrated systems development methodology is a positive step. Such a merger provides an inherently better framework for testing. Moreover, constructing control flow graphs from information in logical process diagrams becomes a straightforward procedure with precise rules.

A particularly good candidate for the merger is the Data Structured Systems Development methodology offered by Ken Orr [9,10], that incorporates the ideas set forth by J. D. Warnier [11]. Orr's method is a data structured approach using modified Warnier diagrams to design both data and process logic structures. An excellent discussion on program design using a data structured approach can be found in Hansen's data structured program design text [2].

The Warnier/Orr diagramming technique is derived from classical set theory, and both data and processes are defined as proper sets and subsets of elements. Process diagrams portray program logic as sets of actions which are abstract pictures of eventual blocks of source code in the finished product. A Warnier/Orr diagram exemplifying the logical design of the previous data validation procedure is shown in Figure 6.8.

In the data editing procedure illustrated in the figure, sets of actions (sequence), and alternating sets of actions (selection) can be conceptualized as equivalent to individual control flow graph nodes. Although this particular diagram has no iterated sets of processes, repeating sets of actions can be conceptualized as single nodes connected to themselves.

In Warnier/Orr diagrams, nesting of sets of actions within other sets of actions creates multiple levels of networks and demonstrates the hierarchical relationship among procedural components (networks). Control flow graphs corresponding to any level or combination of nested levels within the Warnier/Orr hierarchy can be constructed, because control flow graphs, as McCabe described them, are network diagrams. They are excellent for showing the structure within a given hierarchical level.

A Warnier/Orr process set containing hierarchically subordinate sets could (for testing purposes) be represented by a single flow graph node. In this manner, process logic details not required for testing at a particular hierarchical level are omitted. Superordinate sets could be symbolized by nodes containing an empty bracket ({). Such nodes would be "undefined" and contain potential subdiagrams of process logic sets, each of unknown complexity.

Undefined nodes are high-level abstractions that are treated as single nodes for purposes of calculating complexity and ascertaining basis paths (undefined nodes are really the redundant nodes discussed during the calculation of total program complexity). Thus, a hierar-

DATA EDIT PROCEDURE {

  INITIAL ERROR INDICATOR

  STUDENT NUMBER NUMERIC (0,1) { SKIP

  (+)
  STUDENT NUMBER NOT NUMERIC (0,1) { SET NUMERIC ERROR ON
  SELECT ERROR REPORT

  STUDENT NAME BLANK (0,1) { SET NAME ERROR ON
  SELECT ERROR REPORT

  (+)
  STUDENT NAME NOT BLANK (0,1) {
    STUDENT NAME ALPHABETIC (0,1) { SKIP
    (+)
    STUDENT NAME NOT ALPHABETIC (0,1) { SET NAME ERROR O
    SELECT ERROR REPC

  STUDENT SEX ALPHABETIC (0,1) {
    STUDENT SEX VALID (0,1) { SKIP
    (+)
    STUDENT SEX NOT VALID (0,1) { SET SEX ERROR ON
    SELECT ERROR REPO

  (+)
  STUDENT SEX NOT ALPHABETIC (0,1) { SET SEX ERROR ON
  SELECT ERROR REPORT

  STUDENT AGE VALID (0,1) { SKIP

  (+)
  STUDENT AGE NOT VALID (0,1) { SET AGE ERROR ON
  SELECT ERROR REPORT

  STUDENT ALG SCORE NUMERIC (0,1) {
    STUDENT ALG SCORE VALID (0,1) { SKIP
    (+)
    STUDENT ALG SCORE NOT VALID (0,1) { SET SCORE ERROR C
    SELECT ERROR REPC

  (+)
  STUDENT ALG SCORE NOT NUMERIC (0,1) { SET SCORE ERROR ON
  SELECT ERROR REPORT

  STUDENT CHEM SCORE NUMERIC (0,1) {
    STUDENT CHEM SCORE VALID (0,1) { SKIP
    (+)
    STUDENT CHEM SCORE NOT VALID (0,1) { SET SCORE ERROR C
    SELECT ERROR REPO

  (+)
  STUDENT CHEM SCORE NOT NUMERIC (0,1) { SET SCORE ERROR ON
  SELECT ERROR REPORT

}

chical leveling (modularization) of networked flow diagrams can be achieved. The levels chosen would depend on modularization considerations imposed by the designer(s) and/or environmental constraints.

Figure 6.9 contains examples of the Warnier/Orr representations of the basic logical structures and their parallel representations in control flow graph notation. There is essentially a one-to-one relationship between the Warnier/Orr and flow graph portrayals of the basic structures. Complex decision logic, however, is harder to represent. Warnier/Orr diagrams illustrate complex decisions through the logical nesting of conditions. The logical ANDing of conditions in these diagrams translates directly to a corresponding complex of edges and nodes in the control flow graph. The logical ORing of conditions requires repetition of identical sets of actions at differing levels within

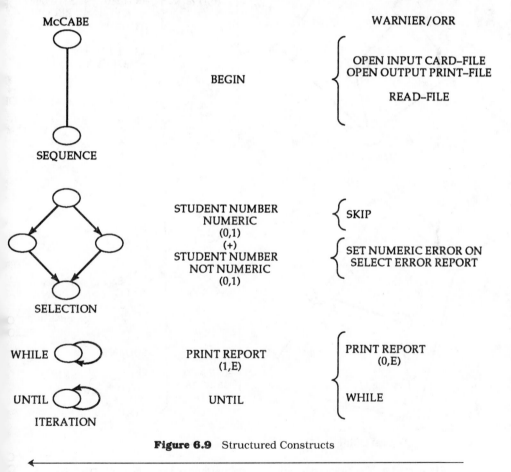

Figure 6.9   Structured Constructs

Figure 6.8   Warnier/Orr Representation of the Data Validation Procedure

the Warnier/Orr process logic model. Negated logically ANDed conditions also result in repeated sets of dependent actions in the diagram. When either of these structures occurs, two control flow graph representations are possible. In one, the duplicated sets of actions are mapped to separate nodes (see Figure 6.10); in the other, a single node represents the redundant sets of actions (see Figure 6.11).

The second representation is recommended and is the basis for a special rule for converting Warnier/Orr complex decision logic to con-

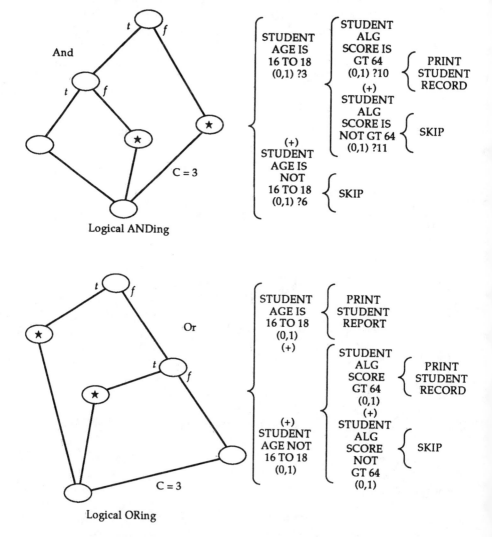

Figure 6.10 Control Flow Graph Representations of Complex Logic Diagrammed with Redundant Nodes

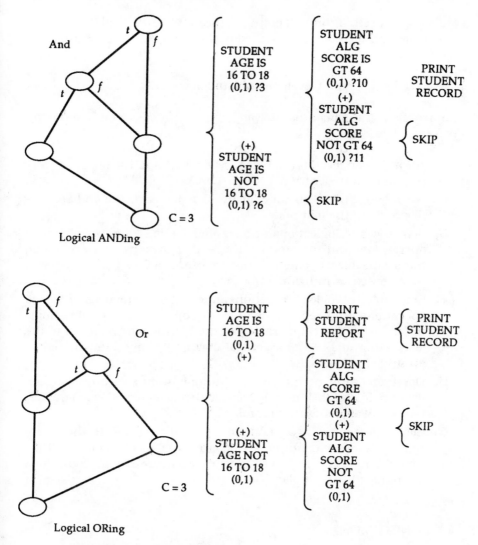

Figure 6.11   Control Flow Graph Representations of Complex Logic Diagrammed without Redundant Nodes

trol flow graph structures: "Show the repeated action sets as a single node within the control flow graph." Doing so in no way affects complexity calculation, because the relationship of edges to nodes within the graph remains constant. It does, however, simplify the diagramatic information.

An important advantage of a data structured approach to control flow graph construction is that it prevents the underestimation of complexity that occurs when decisions with combinations of conditions are mapped to single branch points in the graph [8]. Complex decisions in Warnier/Orr are always presented in their simplest form and all conditions are treated separately.

6.2.1 Flow Graph Development Guidelines

Control flow graphs can be derived from Warnier/Orr diagrams using these guidelines:

1. For a chosen level in the Warnier/Orr diagram, the begin set corresponds to the entry node.
2. For a chosen level in the Warnier/Orr diagram, the end set corresponds to the exit node.
3. Sequences of logical operations, alternative sequences of logical operations, and repetitions of logical operations that are at the hierarchical level being mapped to a control flow graph, are each represented as individual nodes.
4. Sequences of logical operations, alternative sequences of logical operations, and repetitions of logical operations that are subordinate in the logical hierarchy of the Warnier/Orr diagram to the level being mapped to a control flow graph, are summarized as an undefined node ({).
5. Development of nodes from logical operation sets proceeds top-down (left to right) in agreement with the control flow characteristics of Warnier/Orr diagrams.
6. Set to node mapping is a one-to-one relationship with the exception of complex conditions that are negated or logically ORed. Redundant sets of logical actions representing disjoint conditions are mapped to a single node.

6.3 CONCLUSION

Procedures for testing complex software systems should ensure standardization of testing practices and test case design, and promote rigorous testing of software components. Testing should begin early in the development process and should be done within the framework of an established systems development methodology. The ability to calculate complexity while still in the logical design portion of the life cycle allows each design iteration and/or design alternative to be evaluated before construction starts. Thus, test case development strategy becomes an important part of design verification and may impact the selection of a design alternative.

In a staged or phased approach to systems development, the output from a particular stage becomes the input for the succeeding stage. In the normal life cycle progression, input for the testing stage is composed of deliverables from the coding stage. However, control flow graphs built from Warnier/Orr design diagrams use documentation from the logical design phase as an alternative to source listings from the coding stage. The latter approach is better because the logical design is not clouded by physical considerations associated with implementation.

Physical detail is extraneous and not pictured in flow graphs. It does not affect test case generation and is discarded when control flow graphs are drawn from code listings. Test cases based on information in design diagrams have a higher probability of detecting analysis and designerrors because the flow graphs will be a truer representation of the design's logical structure. There will be fewer errors in the flow graphs resulting in more rigorous test cases.

Automating the method of control flow graph construction described previously would eliminate the necessity of converting from Warnier/Orr diagrams to control flow graphs. The logical significance of the control flow is inherent in the relationships established among the sets of actions in the Warnier/Orr process diagram. It should be comparatively easy to develop algorithms to extract the information required to construct test cases directly from the Warner/Orr diagrams.

Automation would also address a general criticism of White Box techniques. Being paper and pencil methods, they are time consuming to use and may not be a viable approach given the amount of time allocated to unit testing.

As both the Warnier/Orr and control flow graph diagramming techniques are soundly based in mathematical theory, their complementary use suggests another possible application. For example, reverse engineering of unstructured programs can be accomplished by creating flow graphs for the modules, integrating them into a program flow graph, and translating it into a a Warnier/Orr diagram. The program could then be restructured and recoded from the Warnier/Orr diagram. Consequently, the costs of maintaining older systems could be substantially reduced. A software to already exist which can do these things i.e., Recorder from KnowledgeWare, Inc.

The structural relationship between control flow graphs and Warnier/Orr diagrams is the basis of a powerful procedure for developing good test cases and determining module complexity for programs designed from a data structured approach. The programs will have fewer errors and the evaluation of structural complexity will optimize modularization. The ultimate result will be an increase in software systems reliability.

REFERENCES

1. Bohm, C., and G. Jacopini, "Flow Diagrams,Turing Machines and Languages with Only Two Formation Rules," *Communications of the ACM,* 9, no. 5 (1966).

2. Hansen, Kirk, *Data Structured Program Design.* Englewood Cliffs, N.J.: Prentice Hall, 1986.

3. Hetzel, William, *The Complete Guide to Software Testing, 2ed.* Wellesley, MA: QED Information Sciences, Inc., 1988.

4. King, David, *Current Practices In Software Development: A Guide to Successful Systems.* New York: Yourdon Press, 1985.

5. McCabe, Thomas, J., "A Complexity Measure," *IEEE Transactions on Software Engineering,* SE-2, no. 4 (1976).

6. McCabe, Thomas, J., *Structured Testing: A Testing Methodology Using the McCabe Complexity Metric.* NBS SPECIAL PUBLICATION, CONTRACT NB82NAAR5518, 1982.

7. Miller, George, "The Magical Number Seven, Plus or Minus Two: Some Limits on Our Capacity for Processing Information," *The Psychological Review,* 63, no. 2 (March 1956), 81–97.

8. Myers, Glenford, "An Extention to the Cyclomatic Measure of Program Complexity," *ACM SIGPLAN Notices* (October 1977), 61–64.

9. Orr, Kenneth, *Structured Systems Development.* New York: Yourdon Press, 1977.

10. Orr, Kenneth, *Structured Requirements Definition.* Topeka, Kansas: Ken Orr and Associates, Inc., 1982.

11. Warnier, J. D., *Logical Construction of Programs.* New York: Van Nostrand Reinhold, 1976.

12. Yourdon, Edward, and Larry Constantine, *Structured Design: Fundamentals of Computer Program and Systems Design.* Englewood Cliffs, N.J.: Prentice Hall; 1979.

7

Equivalence Partitioning, Boundary Analysis, and Error Guessing

For years we have known that 50 percent of the faults we test for arise from errors in the requirements specification.

Dwayne L. Knirk, 1989*

Equivalence Partitioning and Boundary Analysis are complementary Black Box test case design strategies that are very useful early in the development life cycle. They are techniques that translate written specifications into function-based test data. Restrictions on input that are described in the functional specification document are used to define *classes* of input and output. Equivalence partitioning describes categories of input only while boundary analysis can define both classes of input and classes of output.

Both techniques result in *two* basic kinds of input classes, classes that are *valid* and those that are *invalid*. In the majority of instances there will be a single class describing the valid input and one to several classes that describe invalid types of input. Test cases representative of each class are created and added to the test data set.

Myers [1] has established a set of guidelines for identifying equivalence classes and a set of rules for constructing test cases that cover each class. An additional set of rules governs the creation of test cases for the boundaries of the equivalence classes.

---

* From Dwayne L. Knirk, **Specialty**, published in *The Letter T*. Programming Environments, Inc. Trinton Falls, NJ, March, 1989.

7.1 DEFINING EQUIVALENCE CLASSES

Defining equivalence classes is to some extent a trial and error process. It is based largely on intuition and past experience, and is something you may have been or are currently doing as part of your testing activities. There are, however, general guidelines that can expedite the process. As adapted from Myers, they are:

1. For input descriptions that specify a range of possible values (continuous input), identify *one* valid equivalence class that is representative of the values included in the range, and identify *two* invalid equivalence classes, one each, for values that lie above and below the range.

2. For input descriptions that define a set of values, each of which is processed differently (discrete input), identify *one* valid equivalence class for each value and *one* additional equivalence class that represents a value not included in the set.

3. For "data Typed" input (e.g., the COBOL data types NUMERIC and ALPHABETIC) create *one* valid equivalence class representing the correct data type and at least *one* equivalence class representing a data type that would be considered incorrect.

4. For mixed data types (e.g., the COBOL data type Alphanumeric) with specific mandatory conditions (e.g., as in PART-NUMBER where the first position in PART-NUMBER must always be an alphabetic character), identify *one* equivalence class in which the conditions are met and *one* equivalence class in which the conditions are not met.

5. Review the equivalence classes looking for instances where the classes may be further subdivided. The classes are subdivided only if values are discovered in a class which are not all processed in the same manner.

Furthermore, Myers says it is helpful to create a table with three columns, a left-most column where each external input restriction is separately listed, a center column where the valid equivalence classes are described, and a right-most column where the invalid equivalence classes are placed. Arbitrarily number all equivalence classes in the table. Organizing and numbering the equivalence classes in this manner simplifies the test case construction.

7.2 CONSTRUCTING TEST CASES FROM THE TABLED EQUIVALENCE CLASSES

The rules that follow for building test data are predicated on testing economy. [That is they allow for the least number of test cases that can safely be created and executed with a reasonable level of confidence that we are testing effectively.] It is possible to create fewer test cases, but these collapsed test cases will be less effective because of the "error masking" phenomenon.

Error masking can occur when a test case contains more than one invalid value. The system will evaluate each value separately. The situation may arise where the evaluation process is terminated when the first invalid value is discovered. If this happens, the remaining invalid values are not processed, which means we don't know what would have happened had they been processed. An example of this is the COBOL ANDing operation (a Boolean operation) found in conditional actions. If the first condition is in the "false" or "off" state, the state of the second condition is not checked. The problem is that we do not know what the system's behavior regarding the second condition is unless its condition state is evaluated.

An abbreviated version of the test case construction guidelines Myers proposed is:

1. All of the valid equivalence classes can be incorporated into a single test case.
2. Each invalid equivalence class must be represented by a separate test case.

7.3 DEFINING BOUNDARY CONDITIONS FOR EQUIVALENCE CLASSES

Myers has defined boundary conditions as values that fall "on," "above," or "below" the edges of equivalence classes. An immediately obvious conclusion is that those values above and below the edges will have already been identified if the rules set forth above are used to develop the equivalence classes. So, the only new test cases we will create are the ones representing the values on each of the bounds. Consequently, Boundary Analysis is secondary to Equivalence Partitioning in implementation order. In addition, there is one major difference between the two techniques: *Boundary Analysis can also be applied to the output domain.*

The guidelines presented next are once again adapted from Myers's work.

7.3.1 Input Domain

1. For continuous input, write test cases that represent the lowest and highest valid values within the range.
2. For discrete ordered sets of input, construct test cases that represent the first and last elements in the set (e.g., a sequential input file).

7.3.2 Output Domain

1. For continuous output, construct input test cases that will cause output values to be generated for the highest and lowest value in the output range.

2. For discrete ordered sets of output, write input test cases which ensure that the first and last output elements will be processed (e.g., ensure that the first and last detail lines in an output report are printed).

7.4 ERROR GUESSING

Error Guessing is the process of using intuition and past experience to fill in gaps in the test data set. There are no rules to follow. The tester must review the test records with an eye toward recognizing missing conditions. Two familiar examples of error prone situations are division by zero and calculating the square root of a negative number. Either of these will result in system errors and garbled output.

Other areas where experience has demonstrated error proneness are the processing of variable length tables, calculation of median values for odd and even numbered populations, cyclic master file/data base updates (improper handling of duplicate keys, unmatched keys, etc.), overlapping storage areas, overwriting of buffers, forgetting to initialize buffer areas, and so forth. I am sure you can think of plenty of circumstances unique to your hardware/software environments and use of specific programming languages.

Error Guessing is as important as Equivalence Partitioning and Boundary Analysis because it is intended to compensate for their inherent incompleteness. As Equivalence Partitioning and Boundary Analysis complement one another, Error Guessing complements both of these techniques.

7.5 THE ROLLING ROCK POLYTECHNIC STATE UNIVERSITY EXAMPLE REVISITED

Table 7.1 illustrates the Equivalence Classes that could be defined for the College Board reporting program example presented in Chapter Six. Table 7.2 defines the test data records that would be generated for the classes in Table 7.1. Table 7.3 represents the boundary conditions that could be assessed on the input side for the classes in Table 7.1. Table 7.4 depicts the additional test cases that would be added to

TABLE 7.1   Rolling Rock Polytechnic State University Example Equivalence
Classes

Field	Equivalence Class
Student number	1. Numeric
	2. Nonnumeric
Student name	3. Alpha, Nonblank
	4. Blank
	5. Nonblank, Nonalpha
Student sex	6. Alpha, "M" or "F"
	7. Nonalpha
	8. Alpha, not "M" or "F"
Student age	9. Numeric, 15–18
	10. Nonnumeric
	11. Numeric < 15
	12. Numeric > 18
Student Algebra score	13. Numeric, 000–100
	14. Nonnumeric
	15. Numeric, < 000
	16. Numeric, > 100
Student Geography score	17. Numeric, 000–100
	18. Nonnumeric
	19. Numeric, < 000
	20. Numeric, > 100
Student English score	21. Numeric, 000–100
	22. Nonnumeric
	23. Numeric, < 000
	24. Numeric, > 100
Student Physics score	25. Numeric, 000–100
	26. Nonnumeric
	27. Numeric, < 000
	28. Numeric, > 100
Student Chemistry score	29. Numeric, 000–100
	30. Nonnumeric
	31. Numeric, < 000
	32. Numeric, > 100

Note: Equivalence classes 1, 3, 6, 9, 13, 17, 21, 25, 29 are valid classes.

TABLE 7.2   Rolling Rock Polytechnic State University Example Equivalence
Class Test Cases

Equivalence Class	Test Case	
1, 3, 6, 9, 13, 17, 21, 25, 29	9999Paige Mosley	F16098098098098098
2	XXXXPaige Mosley	F16098098098098098
4	9999	F16098098098098098
5	999977777777777.....	7F16098098098098098
7	9999Paige Mosley	916098098098098098
8	9999Paige Mosley	Z16098098098098098
10	9999Paige Mosley	FXX098098098098098
11	9999Paige Mosley	F14098098098098098
12	9999Paige Mosley	F19098098098098098
14	9999Paige Mosley	F16XXX098098098098
15	9999Paige Mosley	F16 -1098098098098
16	9999Paige Mosley	F16150098098098098
18	9999Paige Mosley	F16098XXX098098098
19	9999Paige Mosley	F16098 -1098098098
20	9999Paige Mosley	F16098150098098098
22	9999Paige Mosley	F16098098XXX098098
23	9999Paige Mosley	F16098098 -1098098
24	9999Paige Mosley	F16098098150098098
26	9999Paige Mosley	F16098098098XXX098
27	9999Paige Mosley	F16098098098 -1098
28	9999Paige Mosley	F16098098098150098
30	9999Paige Mosley	F16098098098098 XXX
31	9999Paige Mosley	F16098098098098 -1
32	9999Paige Mosley	F16098098098098150

Expected Output:
The only test case that would be written to the student report is the first one. The remaining test cases would be written to the error report. The invalid classes are underlined as they would appear in the finished error report.

TABLE 7.3   Rolling Rock Polytechnic State University Example
Boundary Conditions

Field	Boundary Condition
Student age	1. < 15 yrs
	2. = 15 yrs*
	3. > 18 yrs
	4. = 18 yrs*
Student Algebra score	5. < 000
	6. = 000*
	7. > 100
	8. = 100*
Student Geography score	9. < 000
	10. = 000*
	11. > 100
	12. = 100*
Student English score	13. < 000
	14. = 000*
	15. > 100
	16. = 100*
Student Physics score	17. < 000
	18. = 000*
	19. > 100
	20. = 100*
Student Chemistry score	21. < 000
	22. = 000*
	23. > 100
	24. = 100*

* Indicates the boundary conditions that would result in additional test cases.

TABLE 7.4   Rolling Rock Polytechnic State University Example Boundary
Test Cases

Boundary Condition	Test Case
2	9999Paige Mosley F15098098098098098
4	9999Paige Mosley F18098098098098098
6	9999Paige Mosley F16000098098098098
8	9999Paige Mosley F16100098098098098
10	9999Paige Mosley F16098000098098098
12	9999Paige Mosley F16098100098098098
14	9999Paige Mosley F16098098000098098
16	9999Paige Mosley F16098098100098098
18	9999Paige Mosley F16098098098000098
20	9999Paige Mosley F16098098098100098
22	9999Paige Mosley F16098098098098000
24	9999Paige Mosley F16098098098098100

Expected Output:
These boundary test cases would all be written to the student report, and
none of the fields underlined.

Input Domain

1. What happens if two students have the same Student Number?
2. What if the Student Number is blank?
3. What happens if a student retakes the exam?
   Does he or she now have two records/two Student Numbers?
4. What happens when two students have the same name?
5. What if Student Sex is blank?
6. What if Student Age is blank?
7. What if any or all of the Scores are blank?

Output Domain

1. What happens when more than one field in the same record
   contains invalid data? Is each underlined?
2. What happens when there are exactly enough detail lines for a
   single page? Does an unneeded page break occur?
3. What happens when there is no input data?

Figure 7.1   Rolling Rock Polytechnic State University Example Error
Guessing Conditions

the test data set as a result of Boundary Analysis. Finally, Figure 7.1 illuminates some of the possible conditions that could result in additional test records when error guessing is completed. The suggestions in Figure 7.1 are not comprehensive. You should use your experience and imagination to discover what other test conditions might also be included.

7.6 CONCLUSION

Equivalence Partitioning, Boundary Analysis, and Error Guessing are complementary methods of test case design and construction. When used together they create a specification-based test data set. This test data should not be executed, however, until it is supplemented with test cases developed through Cause-Effect Graphing, or Basis Testing and Structured Tableaux.

The methods covered in this chapter are somewhat intuitive. I have no doubt that you are already using these procedures to build test data, but possibly not in a formalized way. What these approaches do is formalize the methods making the guidelines for their use overt rather than covert. In other words, making them *repeatable* across testing sessions and across testers. This results in test data that are as complete, as consistent, and as correct as possible.

REFERENCES

1. Myers, Glenford, *The Art of Software Testing.* New York: Wiley-Interscience, 1979.

8

Cause-Effect Graphing

One weakness in boundary-value analysis and equivalence partitioning is that they do not explore combinations *of input circumstances.*

Glenford Myers, 1979 [4]

Cause-effect graphing is a Black Box technique originally developed at IBM System Development Division in Poughkeepsie, New York in the early 1970s by William Elmendorf (now retired) and propagated through the work of Richard Bender, also formerly of IBM, (currently President of Richard Bender & Associates, Inc.). Because it is a Black Box approach, it can be used early in the development process in conjunction with review procedures such as Desk Checking and Walkthroughs. Furthermore, it is a versatile approach because the test cases generated can be used during all subsequent levels of testing from Unit Testing to System Testing.

Elmendorf [2,3] describes the cause-effect graphing method as "disciplined specification-based testing." Based on Elmendorf's work, Myers [4] defines a cause-effect graph as "a formal language into which a natural-language specification is translated." The graph is a "combinatorial logic network" using notation similar to but simpler than standard electronics notation. More precisely, it is a Boolean graph describing the semantic content of a written functional specification as logical relationships between causes (inputs) and effects (outputs).

8.1 THE CAUSE-EFFECT GRAPH

Cause-effect graphs model complex narrative software descriptions as *digital logic* circuits that can easily be used to develop *functional* test cases [4]. Each circuit is a pictorial representation of the semantics portrayed in the written specifications. The semantic information in the cause-effect graphs is translated into Limited Entry Decision Tables (LEDT) which are used to construct the actual test cases. An LEDT is a binary truth table in which each *rule* represents a logical path through a program segment.

The only requirement for using and understanding cause-effect graphs is knowledge of Boolean logical operators. **AND**, **OR**, and **NOT** are the most commonly encountered operators; however, **NAND** and **NOR** may be required in some instances. Tables 8.1, 8.2, and 8.3 are truth tables for the **AND**, **OR**, and **NOT** operators, respectively. Tables 8.4 and 8.5 represent the **NAND** and **NOR** operators, respectively.

The basic cause-effect graph notation is illustrated in Figure 8.1. There are four fundamental configurations and two infrequently used negative forms.

TABLE 8.1   Truth Table for Logical AND

A \ B	1	0
1	1	0
0	0	0

Note: The ANDed variables are "A" and "B."

TABLE 8.2   Truth Table for Logical OR

A \ B	1	0
1	1	1
0	1	0

Note: The ORed variables are "A" and "B."

- **Identity** defines a situation in which node Y is true if node X is true. In Boolean terms, if $X = 1$, $Y = 1$, else $Y = 0$.
- **AND** defines a circumstance where X and Y must be true for Z to be true. Again, in Boolean logic, $Z = 1$ only if $X = 1$ and $Y = 1$, else $Z = 0$.
- **OR** defines a condition in which either X or Y must be true if Z is to be true. In Boolean format, $Z = 1$ if $X = 1$ or $Y = 1$, else $Z = 0$.

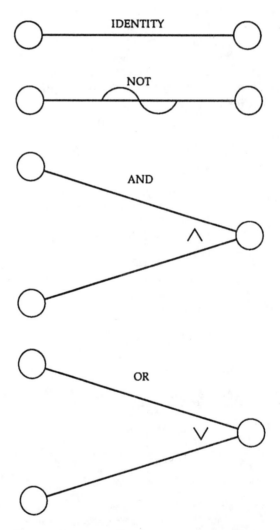

Figure 8.1 Cause-Effect Graphing—Basic Notation

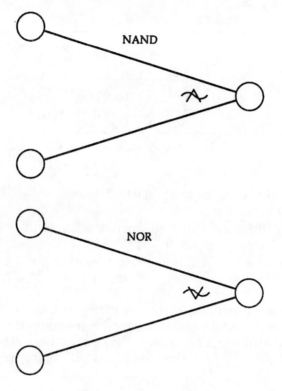

Figure 8.1   (*continued*)

TABLE 8.3   Truth Table for Logical NOT

	B	1	0
A		0	1

Note: The NOTed variables are "A" and "B."

TABLE 8.4   Truth Table for Logical NAND

A	B	1	0
1		0	1
0		1	1

Note: The NANDed variables are "A" and "B."

TABLE 8.5   Truth Table for Logical NOR

A \ B	1	0
1	0	0
0	0	1

Note: The NORed variables are "A" and "B."

- **NOT** defines the instance where Y is true only if X is false. In Boolean logic, $Y = 1$ if $X = 0$, else $Y = 0$.
- **NAND** defines the situation where if both X and Y are false Z is true. In Boolean, $Z = 1$ if $X = 0$ and $Y = 0$, else $Z = 0$.
- **NOR** defines the condition where if neither X nor Y is true, Z is true. In Boolean notation, if $X = 1$ or $Y = 1$, $Z = 0$, else $Z = 1$.

A word of caution about the use of negative logic. Negative logic can lead to unnecessarily complex logical combinations and should be purposely avoided when possible. If the situation is a **NAND** or **NOR**, try to restate the logic in the positive before developing the cause-effect graph.

8.2 GRAPHING CONSTRAINTS

From a cause and effect perspective, some combinations of causes may be impossible because of semantic or syntactic *constraints*. In addition, certain effects may mask other effects and when this occurs it must be indicated on the graph. Consequently, the notation (shown in Figure 8.2) for constraints must be used in conjunction with the basic cause-effect notation.

8.2.1 Constraints on Causes

- **Exclusive** constraint defines the situation where cause X and cause Y cannot simultaneously be true. If $X = 1$, $Y = 0$; if $Y = 1$, $X = 0$. However, both causes X and Y can simultaneously be equal to 0.
- **Inclusive** constraint defines the situation in which either X or Y must always be true. If $X = 0$, $Y = 1$; if $Y = 0$, $X = 1$. Causes X and Y may simultaneously be equal to 1, but the state where $X = 0$ and $Y = 0$ is not a possibility.

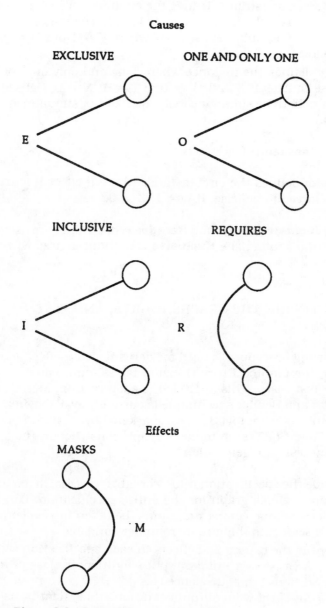

Figure 8.2   Cause-Effect Graphing—Constraint Notation

- **Requires** constraint defines the circumstance where X must be true if Y is to be true. If $X = 1$, $Y = 1$. The states where $X = 0$ and $Y = 0$ simultaneously, and where $X = 1$ but $Y = 0$, are also possible.
- **Only** defines the instance where "one and only one" of X and Y must be true. If $X = 1$, $Y = 0$; if $Y = 1$, $X = 0$. Causes X and Y cannot both be simultaneously equal to 1 or simultaneously equal to 0.

8.2.2 Constraints On Effects

- **Masks** defines the circumstance where if effect V is true, effect Z is forced to be false. If $V = 1$, $Z = 0$.

The **Inclusive, Only,** and **Requires** constraints are used with the logical *and* operator. The **Exclusive** constraint is used with the logic *or* operator.

8.3 DEVELOPING THE GRAPHS, TABLES, AND TEST CASES

The following procedure is used for deriving cause-effect graphs, constructing the Limited Entry Decision tables, and using the tables to compose test cases. This approach is adapted from Myers's work [4]. Elmendorf and Bender's technique is currently available in automated form in the software tool SoftTest marketed by Richard Bender & Associates, Inc. SoftTest automates graph construction, table development, and test case generation.

1. Divide the specification into "workable" pieces. Do not attempt to create a single graph for the entire specification. Large specifications are too complex and must be taken in smaller (less complex) segments that are more understandable.
2. Identify the causes and effects in each specification segment.
    A cause is a unique input condition or class of input conditions (an equivalence class).
    An effect is an output condition or a system transformation (an alteration of the system data base).
3. Translate the semantic relationships in each segment into Boolean relationships linking the causes and effects in a Cause-Effect Graph.
4. Annotate each graph with the constraints affecting the causes and effects.

5. a. Trace the binary condition states (that can be perceived as *true-false* or $1 - 0$ at each node in the graph) and identify each unique combination of binary states that link a cause to an effect.

   b. Draw a Limited-Entry Decision Table summarizing all of the possible condition state combinations (see Chapter Nine for a complete discussion of Decision Logic Tables—DLTs).

   c. List the causes in the Condition Stub of the table and the effects in the Action Stub.

      Describe each combination of condition states (causes) in the Condition Entry quadrant of the table.

   d. Divide the entry side of the table into Rules, one for each unique combination of condition states in the Cause-Effect Graph.

   e. Finally, indicate which state combinations are associated with specific effects by placing an "X" in the column that represents the condition-state combination (rule) next to the invoked effect.

6. Convert each column (rule) in the decision table into a test case.

8.3.1 Some Helpful Hints for Determining the Functional Variations

Identifying each unique combination of condition states (functional variation) in the cause-effect graph (see step 5 above) is a reasonably difficult task. Myers does point out that this exercise can yield information about the completeness because it tends to bring to the surface ambiguities in the specification.There is, however, no recommended mathematical check for completeness as in the DLT procedure described in Chapter Nine, but methodically tracing backwards from an effect through each of the possible combinations of intermediate input values for each of the primary input values will yield a set of distinct condition states. These states can then be used to calculate a total expected table complexity value that can be checked against the sum of the rule complexities as described in Chapter Nine.

The number of functional variations in a function is $n + 1$, where n is the number of logically connected effects [1]. In the situation defined earlier where $\mathbf{Z} = \mathbf{1}$ if $\mathbf{X} = \mathbf{1}$ and $\mathbf{Y} = \mathbf{1}$ there are 3 functional variations because there are 2 logically ANDed effects $\mathbf{X}$ and $\mathbf{Y}$.

1. If $\mathbf{X} = \mathbf{1}$ and $\mathbf{Y} = \mathbf{0}$, then $\mathbf{Z} = \mathbf{0}$.
2. If $\mathbf{X} = \mathbf{0}$ and $\mathbf{Y} = \mathbf{1}$, then $\mathbf{Z} = \mathbf{0}$.
3. If $\mathbf{X} = \mathbf{1}$ and $\mathbf{Y} = \mathbf{1}$, then $\mathbf{Z} = \mathbf{1}$.

The functional variation where **X** = **0** and **Y** = **0** is not required because the error situation causing this would also be detected by functional variations **1** and **2**.

The same axiom is true for logical ORed effects. In the situation where **Z** = **1** if **X** = **1** or **Y** = **1**, there are also three functional variations.

1. **If X = 1 or Y = 0, then Z = 1.**
2. **If X = 0 or Y = 1, then Z = 1.**
3. **If X = 0 or Y = 0, then Z = 0.**

For the ORed effects, the situation where **X** = **1** or **Y** = **1** need not be tested because functional variations **1** and **2** would capture any errors this possible fourth variation would find.

The following procedure for identifying the functional variations is adapted from Myers [4] and Bender [1].

1. Work with a single output or intermediate effect at a time.
2. For an AND, set that effect to the false (0) state.
3. Work through the graph setting each ANDed condition state to 0 while holding all other ANDed states to 1. Last, set all condition states to 1. *The actual number of combinations may be less than n + 1 because of the constraints on the causes.*
4. For an OR, set that effect to the true (1) state.
5. Work through the graph setting each ORed condition state 1 holding other ORed states to 0. Finally, set all ORed states to 0. *As in step 3, the actual number of combinations may be less than n + 1 because of the constraints on the causes.*

Finally, as with Equivalence Partitioning, error masking is a common danger when developing test cases with Cause-Effect Graphing. What this means is that certain combinations of causes can mask errors. Thus, these causes must be packaged in separate test cases in the proper combinations [1]. Bender describes these special combinations as "sensitized" test cases.

Error masking represents a constraint on causes which is in addition to those discussed previously. Potential masking should be identified as soon as possible; however, an inspection of the combinations of causes and effects in the LEDT should reveal any masking conditions. Furthermore, some masking situations should be readily apparent when developing the LEDT.

8.4 THE ROLLING ROCK POLYTECHNIC STATE UNIVERSITY EXAMPLE CONTINUED

We will continue to develop test data for the Rolling Rock Polytechnic State University College Boards data validation example used in Chapter Six. As discussed previously, each validation procedure is really a separate function and if Structured Design principles are followed, each would be implemented in a separate module (COBOL Paragraph) maximizing *cohesion* and minimizing *coupling* [5]. We did not have to decompose the data validation procedure in order to develop test cases using the basis set approach, but to effectively apply cause-effect graphing techniques, it is necessary to view the specification from this decomposed perspective. Table 8.6 shows the causes that can be ascertained as a result of decomposing the functional specification.

In the process of decomposing the specification, each restriction on the input is treated separately. Doing so reduces the amount of structural complexity with which we must cope when constructing the graphs, the corresponding Limited Entry Decision Tables, and the resultant test cases. This is a natural decomposition as each test is really a separate function; however, all of the tests but the check for a valid student number are compound and must be dissected further. Thus, there are nine independent tests but we can deduce seventeen causes.

This is the same number as the Cyclomatic Complexity value we computed using McCabe's approach. They are the same because we

TABLE 8.6   The Rolling Rock Polytechnic State University Example Causes As Enumerated Through Specification Decomposition

Causes
1. Student Number Is Numeric
2. Student Name Is Nonblank
3. Student Name Is Alphabetic
4. Student Sex Is Male
5. Student Sex Is Female
6. Student Age Is Numeric
7. Student Age Is 15–18
8. Student Algebra Score Is Numeric
9. Student Algebra Score Is 000–100
10. Student Geography Score Is Numeric
11. Student Geography Score Is 000–100
12. Student English Score Is Numeric
13. Student English Score Is 000–100
14. Student Physics Score Is Numeric
15. Student Physics Score Is 000–100
16. Student Chemistry Score Is Numeric
17. Student Chemistry Score Is 000–100

TABLE 8.7 The Rolling Rock Polytechnic State University Example Effects As Enumerated Through Specification Decomposition

Effects
101 Write Student Record To Student Report
102 Underline Invalid Values In Student Record
103 Write Student Record To Error Report

Intermediate Effects
90 Intermediate Effect For Student Name
91 Intermediate Effect For Student Sex
92 Intermediate Effect For Student Age
93 Intermediate Effect For Student Algebra Score
94 Intermediate Effect For Student Geography Score
95 Intermediate Effect For Student English Score
96 Intermediate Effect For Student Physics Score
97 Intermediate Effect For Student Chemistry Score

are decomposing on the basis of decision structure, which is what McCabe's complexity measure really indexes. This is why using the two techniques together is not recommended. Cause-effect graphing really does not yield any new and unique test cases with respect to the basis set approach. This conclusion may not be absolute, but it is consistent enough to use in practice.

Further decomposition of the specification with respect to effects reveals the three effects included in Table 8.7. This figure also lists the nodes required to represent intermediate or temporary effects. The necessity of intermediate nodes will become clear as you study the cause-effect graphs for this example.

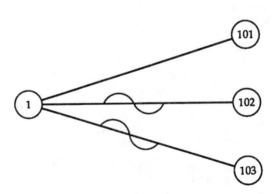

Figure 8.3 Cause-Effect Graph: Student Number

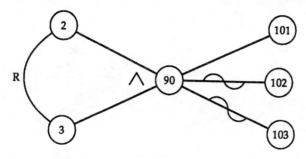

Figure 8.4   Cause-Effect Graph: Student Name

Figures 8.3 through 8.11 are examples of the cause-effect graphs that could be generated for this example. Tables 8.8 through 8.14 represent the Limited Entry Decision Tables that correspond to these graphs. Finally, Table 8.15 is the cumulative test data set developed from the tables.

As an example, Figure 8.3 represents the input condition that student Number must be numeric. If the value of node 1 is "**1**," node 101 is also "**1**" because the relationship demonstrated is that of **Identity**. Nodes 102 and 103 are both "**0**" because the relationships between node 1 and nodes 102 and 103 are that of **NOT**. The latter nodes are "**1**" only if node 1 is "**0**." The limited entry decision table illustrated along with the graph clarifies the possible alternatives (Student Number is NUMERIC; Student Number is NOT NUMERIC).

The left-most rule portrays the occurrence where Student Number is NUMERIC and the remaining rule represents the instance where it is NOT NUMERIC. So, to test this function we must construct two test cases, one for each of the possible situations as shown in Table 8.15.

As an exercise, I suggest that you work through each graph/table/ test cases combination until you understand how they have been developed. Those test data records in Table 8.15 that are followed by an

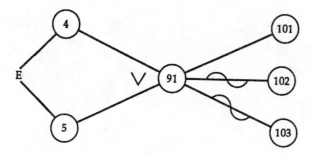

Figure 8.5   Cause-Effect Graph: Student Sex

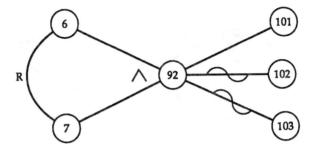

Figure 8.6 Cause-Effect Graph: Student Age

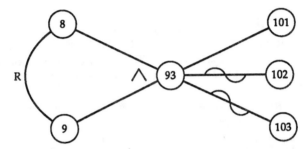

Figure 8.7 Cause-Effect Graph: Student Algebra Score

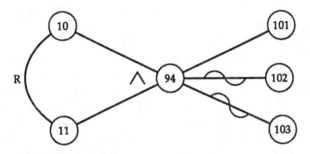

Figure 8.8 Cause-Effect Graph: Student Geography Score

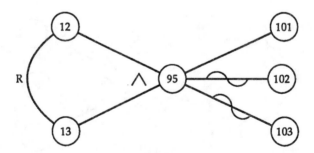

Figure 8.9 Cause-Effect Graph: Student English Score

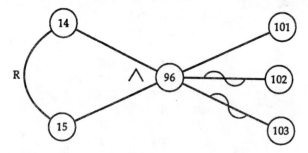

Figure 8.10 Cause-Effect Graph: Student Physics Score

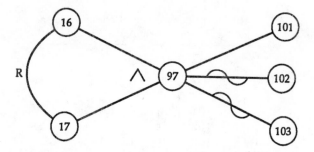

Figure 8.11 Cause-Effect Graph: Student Chemistry Score

TABLE 8.8   Limited Entry Decision Table
For Student Number

	1	0
1	1	0
101	1	0
102	0	1
103	0	1

TABLE 8.9   Limited Entry Decision Table
For Student Name

	1	1	0
2	1	1	0
3	1	0	0
101	1	0	0
102	0	1	1
103	0	1	1

TABLE 8.10   Limited Entry Decision Table
For Student Sex

4	1	0	0
5	0	1	0
101	1	1	0
102	0	0	1
103	0	0	1

TABLE 8.11   Limited Entry Decision Table
For Student Age

6	1	1	0
7	1	0	0
101	1	0	0
102	0	1	1
103	0	1	1

TABLE 8.12   Limited Entry Decision Table
For Student Algebra Score

8	1	1	0
9	1	0	0
101	1	0	0
102	0	1	1
103	0	1	1

TABLE 8.13   Limited Entry Decision Table
For Student Geography Score

10	1	1	0
11	1	0	0
101	1	0	0
102	0	1	1
103	0	1	1

TABLE 8.14 Limited Entry Decision Table
For Student English Score

12	1	1	0
13	1	0	0
101	1	0	0
102	0	1	1
103	0	1	1

TABLE 8.15 The Rolling Rock Polytechnic State University
Example Cause-Effect Test Cases as Derived from the Limited Entry
Decision Tables

STUDENT NUMBER

0131Daniel Mosley   M17100100100100100 *
X131 Daniel Mosley   M17100100100100100

STUDENT NAME

0131**Daniel Mosley**   M17100100100100100 *
0131   M17100100100100100
0131**999999999999999** M17100100100100100

STUDENT SEX

0131Daniel Mosley   **M**17100100100100100 *
0131Paige Mosley   **F**17100100100100100
0131Daniel Mosley   **9**17100100100100100

STUDENT AGE

0131Daniel Mosley   M**17**100100100100100 *
0131Daniel Mosley   M**XX**100100100100100
0131Daniel Mosley   M**19**100100100100100

STUDENT ALGEBRA SCORE

0131Daniel Mosley   M17**100**100100100100 *
0131Daniel Mosley   M17**150**100100100100
0131Daniel Mosley   M17**XXX**100100100100

STUDENT GEOGRAPHY SCORE

0131Daniel Mosley   M17100**100**100100100 *
0131Daniel Mosley   M17100**150**100100100
0131Daniel Mosley   M17100**XXX**100100100

STUDENT ENGLISH SCORE

0131Daniel Mosley   M17100100**100**100100 *
0131Daniel Mosley   M17100100**150**100100
0131Daniel Mosley   M17100100**XXX**100100

STUDENT PHYSICS SCORE

0131Daniel Mosley   M17100100100**100**100 *
0131Daniel Mosley   M17100100100**150**100
0131Daniel Mosley   M17100100100**XXX**100

STUDENT CHEMISTRY SCORE

0131Daniel Mosley   M17100100100100**100** *
0131Daniel Mosley   M17100100100100**150**
0131Daniel Mosley   M17100100100100**XXX**

Note: * indicates redundant correct records that would
result in only test one case.

133

asterisk are redundant occurrences of a completely valid input record that occurs across functions and that can be replaced by a single valid test record as discussed in the Chapter Seven when covering Equivalence Partitioning. In the figure, the test data for Algebra Score, Geography Score, English Score, Chemistry Score, and Physics Score have been combined to elucidate this point.

8.5 CONCLUSION

Cause-effect graphing is an excellent test case design and construction method. It can be applied early in the development cycle and the resultant test data can be used in early review processes. The process of constructing cause-effect graphs is in itself an error revealing exercise. It can identify many of the typical problems that plague written specifications [1].

The common kinds of problems it can bring to light are dangling ELSE clauses, scope of action, ambiguous logical operators, unnecessary use of negation, ambiguity of statements and references, and causes without effects/effects without causes. Thus, cause-effect graphing is an important weapon in your specification-based testing arsenal.

REFERENCES

1. Bender, Richard, *Requirements Based Testing*. Larkspur, CA: Richard Bender & Associates, Inc., Mini Tutorial, 1990.

2. Elmendorf, William R., *Cause-Effect Graphs in Functional Testing*. Poughkeepsie, NY: IBM System Development Division, TR-00.2487, 1973.

3. Elmendorf, William R., "Functional Analysis Using Cause-Effect Graphs," *Proceedings of Share XLIII*, New York, (1974), 567–77.

4. Myers, Glenford, *The Art of Software Testing*. New York, Wiley-Interscience, 1979.

5. Yourdon, Edward, and Larry Constantine, *Structured Design: Fundamentals of Computer Program and Systems Design*. Englewood Cliffs, N.J.: Prentice Hall: 1979.

9

Structured Tableau

A program may be incorrect because of missing
paths. *Exhaustive path testing, of course, would
not detect the absence of necessary paths.*

Glenford Myers, 1979 [12]

The Structured Tableau Design Methodology (STDM) [4,5,6] is a little-
known and used software design method that is applicable to the detailed design phase of development. It has, however, been used extensively at Southwestern Bell Telephone in St. Louis, as well as at the
Washington University School of Medicine, also in St. Louis, with both
instances being described in the trade press [1,8]. It is an approach
based on Decision Logic Tables (DLTs) that are in themselves not considered a "structured" software development tool. DLTs are a tabular
representation of the same kinds of information that can be exhibited
as mathematical Decision Trees.

The Structured Tableau, on the other hand, is a structured approach to program design. The basic tableau format includes all three
of Bohm's and Jacopini's logical programming constructs and their
variations [3,5]. The *Sequence* construct remains unchanged, while
Selection and *Iteration* are represented by an "embedded" DLT.

Tableaux are unique in that they can be constructed from segments of the system's functional specification, or may be based on
program flow charts or constructed from source code listings. From a
testing perspective, this approach could be classed as either White Box
or Black Box; hence, the classification of Gray Box may be applied here.

But Structured Tableau is a design method, so why should it be included in a discussion of test case design strategies? Because Structured Tableau can be viewed as a "logical" path coverage approach that has an advantage Basis Testing does not. The DLT portion of the tableau format allows a test for "completeness" that ensures that none of the "necessary" paths in a particular module are omitted.

The structural complexity of the module is computed as the product of the number of possible states for each condition in a decision. This produces a much larger complexity value than the value of C that would be obtained if McCabe's Cyclomatic Number metric were used. The value that is produced represents the total number of possible logical combinations of conditions states, not the number of independent combinations. Thus, the value of the total table complexity will differ from the cyclomatic complexity. The advantage in knowing the total table complexity is that logical "completeness" can be verified. Thus, the Structured Tableau approach addresses a major criticism of White Box strategies: that they cannot account for missing paths.

A logically complete set of test cases for each program module based on the specifications, design, or code can be created by developing one test case for each rule in the embedded DLT of the tableau. One Structured Tableau diagram is constructed for each program module. Test cases from each tableau are subsequently merged to form a test data set which may in turn be merged with other test data sets created using other White Box and/or Black Box methods.

9.1 DECISION LOGIC TABLES

Before discussing Structured Tableau diagrams, an introduction to DLTs, that make this technique so powerful, is necessary for the novice. Many of you are probably already familiar with DLTs and may wish skip this section; however, if you do read it, it will refresh your knowledge of DLT concepts.

From a testing perspective, the Decision Logic Table is an important tool for software reliability [2,11]. The DLT is a tabular diagram that is used to clarify complex logic which has previously been specified in a design narrative [7]. DLTs deal only with conditional logic, allowing the designer to easily understand a situation that contains many decision steps. Such decisions will ultimately end up as IF/THEN/ELSE form in the final program. A distinct advantage is that the decision making logic of DLTs is void of the IF/THEN/ELSE nesting which often occurs in the narrative description and is perpetuated in the program code. Even Structured English descriptions may contain IF/THEN/ELSE nesting.

The problem with IF/THEN/ELSE nesting is that of increasing structural complexity. Our ability to deal with complexity falls off rapidly after a certain level has been reached [10,14]. When this happens, we begin to introduce errors into our work. The goal of a decision table can be stated formally as follows:

To reduce a narrative to a set of conditions and actions which can easily be implemented in IF/THEN/ELSE form.

Everything except simple sequence can be represented by conditions and the actions dependent on those conditions. In the selection construct, the actions are dependent on the state of the condition being evaluated. Most selections are limited to two mutually exclusive alternatives; however, some decisions involve evaluating conditions with more than two mutually exclusive alternatives. The DLT format does not distinguish between "limited entry" and "extended entry" conditions. It merely organizes the conditions and actions so the proper actions are associated with the right condition state combinations.

The iteration construct can be modeled using conditions and actions. What is a loop? It is a "repeated" set of actions. In some instances the set is repeated if the condition that represents the exit criterion is true (the "while" or pre-test loop) and in others the set is repeated until the condition that represents the exit criterion is false (the "until" or posttest loop). Any loop can be specified if two things are known: what actions are going to be repeated (are conditional on the exit criterion) and the condition state required in order to exit the loop (exit criterion). Consequently, iteration can be portrayed with a DLT.

9.1.1 DLT Format

A DLT is drawn using the format shown in Figure 9.1. There are four quadrants, Condition Stub, Condition Entry, Action Stub, and Action Entry. Conditions are listed in top-down fashion in the Condition Stub in order of their impact on the processing logic. More comprehensive conditions are listed first. For instance (see Example 1), END-OF-FILE is the most comprehensive condition of all because processing stops when it is reached. Consequently, it would be listed first. For instance, in "Control Break" processing, the innermost processing level would be represented in a DLT by being the last condition listed in the Condition Stub and the condition representing the outermost level would be listed first.

Condition state names are placed in the Condition Entry quadrant at the level corresponding to the condition they define. The num-

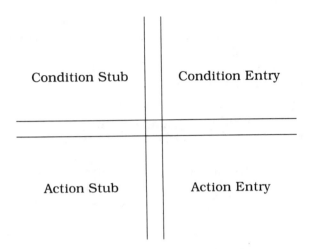

Figure 9.1   Decision Table Format

ber of condition states for a specific condition defines the *Condition Complexity* of that condition.

Actions are entered in the Action Stub. They are listed in the order in which they will execute from top to bottom. Which actions are dependent on what condition state combinations are specified in the Action Entry quadrant, which is divided into *Rules*.

A rule is a vertical column through the entry side (both condition and action) of the table. It represents one unique combination of condition states and the actions that are executed when that combination occurs. The number of rules in a DLT is a function of the product of the Condition Complexities for all of the conditions in the Condition Stub. A DLT containing three conditions and each condition having two possible states would contain 8 rules ($2 \times 2 \times 2 = 8$). The value 8 also represents the *Table Complexity*. Table complexity is a measure of the total number of logic paths through the table.

9.1.2 Enumerating the Rules

1. The rules in a DLT are determined by dividing the entry side of the table into the same number of rules as there are condition states for the first (most comprehensive) condition in the condition stub. See Table 9.1.
2. Divide each of the previously created subdivisions into the same number of rules as there are condition states in the second (next most comprehensive) condition. See Table 9.2.

TABLE 9.1   Enumerating the Rules

End of File?	No	Yes
Process Transaction Exit		

TABLE 9.2   Enumerating the Rules

End of File?	No				Yes			
Transaction Type?	A	C	D	O	A	C	D	O
Process Transaction Exit								

Developing the table in this manner ensures that all possible condition state combinations are present.

9.1.3 Specifying Actions

When all of the rules have been enumerated, the actions dependent on each rule may be specified. More than one action can occur as a consequence of a particular rule. If several actions are dependent on a single rule, they should be listed in top-down sequence in the action stub. Which actions are executed is indicated by placing an "X" in the column that represents the rule across from the action. See Table 9.3.

TABLE 9.3   Indicating the Actions

End of File?	No				Yes			
Transaction Type?	A	C	D	O	A	C	D	O
Process Transaction	X	X	X					
Exit				X	X	X	X	X
Rule Complexity =	1	1	1	1	1	1	1	1

Note: X in column specifies action taken.

9.2 CONDITION STATE INDIFFERENCE

Certain condition states, when they occur, overrule other condition states. When this happens, the dominant condition state is "indifferent" to the values of subsequent condition states that may finish out the logical combination of states defining the rule.

Indifference is important because when it occurs, the table can be "collapsed." A collapsed table is stated more precisely. What is accomplished are rules that have different logical significance, but when they result in the same set of actions, are combined into a single rule. From a software testing standpoint, one test case must be generated for each rule in the table, and when rules can be collapsed because of condition state indifference, fewer test cases have to be constructed.

Collapsing the table in no way changes the total table complexity. Collapsed rules account for more than one logic path. [**Rule Complexity** is defined as the number of logical combinations of condition states (paths) for which the rule accounts.] See Tables 9.3 and 9.4.

Gane and Sarson [7] have defined a set of guidelines for collapsing DLTs.

1. Find a pair of rules for which:
the action(s) is (are) the same
the condition state values are the same except for one condition in which they differ

2. Replace that pair of rules with a single rule using the indifference symbol (~) for the condition that was different

3. Repeat guidelines 1 and 2 for any other pair of rules meeting the indifference criteria

TABLE 9.4   Rule Complexity in Collapsed Table

End of File?		No			Yes
Transaction Type?	A	C	D	O	-----
Process Transaction	X	X	X		
Exit				X	X
Rule Complexity =	1	1	1	1	4

Note: X in column specifies action taken.

9.3 PROOF OF COMPLETENESS

Proof of completeness for a given DLT lies in the fact that the total table complexity can be computed as the product of the condition complexities, or as the sum of the rule complexities. If the product of the condition complexities equals the sum of the rule complexities, the table is proved complete. No logical combinations of condition states are missing.

The reason completeness can be proven is because of the fundamental premise of DLTs, which is:

Given a finite number of conditions with a finite number of condition states, a known number of combinations exist.

9.4 STRUCTURED TABLEAU

The Structured Tableau Design Methodology is an effective program design tool that is used during the Program Design And Development phase of the SDLC [5] (See King's SDLC model [9] in Chapter 2). It is used to model the procedural logic in individual program modules. The modules are, in turn, components in a traditional hierarchical program design. The hierarchical relationship provides the advantage of being able to apply the Yourdon and Constantine measures of design goodness, *Coupling* and *Cohesion* [14,15]. An additional advantage of the Structured Tableau is that it provides an inherent proof of completeness as previously described in the discussion of Decision Logic Tables.

The structured Tableaux (also known as Structured Decision Rule Charts) use a format that closely approximates the way a programmer visualizes the program logic. In this sense, very little conceptual effort is required to convert a tableau to a COBOL paragraph. Because of this relationship, the tableau effectively emulates the paragraph for purposes of generating test cases. Figure 9.2 illustrates the tableau format.

9.4.1 Format Conventions

The *Sequence* construct is represented on the tableau by any imperative action and is put in the form of a simple imperative sentence. There are three areas in the tableau where sequence can be shown: immediately below the function number and name (in COBOL this would be the paragraph name); immediately below the function number and the word "repeat" (in the body of a loop); in the action stub of the embedded DLT.

The Structured Tableau follows this standardized format:

A. Function number and name from the functional hierarchy
B. Any actions, listed in sequence, that are performed once per each invocation of the function
C. Function number plus the word "REPEAT"
D. Any actions, listed in sequence, that are performed repeatedly per each invocation of the function
E. A complete decision table
F. Function number plus the word "EXIT"

The following example illustrates the correct structured tableau format.

(A.) 5060–PROCESS-ONE-SALESMAN.

(B.)   clear salesman-total
          store new-salesman as current-salesman

(C.) 5060–REPEAT

(D.)   action-X
          action-Y

more data?		Y		N
same salesman?		Y	N	~
5066-process-customer		X		
go to 5060-REPEAT		X		
5068-term-salesman			X	X
5060-EXIT			X	X

(E.) marks the decision table. (F.) marks the 5060-EXIT line.

Figure 9.2   Structured Tableau Format

In the first instance, the action is unconditional and it represents something that must be done once and only once upon entering the paragraph. There may be several actions that represent this kind of activity and they should each be represented by an imperative statement at this level in the tableau.

In the latter two instances, the actions are conditional. Actions in a loop are dependent on the execution of the loop. The execution of the loop is, in turn, dependent on the "while" or "until" conditions that control its iteration.

The *Selection* construct is represented by the embedded DLT. Decisions are indicated by the conditions named in the Condition Stub of the table. Note that all decisions within a module (a paragraph) are listed together in a single table. This is possible because the rules represent *independent* logical combinations of the condition states.

The *Iteration* construct is formed by referencing the repeat label from the action stub of the DLT. The repeat label consists of the function number concatenated to the word "repeat" which precedes any inoperative actions that occur repetitively. Reference in the table implies that control flow is returned to the label that marks the beginning of the loop and all subsequent actions are repeated.

This method of modeling repetition does have one drawback. It allows the design to be implemented using unconditional branching (GO TOs); however, stipulations are placed on the branching process. They are that control can be transferred backward to the repeat label, or forward to the paragraph exit.

Just because the design lends itself to this kind of implementation does not mean it has to be so. The logic within the loop (between the label and the action stub to the label) can easily be implemented in pure structured fashion in COBOL 74 using the PERFORM statement and putting the actions in the body of the loop in a separate paragraph that is invoked by the PERFORM statement, and in COBOL 85 using the in-line PERFORM structure (PERFORM —> END-PERFORM). Granted, implementation through the earlier COBOL compiler version is less efficient than in the later version, but it is still better than using unconditional branching.

In the tableau, invocation of subordinate modules is indicated by recording the name of the paragraph anywhere in the tableau where an imperative action can occur.

9.5 STRUCTURED TABLEAU AS A SOFTWARE TESTING TOOL

Structured Tableau is an excellent tool for developing test cases based on path coverage criteria. Because the number of paths is dependent on the number of decisions in a module (see Chapter Six), and because the tableau incorporates all the decisions in a module in a DLT format, every possible combination of condition states (each combination is logic path) is covered [5]. Moreover, the completeness check discussed previously ensures that no paths are forgotten.

Thus, each tableau results in a finite number of test cases being added to the test data set. Because a test case is generated for each of the rules in the table, the tester can be confident of completely testing the module's logic from a path coverage perspective. Furthermore, if the embedded DLT can be collapsed, complete coverage can be attained with even fewer test cases. From the standpoint of testing economics, the smaller the number of test cases required for adequate coverage the better.

9.6 THE ROLLING ROCK POLYTECHNIC STATE UNIVERSITY EXAMPLE AGAIN

Once again the Rolling Rock State University example, discussed earlier in the White Box and Black Box sections, illustrates the Structured Tableau as a test case design tool. If you will remember, the design is too complex having a value for C of 17, but using basis testing methods, test cases could be produced. With the tableau approach, however, the design must be further decomposed before we can construct the tableaux and develop the test cases.

TABLE 9.5   Test Case Construction Example: Student Data

040-EDIT-STUDENT-SAT-DATA.
    041-EDIT-STUDENT-NUMBER.
    042-EDIT-STUDENT-NAME.
    043-EDIT-STUDENT-SEX.
    044-EDIT-STUDENT-AGE.
    045-EDIT-STUDENT-ALG-SCORE.
    046-EDIT-STUDENT-GEO-SCORE.
    047-EDIT-STUDENT-ENG-SCORE.
    048-EDIT-STUDENT-PHY-SCORE.
    049-EDIT-STUDENT-CHEM-SCORE.
040-EXIT.

TABLE 9.6   Test Case Construction Example: Student Number

041-Edit-Student-Number.

Student-Number	Numeric	Nonnumeric
MOVE ALL '-' TO EU-ID		X
MOVE 'E' TO REPORT-SELECT		X
041-EXIT	X	X

TABLE 9.7   Test Case Construction Example: Student Name

042-Edit-Student-Name.

Student-Name	Blank		Nonblank	
Student-Name	Alpha	Non Alpha	Alpha	Non Alpha
MOVE ALL '-' TO EU-NAME.	X	X		X
MOVE 'E' TO REPORT-SEL	X	X		X
042-EXIT	X	X	X	X

Each group of statements which evaluates a different data element can effectively become the crux of a subordinate COBOL module (paragraph) that is invoked from the 040-EDIT-STUDENT-RECORD paragraph through a simple PERFORM statement. The tableau that represents this paragraph is devoid of decisions and loops, and consists of a series of PERFORM statements invoking each of the validation paragraphs. See Table 9.5.

A separate tableau is constructed for each of the subordinate paragraphs. See Tables 9.6 through 9.14. In some instances the embedded DLT can be collapsed. See Tables 9.15 through 9.21. Once all of the tableaux are constructed and collapsed whenever possible, a test case can be created. As before, a test case is actually a record containing entries for all of the data elements in the record.

Using the conventions set forth by Myers [12] concerning the development of test data records using equivalence classes, we can generate heuristics that we can use to fill in the data set.

TABLE 9.8   Test Case Construction Example: Student Sex

043-Edit-Student-Sex.

Student-Sex	Alpha		Nonalpha	
Student-Sex	Valid	Invalid	Valid	Invalid
MOVE ALL '-' TO EU-SEX.		X	X	X
MOVE 'E' TO REPORT-SEL		X	X	X
043-EXIT	X	X	X	X

TABLE 9.9   Test Case Construction Example: Student Age

044-Edit-Student-Age.

Student-Age	Valid	Invalid
MOVE ALL '-' TO EU-AGE		X
MOVE 'E' TO REPORT-SELECT		X
044-EXIT	X	X

TABLE 9.10   Test Case Construction Example: Algebra Score

045-Edit-Student-Alg-Score

STD-ALG-SCR	Numeric		Non-numeric	
STD-ALG-SCR	Valid	Invalid	Valid	Invalid
MOVE ALL '-' TO EU-ALG.		X	X	X
MOVE 'E' TO REPORT-SEL		X	X	X
045-EXIT	X	X	X	X

TABLE 9.11   Test Case Construction Example: Geography Score

046-Edit-Student-GEO-Score

STD-GEO-SCR	Numeric		Non-numeric	
STD-GEO-SCR	Valid	Invalid	Valid	Invalid
MOVE ALL '-' TO EU-GEO.		X	X	X
MOVE 'E' TO REPORT-SEL		X	X	X
046-EXIT	X	X	X	X

TABLE 9.12 Test Case Construction Example: English Score

047-Edit-Student-ENG-Score

STD-ENG-SCR	Numeric		Non-numeric	
STD-ENG-SCR	Valid	Invalid	Valid	Invalid
MOVE ALL '-' TO EU-ENG.		X	X	X
MOVE 'E' TO REPORT-SEL		X	X	X
047-EXIT	X	X	X	X

TABLE 9.13 Test Case Construction Example: Physics Score

048-Edit-Student-Phy-Score

STD-PHY-SCR	Numeric		Non-numeric	
STD-PHY-SCR	Valid	Invalid	Valid	Invalid
MOVE ALL '-' TO EU-PHY		X	X	X
MOVE 'E' TO REPORT-SEL		X	X	X
048-EXIT	X	X	X	X

TABLE 9.14 Test Case Construction Example: Chemistry Score

049-Edit-Student-Chem-Score

STD-CHEM-SCR	Numeric		Non-numeric	
STD-CHEM-SCR	Valid	Invalid	Valid	Invalid
MOVE ALL '-' TO EU-CHEM		X	X	X
MOVE 'E' TO REPORT-SEL		X	X	X
049-EXIT	X	X	X	X

TABLE 9.15   Test Case Construction Example: Geography Name

042-Edit-Student-Name.

| STUDENT-NAME | Blank | Nonblank | |
STUDENT-NAME	-----	Alpha	Non Alpha
MOVE ALL '-' TO EU-NAME.	X		X
MOVE 'E' TO REPORT-SEL	X		X
042-EXIT	X	X	X

TABLE 9.16   Test Case Construction Example—Collapsed Version: Student Sex

043-Edit-Student-Sex.

| STUDENT-SEX | Alpha | | Nonalpha |
STUDENT-SEX	Valid	Invalid	-----
MOVE ALL '-' TO EU-SEX.		X	X
MOVE 'E' TO REPORT-SEL		X	X
043-EXIT	X	X	X

TABLE 9.17   Test Case Construction Example—Collapsed Version: Algebra Score

045-Edit-Student-Alg-Score

| STD-ALG-SCR | Numeric | | Nonnumeric |
STD-ALG-SCR	Valid	Invalid	-----
MOVE ALL '-' TO EU-ALG.		X	X
MOVE 'E' TO REPORT-SEL		X	X
045-EXIT	X	X	X

TABLE 9.18   Test Case Construction Example—Collapsed Version: Geography Score

046-Edit-Student-Geo-Score

STD-GEO-SCR	Numeric		Nonnumeric
STD-GEO-SCR	Valid	Invalid	-----
MOVE ALL '-' TO EU-GEO.		X	X
MOVE 'E' TO REPORT-SEL		X	X
046-EXIT	X	X	X

TABLE 9.19   Test Case Construction Example—Collapsed Version: English Score

047-Edit-Student-Eng-Score

STD-ENG-SCR	Numeric		Nonnumeric
STD-ENG-SCR	Valid	Invalid	-----
MOVE ALL '-' TO EU-ENG.		X	X
MOVE 'E' TO REPORT-SEL		X	X
047-EXIT	X	X	X

TABLE 9.20   Test Case Construction Example—Collapsed Version: Physics Score

048-Edit-Student-Phy-Score

STD-PHY-SCR	Numeric		Nonnumeric
STD-PHY-SCR	Valid	Invalid	-----
MOVE ALL '-' TO EU-PHY.		X	X
MOVE 'E' TO REPORT-SEL		X	X
048-EXIT	X	X	X

TABLE 9.21 Test Case Construction Example—Collapsed Version: Chemistry Score

049-Edit-Student-Chem-Score

STD-CHEM-SCR	Numeric		Nonnumeric
STD-CHEM-SCR	Valid	Invalid	-----
MOVE ALL '-' TO EU-CHEM		X	X
MOVE 'E' TO REPORT-SEL		X	X
049-EXIT	X	X	X

1. For all tableaux, assign an arbitrary number to each rule in the embedded DLT, continuing until all of the rules across tableaux are uniquely identified.

2. Until each rule that represents a valid input value is covered, write a single test record covering as many of the valid rules as possible.

3. Until each rule that represents invalid input value is covered, write a single test record covering one and only one of the rules.

TABLE 9.22 Structured Tableau
Test Data Set

```
 1. 9999Paige Mosley    F16098098098098098
 2. XXXXPaige Mosley    F16098098098098098
 3. 9999               F16098098098098098
 4. 9999888888888888F16098098098098098
 5. 9999Paige Mosley    916098098098098098
 6. 9999Paige Mosley    T16098098098098098
 7. 9999Paige Mosley    F19098098098098098
 8. 9999Paige Mosley    F16150098098098098
 9. 9999Paige Mosley    F16XXX098098098098
10. 9999Paige Mosley    F16098150098098098
11. 9999Paige Mosley    F16098XXX098098098
12. 9999Paige Mosley    F16098098150098098
13. 9999Paige Mosley    F16098098XXX098098
14. 9999Paige Mosley    F16098098098150098
15. 9999Paige Mosley    F16098098098XXX098
16. 9999Paige Mosley    F16098098098098150
17. 9999Paige Mosley    F16098098098098XXX
```

TABLE 9.23   Structured Tableau
Expected Output for Test Data

Record Number	Expected Result
1.	Student Report
2.	Error Report Underline ID
3.	Error Report Underline Name
4.	Error Report Underline Name
5.	Error Report Underline Sex
6.	Error Report Underline Sex
7.	Error Report Underline Age
8.	Error Report Underline Alg Scr
9.	Error Report Underline Alg Scr
10.	Error Report Underline Geo Scr
11.	Error Report Underline Geo Scr
12.	Error Report Underline Eng Scr
13.	Error Report Underline Eng Scr
14.	Error Report Underline Phy Scr
15.	Error Report Underline Phy Scr
16.	Error Report Underline Chem Scr
17.	Error Report Underline Chem Scr

A test data set has been generated for our example using these guidelines. See Table 9.22. The expected output is defined in Table 9.23.

9.7 CONCLUSION

The rules set forth by Myers [12] for creating test cases for equivalence classes are also applicable to the tabular format of the Structured Tableau diagram. A set of test data which are similar and in some instances redundant with the test data from equivalence classes is produced. The advantage of the tableau method over the equivalence class method is primarily the ability to prove completeness. [In equivalence partitioning there is not an inherent way to determine that all possible classes have been identified.] From Black Box perspective, each equivalence class identifies a unique type of input to the module and each unique kind of input will invoke a distinct pathway through the module. A rule in a DLT identifies a unique set of circumstances (which, in turn, defines a unique kind of input). In this sense, the two test case design methods are equivalent, the difference being in the guidelines for establishing equivalence classes versus the guidelines for enumerating the rules in the DLT of the Structured Tableau.

REFERENCES

1. Bartusiak, Marcia, "Designing Drugs With Computers," *DISCOVER* (August 1981).
2. Beizer, Boris, *Software Testing Techniques, 2ed.* New York: Van Nostrand Reinhold, 1988.
3. Bohm, C., and G. Jacopini, "Flow Diagrams, Turing Machines and Languages With Only Two Formation Rules," *Communications of the ACM*, 9, no. 5 (1966).
4. Couger, Daniel, "The Structured Tableau Design Methodology (STDM)," *Computer Newsletter* (1983), University of Colorado, Colorado Springs.
5. Franz, Don, *Information Systems File Structure and Program Design Workbook and Problems.* Unpublished.
6. Franz, Don, and D. Gamble *Structured Tableau Design Methodology.* Specialized OnLine Systems, Inc., 1981.
7. Gane, Chris, and Trish Sarson, *Structured Systems Analysis: Tools and Techniques.* Englewood Cliffs, N.J.: Prentice Hall, 1979.
8. Kearney, Julia, "SORD Has a Better Idea." Source of publication unknown.
9. King, David, *Current Practices In Software Development: A Guide to Successful Systems.* Englewood Cliffs, N.J.: Prentice Hall, 1984.
10. Miller, George, "The Magical Number Seven, Plus or Minus Two: Some Limits on Our Capacity for Processing Information," *The Psychological Review*, 63, no. 2 (March 1956), 81–97.
11. Myers, Glenford, *Software Reliability.* New York: Wiley, 1977.
12. Myers, Glenford, *The Art Of Software Testing.* Englewood Cliffs, N.J.: Prentice Hall, 1979.
13. Poole, Bernard, and Noreen Prokop, "Miller's Magical Number: A Heuristic Applied to Software Engineering," *Information Executive* (1989).
14. Stevens, Wayne, Glenford Myers, and Larry Constantine, "Structured Design," *IBM Systems Journal*, 13, no. 2, (1974).
15. Yourdon, Edward, and Larry Constantine, *STRUCTURED DESIGN: Fundamentals of a Discipline of Computer Program and Systems Design.* Englewood Cliffs, N.J.: Prentice Hall, 1979.

10

Integration Testing

A software error is present when the program does not do what its end user reasonably expects it to do.

Myers, 1976 [2]

Integration and Function Testing are the first of the levels of "higher-order testing" [3] we will confront. Integration Testing, Function Testing, System Testing, and Acceptance Testing have also been dubbed "testing in the large" [1]. These tests are very important because they occur during the later stages (the Program Design and Development phase, and the Testing phase) of systems development, and thus, are the last battery of tests to be executed.

Errors found through higher-order tests are of the type described in Myers's statement which begins this chapter. Errors of this nature are the result of improper analysis and design of the system. As was stated much earlier in this book, these errors are the most expensive to correct. This is so because they are made during the early phases of development and are usually found just before, during, or after installation. Once identified, each error must be traced backwards through the development process until the cause is determined. Finally, after the cause has been discovered, all of the subsequent development tasks must be redone. This results in a "rework cycle."

One way to avoid rework cycles is to concentrate on the development process itself. Ask why the error was made in the first place, and the answer should tell you how to modify the development process so that type of error will be unlikely to occur again. This means that the first step to "quality" through testing is to constantly monitor and adjust analysis and design activities so that they are more *effective*.

If you are already doing this, kudos to you. If you aren't, you will be in the future because the customer base, whether it is an internal group within your company or whether you are selling software systems to the general public, is becoming more sophisticated and more quality conscious. Regardless, the only other alternative is to use higher-order testing to correct the errors that were not prevented earlier.

10.1 INCREMENTAL VERSUS NONINCREMENTAL TESTING

10.1.1 Nonincremental Testing

Nonincremental testing as defined by Myers [2] is the process of testing each program module independently and then combining them to form a program. He termed this nonintegrated approach "Big Bang" testing. This is similar to, but not exactly how COBOL programs are usually tested.

COBOL programmers build a PROCEDURE DIVISION composed of paragraphs and sections. The complete PROCEDURE DIVISION is finished before any testing is done. This means the COBOL modules (usually defined as one paragraph = one module, or as a section = a module) are neither tested independently nor tested in incremental fashion.

10.1.2 Incremental Testing

Incremental testing was defined by Myers as combining each new module being tested with a set of previously tested modules and then retesting the set. The result of this approach is that the only module tested in isolation is the first one in the set. By definition, incremental testing is Integration Testing. The types of Incremental Testing and the types of Integration Testing are one and the same. So, our discussion will center on and use the label Integration Testing.

Integration Testing is the testing of modules, programs, subsystems, and even systems to prove that they interact properly. The common link among modules, programs, subsystems, etc. is that they can (1) share data globally and (2) share data locally defined data through specially designed and constructed interfaces.

Global Data

Global data are known to all system components through a single interface. In COBOL this is accomplished through the DATA DIVISION, which defines every piece of data that will be used by the program. All of the defined data structures are "seen" by all of the paragraphs and sections in the PROCEDURE DIVISION. This is why once an error has been identified in a COBOL program, it is extremely difficult to locate. Because the procedures all have access and could potentially manipulate any or all of the data elements, the error could be in virtually any paragraph or section. Furthermore, the manner in which COBOL programs are usually tested (described earlier) makes matters worse. Once an error has been identified, it could still be in virtually any paragraph or section.

During my programming days, I was given the responsibility of rearranging the "control breaks" in a moderately sized COBOL program (about 8,000 lines). The program generated several very important sales reports. After completely rewriting the totaling logic according to the new control break sequence, the report totals would not balance. For several days I scrutinized the totaling logic to no avail. It all looked correct to me. Finally, while thumbing through the source code listing, I noticed a single line of code adding to one of the totals that I had not seen before. Guess where it was. I found it in a paragraph hidden deep in the listing which formatted a report header for printing. Oh, well.

In another instance, I was sequestered to find an error in another programmer/analyst's program. Because of the global nature of the data and the way COBOL programs are tested, the only way we managed to find this particular problem was to remove the "guts" of each paragraph one at a time until the error disappeared. When it did, we knew it was in that paragraph.

Local Data

Other languages such as the newer COBOL 85, and FORTRAN, PL/1, Pascal, and C, the block-structured languages, allow locally defined data elements known only to the specific procedure in which they are defined and used. It is much easier to isolate an error when it occurs in distinctly defined "PROC's" because you only have to investigate the module that described and used the data. Furthermore, if the modules are tested incrementally, the last module introduced into the set is the likely suspect.

The language used, the type of system component being integrated, and so on, can influence the choice of testing strategy. Systems written in earlier versions of COBOL can be nonincrementally tested only at the program level. Although a paragraph can be formally defined as a module, in practice, testing does not begin until the entire PROCEDURE DIVISION is complete.

Each program, however, can be integrated into the job stream and tested in conjunction with the other programs that have already been integrated (sometimes this is called JCL testing, which is not entirely correct because the purpose is not just to test JCL, but also module interfaces). The only program that is tested in isolation is the first one to be integrated. Consequently, COBOL software is nonincrementally tested at the module (paragraph) level and incrementally tested at the program level and above.

In the languages listed above, a module is normally defined as *a separately compilable unit.* In this situation there is a choice that must be made concerning the kind of testing and integration strategy that is best. The separately compiled components can be combined all at once or integrated individually or some combination of these options.

Myers [2] summarized the advantages and disadvantages of nonincremental and incremental approaches to Integration Testing.

1. Nonincremental requires more initial effort and more work overall because drivers and stubs must be coded.
2. Nonincremental will not detect interface errors as early as incremental because the modules do not interact until late in their development.
3. Debugging is easier if incremental integration is used because errors can be associated with the "last" module that was integrated.
4. Incremental testing is more thorough because the modules are tested under many more different conditions.
5. Nonincremental testing allows more parallel development work to be done than does incremental testing.

Myers [2] also says it has been argued that nonincremental testing requires less machine time, but he feels that the machine time devoted to the initial work developing driver and stub modules makes nonincremental and incremental testing about even in terms of machine resources they use. Because machine cycles are much less expensive than in the past, they are not a major testing consideration today.

Finally, Myers classified integration strategies into one kind of nonincremental testing and five kinds of incremental testing.

NONINCREMENTAL	INCREMENTAL
Big bang testing	Top-down testing
	Bottom-up testing
	Modified top-down testing
	Sandwich testing
	Modified sandwich testing

10.2 NONINCREMENTAL TESTING

10.2.1 Big Bang Testing

The big bang approach is the most used strategy; however, because of the properties of the COBOL language we have already discussed, this type of testing occurs at the program integration level. It is first Unit Testing all of the programs in isolation, followed by integrating all of the tested programs at once. The programs represent separately compilable units which are independently tested (usually by the programmer). After independently testing each program, they are simultaneously introduced into the job stream and tested as described earlier.

The same logic as was applied to COBOL paragraphs and sections also applies here regardless of the particular programming language. If an error occurs, it will be much more difficult to isolate because it could be in any of the programs that were communally integrated. Granted, there will be times when the program that contains the error is obvious, but you can't always count on that.

Compared to the incremental testing approaches, Big Bang testing has another disadvantage. It requires that *JCL* for programs, or *Drivers* and *Stubs* for module "scaffolding" be constructed in order to test them separately.

Drivers are modules that emulate superordinate (higher-level) modules which invoke and control subordinate (lower-level) modules. Stubs are modules that pretend to be missing subordinate modules when testing higher level modules.

Both drivers and stubs are approximations of modules that have not yet been constructed. Drivers, however, can be structurally simpler than stubs, which must at times almost be coded with the sophistication of the later module. Drivers and stubs will be discussed further when we review top-down and bottom-up Integration Testing.

10.3 INCREMENTAL TESTING

The two basic integration strategies in incremental testing are *Top-Down* and *Bottom-Up*. Everything else is either a modification of, or a combination of these approaches. Myers's [2] comparison of the two is discussed in Sections 10.3.2 and 10.3.3.

Myers's incremental testing approach differs from Hetzel's [1] in that Myers does not require independent Unit Testing prior to module integration, while Hetzel says that modules should be Unit Tested separately before being combined. Even though it is more work to use Hetzel's advice, I agree with him. Modules should be tested independently before integration. The success of Integration Testing depends on the initial quality of the modules being integrated. They should be as error-free as possible when integrated testing at the pre-integration level is the responsibility of the programmer (tested to prove that they do what they were intended to do).

10.3.1 Integration Testing Heuristics

Thus, the first rule of thumb of Integration Testing should be: *Each module is tested in isolation before integration begins.*

A very important second heuristic which should be common to all incremental testing approaches is: *Each module being integrated should be thoroughly tested before moving on to the next one.*

A third rule is: *Structurally complex modules should be integrated and tested first.*

The fourth rule of thumb is: *Integrate and test I/O modules as soon as possible.*

10.3.2 Top-Down Testing

Top-down testing begins with the development and test of the mainline or executive module which controls all of the lower-level modules (this model assumes a hierarchical design that is based on the tenets of Structured Design [4] not a networked design). Thus, top-down design must have been completed before testing begins; however, as Myers pointed out, top-down testing and top-down development can occur simultaneously.

It is possible, particularly in top-down testing, to defer the testing of some modules when top-down design has not been completed before commencing testing. This is a bad practice because the program could be completed without ever going back and testing those modules.

Assuming a completed top-down design and once the mainline module has been coded and tested, the subordinate modules can be constructed and tested with some degree of parallelism. The choice of which modules are forged and tested simultaneously depends on the integration criteria. Myers suggests that, as the primary consideration, "critical" sections of the program be "added as early as possible." If the nucleus of the system or program can be identified, these sections should be constructed and tested first. Each group being tested is a system "build."

Obviously, these core build modules will differ depending on the nature of the program or system, but I would offer a suggestion for establishing which modules should be considered critical. Modules that have higher structural complexity levels as indicated by McCabe's cyclomatic complexity metric (refer to Chapter Six) should be constructed and tested first. This is because these modules tend to be error prone, and must be tested and debugged as much as possible before they are combined with modules of lesser structural complexity.

Myers's second consideration for determining module integration is I/O modules should be constructed and integrated as soon as possible. One problem with the top-down approach is getting input to the program "skeleton" and output from it. Until these modules are present, inputs and outputs must be created or "hardwired" in the stub modules. This can cause the complexity of a stub to approach that of the module it emulates. A stub in most situations is not just an "empty" module.

A procedure I used as a programmer writing COBOL PROCEDURE DIVISION code was to begin with empty subordinate paragraphs which simply displayed a message when invoked. One by one I would add the process to each paragraph. This worked fairly well; however, in some cases the paragraphs were so dependent on one another that they had to be constructed completely in order to gage their interactions. I did use top-down development in conjunction with top-down testing as much as is possible when programming in COBOL.

A final problem with top-down testing is that input values are frequently transformed many times before they reach the module (paragraph) they are intended to test. This makes the initial value critical. An input value must be selected which will result in the desired value at the appropriate level in the program skeleton (after transformation) that will adequately test the module in question.

The degree of difficulty increases as modules are added which are furthest removed from the input modules. What this means is that testing from a top-down perspective is sometimes at best an indirect test.

10.3.3 Bottom-Up Testing

Bottom-up integration begins with the modules in the lowest level in the hierarchy and works toward the higher levels. An advantage that is common to bottom-up testing and big bang testing is the capacity to do parallel work. The lower level modules representing different "arms" of the hierarchy can be constructed simultaneously.

Each of the bottom-level modules requires a driver to feed it input and control its actions. This is usually considered an advantage over top-down testing because drivers are normally less complex structurally than stubs.

Bottom-up testing has the additional advantage of drivers being able to input untransformed values directly into the module being tested. This ensures that what the tester thinks is being tested is in fact being tested. In bottom-up testing, the drivers can be thought of as "test probes."

10.3.4 Modified Top-Down Testing

Modified top-down testing is simply top-down integration with modules that have been Unit Tested first. This, as discussed earlier, is the approach recommended by Hetzel [1].

10.3.5 Sandwich Testing

Sandwich testing combines both top-down and bottom-up module construction and integration from a testing posture. It has advantages general to both of the previous types of testing. For instance, the top-down advantage is an early program skeleton is retained and the bottom-up ability to directly test conditions also remains.

   The disadvantage that I see for sandwich testing is that the middle level modules which do the most processing and which are often the most complex structurally are not developed and tested until last. The heart of the program or system does not exist until these modules do. If the strategy is to work to a functioning program skeleton, a portion of these nuclear modules will have been developed.

   It may be that a "middle out" testing approach could be defined where the filling of the sandwich is completed first. It would be followed by concurrent work on the top and bottom portions with a strategy of producing a functioning skeletal structure, the primary advantage being construction and testing of the complex transaction processing modules first.

10.3.6 Modified Sandwich Testing

Modified sandwich testing is identical to sandwich testing except the modules are independently Unit Tested before integration begins.

10.4 CONCLUSION

All things considered, incremental testing appears to be much better than nonincremental testing. Furthermore, of the types of incremental testing, some form of modified sandwich/middle out testing is preferable. Bottom-up testing portends to have the edge over top-down testing [2,3].

   If you are developing COBOL-based information systems, and the majority of you are, the COBOL programming standards should be followed to ensure that quality is built into each software unit before it goes into the testing process.

REFERENCES

1. Hetzel, William, *The Complete Guide to Software Testing, 2ed*. Wellesley, MA: QED Information Sciences, Inc., 1988.
2. Myers, Glenford, *Software Reliability: Principles and Practices*. New York: Wiley-Interscience, 1976.
3. Myers, Glenford, *The Art of Software Testing*. New York: Wiley-Interscience, 1979.
4. Yourdon, Edward, and Larry Constantine, *Structured Design: Fundamentals of Computer Program and Systems Design*. Englewood Cliffs, N.J.: Prentice Hall, 1979.

11

System Testing

If you do not have written objectives for your product, or if your objectives are unmeasurable, then you cannot perform a system test.

Glenford Myers, 1979 [5]

Integration Testing and System Testing are both Black Box oriented. The difference between Integration Testing and System Testing is often not distinct. The question that does not always have a clear answer is, "when does Integration Testing stop and System Testing begin?" The answer is not, as suggested by some [2], that the final Integration Test constitutes the System Test or that System Testing is the "sum total" of all the conditions tested during the Unit Tests [1]. The true answer actually lies in the purposes of Integration and System Testing, as there are many differences between these two kinds of tests. The most important of these are discussed in the text that follows.

The purpose of Integration Testing (a.k.a string testing, interface testing) is to demonstrate that combined system components interact properly. The tester's concern is that the values sent and received are correct. Thus, the important dimension of Integration Testing is determining that the modules talk to one another properly. In a more technical sense, Integration Testing is designed to detect situations where *data and control messages* are incorrectly passed across module or subsystem interfaces.

Consequently, Integration Testing begins during the "construction" phase of the SDLC. King [3] refers to this stage as the *Program*

Design And Development phase. According to Structured Design doctrine, top-down design, which began in the previous stage, is continued to a much lower level of detail, and *top-down construction* and *top-down testing* are begun. Of course, top-down integration may not be the chosen approach. As discussed in the preceding chapter, there are several approaches to integration, top-down being only one.

Integration issues are not confined to module integration. This concept also applies to the integration and interface testing of functional subsystems and to tests of system-system interfaces. Although considered to be near the Black Box end of the testing spectrum, Integration Testing represents an "internal" view of system functionality.

A second difference between Integration and System Testing is that System Testing very rarely involves the invocation of a single system function. Integration Testing can and often does incorporate Function Testing as a part of the levels of testing. System components which implement a particular function may form a "natural" grouping for integration. In the vernacular, these natural groupings have been termed "builds."

A third and very important difference between these two types of testing is that of the nature of the test cases used. In Integration Testing, the test data are designed and constructed using Equivalence Partitioning, and Boundary Analysis. It is important to supplement this basic test data with additional test records created through Basis Testing and Error Guessing. Additional volume may be created by copying some production data (if available) into the test data set. This is not going against earlier arguments that production data have very little chance of finding an error because we have included records that are specifically designed to ferret out errors.

11.1 SYSTEM TESTING

System Testing is carried out during the formal *Testing Phase* of the SDLC. As far as testing is concerned, this stage consumes the largest chunk of testing resources. As indicated in Chapter Two, that amounts to approximately 12.5 percent of allocated reserves. Our discussion of system testing will refer to the activities of this stage of development.

System Testing activities are controlled by the *System Test Plan*, which was developed much earlier during the SDLC in the *System Design* phase, but is now implemented. The System Test Plan is, as discussed in Chapter Four, a detailed document which is constructed using Section Five of the Test Plan Table of Contents offered in the same chapter.

These activities are intended to prove that the system meets its *objectives*. Some experts argue that the purpose of System Testing is to prove that the system meets its *requirements*. This is not entirely true unless you consider Acceptance Testing as a type of system testing, because the purpose of Acceptance Testing is to demonstrate that the system meets the user's requirements.

Acceptance Testing is a *validation* process. System testing, in the strictest sense, is a *verification* process. Regardless of whether it represents verification or validation, System Testing represents an "external" view of the system.

This is true because requirements represent the eventual system user's view of the system. Users do not understand nor do they care about how the system works as long as it is "usable." Their opinions of the system are formulated strictly from what their senses tell them when they use the system. They interact with the system via a user interface using a set of manual procedures designed to invoke specific responses from the system. If the interface is difficult to master or the system's responses are inappropriate, the system is not usable. System Testing should be approached from this perspective. An excellent source for designing and constructing System Test cases is either the system user's manual or user training materials.

You are probably saying to yourself, "but objectives are specified internally by the design team," and you are correct. However, objectives are direct translations of requirements into design goals that must be achieved. Therefore, objectives are formulated from external system considerations. If this basic translation process results in objectives that do not reflect the requirements, a discrepancy exists which must not be allowed beyond System Testing.

For clarity in our discourse on System Testing, we will define and discuss three types of system testing, one of which will incorporate what is known as acceptance testing. They are *System Verification Testing*, *Customer Verification Testing*, and *Customer Validation Testing*.

The first two kinds of system tests are verification procedures designed to assure that the system does meet its design objectives. They are destructive in nature and intended to find areas where the system does not accomplish its objectives so that corrections can be made. The third type is designed to validate the system and is intended to be a positive (confidence building) experience demonstrating how the system fulfills its requirements (this is the unrealized true purpose of User Acceptance Testing).

The key words here are "verify" and "validate." Testing is a verification process when it occurs in a nonlive test environment using nonlive test data. This is exactly what happens when we do what we commonly call System Testing. A test team consisting of members of the development group, system operations staff, quality analysts, auditors, and end user representatives is at the helm during the test. The project team leader directs this test. The test is actually conducted by the MIS staff with input from the quality analysts, users, and the like who are present. This is more properly termed System Verification Testing.

Another instance of testing as a verification procedure involves repeating the previous test with the users conducting it. The test, as was the one before, is executed in a simulated nonproduction environment, hence the name Customer Verification Testing. In fact, this test is conducted in the same environment as the previous System Test, detail for detail. The same typical processing day is used together with the previously used scripts. In this case, the MIS staff acts in an advisory capacity.

Validation means that something actually works as it was intended to work. If this is so, then the product being tested meets its requirements. The purpose of Customer Validation Testing is to demonstrate that the system works:

The only way to prove that a product functions correctly is to use it in the real world on real data.

So, this kind of System Testing occurs using live production data with the users conducting the test. Sounds a lot like Acceptance Testing, doesn't it? Consequently, the things we have said about Acceptance Testing Apply to this type of System Test.

The common thread among the three kinds of System Tests is that they are formally implemented. "Formal" means according to a written plan. A major criticism of System Testing in general is that it is frequently done in an informal manner. This results in some portions of the system being tested more thoroughly than others, or even, in some portions not being tested at all. Scripts (discussed below) impose the formality of a specific scenario on the testing process, making the testers actors in the play who are compelled to learn and execute their lines. Of course some improvisation is acceptable, but only within strict prespecified limits.

11.2 DEVELOPING SYSTEM TEST CASES

Test cases for system testing consist of scripts that enact a specific information processing scenario. If we think of system testing as a "play," each script can be considered an act in the play. A script most often represents a typical user's session on an on-line system or a typical transaction processing event in a batch system. For both types of system, the play would conclude after enough scripts were executed to represent a normal processing day, week, month, quarter, etc.

As an example of the kinds of events a script might include, let's consider an on-line system which creates and services customer accounts for a cable TV company. In a normal day, customers are added to the system data base, as well as removed from that data base; new customers must be authorized and deleted customers must be deauthorized; some customers may require reauthorization and credits for lost viewing time; customers call and request pay-per-view authorization for special movie and sporting events, and so on. A System Test of these activities must be comprised of scripts intended to thoroughly exercise each one. Furthermore, the scripts must be "destructive." They must include attempts to make the system do things it is not supposed to do.

Because test scripts are fairly complicated and several may be implemented during the System Test, it is best to organize them in test case *folios*. The test cases in the folio can be conveniently grouped according to the design objectives or requirements of the system. Based on Hetzel's [2] previous description, test case folios should minimally contain:

1. A section detailing the objectives and requirements to be tested.
2. Restrictions and limitations on how each group of scripts may be used.
3. A description of the overall test scenario explaining how the groups are related.
4. Groups of test scripts organized according to purpose.
5. Expected system behaviors for each group of scripts.

Examples of scripts written for a real system by MIS practitioners in partial fulfillment of the credit requirements for my Software Testing course can be found in the *Hardware Tracking System* (HTS) Test Plan included in Appendix C.

Scripts are formulated by considering the objectives, but are constructed from details contained in the user and operator manuals, as well as other system documentation. Since the value of the test cases will depend on the correctness of these documents, steps should be taken to ensure their integrity during earlier development phases. Walk-throughs and/or Inspections of all system documentation is highly recommended as a preventive measure.

11.3 PURPOSES OF SYSTEM TESTING

The title of this subsection could have been "Types Of System Tests," but I feel "purposes" is better. What are traditionally touted as kinds of System Tests [5] are really *specific* purposes of the System Test which do not necessarily have to be separate tests, but rather, can be tested in parallel during one of the two types of system verification tests. Each specific purpose should be represented by a group of scripts aimed at the facet of the system to be tested.

Thus, there are several kinds of situations which the scripts may be designed to invoke during the three kinds of System Tests. Two important ones that can be used during System Verification and Customer Verification Testing are Volume Testing and Stress Testing.

The purpose of *Volume Testing* is to find weaknesses in the system with respect to its handling of large amounts of data during short time periods. This kind of testing ensures that the system will process data across physical and logical boundaries such as reels of tape and disk partitions. Thus, a script may include some activities which require a particular tape reel be mounted and others which require that a different reel be mounted at a different time but within the same session.

With the advent of distributed processing and "groupware," processing activities no longer just span the physical boundaries of data storage media, but also span networked processors and intelligent work stations. Testing must also assure that volumes of data are processed correctly across these processing interfaces.

The purpose of *Stress Testing* is to show that the system has the capacity to handle large numbers of processing transactions during peak periods. An example of a peak period is when everyone is logging back onto an on-line system after it has been down. In a batch environment, a similar situation would exist when numerous jobs are fired up after down time.

As an example, a script might require a user to log on and proceed with his/her daily activities while at the same time require that a Batch Terminal Simulation (BTS) program be executed emulating a number of other system users. The script should include activities purposely designed to compete for system resources with the activities executed through the BTS.

Performance Testing can be accomplished in parallel with Volume and Stress Testing. System performance is generally assessed in terms of response times and throughput rates under differing processing and configuration conditions.

Configuration Testing is another important purpose of System Testing. Perhaps the system will run under different versions of the operating system. If so, it must be tested in all of those operating environments. Furthermore, if the system could possibly be installed on several hardware platforms, it must be tested in those environments too.

I once had the pleasure of installing a construction cost estimating system for a major construction/engineering firm. The system was written in FORTRAN and was commented in the German language. It was shipped from the parent company office in Germany to the local office where I worked. I could not make it work on our minicomputer, which was identical to hardware on which the system was developed. As it turned out, our office was running Version 3.0 of the operating system software and the home office was still using Version 2.0.

A simple problem was our downfall. In the older version, user log-on id's were two positions in length, while the newer version stored id's as a three-position field. When the application software was changed to correct this single problem, everything worked.

By the way, I hope you never have to support software commented in a language you do not speak, read, or write. I can tell you it was a wonderful experience!

From a maintenance perspective, *Compatibility Testing* is very important. People become accustomed to certain consistencies in life, and work life is no different. Individuals who have invested time and effort in learning the appropriate procedures to use when working with a particular applications system can be very unhappy if a system modification requires relearning the system interface. Compatibility Testing is designed to assess the level of "sameness" that exists between the modified system and the previous system.

For example, if an on-line system is menu driven and all of the menus are designed to have the same look and feel, any changes that might result in a different look and feel must be carefully considered and tested as part of the System Test. Scripts that force the changed menu to be used are absolutely a must.

This is particularly important if the procedure used to interact with the system via the menu has been changed. If the previous menu required the user to hit the return key to execute a command and the new menu requires that the user press a function key to execute the command, there will be many mistakes before this subtle change is incorporated into the user's set of programmed (learned) responses.

Recovery Testing is an extremely important reason for doing System Testing. Scripts which investigate data recovery and system re-start capabilities can save a lot of money and time once the system is in production. As an illustration of what can happen, a particular master file which records transactions for a respected publishing company did not have recovery capabilities built into the application that updated this file. This was discovered only after the monthly update which handled two million plus transactions blew up. Each processing cycle required 60 hours to completion. When the software encountered a corrupt data record after 40 hours of processing, it went down.

This should not have happened, and if adequate System Testing procedures had been in place it would not have happened. Alas, the poor programmer/analyst! He was called in during the weekend, but could only recommend restarting the job. After a premature termination of the second run, he was in definite hot water. Monday morning the MIS director and the MIS applications development manager swarmed around his cubicle and after three maddening days the system was rewritten to include recovery and restart capacity.

There is one final aspect to this sad story. System recovery and restart procedures should be complemented with "error trapping" capabilities which allow an orderly shut down of the application and not just allow operating system errors to be generated, as is frequently the case in an IBM environment. Error trapping logic could even record the problem, bypass the corrupt data and continue processing as an alternative to an orderly shutdown.

Finally, *Documentation Testing* is an important part of the System Test. Evaluating user and operator manuals for completeness, correctness, and consistency is important for system usability. This is accomplished by using the documents during the three kinds of System Tests we have discussed.

Just as important is *readability*, a concept unheard of in one major hardware vendor's (I think most of you know which one) publications. The manual must be written in unambiguous English using CLEAR, CONCISE, and COMPLETE sentences which are organized into paragraphs expressing single thoughts. Remember the "one function, one module" rule of Structured Design. Well, it can be rephrased as "one thought, one paragraph" when applied to system documentation.

I have taught MIS graduate students for several years now, and I am appalled at their lack of ability to write in a clear and organized manner. These are future MIS managers who cannot communicate, or can only communicate in a disorganized way. Unfortunately , most of the documentation I confronted during my career in MIS must have been written by individuals of similar talent. I understand that writing is tough, but if I can do it (and this book should be some proof), so can you.

11.4 CONCLUSION

The importance of System Testing cannot be overemphasized. It is so important because it is the last line of defense before the system is put into production. Furthermore, it is at the point of System Testing that we must vigorously attempt to find remaining errors which were caused by inadequate analysis and design procedures. If you will remember the discussion on the cost of errors, you should recall that errors which leak through into production systems are very costly to fix, and the majority of those errors are due to faulty analysis or design.

System Testing, being a Black Box approach, is specifically geared toward finding errors in analysis and design. The reason so many of these errors are found in functioning information systems is the informal approach most organizations have when it comes to System Testing. The most profitable testing activities are those of a *formal* System Test.

The burden of System Testing can be reduced through the use of Computer-Aided Software Engineering (CASE) analysis and design workbench products. There is evidence [4] that CASE use reduces the number of analysis and design errors found in implemented information systems. A word of caution: This does not imply that System Testing will not be necessary as more and more software is developed using CASE. CASE reduces but does not eliminate these kinds of errors.

REFERENCES

1. Armour, Philip, *Structured Unit and System Testing: A Test Construction Methodology*. Note: Author was with United Airlines at the time of publication; The date of publication and journal are not known.

2. Hetzel, William, *The Complete Guide to Software Testing*, 2ed. Englewood Cliffs, N.J.: Prentice Hall, 1988.

3. King, David, *Current Practices in Software Development: A Guide to Successful Systems*. Englewood Cliffs, N.J.: Prentice Hall, 1984.

4. Lempp, P., and R. Lauber, "What Productivity Increases to Expect from a CASE Environment: Results of a User Survey," *Productivity: Progress, Prospects, and Payoff* (June 1988), 13–19.

5. Myers, Glenford, *The Art of Software Testing*. New York: Wiley-Interscience, 1979.

12

Human Testing: The Walk-Through and the Inspection

With a renewed interest in the quality of information systems around the world, walk-throughs should become a universally practiced technique in the industry.

Edward Yourdon, 1989

Human Testing is a legacy from the "structured revolution" of the late 1960s through the 1970s and early 1980s. The basic premise of the structured approach is the structured theorem, which was proposed by Bohm and Jocopini in 1962 and again in 1966 [1]. The fundamental idea is that the logic of any program can be designed using three logical constructs: Sequence, Selection, and Iteration. Bohm and Jacopini proved this axiom mathematically.

I am not sure, however, that they saw the complete significance of their work. What they did was develop a mathematical proof that we can construct software which models the way we do things in the real world. We carry out our activities in three ways. We do things in the order in which they occur (sequence); we make decisions to do some things and not others (selection); we do some things over and over until we can determine that it is time to stop (iteration).

The consequence of the idea that programs should be structured has had an impact extending above and beyond just structuring code. Structured Design [11] and Structured Analysis [2] are the logical extensions that have evolved. The essence of the "structured" revolution is that relating software structure to the real world processes through rigorous application of structured analysis, design, and coding makes the software understandable to a lot of people, not just the software builder. Hence, structured programs are considered readable by anyone trained in the principles and constructs of Structured Programming. The idea that programs are readable by human beings, and not just machines, leads to the concept of Human Testing. Readability is important because the large complex software systems of today are developed by groups of people who must communicate.

The idea of humans reading systems development products does not stop with programs. The concept of Human Testing has been extended to include the products of Structured Design and Structured Analysis. Requirements documents, system specifications and designs including analysis and design diagrams should also be considered readable. *If it's readable it's testable!* So, various kinds of Human Testing can be applied at every stage of systems development.

The major problem with Human Testing is that reading is an informal activity which is usually done by individuals. If there has been a consistent criticism of Human Testing, it is that it is frequently an informal process. An example of Human Testing that is completed by an individual is Desk Checking.

Desk Checking, however, does not have to be an informal activity. It is not simply reading the source code, as many programmers think, but rather the paper and pencil execution of the program by the programmer, or someone else who understands the logic (or can read the source code if the program has been coded following the structured theorem). Consequently, Desk Checking a program requires the construction of a set of "paper" test cases which may or may not actually be written down on paper, and which are "mentally" executed by the person who is "playing computer."

Desk Checking and Code Inspections differ in several aspects. First, an Inspection is a formal group activity consisting of separate and distinctly defined phases. Second, inspections require preparation because participants review and use checklists of known errors while reading the source code aloud. Third, inspections are not limited to source code. Other development products such as design specifications can be reviewed using this process. So, a code inspection, while the most widely known type [4,5], is not the only kind of inspection.

The Walk-through, is a formalized group activity, as is the inspection. It differs from inspections and is related to Desk Checking in that the group "plays computer." The Walk-through is similar to the inspection because error checklists are also used to bolster the "mock" execution of the software. Walk-throughs, like inspections, can occur for other system development products in addition to source code.

Regardless of the type of Human Testing used, there are two important advantages. First, as discussed in Chapter Two, the earlier an error is found, the cheaper it is to repair. Inspections and Walk-throughs can identify errors in requirements before they are translated into design specifications. They can also assess designs with respect to *completeness*, *correctness*, and *consistency*, prior to coding and implementation. The sooner an error is found, the less rework that has to be done. The less rework, the greater the development team's productivity.

The second advantage is the earlier an error is found, the greater the probability of correcting it *correctly*. Late in the development process when the requirements and design are already in the form of completed code, there is tremendous pressure to correct any problems that might occur. This forces the programmers, etc. to place great psychological pressures on themselves to "fix" the problem. In this kind of crisis resolution situation where a problem must be corrected "or else" and individuals are called to work at odd hours, the stress can cloud their judgment. Thus, there is a much greater chance of overlooking an important aspect of the problem and failing to correct it. In addition, the fix may actually introduce new errors into the software because it is not carefully thought out.

This is really a management problem [3]. When an error is identified late in development, we go into "crisis" mode in order to find and repair that error. Most project managers, however, do not build time into the development schedule for crisis resolution, and consequently, development falls behind. When this happens, *we all look bad!* As a component of an integrated testing and development life cycle, crisis resolution activities should be specifically defined along with revised development schedule estimates as a part of the form test planning process.

12.1 THE WALK-THROUGH

King [7] formally defines a Walk-through as:

a process in which a product or a partial product of a data processing system development activity is examined component by component.

He says that Walk-throughs can be performed for requirements definition documents, system specification documents, program specification documents, and program source code, and he designed a formal, yet simple, walk-through procedure which I highly recommend. He stresses the importance of having a "standardized" walk-through procedure defining the stages, participants, timing, input documentation, and output documentation.

King's view of a Walk-through is that it occurs in three stages: The *Review Stage*, the *Walk-Through Stage*, and the *Follow-up Stage*. Figure 12.1 is a diagram depicting the flow of activities in a Walk-through.

King suggests that Walk-through attendees be kept to a minimum, but adequate, number, with 12 as a maximum. The attendance of any person must be justified by what that person can contribute to the session. (See Table 12.1)

He defined a specific set of attendee roles and responsibilities.

The Moderator	The moderator is the chairperson of the group who facilitates the session. He or she can be a senior member of the project team who has management experience but who is not a manager directly involved in this project.
The Presenter	The presenter is the author of the product. If the product was developed by a team, a member is selected to present.
The Recorder	The recorder compiles a written list of criticisms and comments about the product and records the schedule for product modifications.
The Attendees	The rest of the group can consist of project team members, representatives from the user departments where the system will be implemented, operations staff members, developers from interrelated projects, EDP auditors or quality assurance analysts, and so on.

The actual make-up of the group will vary according to the nature of the product. For example, a strategic planner might be invited to a Walk-through for a product from a "mission critical" system. If this

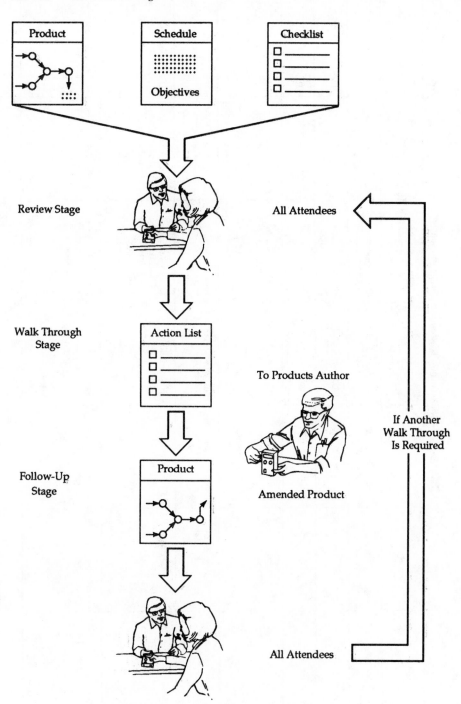

Figure 12.1 Flow of Walk-Through Activities

TABLE 12.1 Walk-Through Attendees: Stage by Stage

Stage / Role	Requirements Definition	System Specification	System Design	Program Design & Development	System Test	Implementation & Production
Moderator	Sensor User	Sensor User	Sensor DP System Analyst	Chief Programmer (Project Leader)	Chief Programmer	Senior User
Presenter	Business System Analyst	Business System Analyst	DP System Analyst or Designer	Program Designer	Testers	Business System Analyst
Recorder	Another Business System Analyst	Another Business System Analyst	Project Librarian	Project Librarian	Project Librarian	Another Business System Analyst
Team members	More Business System Analysts	Business & DP System Analysts & User Representatives	DP System Analysts & Designers	Programmers & System Analysts	Programmers & DP System Analysts	Business & DP System Analysts, Programmers, Testers
User represenative	DP System Analyst & User Business System Analyst	User Representative	Business System Analysts	Business System Analysts	Senior User, Business System Analysts	User Representative
Outsiders	DP Operations, Quality Assurance, DP Audit, Data Administration, Strategic Planning	DP Operations, Quality Assurance, DP Audit, Data Administration, Strategic Planning	DP Operations, Quality Assurance, DP Audit, Data Administration, Strategic Planning	Quality Assurance, Database, Administration, DP Audit	Quality Assurance, DP Audit, DP Operations	DP Operations, Quality Assurance, DP Audit
Product to be walked through	Requirements Definition Document & Cost-Benefit Analysts	System Specification Document & Cost-Benefit Analysts	System Design Document System Test Plan Database Design Installation Test Plan	Program Design & Code, Program Test Results Data Design	System Test Results	Implementation Results Production Review Report

kind of system fails, the company might go out of business or lose a large amount of money. An example of one such failure is the recent AT&T long distance service faux pas. A little prevention here could have saved millions of dollars. One way to develop an attendee list is to conduct a risk analysis as described by Perry [9].

12.1.1 The Review Stage

The purpose of this stage is to familiarize the walk-through participants with the product being reviewed. This is important because the actual walk-through adheres to a strict time limit. If the participants are not prepared, then the entire time would have to be used to develop an understanding of the product. If this is the case, the walk-through will be a failure and the attendees will probably become confused, and ultimately, angry with one another.

Review materials include a copy of the product, review checklists, and guidelines describing the walk-through activities and how they will occur (the guidelines should be based on previously established standards for conducting walk-throughs).

The time allocated to the review stage varies as a function of product size. For example, King recommends a 14-day review period for development products such as the requirements definition document and the system specification document, but only a 4-day review period for program designs. Weinberg and Freedman [10], however, have determined that on the average spending more than a total of 6 hours reviewing a product is a waste of time because preparedness levels off after that, and the law of diminishing returns prevails.

This is an example of the Pareto Principle mentioned later and discussed in Chapter Fourteen. Eighty percent of the preparation is accomplished on the average within 6 hours, while the remaining 20 percent could take an additional 24 hours to complete. Thus, it is not worth the additional effort to approach 100 percent preparedness.

Table 12.2 contains a summary of recommended walk-through stage timing (in days) for different phases and the products they deliver.What it does not contain is the 80/20 break point for each different product. These points must be determined as you apply different review processes and incorporated into your review standards.

12.1.2 The Walk-Through Stage

The function of this stage is to conduct a detailed product assessment. The product's author or a member of the project team presents the product to the group. The essence of the product is summarized as

TABLE 12.2 Walk-Through Timing: Stage by Stage

Life Cycle Stage	Requirements Definition	System Specification	System Design	Program Design & Development	System Test	Implementation & Production
Typical Product of Life Cycle Stages	Requirements Definition Document	System Specification Document	System Design Document	Program Design	System Test Results	Production Review Document
			Days Required to Review the Product			
Review	14	14	30	4	14	30
Walk-through	1	2	2	1	1	2
Follow-up	45	29	30	5	15	30
Total Elapsed Days	60	45	62	10	30	62

opposed to a "line-by-line" reading of the product. During this process, the participants offer constructive criticism.

The atmosphere during this stage must be an impersonal one. I have personally attended product Walk-throughs where the session became highly agitated and the product's authors felt they were being impuned by the group. It is the moderator's responsibility to see that this does not happen. If a session goes out of control it should be terminated immediately, and resumed only after a cooling-off period of at least overnight.

The attendees should look at the product with respect to completeness, correctness, and consistency, their purpose being to generate an *Action List*. This document will subsequently be used by the author to modify the product. It is important to keep the group from suggesting solutions for the problems they find because there is not enough time in a walk-through session to both find and solve problems. The group should, however, generate a schedule for resolving the problems. It is the author's responsibility to see that the appropriate product changes occur within the allocated time or have "damn" good reasons why the problems can't be resolved in the specified time.

If the product being reviewed is a design diagram (Flow Chart, Warnier/Orr Diagram, Nassi-Schneidermann Chart, etc.) or source code, the participants "play computer." One attendee is designated as a *tester* who brings a set of "paper" test cases. The group then mentally executes the program logic according to the paper design or the source listing.

The length of the actual walk-through session is dependent on the product being evaluated. The maximum time for a single session is 2 hours. If the product is large or complex enough to require more time, the walk-through stage can be broken into several sessions. The sessions can be held on successive days. The reason for a time limit is that the ability of humans to concentrate on a particular problem deteriorates as a function of time. At the end of a 2-hour stint, everyone will be sufficiently fatigued and ready for a break.

12.1.3 The Follow-Up Stage

The purpose of this stage is to ensure that the requested product changes are implemented. This requires a written report of the changes made and if some changes were not implemented, a written defense of the lack of action. The report is the product author's responsibility.

An important rule of thumb is that a product that is changed by 25 percent or more is to be considered a new product. Products modified this extensively should be re-reviewed. This means a second walk-through stage session as indicated by the flow of the diagram in Figure 12.1.

12.2 THE INSPECTION

The procedure for doing an inspection is the same as that of the Walk-through. There is an initial *Review Stage*, an *Inspection Stage*, and a *Follow-Up Stage*. The major differences are a smaller number of attendees and the inspection stage is a reading of the product.

As an example, let's look at the Code Inspection. The inspection team is composed of a moderator, a programmer, a program designer, and a testing specialist. The moderator's role and responsibilities are the same as before. The programmer functions as the reader and should be the program's author or another programmer familiar with the program's structure. The program designer should be the program's original designer if possible. The testing specialist is there as a technical advisor who can help guide the proceedings.

12.2.1 The Inspection Stage

The Inspection Stage is twofold. First, the programmer narrates the program logic statement by statement while the other group members offer comments and constructive criticism. Second, the group evaluates the program against a list of known errors and for error proneness. Litecky and Davis [8] have identified several common types of errors committed when writing COBOL programs, and they identified weaknesses in the language which cause certain constructs to be error prone. Refer to the data in Table 14.1 and to the Pareto chart illustrated in Figure 14.1 of Chapter Fourteen for a summary of their findings.

Some traditional points to check are omission of a portion of the program, branching the wrong way at a decision, using the wrong format for reading data (this one will save you those SOC -7's if you're an IBM'er), uninitialized variables, incorrect variable references, and truncating of data. Set the compiler option and use the CX list to locate data names defined but never used, and if GOTO's are the norm in your shop, look for unused labels.

The output of the Inspection Stage is once again an Action List which contains the team's recommendations for modifications during the Follow-Up Stage. Furthermore, the previous heuristic still applies. If the product is changed by 25 percent or more, it must be re-inspected.

The length of the Code Inspection session should be held to approximately 1 hour, and absolutely, not more than 2 hours.

12.3 HUMAN CONFLICT AND REVIEW EFFECTIVENESS

Where Human Testing is most valuable is evaluating specifications for "reasonableness," for the inclusion of restart and data recovery capabilities, where test data are insufficient or impractical, and to facilitate debugging situations. The effectiveness of the review process in these areas can be drastically reduced because of squabbling among the participants.

When these conflicts do tend to reduce the effectiveness of Human Testing, stop the review immediately and report the results (or lack of results) to management [10]. Sometimes a little pressure applied to the right people from their superiors is all that is required to turn things around. In one major financial institution where "peer" reviews were implemented, the participants were rotated in and out of review team duties, serving for 12 months when assigned. The team members were expected to continue to fulfill their normal work activities, and in addition prepare for and attend the reviews.

Needless to say, some individuals did not take their roles as reviewers seriously. They did not prepare and were not productive during the review. The Quality Assurance group which conducted the reviews proceeded to inform the managers of the unproductive attendees concerning the quality of their work. Well, the worst reviewers suddenly became the best reviewers because their jobs were on the line.

Conflicts can also happen because of the mental "games" people play with one another in team situations [12]. The problems arise because the games are almost always competitive, and competition among review attendees is counterproductive. The review process must have an atmosphere of cooperation if it is to succeed. Thus, the training and experience of the review facilitator are very important because he or she must identify when attendees are playing games and must stop the unproductive behavior. The facilitator should not be afraid to "eject" uncooperative attendees from the review if necessary.

When conflicts are severe enough that the review session has to be terminated, all parties should attend a conflict resolution session. These sessions should include management, users, and operations personnel because of their perspectives. At the end of the session, all attendees must sign off on the conflict resolution.

Further conflict may occur after the review stage during the follow-up phase. Just because a potential problem is included in the Action List does not mean that the product's author must agree that it is a problem. The author may choose to ignore some Action List items. Thus, some further discussion of these items is necessary to determine if the author is justified in his/her actions. Ultimately, someone with higher authority may make the determination for the group.

12.4 CONCLUSION

Human Testing is a "legitimate" form of software testing. It realizes the preventive potential of the testing process because it is applicable to a diverse range of development products in all stages of the development process. In this sense, it adds a quality assurance component to software testing which supplements the quality control aspects of what has traditionally been considered testing.

Furthermore, Human Testing is more effective at preventing analysis and design errors than Unit, Integration, and System Testing are at removing them. Thus, a substantial portion of the testing resources should be devoted to it in each stage of development. As was indicated in Chapter Two, this is currently not the situation. Fifty percent of development resources are allocated to testing in the corrective form.

This is far and away too much emphasis on error removal. As was previously discussed, testing should only account for 30 percent of development resources, and the 30 percent should be spread among development phases, not poured into a single testing phase. If the allocation guidelines presented in Chapter Two are followed, at least 2 percent of the testing resources in each stage should be for Human Testing.

REFERENCES

1. Bohm, C., and G. Jacopini, "Flow Diagrams, Turing Machines, and Languages with Only Two Formation Rules," *Communications of the ACM*, 9, no. 5 (1966).

2. DeMarco, Tom, *Structured Analysis and System Specification*. Englewood Cliffs, N.J.: Yourdon Press/Prentice Hall, 1978.

3. Evans, Michael, *Productive Software Test Management*. New York: Wiley-Interscience, 1984.

4. Fagan, Michael, "Design and Code Inspections to Reduce Errors in Program Development," *IBM Systems Journal*, 15, no. 3 (July 1976), 182–211.

5. Fagan, Michael, "Advances in Software Inspections," *IEEE Transactions on Software Engineering*, SE-12, no. 7 (July 1986), 744–51.

6. Gane, Chris, and Trish Sarson, *Structured Systems Analysis: Tools and Techniques*. Englewood Cliffs, N.J.: Prentice Hall, 1979.

7. King, David, *Current Practices in Software Development: A Guide to Successful Systems*. Englewood Cliffs, N.J.: Prentice Hall, 1984.

8. Litecky, Charles R., and Gordon Davis, "A Study of Errors, Error Proneness, and Error Diagnosis on COBOL," *Communications of the ACM*, 19, no. 1 (January 1976), 33–37.

9. Perry, William, *A Standard for Testing Application Software 1992*. Boston, MA: Auerbach, 1992.

10. Weinberg, Gerald, and Daniel Freedman, *Handbook of Walk-Throughs and Inspections*. Boston, MA: Little Brown, 1982.

11. Yourdon, Edward, and Larry Constantine, *Structured Design: Fundamentals of Computer Program and Systems Design*. Englewood Cliffs, N.J.: Prentice Hall, 1979.

12. Yourdon, Edward, *Structured Walk-Throughs, 4ed*. Englewood Cliffs, N.J.: Yourdon Press Computing Series, 1989.

13

Software "Tools" for Software Testing

Tool:
Something (as an instrument or apparatus) used in performing an operation or necessary in the practice of a vocation or profession

Webster's Ninth New Collegiate Dictionary

In a survey of software engineering practices, Beck and Perkins [3] determined that software testing is one of the least defined areas of systems development in terms of *methods, techniques,* and *tools.* That's the good news. Now the bad news. This is still the status of software testing today. The Center for the Study of Data Processing offers its Software Testing seminar once every quarter and that is not often enough. Every session has at least 25 attendees plus a waiting list of 10 to 15 more. These enrollment figures have remained stable for five years now. These figures plus Beizer's [4] analysis of sales of software testing books corroborate Beck and Perkins's findings. Indeed, software testing is an area wide open to improvement.

There is renewed interest in software testing because automation is reviving interest in the "structured methodologies" including testing methods. We are on the verge of the *industrialization* of software development. Computer-Aided Software/Systems Engineering (CASE) is "an integrating technology that will pull together and focus the many methods, techniques, and tools software developers are using" [15]. In a corresponding sense, Carma McClure [14] sees CASE as being built upon "techniques and tools that have been proven in practice." She

184

defined CASE as "a repackaging of structured concepts and methodologies with a new twist. The new twist is automation."

CASE primarily represents the automation of analysis and design activities through *Analysis/Design* workbenches which are analogous to Computer Aided Design (CAD) Software tools in the engineering community, and construction activities through *Programmer Productivity* workbenches analogous to Computer Aided Manufacturing (CAM) software tools. A *workbench* is an integrated set of software tools ("tools" refers to software utility programs that are part of a complete system of utilities to assist software development activities and their management) that automate software development, maintenance, and project management activities [12,14].

13.1 IS INDUSTRIALIZATION AND TESTING

According to Appleton [2], industrialization occurs when the present mode of production is no longer able to meet the demand for product. Consequently, the backlog of new application development projects, that is estimated to be as long as 88 months by Dr. Carma McClure, is forcing systems development along the path toward industrialization.

To describe the systems development process, Appleton applies a "manufacturing" metaphor. In doing so, he depicts the current "mode of production" as that of the "job shop." In job shop mode information systems are built from scratch according to the customer's (user's) specifications. In essence, the customer's needs drive the development process. While in the "standard production" mode, product is manufactured prior to a request from a specific customer, and when a purchase is imminent, the manufacturer offers the customer one of two options. The manufacturer can customize the existing product so it fits the customer's needs, or the customer can purchase the product and customize it him/herself.

Thus, an important difference between the two modes is "needs" management versus "assets" management. In the job shop, customer requirements "drive" the manufacturing process. Isn't this exactly what happens in the majority of MIS development shops? *Absolutely!* This means that most MIS development is done in job shop mode, and that is why the development of information systems is extremely inefficient and ineffective.

If systems development were in standardized mode, off-the-shelf components would be assembled to meet customer needs. Previously created software components are assets that are used to meet customer demand in a timely fashion. The term that is in vogue is "reuse." Analyses, designs, and code modules can be stored in libraries as assets that can be used over and over again. Reuse in the standardized production shop results in a manufacturing process that is much simpler and is repeatable (executed the same way each time). In contrast, in the job shop, the process is complex and is executed differently for each development project.

The reason CASE technology cannot be ignored is because it offers developers the opportunity to simplify and standardize the development process, and thereby move from the job shop mode to the standardized production mode [16]. From a testing perspective, standardizing production via CASE is an important step in the right direction because it would prevent many of the kinds of errors we now find in software systems.

Because industrialization would generate an overall increase in product quality, some experts argue that CASE will eliminate the need for testing. This is simply not true! CASE will allow us to "engineer" our systems, and as engineers already know, *predictability* is an important aspect of engineering [22]. It is also an important component of software testing.

Technology is "applied" science, and engineers are "applied scientists." The characteristic that distinguishes science from art or religion is attitude (according to Popper [20], a scientist tries to *disprove* scientific theories). Thus, testing, that according to Myers [17] is the process of disproving information system quality (identifying errors), is an integral part of the development process which cannot be omitted. Furthermore, testing to find or prevent discrepancies in information systems that could prevent them from performing as expected (predicted) adds value to the finished system.

Even CASE technology cannot ensure that systems requirements are correctly specified. If they are not, you have built the wrong system! How valuable is the wrong system to a "paying" customer? The only way to determine that you have built the right system is to apply verification and validation processes.

Partially because of the erroneous belief that testing is not necessary, and partially because the testing process has not been adequately defined (refer to the previous discussions on process maturity in Chapter Two and the automation panacea in Chapter Three), CASE has not yet embraced the range of testing activities it must if we are to include software testing as part of the CASE *revolution*. Some CASE vendors are currently rushing to rectify this situation.

So, software products designed to assist the testing process exist for the most part independent of the current CASE products. The kinds of software products that are used to assist the testing process in many instances are not new, but have been around and have been used by two decades of programmers, while other products represent more recent developments.

13.2 A TOOL IS A TOOL IS A TOOL

In this age of automation, the *path* to improvement is the use of automated testing aids. I decided to avoid as much as possible using the word "tools" because in the development process we frequently use the terms "method," "technique," and "tool" inconsistently, which has caused much confusion.

For example, in a recent article on software testing[19], the author offered a list of "tools used to help perform and automate the [testing] process." In that list (refer to Figure 13.1), he included "testing methodologies." In another instance [5], classification of application development productivity tools has also included "management policies," "organizational factors," and "development methodologies."

William Perry [18] defines "testing tools" as "the aids used by individuals with testing responsibility to fulfill that responsibility." Again, an unclear use of the word "tools." He continues to describe testing "tools" as "techniques," manual and automated, that perform static tests, dynamic tests, and that evaluate system structure and function.

To avoid confusion and for purposes of discussing software products and important product features that increase the *productivity* and *quality* of the testing process, I want to clarify and restrict the meanings of the terms methods, techniques, and tools, in particular, the rather indiscriminate use of the word "tools."

- Testing methodologies
- Program analyzers
- Interactive debuggers
- Test data generators/editors
- Test coverage monitors
- File comparers
- Dump formatter/analyzers
- Capture/replayers
- Regression/automatic testers

Adapted from [19].
Figure 13.1 Software Testing Tools

13.2.1 What Is a Tool?

Methodologies employ sets of methods, techniques, and tools when implemented (i.e., a software testing methodology would dictate the use of specific software testing methods, techniques, and tools).

A "method" is a set of *procedures* used to guide the systems development activities (including testing activities).

The *ANSI/IEEE STD 729–1983, Glossary of Software Engineering Terminology* (ANSI/IEEE, 1983) defines a procedure as "a set of manual steps to be followed to accomplish a task each time the task is to be done."

A "technique" is a *technical procedure* outlining specific steps involved in a development activity.

Finally, a tool is an extension of the human body that assists us in our work; therefore, a development "tool" is a narrative or diagram (a model, logical and/or physical, that enhances visualization of the system: an extension of the human mind) which aids the analysis, design, construction, and testing of an information system.

I am sure that these definitions will conflict with those of other authors (e.g., see Martin, [13]; Perry, [18]), but they will help us maintain consistency within our discussion of *software tools* that aid the testing process.

Consequently, a chapter about software testing "tools" in the sense of Perry's previous definition would include software tools that assist the testing process, as well as diagrams, etc. that are "an aid to clear thinking," [13] and that model such things as the independent paths in program modules (Control Flow Graphs) or the program's functional specifications as digital logic circuits (cause-effect graphs). But the latter, being representative of tools as I have defined them and their use, is not the topic of this chapter (see Chapters 6 through 9 for discussions of these kinds of tools).

It is about *software tools* (software tools in the sense of the ANSI/IEEE and National Bureau of Standards—*NBS*—definitions below) which automate the use of software testing methods, techniques, and tools.

13.2.2 What Is a Software Tool?

ANSI/IEEE STD 729–1983, SOFTWARE ENGINEERING STANDARDS, 3rd ed., [1] defines a software tool as "a computer program used to help develop, test, analyze, or maintain another computer program or its documentation." This definition is very similar to and probably based on an earlier definition published by the NBS [9] for software development tools (NBS is currently the National Institute for Standards and Technology—NIST).

Software development tools are computer programs that aid the specification, construction, testing, analysis, management, documentation, and maintenance of other computer programs.

13.3 SOFTWARE TOOLS FOR SOFTWARE TESTING

Little of the effort to improve the development process over the years has been directed toward improving the testing portion of that process [18]. The result is manual testing procedures that are largely inefficient and ineffective, and thus, not very productive. Bill Silver [25], editor and publisher of *Software Quality World* and the president of ProQual, Inc., stresses the economic importance of automating the testing process.

The major effort of a test person should be the design and creation of automated tests. Testing is not something done once or twice prior to release. An automated test suite has value throughout the life of the software.

Historically, as discussed in Chapter Three, software testing has evolved from a *debugging/demonstration* oriented process to that of a *destruction/evaluation/prevention* oriented process [19]. These phases represent the philosophy of software testing and how it has changed over the years. As the conceptualization of testing has evolved, so have the software tools that are used to assist the process.

For purposes of discussion, we will describe a classification scheme for testing aids that has evolved in conjunction with, yet independently of, other schemes for categorizing software tools including CASE. We can then use this basic software tools classification framework as a template for evaluating frameworks that describe software tools for software testing. Because several frameworks for classifying the software tools for testing are available (Gelperin [7], Myers [17], Perry [18], Poston [21], Scott and Farley [23], Software Quality Engineering [26]), no one framework represents the generally accepted classification scheme. As we cannot discuss all of these schemes, we will look in depth at the two that have the most potential for practical application, the Software Quality Engineering (SQE) and the Poston frameworks.

13.3.1 Classification Criteria

Several classification criteria for software tools are possible [19]. The simplest and most convenient criterion is the function that is supported. Supported functions are manifested as "tool features." Another approach is to group software tools by the life cycle step in which they have the greatest use or influence. And finally, the way CASE workbenches are classified is by the personnel function they support, i.e., *Analyst Workbenches* support analyst activities and *Programmer Workbenches* support programmer activities.

NBS Special Publication 500–74, *Features of Software Development Tools* [9] describes a taxonomy of software tools in general that is based on software tool features. Tool "features" describe the functionality of a given software tool. The taxa (classes) of tool features are organized in four hierarchical levels (see Figure 13.2). The fourth level consists of 52 tool features, which are described in detail. The tool features are in turn put into classes at the third level and grouped by "basic" processes at the second level, input-function-output.

13.3.2 A Framework

The NBS framework is awkward and difficult to use, and it is not of much assistance for classifying testing aids. In a recent article on testing "tools" [7], David Gelperin, president of Software Quality Engineering of Jacksonville, Florida, offered a functional categorization of testing aids that may prove to be more useful to information systems practitioners than classifications based on the other criteria, and which is more practical than the NBS taxonomy described earlier.

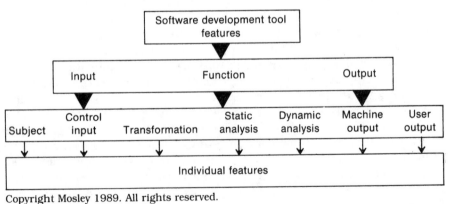

Figure 13.2   Software Development Tools: The NBS Taxonomy

His framework is simple (containing only five categories) and seems to capture, at the procedural level, the functionality of commercially available testing aids. The classes are:

1. Data Utilities
2. Simulators
3. Data Comparators
4. Capture-Replay Systems
5. Execution Tracers

Data Utilities

Data utilities are software utility programs that can describe the "characteristics and conditions" of data structures and data elements associated with the software being tested. Dictionary (known as the "repository" in CASE jargon) facilities that can store descriptions of the data and nonprocedural query-based languages that can access (display or print the content of) the data descriptions fall into this category.

ANSI/IEEE STD 729–1983 does not define a data utility but it does define what is meant by utility software.

Computer programs or routines designed to perform some general support function required by other application software, by the operating system, or by system users.

So, we can infer that data utilities are computer programs designed to perform data support functions. Anything from vendor supplied file access routines and sort/merge packages to fourth generation query-based languages, etc. could fall into this category.

Simulators

Simulators are used to create varying kinds of test execution environments. An important aspect of a simulation software [7] is that it reduces the interdependencies of development and testing. Simulators can represent portions of the system that have not yet been constructed or simulate the interaction of the system with users and/or other systems. Accordingly, simulators can emulate software, hardware, and people.

Simulators can invoke the software being tested, be invoked by the software being tested, interrupt test execution, and/or manipulate test data. Drivers and stubs are examples of simulators used during Unit and Integration testing to emulate missing program modules.

Drivers and stubs may be required to pass and receive data values (arguments and parameters) during test execution.

ANSI/IEEE STD 729–1983 defines a simulator as:

A device, data processing system, or computer program that represents certain features of the behavior of a physical or abstract system.

Data Comparators

Comparators assist in the comparison of observed and expected results in testing. File contents can be observed "before" and "after" test execution. It has been my experience that data comparators are among the most useful and indispensable of the software aids.

ANSI/IEEE STD 729–1983 defines a comparator as:

A software tool used to compare two computer programs, files, or sets of data to identify commonalities or differences.

Capture-Replay Systems

A capture-replay system is a complete testing facility which includes the capability to capture data structures as they are passed "to and fro" in the input and output data flows, to edit input and output data structures, to capture the flow of test execution so that it may be repeated, and to compare expected to observed outputs. A capture-replay system is a key component in a software tester's testing workbench.

The *ANSI/IEEE STD 729–1983* does not contain a definition of a capture-replay system; however, the definition of a *Test Bed* contains the essence of a capture-replay system definition.

A test bed is:

A test environment containing the hardware, instrumentation tools, simulators, and other support software necessary for testing a system or system component.

Execution Tracers

Execution tracers assist the tester in tracking which program statements have been executed, which remain to be executed, and what is happening as the current statement is executing. Execution tracers may work in both on-line and off-line modes as required by the test environment. Many compilers offer execution tracing capabilities as compiler options, and some programming languages have internal language statements that invoke execution tracing capacities, e.g., the READY TRACE statement, and the DISPLAY and COUNT verbs in COBOL.

The combined *ANSI/IEEE STD 729–1983* definitions of a tracer and a trace serve to define a tracer as it is used above.

A software tool used to trace. A record of the execution of a computer program; it exhibits the sequences in which the instructions were executed.

SQE currently classifies testing aids by the testing activities they support [26]. This approach is a high-level classification scheme that is a refinement of Gelperin's categories.

13.4 THE SQE FRAMEWORK

The Software Testing Life Cycle (STLC) can, as in the Systems Development Life Cycle (SDLC), be broken into several gross phases (as you may remember from Chapter Two, it is my position that software testing activities should be integrated via the SDLC framework, not separately and not with a distinct STLC). SQE advocates an STLC consisting of three phases: *test planning, test set acquisition, and software measurement.* Other authors have offered differing versions of the STLC (for example see Hetzel, [8]), but SQE has used theirs as a basis for classifying automated testing aids.

Test planning aids assist in the planning and coordination of the testing process. Such products assist in the establishment of testing objectives, identifying the best testing method to use, and scheduling of the testing activities. Test planning is a complicated project management problem. There are tests to be selected, test cases to be designed and constructed, hardware and software resources to be allocated, test runs to be logged and analyzed, test results to be reported, and problems resulting from the test results which will have to be resolved [8]. Adequate planning can avert the potential crises that can arise when major flaws are discovered in the system [6].

Test set acquisition aids help in the design and construction of test cases, and establishment of testing procedures. In addition, they may assist in the development of test harnesses and test simulators.

Software measurement aids assist in test execution and regression test execution, evaluation and reporting of test results, and management and control of testing activities.

SQE has further refined and formalized this classification framework to include the following categories of software testing aids:

1. Data acquisition. Assist in the acquisition or creation of test data.
2. Static measurement. Perform analysis of static (time-independent) information.

3. Dynamic measurement. Perform analysis of dynamic (time-dependent) information.

4. Simulator. Simulate an activity or function of the software being tested (e.g., a batch terminal simulator).

5. Test management. Assist in the development, execution, review, and control of test activities.

6. Multidimensional aids. Aids that can fit into several different categories.

7. Other aids. Those that do not fall under the categories above, but which still contribute to the productivity of the testing process.

These categories overlap significantly with the classes of tool features constituting the third level of the NBS taxonomy; however, SQE's categories may contain aids that have features from several of the NBS classes. For example the NBS class "Transformation" lists such features as *editing input* and *instrumentation*. Accordingly, within the SQE framework these features would be placed in the Data-Acquisition and Dynamic Measurement categories, respectively.

13.5 POSTON'S FRAMEWORK

Robert Poston, president of Programming Environments, Inc., Trenton Falls, N.J., classifies software tools for testing within the traditional SDLC. He has identified classes of "old" and "new" testing aids for each phase of software development.

13.5.1 Requirements Phase Tools

Poston classes *Requirements Recorders* as older software tools that have been in use for some time, but that have recently been updated and popularized by CASE vendors as analysis workbench products. These products have evolved from formal specification languages to high-resolution graphic based diagramming editors.

    Requirements Verifiers are a recent development. They can check for ambiguity, inconsistency, and completeness in requirements statements. The limitation of this category of software testing aids is that they can check only what has been entered into the requirements documentation. If some important information is missing, they cannot alert the developer. Thus, requirements verification is still dependent to a great extent on manual activity.

    Specification-Based Test Case Generators is another recent development. These software tools produce test cases from requirements specifications by random, algorithmic, and/or heuristic methods. Poston says a good product should use all three means.

Random test case generation uses statistical sampling procedure to choose the test case, while *algorithmic* test case generation is based on techniques Cause-Effect Graphing, Equivalence Partitioning, and Boundary Analysis (all discussed in earlier chapters of this book), and *heuristic* test cases are constructed based on the tester's skill and past experience with system failures (Error Guessing, also covered in this test).

Requirements To Test Tracers are new software tools that trace specific test cases back to a particular requirement statement. This linkage is particularly important when Regression Testing because test cases must be developed for new requirements or changed for modified requirements.

Expected Output Tools are on Poston's wish list but are not yet available. He says that most testers use a procedure he terms *Reference Testing* to develop a set of expected outputs because others methods are so time consuming and costly. Reference Testing simply involves executing the test cases the first time without developing a set of expectations. The actual outputs are then judged by the tester as "right" or "wrong," and thereafter, used as expected outputs. The general category of *Simulators* as previously described would be included here.

13.5.2 Design Phase Tools

Poston argues that the same software tools that are used in the requirements phase from a system-level perspective can also be used in the design phase from a program-level perspective. The advantage of this is that the majority of the test cases are already designed and constructed before entering the design phase. So the test cases can not only be used to test software, but also to test designs prior to software construction.

13.5.3 Programming Phase Tools

Metrics Reporters are software tools that are not new, and that are used to analyze existing source code and generate metrics on data flow, data structure, control flow, and process structure. These tools may also include size metrics (e.g., Lines of Code).

Code Checkers are static analyzers that look for such things as uninitialized variables, out of range subscripts, etc. Poston recommends these for code checking prior to formal Code Inspections. Code Checkers can be used to enforce programming standards. ANSI Standard COBOL 85 includes the capacity to enforce coding standards directly through its recommended compiler options. Whether COBOL compiler vendors choose to implement these options is at their discretion.

Product-Based Test Case Generators are testing aids that attempt to obtain structural coverage, that is, cause every statement to be executed, every decision branch to be exercised, all of the conditions within a decision to be tested, and each path covered. Poston does not reccommend these tools because they use the code as the basis of the test cases, and he argues that the quality of the code will affect the quality of the test cases. I, however, believe that there is still some merit in their use as long as tools such as code checkers are first used to ensure adherence to programming standards.

Code Instrumentors are code coverage analyzers. These software tools have been in use for almost two decades and their functionality is now commonly seen in the form of tools that are called "symbolic debuggers."

13.5.4 Testing Phase Tools

Capture/Playback Systems are testing session recording and replay facilities, and have been available to testers for a long time. They capture the testing events at the level of the keyboard and can be replayed as if the key strokes are being re-entered. The major capabilities and characteristics of these systems were described earlier.

A *Test Harness*, as defined by Poston, is an environment-specific capture/playback system. The term, however, is generally used to describe purchased or fabricated software that is used during integration testing to control and monitor the behavior of "drivers" and "stubs," that are used to simulate missing calling and missing called modules, respectively. So a test harness facilitates the testing of intermodular interfaces.

Testing Comparators are, as previoulsy described, used to compare actual outputs with expected outputs. The compare functions provided by most proprietary operating systems can be used, or commercially available comparator packages that have more functionality can be purchased.

Structure Coverage Analyzers are either "nonintrusive" or "intrusive." Intrusive analyzers instrument the software by placing extra commands that are compiled along with the program. Nonintrusive analyzers run on separate but parallel processors gathering information about structural coverage of the test cases.

Requirements Coverage Analyzers gather information about what code has been exercised and which requirements were represented in the executed code.

13.5.5 Maintenance Tools

The testing aids associated with each of the development phases should all be used during the maintenance phase. The proper approach to maintaining software systems is to analyze the requirements for specific maintenance projects, modify the existing design according to the new requirements, incorporate the change in the software, and do Regression Testing. Thus, each level of testing aids can be of use in a maintenance environment.

Because many organizations are primarily in a maintenance or production support mode, their testing needs are primarily those of Regression Testing. The dilemma these organizations face is further complicated by the fact that many of these "legacy" systems were not properly tested when developed. Thus, many professionals are struggling with this situation and believe that testing methods and testing tools cannot help in maintenance because they were neglected during development.

This is a completely false assumption. You have to start somewhere, and if where you are is in production support, that is where you begin. In my experience, testing production systems that were previously not tested or tested very ineffectively, implementation of both testing methods and testing aids has paid tremendous dividends. Many severe errors that were silently hidden in the original systems were suddenly made obvious when new or modified components were Regression Tested. It is never too late to begin a rigorous program of formal testing methodology.

13.5.6 Poston's Tool Checklist

Poston has devised a Software Testing Tool Checklist which separates the software tools according to what testing objectives they accomplish. His list allows the consumer to decide what aids are needed for each level of testing Unit, Build (Integration), and System (see Figure 13.3). I believe this two-dimensional checklist is helpful, but it would be even more beneficial if it categorized the testing activities it lists across SDLC phase as a third dimension, as he has done in his classification scheme. Figure 13.4 shows this additional view.

13.6 SOFTWARE TOOL INTEGRATION CONSIDERATIONS

A problem common across a great number of the commercially available software tools, including those that assist testing, is a lack of *integration*. Integration refers to the inter-tool communication, the presence

Legend: Low ○   Average ◐   High ●

	Tool: _____ Level Usage			Tool: _____ Level Usage			Tool: _____ Level Usage		
	Unit	Build	System	Unit	Build	System	Unit	Build	System
Managing Testing									
☐ Predict cost and schedule for testing	○	○	○	○	○	○	○	○	○
☐ Plan testing work products, activities, and resources . . .	○	○	○	○	○	○	○	○	○
☐ Monitor testing work products, activities, and resources ..	○	○	○	○	○	○	○	○	○
☐ Report testing work products, activities, and resources ..	○	○	○	○	○	○	○	○	○
Defining Requirements and Test Objectives									
☐ Record requirements and/or test objectives	○	○	○	○	○	○	○	○	○
☐ Verify requirements for testability	○	○	○	○	○	○	○	○	○
Designing Tests									
☐ Design, generate, and document specification-based test cases	○	○	○	○	○	○	○	○	○
☐ Trace requirements, inputs, outputs to/from test cases	○	○	○	○	○	○	○	○	○
☐ Design, generate, and document product-based test cases	○	○	○	○	○	○	○	○	○
☐ Trace paths, branches, and statements to test cases . . .	○	○	○	○	○	○	○	○	○
☐ Predict expected-outputs	○	○	○	○	○	○	○	○	○
Constructing Test Execution Environments									
☐ Check code	○	○	○	○	○	○	○	○	○
☐ Generate test harness (interfaces, stubs, drivers, etc.) . . .	○	○	○	○	○	○	○	○	○
☐ Instrument code for tracing data-flow and control-flow ..	○	○	○	○	○	○	○	○	○
Executing the Tests									
☐ Control test case and script libraries	○	○	○	○	○	○	○	○	○
☐ Record executions of test cases and scripts	○	○	○	○	○	○	○	○	○
☐ Replay executions of test cases and scripts	○	○	○	○	○	○	○	○	○
☐ Record test case and script actual outputs	○	○	○	○	○	○	○	○	○
☐ Trace data-flow and control-flow	○	○	○	○	○	○	○	○	○
Evaluating Tests and Software									
☐ Evaluate test case pass/fail (compare actual and expected outputs)	○	○	○	○	○	○	○	○	○
☐ Evaluate failure statistics (total failures, failure detection rate, etc.)	○	○	○	○	○	○	○	○	○
☐ Evaluate testing work (test cases created, passed, etc.) ..	○	○	○	○	○	○	○	○	○
Evaluate Test Quality (TQ)									
☐ Requirements coverage	○	○	○	○	○	○	○	○	○
☐ Input coverage (valid, invalid, etc.)	○	○	○	○	○	○	○	○	○
☐ Output coverage (normal and error outputs)	○	○	○	○	○	○	○	○	○
☐ Structure coverage (interrupt, DU path, branch, statement, etc.)	○	○	○	○	○	○	○	○	○
Evaluate Software Quality (SQ)									
☐ Functionality	○	○	○	○	○	○	○	○	○
☐ Performance	○	○	○	○	○	○	○	○	○
☐ Usability	○	○	○	○	○	○	○	○	○
☐ Availability	○	○	○	○	○	○	○	○	○
☐ Reliability	○	○	○	○	○	○	○	○	○
☐ Maintainability	○	○	○	○	○	○	○	○	○
☐ Metrics reporter (size, complexity, etc.)	○	○	○	○	○	○	○	○	○

Figure 13.3   Software Testing Tools Checklist

Figure 13.4   Revised Software Tools Checklist: Indicating Tool Use Across SDLC Stages

Maintenance
Testing
Program Construction
Program Design
System Design
System Specification
Requirements Definition

Legend:	Low ○	Average ◐	High ●

	Tool: _____ Level Usage	Tool: _____ Level Usage	Tool: _____ Level Usage
Managing Testing			
☐ Predict cost and schedule for testing	○	○	○
☐ Plan testing work products, activities, and resources	○	○	○
☐ Monitor testing work products, activities, and resources	○	○	○
☐ Report testing work products, activities, and resources	○	○	○
Defining Requirements and Test Objectives			
☐ Record requirements and/or test objectives	○	○	○
☐ Verify requirements for testability	○	○	○
Designing Tests			
☐ Design, generate, and document specification-based test cases	○	○	○
☐ Trace requirements, inputs, outputs to/from test cases	○	○	○
☐ Design, generate, and document product-based test cases	○	○	○
☐ Trace paths, branches, and statements to test cases	○	○	○
☐ Predict expected-outputs	○	○	○
Constructing Test Execution Environments			
☐ Check code	○	○	○
☐ Generate test harness (interfaces, stubs, drivers, etc.)	○	○	○
☐ Instrument code for tracing data-flow and control-flow	○	○	○
Executing the Tests			
☐ Control test case and script libraries	○	○	○
☐ Record executions of test cases and scripts	○	○	○
☐ Replay executions of test cases and scripts	○	○	○
☐ Record test case and script actual outputs	○	○	○
☐ Trace data-flow and control-flow	○	○	○
Evaluating Tests and Software			
☐ Evaluate test case pass/fail (compare actual and expected outputs)	○	○	○
☐ Evaluate failure statistics (total failures, failure detection rate, etc.)	○	○	○
☐ Evaluate testing work (test cases created, passed, etc.)	○	○	○
Evaluate Test Quality (TQ)			
☐ Requirements coverage	○	○	○
☐ Input coverage (valid, invalid, etc.)	○	○	○
☐ Output coverage (normal and error outputs)	○	○	○
☐ Structure coverage (interrupt, DU path, branch, statement, etc.)	○	○	○
Evaluate Software Quality (SQ)			
☐ Functionality	○	○	○
☐ Performance	○	○	○
☐ Usability	○	○	○
☐ Availability	○	○	○
☐ Reliability	○	○	○
☐ Maintainability	○	○	○
☐ Metrics reporter (size, complexity, etc.)	○	○	○

of an accepted data interchange standard. At last report, there were nine different standards efforts under way to develop a CASE data interchange standard.

Simply put, software tools that are integrated can use the output from other software tools as input to the processes they support, and this can be done without human intervention. When the presence of a human is required to rekey input data, etc., the tools are not integrated. Philips [19] wrote, "Tools, even from the same vendor, often have their own unique human interfaces and do not talk to other tools [i.e., tools from the same vendor]."

The absence of integration means more work which, in turn, means lower development (testing) productivity. Just as King [10] pointed out that the use of several nonintegrated diagramming tools could add to the cost of maintenance, the use of several nonintegrated software tools can also increase maintenance costs. The production support programmer must be familiar with each of the different software tools in order to maintain the system.

Consequently, it is very important that software tools that assist the testing process be integrated. If maintenance is to be performed properly, Regression Testing must be a part of the maintenance activities. Regression Testing requires that pre-existing portions of the system be tested exactly as they were when the system was first developed, and that corrections, modifications, and enhancements are also specifically tested. The only way this can be accomplished efficiently and effectively is through the use of a test bed of integrated testing tools.

Integration will not only strengthen Regression Testing, but will also impact Unit, Integration, Function, and System Testing. Some CASE vendors are already working on integrated testing functions in their workbench products [19]; however, more progress is urgently needed.

Recently announced IBM strategies may provide the needed catalyst for tool integration. In IBM installations, the IS organization must be aware of the Systems Application Architecture (SAA) and AD/Cycle framework for supporting SAA. The official announcement of AD/Cycle is IBM's blessing of CASE technology and offers automated support through *DevelopMate*, IBM's application development workbench. AD/Cycle also includes verification and validation products *Workstation Interactive Test Tool* and *Software Analysis Test Tool* which should have been released by the time this book is published.

Having more of a marketing bent than a technology bent, IBM is saying, play the game our way or don't play. This means any software tools for testing that you might purchase from an independent vendor should conform to SAA's suite of interfaces, protocols, and operating environments [11]. For your protection ask vendors how many of the 32 SAA components are included in their products. This will provide some feel for the vendor's compliance with SAA. The positive side of this situation is SAA compliance by vendors as a significant step toward tool suite integration. IBM is establishing a de facto standard for tool integration.

13.7 CONCLUSION

As you can see, classifying automated software testing aids is a rather difficult process, and furthermore, is one that depends on your perspective (functionality, life cycle, etc.). Which framework you choose to accept and which software tools you select will probably depend on your professional environment and/or background. Moreover, these considerations will ultimately affect the productivity of the testing process. Although I feel that both the Poston and the SQE frameworks are valuable, the SQE taxonomy has a distinct advantage. SQE publishes and updates, yearly, a comprehensive catalogue of software tools that serve as testing aids. The existence of the SQE catalogue is the reason I did not attempt to list here all of the commercially available testing aids. Such lists are out of date before they are published.

The latest of the SQE Testing Tools Reference Guide [26] contains in-depth descriptions of software tools for testing that have been certified by SQE; however, there is also a listing of software tools that are not SQE certified among the guide's indexes. The kinds of information contained for certified tools are a brief narrative description and other items, some of which are listed below.

1. Hardware supported
2. Software supported
3. Testing activities supported
4. Major tool classification
5. Descriptor
6. Documentation supplied
7. Training supplied
8. Demo availability

The SQE testing tool guide is by no means perfect, but it is a good place to begin your search for software testing tools. Its strength lies in its organization. The index contains a tools by testing activities matrix, as well as cross references by tool classification, hardware supported, software supported, and vendor.

Another resource that is available is the latest version of *The CASE Locator for Software Tools*, published by CASE Associates, Inc., a member of the CASE Technology Group [24]. It is but one of a series of guides to software tools for automating the systems development process. This guide is a listing of software testing tools containing vendor, price, and technical specification information. The tools are categorized as Debugger/Editor, Performance/Coverage Analyzer, Test Generator/Utility, Test Case Manager/Version Control, and Software Monitor.

Either of these publications will be very useful to the Testing Specialist and Testing Manager. Both can be obtained for a total cost of less than $200.00.

REFERENCES

1. ANSI/IEEE Std 729–1983. *Glossary of Software Engineering Terminology*. New York: IEEE, 1983.

2. Appleton, Daniel, S., "Applying Lessons from the Industrial Revolution to the Information Revolution," *Chief Information Officer Journal*, 2, no. 3 (Winter 1990), 10–16.

3. Beck, Leland, and Thomas Perkins, "A Survey of Software Engineering Practice: Tools, Methods, and Results," *IEEE Transactions on Software Engineering* (September 1983).

4. Beizer, Boris, "On Becoming the Mainstream," *American Programmer*, 4, no. 4 (April 1991), 11–21.

5. Doke, Reed, "Application Development Productivity Tools: A Survey of Importance and Popularity," *Journal of Information and Systems Management* (Winter 1989).

6. Evans, Michael, *Productive Software Test Management*. New York: Wiley-Interscience, 1984.

7. Gelperin, David, "Divining Five Types of Testing Tools," *Software News* (August 1987).

8. Hetzel, William, *The Complete Guide to Software Testing*, 2ed. Wellesley, MA: QED Information Sciences, 1988.

9. Houghton, Raymond, *Features of Software Development Tools*. NBS Special Publication 500–74, Washington, D.C.: National Bureau of Standards, 1981.

10. King, David, *Current Practices in Software Development: A Guide to Successful Systems*. Englewood Cliffs, N.J.: Prentice Hall, 1984.

11. Majkiewciz, Jane, "A Test for SAA," *DATAMATION* (October 1989).

12. Martin, James, and Carma McClure, "The Latest Look in Programmer Productivity Tools," *Business Software Review* (May 1986).

13. Martin, James, *Recommended Diagramming Standards for Analysts and Programmers: A Basis for Automation.* Englewood Cliffs, N.J.: Prentice Hall, 1987.

14. McClure, Carma, *CASE Is Software Automation.* Englewood Cliffs, N.J.: Prentice Hall, 1989.

15. Mosley, Daniel, "Are We Ready for CASE?" *American Programmer* (September 1989).

16. Mosley, Daniel, J., "Getting CASE Straight: Can You Use It or Not?" *CIO Journal*, 3, no. 2 (Fall 1990), 55–59.

17. Myers, Glenford, *The Art of Software Testing.* New York: Wiley-Interscience, 1979.

18. Perry, Bill, *A Structured Approach to Systems Testing, 2ed.* Wellesley, MA: QED Information Sciences, 1988.

19. Philips, Roger, "No-Test Software Is 'Unobtainable.' " *Software Magazine,* (December 1988).

20. Popper, K. R., Conjectures and Refutation. *The Growth of Scientific Knowledge.* New York: Harper & Row, 1968.

21. Poston, Robert, "A Complete Toolkit for the Software Tester," *American Programmer,* 4, no. 4 (April 1991), 28–37.

22. Ryan, Hugh, W., "Why CASE Is Not a Cure for Testing," *Journal of Information Systems Management,* 7, no. 3 (Summer 1990), 63–66.

23. Scott, Tony, and Dennis Farley, "Slashing Software Maintenance Costs," *Business Software Review* (March 1988).

24. Sharon, William, D., *The CASE Locator for Software Testing Tools.* Oregon City, Oregon; CASE Associates, Inc., 1991.

25. Silver, Bill, "Symbols of Quality," *Software Quality World; Guided Tour* (1989).

26. Software Quality Engineering. *Testing Tools Reference Guide: A Catalog of Software Quality Support Tools,* Version 5. Jacksonville, FL: Software Quality Engineering, April 1991.

14

Controlling and Improving the Software Testing Process: A Process Metrics Approach

Every manufacturing operation has problems. Some are painfully obvious; others require ingenuity and hard work to identify.

Dr. Ellis R. Ott, 1975 [12]

Measurement is an integral component in the arsenal of scientific tools and has been so since the earliest scientific endeavors. It is only through measurement that we understand the phenomena that surround us. We cannot rely on our perceptions alone for they are frequently given to distortion. Our senses are more than adequate for most aspects of day-to-day functioning, but we cannot trust them in the conditions under which scientists work.

Furthermore, scientific knowledge that is based in numbers has proven successful when applied to identification and resolution of practical real-life problems. Success comes because the practitioners (engineers) also understand and use the mathematical principles that the scientists have uncovered and proven. Thus, measurement is basic to engineers because they are in fact applied scientists.

In the Information Systems (IS) profession, measurement has played only a cursory role. It has been so because our profession is still very young and the scientific foundations have been only partially laid.

Even so, we find ourselves being thrust into the 1990s and directed to "engineer" very large and complex information systems using skills that are much more art than science. Thus, the practical problems of systems development IS professionals are experiencing have increased by several orders of magnitude as the demand for information has grown.

IS science has evolved in a rather multidisciplinary fashion borrowing from Computer Science, Systems Science, and even from human psychology, but it has failed in one major respect. Measurement is not considered a basic tool for discovering concepts, or for implementing existing IS principles. Far and away, the vast number of Management Information System (MIS) professionals are ill-trained in this area.

Structured Programming, Structured Design, Structured Analysis, and most recently the comprehensive concept of Enterprise-Level Information Engineering have emerged over the last 40 years as the basis of an IS problem-solving discipline using project management principles integrated in a System Development Life Cycle (SDLC) approach. These constructs (with the exception of structured programming) have not been put to rigorous scientific proofs of their validity and should be perceived as merely unsubstantiated hypotheses. They are, however, accepted as the very fabric of the IS development process. Some important scientific efforts have attempted, and are yet attempting, to establish that concepts are valid, but most of us work on faith alone.

Even though we are applying, and automating, unproven development methods, techniques, and tools, we can implement a comprehensive regimen of measures that will allow IS professionals to understand, control, and improve the process of developing computer software for corporate information systems. We can achieve this through the application of proven manufacturing control and improvement methods to the IS development process.

The structured methods, techniques, and tools of the MIS discipline can be strengthened through the application of Statistical Quality Control (SQC), which is an industrial concept employing Statistical Process Control (SPC) methods. (Note: SQC is sometimes used synonymously with SPC.) SQC implementation should be an integral component of a corporate Total Quality Management (TQM) program. TQM is an enterprisewide state of mind that employs feedback from SPC to set the stage for quality improvement through SQC. TQM philosophy may be different in each company, but SQC is very basic statistical process analysis, control, and improvement, and within limits, this same basic approach to process trouble shooting can be applied in SQC ventures across organizations and professions.

Testing is an integral component of the MIS development process and *is the activity that differentiates art from science* [16]. The methods, techniques, and tools of software testing readily lend themselves to principles of SPC. Many questions concerning the effectiveness of software testing process could be answered if SPC were applied. For example, Parnas's [13] problem of software "trustworthiness" could be addressed, as well as the related, practical, and long debated question [11] of "when to stop testing."

14.1 WHY DO WE MEASURE?

In order to acquire the proper purview for software metrics, and their application in software testing, it is important to have a fundamental knowledge of what measures are currently used in IS organizations, when they are applied, and what they can tell us: *we must understand why we measure.*

IS professionals, who measure, do so for three primary reasons. First, we measure for *predictability* purposes. Second, we measure for *evaluation/justification* purposes. Third, we measure for *control* purposes. The most frequent uses of popular software metrics (e.g., Function Points, Lines of Code) are for purposes of predictability and evaluation/justification. The use of software metrics for process control is at best infrequent.

Three unique reasons for measuring suggest the preeminence of three major divisions of software metrics. However, from a SQC perspective, three motives for measurement are not sufficient. A fourth, *software process analysis and improvement*, has to be defined. Metrics used for process improvement purposes could be considered variations of process control measures, but variations that are interpreted within a different context from the parent measures, their purpose being to streamline the IS systems development process and assist in automating the resultant refined process.

A fifth purpose of software metrics should be to measure the business value of information to the enterprise [15]. This topic is beyond the scope of this chapter, but should be recognized for its importance in the overall picture of what metrics must be collected.

While working at Hewlett Packard (HP), Grady and Caswell [4] published one of the most important recent works on software metrics entitled, *Software Metrics: Establishing a Company-Wide Program* in 1987. Their program goal was to use measurement to demonstrate that the company's efforts (a portion of HP's TQM program) to improve software development had worked.

The problems they encountered were *definition* and *classification* of software metrics. Both are extremely enigmatic issues. They are so because of the number of dimensions within which metrics can be described. Metrics can be intraproject and/or interproject. They can also be classed as either process or product metrics, and product metrics can be further broken down into size and cost metrics. So, out of necessity, they developed a metrics classification that is simple and easy to understand and use.

Drawing on the HP perspective, a simplistic definition of the term *metric* can be deduced:

> **A software metric is a process indicator; a simple count of a process attribute or a mathematical equation that represents process attribute interactions.**

Grady and Caswell formally defined two classes of software metrics, *primitive* and *computed*, that can be applied to each of the four divisions of metric use described earlier. Primitive metrics are counts of directly measurable characteristics (e.g., Lines of Code, Defects), while computed metrics are a mathematical combination of two or more primitive metrics (e.g., Defect Count per Line of Code).

They refined their classification further by defining two levels of metrics application, *primary* and *secondary*. Whether a metric is primary or secondary can affect the information it contains and thus determine its appropriateness for a particular usage class. Primary measures are used for interproject comparisons at the project level. Secondary metrics are intraproject "real-time" measures that are used to monitor and control the systems development process in the short term, and to improve that process in the long term. Hence, primary metrics can be thought of as project-level metrics and secondary metrics can be conceptualized as process-level metrics.

Primary-level metrics are really product-based measures of development process *efficiency*. Their intent is to provide product size parameters that can be used to compare projects of similar size and complexity, and that can also be used as a basis for estimating the resource requirements of future projects. They can tell us something about our abilities to deliver a certain size product in a prespecified time span and within a prespecified budget. This is efficiency (productivity) measurement.

Secondary metrics, on the other hand, are process-based measures. Their intent is to open a window into the development process that can provide process parameters that can be adjusted during the project (process control), or prior to subsequent projects (process improvement), to ensure that the process leads to a *complete, consistent,* and *correct* product. They are aimed at improving the *effectiveness* of the development process.

The Function Point [1,2,3,6] (a sophisticated computed metric) can be used for cross-project comparisons, but not for process control or process improvement, and should be classed as a primary-level metric. Consequently, Function Points are appropriate for purposes of IS development project *evaluation* in terms of *resource estimation* and *justification* within and among different systems projects.

Lines of Code, Cost per Defect, and Percentages have also been used [2,6], albeit unsuccessfully, as primary *productivity* metrics for interproject comparison and intraproject estimation. Capers Jones [6] made the IS public aware of this lack of success through an attack on current IS productivity measures in which he pointed out three mathematical paradoxes that invalidate the measures.

The Lines of Code paradox is that each succeeding generation of higher level language (second, third, fourth, fifth generation, etc.) requires, and hence, produces fewer lines of code to complete the same amount of programming work as its predecessors. Therefore, Lines of Code has an inverse relationship to productivity when considered across programming language levels (higher level languages appear to be less productive than lower level equivalents).

The "Cost per Defect" paradox is that the cost to repair defects is lowest in the development stage where defects are the greatest in number. This is based on the fact that the number of software defects is always higher in development than in maintenance.

The "Percentage" paradox is that percentages are ratios which like Lines of Code are subject to the inverse relationship effect the generation of the programming language has on productivity.

The truth is that these paradoxes do not exist. They are artificially created through misapplication of Lines of Code, Cost per Defect, and Percentages as primary (project-level) software metrics. As Grady and Caswell learned from their experiences at Hewlett Packard, these measures are secondary (process-level) metrics, and are only useful for process control, or process analysis and improvement. This becomes obvious when we view development process improvement in terms of efficiency and effectiveness.

In addition, a single process parameter alone is not sufficient to identify trends and make judgments concerning process control and process improvement. A set of secondary-level process measures sets the stage for assessing process parameter interactions which can reveal much more process information.

14.2 PROCESS IMPROVEMENT

An *effective* process is one that delivers a *quality* product. From an external perspective, a quality product is one that (1) is the product the user requires, (2) is in the form the user needs, and (3) works properly when it is used. Internally speaking, a quality product is one that contains features representing a negotiated settlement of applicable product requirements (a complete product); is one in that the implemented features map directly back to specific product design objectives (a consistent product); is one in which the features function in the intended manner and do not have any unexpected side effects (a correct product). The only way to ensure that systems development products meet these external and internal quality criteria is to implement a rigid process measurement/improvement program.

Continuous process improvement in IS, however, is only possible if we are able to precisely define the development process *product*. The question is which perspective do we adopt in our product definition, an external or an internal one? Although it may seem more sensible to the IS professional to embrace an internally oriented product definition, an externally defined product proves the better approach. Refer back to Chapter One for a complete explanation of why this is true.

From an external perspective, Appleton (1990) defines the product of the information systems development process as *information*, not software. Thus, quality information can be defined as information containing everything necessary and sufficient to make the proper decisions when conducting business (complete), information presented in the proper context (consistent), and information containing value (correct).

In Appleton's sense, information is a communication (a signal) which, in a specific context, becomes knowledge that solves someone's business problem. The signal to noise ratio is related to effectiveness (again refer to Chapter One for a refresher on information effectiveness). The higher the signal and the lower the noise, the more effective (useful) the information. Traditionally, information systems have had high noise levels which interfere with the quality of the information product. An information signal that has a high signal to noise ratio is complete, correct, and consistent.

The approach taken to address the information signal to noise problem illustrates a basic difference between software engineering and information engineering. Current software engineering thinking (measuring and improving productivity/efficiency) reflects a severe case of industry "tunnel vision." We want to output the same noisy signal, but to be able to create that signal faster and cheaper than ever before! Furthermore, our industry is determined to measure everything in terms of dollars, and quality cannot be defined in financial terms. All of this is the result of approaching quality from an internal perspective.

In contrast, an enterprise-level information engineering approach is aimed at producing effective information systems, those systems that provide the information knowledge workers need to carry out their daily/weekly/monthly/yearly business activities. This requires measures not tied to the project's financial resources but rather indicators of process-level activities. Thus, secondary-level software metrics fit here extremely well.

14.2.1 A Process Improvement Example

Suppose we were counting Lines of Code in an imaginary project and were not satisfied with the baseline levels over time. So, we implemented a new coding strategy aimed at improving the production rate of Lines of Code. As we continue to monitor, the baseline level increases substantially. This is proof that the new strategy changed the development process and increased the programmers' output. Is this a change for the good?

Imagine we are also counting the numbers and kinds of errors discovered as the software is tested. After the new coding strategy is introduced, we note increased numbers and kinds of errors during the testing process (coding errors and analysis/design errors). Thus, more testing is required. Did we really gain anything? The numbers say no. We increased efficiency but sacrificed effectiveness.

Let's consider the same imaginary example, but this time the process change we introduce is a "code generation" software tool. Again we see an increase in the Lines of Code produced, but there is not a corresponding increase in the number and kinds of errors discovered during testing. Did this change work? Yes, to an extent. It increased process efficiency and did not reduce process effectiveness. Is this enough?

Taking this example one step further, suppose that the code generator instead resulted in a decrease in the numbers and kinds of errors. This would indicate not only an increase in efficiency but also an increase in effectiveness.

So, which point of view makes the most sense? Should we implement a process change to improve efficiency or to improve effectiveness? We can turn to our imaginary example to find the answer. If we had simply concentrated on collecting data about Lines of Code and our goal was to increase efficiency, we would have believed that the change worked. Looking at error rate (focusing on effectiveness), we discovered that in each of the three instances where the example was modified, there were three different outcomes. Thus, we could have made a serious mistake if we had focused solely on efficiency because increases in efficiency are directly proportional to increases in effectiveness. Without increased effectiveness, increased efficiency is a dead-end street.

We have just identified the real paradox: even though it seems sensible, and even more logical, to approach the IS development productivity problem directly by addressing process efficiency, productivity gains are realized only through attacking process effectiveness as a *continuous process improvement* strategy.

Thus, to improve the overall development process, we must thoroughly understand what that process is supposed to produce and focus on implementing a *defined process* that will achieve that product. Collection of process-level metrics that are interpreted in light of what the process is manufacturing is the sensible approach.

The function of secondary-level process metrics should be to determine where in the process we are introducing noise, and to change those process steps so the components of the information system they manufacture output the cleanest possible information signals.

14.3 THE SOFTWARE TESTING PERSPECTIVE

Testing is not a phase or process step to be implemented at a predetermined point in SDLC, but is rather an ongoing philosophy of *prevention* and *correction*. It is best to prevent errors (discrepancies in the software arising from its design specifications/objectives and requirements that cause noise or that can cause certain aspects of the signal to be omitted) through process inspection and improvement followed by a final program of product inspection (traditionally thought of as testing) that will identify errors that may have slipped through the preventive actions.

Software testing must have improved MIS effectiveness as its primary objective. The products of the testing activities must focus on improving the development process, not just on cleaning up the product after it is produced. Furthermore, testers must realize that the product is not the software system itself but the information the system provides.

What this all means is the products of testing activities should be considered as indicators (metrics) of the software development effectiveness. They should be used primarily to trace and remove problems in the process steps, and secondarily, to correct product defects after the fact. Furthermore, measures of the testing activities should be used to control and improve software testing.

In an enlightening article titled, "The Power of Simple Software Testing Metrics" which appeared in *The Letter T* [14], Robert Poston makes a distinction between the work product and work process metrics. He says software testers perform testing activities (the work process) and produce testing products (the work products). The activities they perform include test case design, test case execution, test results analysis, test reporting, and so on. The products testers produce are test plans and procedures, test cases, test logs, test results, test reports, and the like. So, both testing activities and test products are areas where testing metrics could be developed and implemented.

Categorizing testing metrics as process metrics and product metrics clearly demarcates the different objectives of software testing that were discussed earlier. First, testing process metrics are indicators of our knowledge and skills used to plan, design, construct, execute test cases, and analyze and record the results during software testing. These metrics can be used to improve specific testing activities. Second, testing product metrics are indicators of both software testing and software development performance. They contain information that can control and improve testing, as well as information that can control and improve development activities.

It is as simple as this: the better we can track and measure testing activities, the more confidence we can place in the testing products. The more reliable the testing products, the greater the probability that a change to the software development process based on specific test results will enhance development process effectiveness.

14.4 THE SOFTWARE TESTING METRICS STATUS QUO

In a 1990 survey [17] on the evolution of software strategies in the 1990s conducted by TRAVTECH, Inc., participants were asked to rate their use of specific testing practices including measurement. Sixty-six percent indicated that they never measure code coverage, and only 23 percent measure code coverage sometimes, while 6 percent usually measure code coverage.

Thirty percent responded they never measure/audit coding standards, 43 percent sometimes measure/audit coding standards, 19 percent usually measure/audit coding standards, and only 8 percent always measure/audit coding standards.

Thirty percent never measure the time spent on testing, 30 percent sometimes measure testing time, 23 percent usually measure testing time, and 17 percent always record testing time. Forty-two percent never track the cost of testing, 32 percent sometimes track the cost, 23 percent usually track the cost, and 9 percent always track testing cost.

It is somewhat comforting to note that 83 percent of the respondents sometimes, usually, or always produce testing summary reports, and that 87 percent sometimes, usually, or always track defects.

These responses to questions about testing practices indicate that measurement of even primitive elements of the testing process is typically overlooked. As a profession, we have a long way to go before our approach to testing can be called scientific.

To date, most of the metrics suggested for testing purposes are primary metrics such as *Mean Time Between Failures*, which can be collected only during volume testing, or *Errors per Function Point Delivered*, and so forth. While these measures do have their place in software testing, what is absolutely necessary, but not yet in place, is a set of secondary-level testing metrics beginning with elemental primitive baseline counts of testing activities and their products, and when meaningful, simple computed metrics.

14.5 THE CRITICAL SET CONCEPT

Once we make a commitment to improve our testing, where do we begin? The place to start is with a small set of primitive secondary metrics; from them we can determine which are meaningful for improving the testing process. Making such a determination requires periodic evaluation of the metrics being collected if we are to develop a dynamic set of "critical" testing metrics. Watts Humphrey [5] of the Software Engineering Institute at Carnegie Mellon University, and HP's Grady and Caswell team, are in accord in recommending establishment of a small critical set of software metrics as the cornerstone of any metrics program.

Humphrey [5] warns us not to become enamored of metrics because the metrics are not an end in themselves. Metrics are indicators of things that are happening that require our attention. The mistake that many IS organizations make is trying to measure too many things. This makes the process of collecting metrics data extremely difficult, the calculation of software metrics cumbersome, and the interpretation of the metrics confusing. The implementation of a small set of focused software metrics avoids these problems.

The idea of the critical set can best be understood if we apply Appleton's information as a product analogy to software metrics development and use. We can view individual metrics as the outputs of a specific metrics data gathering and computation process (a metrics system that should be integrated with the systems development process). We rely on the metrics to make decisions as we conduct business, the business of manufacturing information systems. Thus, the metrics contain *information* we use to control and improve the software development process. Some of the metrics will be meaningful and useful for process control or improvement (signal metrics) and the rest will not be useful (noise metrics). The challenge is to fine tune the critical set until it contains only signal metrics.

As described so far, this is an heuristic process. *Try collecting some metrics; determine if they are useful; replace the ones that aren't useful.* It must stay to some extent a trial-and-error process, but we can establish criteria for the initial entries in the set.

Poston says critical testing activity and process metrics should be centered around test cases. He suggests using counts of the total number of test cases: the number of test cases that led to the discovery of an error, the number of test cases that did not discover an error, the number of test cases actually executed during testing, and the number of test cases not executed. These are excellent suggestions and should be considered for inclusion in the basic set of testing metrics, but we need something more than just advice from industry experts.

14.5.1 Pareto Analysis

A more rigorous method is the use of *Pareto analysis* to determine the initial composition of the critical set. Dr. Joseph Juran identified the Pareto distribution (originally a concept of economic theory) as a "universal" concept that could be used in many diverse disciplines. He coined the catch-word phrases *vital few* and *trivial many*. This has since become the 80/20 rule.

A Pareto distribution is simply put: an ordered frequency distribution where data classifications are ranked in descending order of frequency of occurrence. It has many applications. For example, Myers's [11] suggestion that errors tend to cluster in specific software modules probably has a Pareto distribution. Therefore, it could be restated as "errors found in 20 percent of the software modules in a given system account for 80 percent of all the errors found in that system." Notice that the Pareto Principle does not say why this is most likely true. It simple says that it is true. Furthermore, the proportions may vary. The vital few may be less than 20 percent or in some instances slightly more than 20 percent.

Litecky and Davis [8] demonstrated that 20 percent (18 of 88 error classes) of COBOL error types account for 80 percent of the total numbers of errors COBOL programmers tend to make (refer to the data in Table 14.1 and the Pareto Chart in Figure 14.1). Furthermore, they determined COBOL spelling errors are high-frequency errors, that 80% of the spelling errors could be localized in four classes of spelling errors.

Thus, Pareto analysis provides a way (provided we are willing to do some minimal level of data gathering up front) to intelligently decide

TABLE 14.1   Cobol Error Frequencies for Top 20 Percent of Errors

Rank	Code	Frequency	Description of Errors or Grouped Errors
1	2B	253	Misspelling of nonstructurals
2	6A–6B	176	Hyphenation error
3	3A	154	Period missing
4	20F2	117	Name not defined
5	20A1	89	Reserved word used as data name
6	3B	88	Period added
7	4A–4E	81	Data description error
8	20F1	67	Multiple definition of name
9	31A3	58	Incompatible class in arithmetic statement
10	2A	47	Misspellings of structural
11	1A3	46	B margin coded to left of column 12
12	1B2	42	Invalid word delimiters, e.g., comma without a space
13	31A1	38	Incompatible class in move statement
14	1B1	37	Words run together without blank as delimiter
15	1A2	34	A margin coded to right of column 8
16	32A2	32	Keypunching shift error, e.g., numeric instead of alphanumeric
17	20E3	28	Continuation error on alphanumeric literal
18	1A4	27	Coding beyond column 72

Total 1,414   = 79.6% density

$N = 88$ error classes (20% $\times N = 18$)

what product or process characteristics we want to include in the critical set of metrics. The information in Figure 14.1 indicates that we should include at least one metric for each of the 18 COBOL error categories in our software testing metrics set (this type of analysis can be completed for any programming language). We can then institute procedural changes to reduce these classes of errors and track the results of our efforts via Shewhard Control Charts (aka Control Charts, Statistical Quality Control (SQC) Charts).

We could extend this framework by collecting data about errors using Li's [7] language-independent general error classification frame-

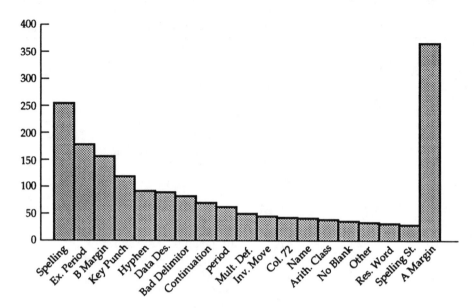

Figure 14.1   Pareto Chart for COBOL Error Frequencies

work, do the Pareto Analysis, and add to our critical set those that represent the "vital few" kinds of errors to monitor with control charts.

14.5.2 Shewhard Control Charts

Software testing metrics are more meaningful if plotted in Shewhard Control Charts as functions of either time or test runs. SPC focuses on controlling variation in process/product parameters. SQC charts paint a picture of the variation around average values within prespecified control limits.

Traditionally, SOC charts are plots of the Mean and Standard Deviation of a process variable. The plot includes "control limits" that represent ±3 standard deviations about the mean. If the process plotted variables remain within their specific control limits, the process is said to be "under control." Figure 14.2a shows a software testing process that is under control. In practice, this is a limited assumption because shifts can occur within the control limits that can drastically affect the process. An idea process fluctuates very little about the mean.

Figure 14.2b presents a software testing process that is out of control; however, the shift is in a positive direction (the process is now finding more errors on the average). The average number of weekly errors is re-establishing itself at a higher level. This is what testers want: to find as many errors as possible. The tester's responsibility is

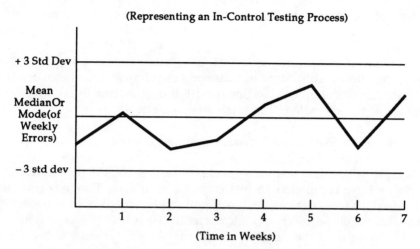

Figure 14.2a   Example Shewhard Control Chart for Average Weekly Errors During Testing (Representing an In-Control Testing Process)

to determine why this is happening so that the higher average level of error identification can be maintained.

Many software development process variables may not lend themselves to calculation of mean values as a computed metric, and therefore, will not allow the establishment of control limits. Even so, the simple counts or ratios must still be presented in the control chart as

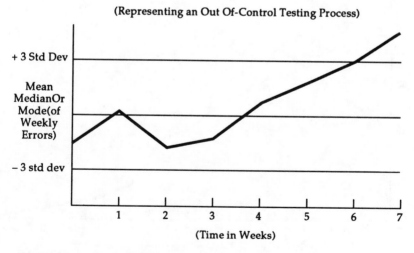

Figure 14.2b   Example Shewhard Control Chart for Average Weekly Errors During Testing (Representing an Out-of-Control Testing Process)

a "baseline" of activity for the variables. Control charts, even in this modified form, are still valuable for understanding the development process.

Thus, it is reasonable to look at charted trends with respect to baseline "shifts" that could indicate process change. These can consist of baseline shifts upward or downward, large baseline fluctuations, or failure of the variable to establish a consistent baseline.

14.5.3 An SQC Chart Software Testing Example

Suppose we are unit testing a small program [9,10]. Furthermore, suppose we have completed 15 test executions to date. The first test run required 50 test cases be designed and implemented, and subsequent test runs each required modifications to the initial test case data set but keeping the total number of test cases to 50 for each subsequent test run. Finally, suppose the test data set modifications were based on the number of and kinds of errors found in the preceding run. Discrepancies found by each run were corrected prior to subsequent runs.

If we simply count and plot the number of errors per test run across test runs as in Figure 14.3, what does it show us? The decreasing numbers of errors seen in later test trials is an indication that these test runs may not have returned much in the way of adding value to our program because the number of errors discovered drops off substantially. Furthermore, an upward trend in the number of errors identified is apparent in the intermediate test runs. We can clarify, and

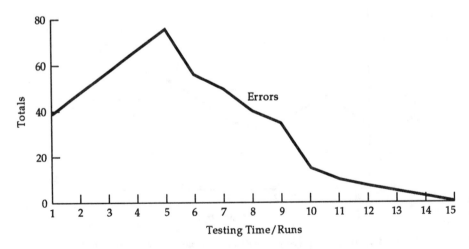

Figure 14.3　SQC Chart for Error Totals by Time Unit/Test Run

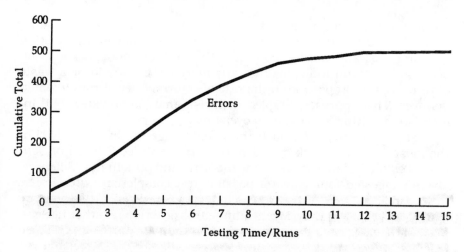

Figure 14.4 SQC Chart of Cumulative Errors Across Time/Test Runs

improve, the picture of what is happening if we plot the errors discovered with respect to the accumulating number of test cases across
test runs (see Figure 14.4) and if we develop a final plot (see Figure
14.5) of the ratio of errors to test cases (the number of errors in a given
test run divided by the number of test cases for that run) over the 15
runs.

What we see in Figure 14.4 is that the number of errors, in proportion to the total number of test cases, accelerates during the early

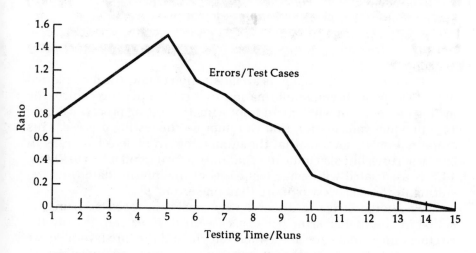

Figure 14.5 SQC Chart of Errors to Test Cases Ratio Per Time Unit/Test
Run

and intermediate test runs and rapidly decelerates in the late test runs. This "plateaued" curve is a good indication that we can stop testing this program, and yet, feel confident that we have done a "good" job because the graph indicates that any more testing would be a waste of resources in proportion to the rate of return of new errors it would discover. This approach coupled with risk analysis provides solid indication of testing effectiveness over time.

This is a better approach than that suggested by Myers [11] in the most respected work on software testing entitled *The Art of Software Testing* because it takes out the "Art" and puts in the "Science." Myers suggested four types of possible test completion criteria. The first, and least useful, approach is to stop when the allocated time for testing has elapsed. Even Myers admits this criterion is rather useless. Second, he suggested basing completion on the use of specific proven test methods that are used until they are no longer successful (no longer identifying new errors). The outstanding problem with this approach is that it represents a subjective measure. Third, he proposed estimating the number of expected errors and testing until that number is found or until a specific amount of time has elapsed. The first problem is the third criterion relies on estimates. Estimates are just that, estimates. The second problem is that this approach does not assure that the software is "thoroughly" tested, whereas, a statistical process control approach does give an indication of how completely the program has been tested (a numerical indication of the trustworthiness of the software). The fourth type of criterion he proposed is by far the best, but Myers's version did not go far enough. He suggested charting errors across weeks of testing for specific types of tests. What he did not suggest is that this should be done in conjunction with a statistical quality control program as a component of statistical process control. Furthermore, he did not fathom charting for continuous process control.

The previous discussion is an illustration of how the data plotted in an SQC chart become information that can be used to control the testing process, but what about improving the testing process? Figure 14.5 provides information that can improve the testing process. This graph not only shows us that the number of errors detected drops in later test runs, but also indicates that the upward trend noted in Figure 14.3 is associated with some test cases in the intermediate runs, resulting in the discovery of more than one error.

We should strive to discover why those test cases/test runs resulted in the higher error per test case yield. If we can identify the circumstances that caused the high return, and they are favorable, we can endeavor to ensure that future testing is conducted under similar circumstances. If, on the other hand, they indicate a problem that was occurring during those tests, we can use that information to avoid the problem in future test runs. We can turn to the Ishikawa diagram to plot possible causes for specific problems we have identified using Pareto Analysis and Control Charting.

14.5.4 Ishikawa Diagrams

An Ishikawa diagram is a picture of potential causes for a particular known effect. It is generically termed a "Cause-and-Effect" diagram or a "Fishbone" diagram. See Figure 14.6. Ishikawa diagrams are traditionally used in the manufacturing sector to investigate a bad effect and correct its cause(s), or to investigate a good effect and learn how to perpetuate its cause(s).

Causes are broken down into a few categories of "major" causes (traditionally including process, materials, environment, people, and management) and each major cause is further subdivided into several "minor" causes. For example people might be broken down into education, training, ability, motivation, and so on.

Ishikawa diagrams should be created as a result of a formal review of the metrics values collected in the critical set and illustrated in the Control Charts. The review process should follow that described in Chapter Eleven of this book. The values and charts would be included during the pre-review stage work. The review stage itself would occur as two short group meetings, one in that the Ishikawa diagram is assembled, and a second one in that the most likely causes are determined and inscribed in an action list to be used during the follow-up stage. The follow-up stage as discussed in the previous chapter would provide control over corrections.

The one weakness in the Ishikawa technique is that reviewers determine the causes to pursue by voting on them. A majority vote does not mean that the majority knowledge about which causes are creating the effect is accurate. A better procedure is to use either the

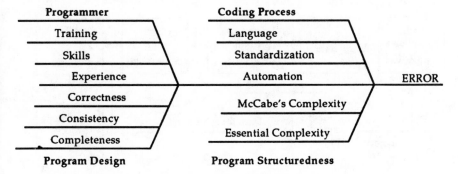

Figure 14.6 Generic Ishikawa Diagram Charting Possible Causes for a Known Error in a Specific Program

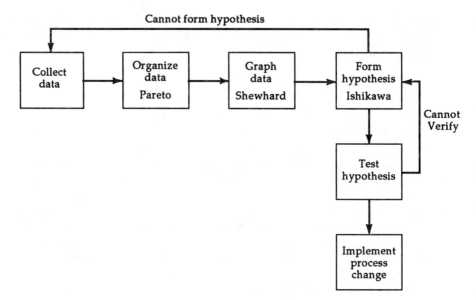

Figure 14.7   Inductive Hypothesis Formulation and Verification

"inductive" or "deductive" approaches suggested by Myers [11] as an aid to debugging known software errors. These two techniques result in the formulation and verification of hypotheses concerning the cause of the error. See Figures 14.7 and 14.8.

Combination of Cause and Effect charting and either inductive or deductive hypothesis formulation and testing results in a powerful technique for systematic elimination of all but the real cause or causes of the effect.

As illustrated, a critical set approach based on integrated Pareto Analysis, Shewhard Control Charting, and Ishikawa Charting ap-

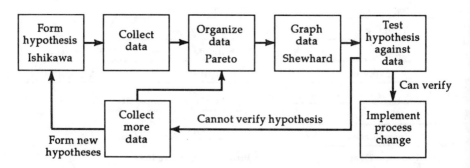

Figure 14.8   Deductive Hypothesis Formulation and Verification

proaches is the best procedure for collecting and analyzing software testing metrics. The advantage of combining these techniques is that together they present a related and unified "picture" of what is happening.

From a testing perspective, simple primitive counts and/or simple computed metrics which identify faulty development process activities are signal metrics, but we must be able to see the whole picture in order to (1) properly interpret what is happening, and (2) be convinced that differences (deviations from the process norms) do in fact exist [12]. Thus, each member of the critical set of testing process metrics should take on one or more of these graphical forms.

14.6 CONCLUSION

The late Professor Emeritus, Dr. Ellis R. Ott, advanced a set of troubleshooting principles for industrial processes [12]. The second and third of his principles are readily applicable to the use of software metrics for controlling and improving the process of developing information systems software from an information effectiveness perspective.

- Gather data on the problem.
- Always graph your data in a simple way.

Because software testing is an integrated part of the overall software development process, any process improvement effort should also scrutinize testing activities. As process measurement is the key to process improvement, measuring the testing process is a necessary evil. A critical set of secondary-level software testing metrics is necessary for controlling and improving the software testing process. The critical set can contain both primitive and computed metrics. The key to interpretation of the resulting testing metrics is to present them in SQC charts and to observe changes in the baseline levels. Obvious trends (differences) over time/test runs should be investigated for purposes of process control and improvement.

Primary testing metrics such as Defects per Function Point should also be computed, but should be used for high-level evaluation of the overall testing process and for predicting future testing resource utilization, or comparison of testing efforts across independent development projects.

As a final note, the advent of "information engineering" and "enterprise-level" information delivery as the product of system development has broadened the scope of software metrics. A third level of metrics application, enterprise-level metrics, must now be considered which measures the business value of the information delivered to the enterprise [15].

REFERENCES

1. Albrech, Allan J., and John E. Gaffney, "Software Function, Source Lines of Code, and Development Effort Prediction: A Software Validation Science," *IEEE Transactions on Software Engineering*, SE-9, no. 6 (1983), 639–48.

2. Albrech, Allan J., "Measuring Application Development Productivity," *Proceedings of the Joint IBM/SHARE/GUIDE Application Development Symposium* (1979).

3. Dreger, Brian J., *Function Point Analysis.* Englewood Cliffs, N.J.: Prentice Hall Advanced Reference Series, Computer Science; 1989.

4. Grady, R., and D. Caswell, *Software Metrics: Establishing a Company-Wide Program.* Englewood Cliffs, N.J.: Prentice Hall, 1987.

5. Watts, Humphrey, "Characterizing the Software Process: A Maturity Framework," *IEEE Software*, 5, no. 2 (March 1988), 73–79.

6. Jones, T. Capers, *Programming Productivity.* New York: McGraw-Hill, 1986.

7. Li, Elden, *Structured Software Testing: An Introduction.* San Luis Obispo, CA: The Working Paper and Reprint Series; Center for Business and Economic Research, School of Business, California Polytechnic State University.

8. Litecky, Charles R., and Gordon B. Davis, "A Study of Errors, Error Proneness, and Error Diagnosis In COBOL," *Communications of the ACM*, 19, no. 1 (January 1976), 33–37.

9. Mosley, Daniel J., "Software Testing: A Process Metrics Approach," *System Development*, 11, no. 3 (March 1991), 5–9.

10. Mosley, Daniel J., "Improving the Software Testing Process: A Process Metrics Approach," *The Center for the Study of Data Processing Working Paper Series*, 4, no. 3 (1991), WP 88–33.

11. Myers, Glenford, *The Art of Software Testing.* New York: Wiley-Interscience, 1979.

12. Ott, Ellis R., and Edward G. Schilling, *Process Quality Control: Trouble Shooting and Interpretation of the Data*, 2ed. New York: McGraw-Hill, 1990.

13. Parnas, David, "Software Aspects of Strategic Defense Systems," *American Scientist*, 73 (1985).

14. Poston, Robert, "The Power of Simple Software Testing Metrics," *The Letter T* (1990), Programming Environments, Inc.

15. Rubin Howard, *IS And Its Business Value: The Metrics Connection.* ShowCASE Conference VI Tutorial: St. Louis MO, September 26, 1991.

16. Ryan, Hugh W, "Why CASE Is Not a Cure for Testing" *Systems Development* (Summer 1990), 63–66.

17. TRAVTECH, Inc. *TRAVTECH User Survey: Testing Practices Summary.* TRAVTECH, Inc.: One Tower Square, Hartford, CT.

Appendix A

Software Testing Bibliography

ACM. "Software Engineering Notes." *Proceedings of the Software Quality Assurance Workshop*, 3, no. 5 (November 1978), 187 pp. Note: Most of the papers are general, not on specific techniques.

ACREE, ALLEN T., et al. *Mutation Analysis* (GIT-ICS-70/08). Atlanta, GA: Georgia Institute of Technology (September 1979), 86 pp. Note: Mutation testing.

ADAM, JOHN A. "Star Wars in Transition." *IEEE Spectrum* (March 1989), 32–38.

ADRIAN, W. R., M. A. BRANSTAD, and J. C. CHERNIAVSKY. "Validation, Verification, and Testing of Computer Software." *ACM Computing Surveys*, 14, no. 2 (June 1982), 159–92.

ALBRECHT, A. J. "Measuring Application Development Productivity." *Proceedings of the Joint IBM/SHARE/GUIDE Application Development Symposium*, 1979.

ALBRECHT, A. J., and J. E. GAFFNEY. "Software Function, Source Lines of Code and Development Effort Prediction." *IEEE Transactions on Software Engineering*, SE-9, no. 6 (1983), 639–48.

ANDRIOLE, STEPHEN, ed. *Software Validation, Verification, Testing, and Documentation*. New Jersey: Petrocelli Books, 1986.

ANSI/IEEE Standards Board. *IEEE Standard for Software Test Documentation Std 829–1983*. New York: The Institute of Electrical and Electronics Engineers, Inc., 1983.

ANSI/IEEE Terminology Task Group. *IEEE Standard Glossary of Software Engineering Terminology Std 729–1983*. New York: The Institute of Electrical and Electronics Engineers, Inc., 1983.

ANSI/IEEE. *Software Engineering Standards, ANSI/IEEE Standards*. New York: IEEE, 1987.

APPLETON, DANIEL, S. "Applying Lessons from the Industrial Revolution to the Information Revolution." *Chief Information Officer Journal* (Winter 1990), 10–16.

ARMOUR, PHILIP. *Structured Unit and System Testing: A Test Construction Methodology*. Note: Author was with United Airlines at the time of publication. The date of publication and journal are not known.

ASCOLY, J., M. CAFFERTY, S. GRUEN, and O. KOHLI. *Code Inspection Specification*. Kingston, N.Y.: IBM System Communications Division; TR-21.630, 1976.

ASTRAND, THOMAS, and MARC BALCCR. "The Category-Partition Method for Specifying and Generating Functional Tests." *Communications of the ACM* (June 1988).

BARBUTO, PAUL F., and JOE GELLER. "Tools for Top-Down Testing." *Datamation*, 24, no. 10 (October 1978), 178, 182.

BARTUSIAK, MARCIA. "Designing Drugs with Computers." *Discover* (August 1981).

BASILI, V. R., and B. T. PERRICONE. "Software Errors and Complexity: An Empirical Investigation." *Communications of the ACM*, 24, no. 1 (1984), 42–52.

BASILI, V. R., and R. W. SELBY. "Comparing the Effectiveness of Software Testing Strategies." *IEEE Transactions on Software Engineering* (December 1987), 1278–96.

BECK, L., and T. PERKINS. "A Survey of Software Engineering Practice: Tools, Methods, and Results." *IEEE Transactions on Software Engineering*, SE-9, no. 5 (1983).

BEHRENS, CHARLES. "Measuring the Productivity of Computer Systems Development Activities with Function Points." *IEEE Transactions on Software Engineering*, SE-9, no. 6 (November 1983), 648–52.

BEIZER, BORIS. *Software Testing Techniques, 2ed*. New York: Van Nostrand Reinhold, 1988.

BEIZER, BORIS. "On Becoming the Mainstream." *American Programmer*, 4, no. 4 (April 1991), 11–21.

BELANGER, DAVID, DAVID BERGLAND, and MIKE WISH. "Some Research Direction for Large-Scale Software Development." *AT&T Technical Journal*, 67, no. 4 (1988), 77–92.

BELLMAN, KIRSTIE L. "Testing and Evaluating Knowledge-Based Systems." *Software Maintenance News: Special Quarterly Issue on Testing*, 7, no. 12 (December 1989), 19–20.

BENDER, RICHARD. "Requirements-Based Testing." Larkspur, CA: Richard Bender & Associates, Inc.; Mini-Tutorial.

BENSON, JAMES D. "Managing Beta Testing." *Software Maintenance News: Special Quarterly Issue on Testing*, 7, no. 12 (December 1989), 18–20.

BENYON-TINKER, G. "Complexity Measures in an Evolving Large System." *Proceedings of the Workshop on Quantitative Models* (1979), 81–88.

BESTERFIELD, DALE H. *Quality Control, 3ed.* Englewood Cliffs, N.J.: Prentice Hall, 1990.

BLAUSTEIN, ERIC. "The 10 Commandments for Preparing Software Plans." *Quality Data Processing*, 2 (July 1988), 28–30.

BLOOMBECKER, J. J. "Malpractice In IS?" *Datamation* (October 1989), 85–86.

BOEHM, BARRY. "Software Engineering." *IEEE Transactions on Computers*, C-25, no. 12 (December 1976), 1226–41.

BOEHM, B. W. *Software Engineering Economics.* Englewood Cliffs, N.J.: Prentice Hall, 1981.

BOEHM, BARRY. "Improving Software Productivity." *IEEE Computer*, 20, no. 9 (September 1987), 93–107.

BOEHM, BARRY, and PHILIP PAPACCIO. "Understanding and Controlling Software Costs." *IEEE Transactions on Software Engineering*, 14, no. 10 (October 1988), 1462–72.

BOHM, C., and G. JACOPINI. "Flow Diagrams, Turing Machines, and Languages with Only Two Formation Rules." *Communications of the ACM*, 9, no. 5 (1966).

BOWEN, J. B. "Module Size: A Standard or Heuristic." *Journal of Systems and Software*, 4 (1984), 327–32.

BOX, GEORGE, E. P. HUNTER, G. WILLIAM, and J. STUART HUNTER. *Statistics for Experimenters: An Introduction to Design, Data Analysis, and Model Building.* New York: Wiley, 1978.

BOYER, ROBERT S., BERNARD ELSPAS, and KARL N. LEVITT. "SELECT—a formal system for testing and debugging programs by symbolic execution." *SIGPLAN Notices*, 10, no. 6 (June 1975), 234–45.

BRANSTAD, M. A., J. C. CHERNIAVSKY, and W. R. ADRION. "Validation, Verification, and Testing for the Individual Programmer." *Computer*, 13, no. 12 (December 1980), 24–30.

BRANT, RICHARD, EVAN SCHWARTZ, and NEIL GROSS. "Can the U.S. Stay Ahead in Software?" *Business Week* (March 1991), 98–105.

BROCKA, B. "Measuring Software Quality." *Government Data Systems*, 14, no. 1 (January 1985), 44–45.

BROOKS, FREDERICK. *The Mythical Man-Month: Essays on Software Engineering.* Reading, MA: Addison Wesley, 1975.

BRYCE, TIM. "Building Quality into Systems." *System Development* (September 1988).

CARD, D. N., and W. W. AGRESTI. "Measuring Software Design Complexity." *Journal Systems and Software*, 7 (1988).

CARLYLE, RALPH. "High Cost, Lack of Standards is Slowing Pace of CASE." *Datamation*, 33, no. 23/24 (August 1987), 23–24.

CARRUBBA, EUGENE R. *Product Assurance Principles, Integrating Design Assurance & Quality Assurance.* New York: McGraw-Hill, 1988.

CARVER, D. L. "Criteria for Estimating Module Complexity." *Journal of Systems Management,* 37, no. 8 (1986), 18–23.

CARVER, DORIS. "Acceptable Legal Standards for Software." *IEEE Software,* 5, no. 3 (May 1988), 87–93.

CELKO, JOE. "Faster Development Means Higher Maintenance Costs." *Software News,* 7, no. 11 (October 1987), 83–84.

CHANDRASEKAREN, B., and S. RADICCHI, eds. *Computer Testing.* New York: North-Holland, 1981; ISBN: 326 pp. Note: Proceedings of a wide ranging conference.

CHIKOFSKY, ELLIOT, and BURT RUBENSTEIN. "CASE: Reliability Engineering for Information Systems." *IEEE Software,* 5, no. 2 (March 1988), 11–16.

CHO, CHIN-KUIE. *An Introduction to Software Quality Control.* New York: Wiley, 1980; ISBN: 445 pp. Note: A statistical quality control approach.

CHO, CHIN-KUEI. *Quality Programming: Developing and Testing Software Using Statistical Quality Control.* New York: Wiley, 1987.

CHOW, T. S. *Software Quality Assurance—A Practical Approach.* Washington, D.C.: IEEE Computer Society Press, 1985.

CHUNG-FERN WU, REBECCA. *The Impact of Information System Quality Assurance Audits on Software Maintenance.* Information Systems Working Paper No. 4-86, UCLA Graduate School Of Management, November 1985.

COBB, R. H., and HARLAN MILLS. "Engineering Software Under Statistical Quality Control." *IEEE Software* (November 1990), 44–54.

CONNELL, JOHN, and LINDA BRICE. "Practical Quality Assurance." *Datamation,* 31, no. 5, 106–14.

CONTE, S., H. DUNSMORE, and V. SHEN. *Software Engineering Metrics and Models.* New Jersey: Benjamin Cummings Publishing Co., 1986.

COOK, MICHAEL. "Software Metrics: An Introduction and Annotated Bibliography." *Software Engineering Notes,* 7, no. 2 (April 1982), 41–60.

COUGAR, DANIEL. "The Structured Tableau Design Methodology (STDM)." *Computer Newsletter* (1983), University of Colorado, Colorado Springs.

CROSBY, PHILIP. *Quality Is Free: The Art of Making Quality Certain.* New York: McGraw-Hill, 1979.

CURRIT, P.A., M. DYER, and HARLAN D. MILLS. "Certifying the Reliability of Software." *IEEE Transactions on Software Engineering,* SE-12, no. 1 (1986), 3–11.

CURTIS, B. "Measurement and Experimentation in Software Engineering." *Proceedings of the IEEE,* 68, no. 9 (1980), 1144–57.

CURTIS, B., S. B. SHEPPARD, P. MILLIMAN, M. A. BORST, and T. A. LOVE. "Measuring the Psychological Complexity of Software Maintenance Tasks with the Halstead and McCabe Metrics." *IEEE Transactions on Software Engineering,* 5, no. 2 (1979), 96–104.

DE LA TORRE, JOSE. "Quality-Assured Software in 4GL/CASE." *Business Software Review,* 7, no. 3 (March 1988), 30–33.

DEBNATH, N. C. "On the Relationship of a New Approach to Measuring Software Effort." *Software Engineering: Practice and Experience*, 1984. Nice, France: 2nd Softw. Eng. Conference: pp. 189–93.

DEBNATH, N. C. "On the Relationship Among Software Complexity Metrics in the COBOL Environment." *Proceedings, 1st Int'l. Conf. on Comp. & Appl.*, 1984. Beijing: IEEE: pp. 624–32.

DEMARCO, TOM. *Structured Analysis And System Specification.* New Jersey: Yourdon Press/Prentice Hall, 1978.

DEMILLO, RICHARD A., RICHARD J. LIPTON, and FREDERICK G. SAYWARD. "Hints on Test Data Selection: Help for the Practicing Programmer." *Computer*, 11, no. 4 (April 1978), 34. Note: Selective testing.

DEMILLO, RICHARD A., W. MICHAEL MCCRAKEN, R. J. MARTIN, and JOHN F. PASSAFIUME. *Software Testing And Evaluation.* Menlo Park, CA: Benjamin Cummings, 1987.

DEMING, W. EDWARD. *Out of the Crisis.* Cambridge, MA: MIT Center for Advanced Engineering Study, 1982.

DEMING, W. EDWARD. *Quality, Productivity, and Competitive Position.* Cambridge, MA: Massachusetts Institute of Technology, 1982.

DEO, N. *Graph Theory with Applications to Engineering and Computer Science.* Englewood Cliffs, N.J.: Prentice Hall, 1974.

Department of Defense. *DOD-STD-2167A.* Washington, D.C.: The United States Department of Defense, 1987.

DEUTCH, MICHAEL, and RONALD WILLIS. *Software Quality Engineering: A Total Technical and Management Approach.* Englewood Cliffs, N.J.: Prentice Hall, 1988.

DIJKSTRA, E. W. "Structured Programming." *Software Engineering Techniques*, April 1970. Report on a conference sponsored by the NATO Science Committee, Rome, Italy: pp. 84–88.

DIJKSTRA, E. W. "Programming Considered as a Human Activity," in *Classics In Software Engineering*, Edward Nash Yourdon, ed. New York: Yourdon Press, 1979.

DOKE, REED. "Application Development Productivity Tools: A Survey of Importance and Popularity." *Journal of Information and Systems Management* (Winter 1989).

DRAKE, H. D. "Reliability Theory Applied to Software Testing." *Hewlett-Packard Journal* (April 1987), 35–39.

DREGER, BRIAN J. *Function Point Analysis.* Englewood Cliffs, N.J.: Prentice Hall Advanced Reference Series, Computer Science, 1989.

DRESSLER, FRITZ. "CASE Standards: A Grab Bag of Good Intentions." *PC Week*, 5, no. 35 (August 1988), 90–91.

DYNHAM, JANET R. "V&V in the Next Decade." *IEEE Software* (May 1989), 47–53.

DUNCAN, ACHESON J. *Quality Control and Industrial Statistics, 5th ed.* Homewood, IL: Irwin, Inc., 1986.

DURANT, JERRY. "Classifying Software Tools." *Software Maintenance News: Special Quarterly Issue on Testing*, 7, no. 12 (December 1989), 16–17.

DURANT, JERRY, and S. C. NATFOS. "An Evaluation of Random Testing." *IEEE Transactions on Software Engineering*, SE-10, no. 4 (1984), 438–44.

DURANT, JERRY. *Testing Tools Reference Guide*. Jacksonville, FL: Software Quality Engineering, 1991. (Note: See also Software Quality Engineering below.)

DYKSTRA, EDSKER. "Programming Considered as a Human Activity," in *Classics In Software Engineering*, Edward Yourdon, ed. New York: Yourdon Press, 1979.

EISSENBERG, TOM, and GINNY REDISH. "First a Controlled Evaluation, then a Test." *Software Maintenance News: Special Quarterly Issue on Testing*, 7, no. 12 (December 1989), 12–14.

ELMENDORF, WILLIAM R. *Cause-Effect Graphs in Functional Testing*. Poughkeepsie, NY: IBM System Development Division; TR-00.2487, 1973.

ELMENDORF, WILLIAM R. "Functional Analysis Using Cause-Effect Graphs." *Proceedings of SHARE XL111*, 1974. New York: SHARE<: pp. 567–77.

EVANGELIST, W. M. "Software Complexity Metric Sensitivity to Program Structuring Rules." *Journal of Systems and Software*, 3 (1983), 231–43.

EVANS, MICHAEL. *Productive Software Test Management*. New York: Wiley-Interscience, 1984.

EVANS, MICHAEL. *The Software Factory: Concepts and Environment*. New York: Wiley, 1987.

EVANS, MICHAEL, P. H. PIAZZA, and J. B. DOLKAS. *Principles of Productive Software Management*. New York: Wiley, 1983.

EVERETT, JOHN. "Independent Information Professionals and the Question of Malpractice Liability." *Online* (May 1989), 65–70.

FAGAN, M. E. "Design and Code Inspections to Reduce Errors in Program Development." *IBM Systems Journal*, 15, no. 3 (1976), 182–211.

FAGAN, M. E. "Advances in Software Inspections." *IEEE Transactions on Software Engineering*, SE-12, no. 7 (July 1986), 744–51.

FEUER, A. R., and E. B. FOWLKES. "Relating Computer Program Maintainability to Software Measures." *Proceedings of the National Computer Conference* (1979), 1003–12.

FICKAS, STEPHEN, and P. NAGARAJAN. "Critiquing Software Specifications." *IEEE Software* (November 1988), 37–47.

FISHER, ALAN. *CASE: Using Software Development Tools*. New York: Wiley, 1988.

FLAHERTY, M. J. "Programming Process Productivity Measurement System for System/370." *IBM Systems Journal*, 24, no. 2 (1985), 168–75.

FLOWER, PRISCILLA. "In-Process Inspections of Workproducts at AT&T." *AT&T Technical Journal*, 65, no. 2 (1986), 102–12.

FRANKL, PHYLLIS, and ELAINE WEYUKER. "An Applicable Family of Data Flow Testing Criteria." *IEEE Transactions on Software Engineering*, 14, no. 10 (October 1988), 1483–98.

FRANZ, DONALD. *Information Structures and Program Design Student Text Workbook and Problems.* Unpublished.

FRANZ, DONALD, and D. GAMBLE. *Structured Tableau Design Methodology.* Specialized Online Systems, Inc., 1981.

FREEDMAN, DANIEL P., and GERALD M. WEINBERG. *Walkthroughs, Inspections and Technical Reviews.* Boston, MA: Little, Brown & Co., 1982. 450 pp.

FREEMAN, PETER. *Software Reusability, Tutorial.* Washington, D.C.: IEEE Society Press, 1987.

GANE, CHRIS, and TRISH SARSON. *Structured Systems Analysis: Tools and Techniques.* Englewood Cliffs, N.J.: Prentice Hall, 1979.

GANNON, J. D., and J. J. HORNING. "Language Design for Program Reliability." *IEEE Transactions on Software Engineering,* 1, no. 2, 179–91.

GELPERIN, DAVID. "Divining Five Types of Testing Tools." *Software News,* 7, no. 9 (August 1987), 42–47.

GELPERIN, DAVID, and DAVID HETZEL. "The Growth of Software Testing." *Communications of the ACM* (June 1988).

GILB, TOM. *Software Metrics.* Cambridge, MA: Winthrop, 1977.

GILB, TOM. *Principles Of Software Engineering Management.* Workingham, England: Addison-Wesley, 1988.

GILB, TOM. "Advanced Defect Prevention Using Inspection, Testing & Field Data." *American Programmer,* 4, no. 5 (May 1991), 38–45.

Glass, Robert L. "The Universal Elixar, and Other Computing Projects which Failed." *Computerworld* (1976).

GLASS, ROBERT L. *Software Reliability Guidebook.* Englewood Cliffs, N.J.: Prentice Hall, 1979.

GOEL, A. L. "Software Error Detection with Applications." *Journal of Systems and Software,* 1 (1980), 243–49.

GOOD, DONALD I., RALPH L. LONDON, and W. W. BLEDSOE. "An Inter-active Program Verification System." *Software Engineering,* SE-1, no. 1 (March 1975), 59–67.

GOODENOUGH, JOHN B., and SUSAN L. GERHART. "Toward a Theory of Test Data Selection." *Software Engineering,* SE-1, no. 2 (June 1975), 156–73.

GORDON, R. D. "Measuring Improvements in Program Clarity." *IEEE Transactions on Software Engineering,* 5, no. 2 (1979), 79–90.

GRADY, R., and D. CASWELL. *Software Metrics: Establishing a Company-Wide Program.* Englewood Cliffs, N.J.: Prentice Hall, 1987.

GRADY, ROBERT. "Measuring and Managing Software Maintenance." *IEEE Software,* 4, no. 5 (September 1987), 35–45.

GRADY, ROBERT. "Dissecting Software Failures." *Hewlett-Packard Journal* (April 1989), 58–63.

GRIES, D. "An Illustration of Current Ideas on the Derivation of Correctness Proofs and Correct Programs." *Software Engineering,* SE-2, no. 4 (December 1975), 238–44. Note: Proofs of correctness.

GRUENBERGER, FRED. "Program Testing and Validation." *Datamation,* 14, no. 7 (July 1968), 89–47.

GUIDE PUBLICATIONS. *How to Build and Run a Standards Program*. Anaheim, CA: Guide International Corp., 1982.

GUIDE PUBLICATIONS. *Performing Systems Quality Assurance*. Anaheim, CA: Guide International Corp., 1982. Note: Publication No. GPP-83.

GUIDE PUBLICATIONS. *Reusable Design/Code Productivity Techniques*. Anaheim, CA: Guide International Corp., 1983. Note: Publication No. GPP-104.

HALSTEAD, M. H. *Elements of Software Science*. New York: Elsevier, 1977.

HAMILTON, ROSEMARY. "Standard for CASE Offered." *ComputerWorld*, 21, no. 27 (1987), 27–29.

HANFORD, K. V. "Automatic Generations of Test Cases." *IBM Systems Journal*, 9, no. 4 (1970), 242–47.

HANSEN, KIRK. *Data Structured Program Design*. Englewood Cliffs, N.J.: Prentice Hall, 1986.

HARRISON, W., and C. COOK. "Are Deeply Nested Conditionals Less Readable?" *Journal of Systems and Software*, 6 (1986), 335–41.

HARRISON, W., and C. COOK. "A Micro/Macro Measure of Software Complexity." *Journal Systems and Software*, 7 (1987), 213–19.

HENRY, SALLIE, and ROGER GOFF. "Complexity Measurement of a Graphical Programming Language." *Software—Practice and Experience*, 19, no. 11 (November 1989), 1065–88.

HENRY, S. M., and D. KAFURA. "The Evaluation of Software Systems' Structure Using Quantitative Software Metrics." *Software—Practice and Experience*, 14, no. 6 (1984), 561–73.

HENRY, S. M., D. KAFURA. and HARRIS. "On The Relationships Among Three Software Metrics." *Performance Evaluation Review*, 10, no. 1 (1981).

HERBERT, MARTIN, and THOMAS BROWDY. *The CASE Studies Consortium Survey Analysis Results*. St. Louis, MO: The Center for the Study of Data Processing, School of Technology and Information Management, School of Engineering and Applied Science, Washington University, 1989.

HETZEL, WILLIAM C., ed. *Program Test Methods*. Englewood Cliffs, N.J.: Prentice Hall, 1973. Note: 321 pp.

HETZEL, WILLIAM. *The Complete Guide to Software Testing*, 2ed. Wellesley, MA: QED Information Sciences, 1988.

HETZEL, WILLIAM, and DAVID GELPERIN. "Software Testing: Some Troubling Issues." *American Programmer*, 4, no. 4 (April 1991), 22–27.

HOMER, WILLIAM, and RICHARD SCHOOLER. "Independent Testing of Compiler Phases Using a Test Case Generator." *Software—Practice and Experience*, 19, no. 1 (January 1989), 53–62.

HORCH, JOHN W. "Test Management." *System Development* (March 1988), 7–10.

HORCH, JOHN. "Quality Makes Sense." *System Development* (September 1988), 1–2, 7–9.

HOUGHTON, RAYMOND. *Features of Software Development Tools — NBS Special Publication 500–74*. Washington, D.C.: National Bureau of Standards, 1981.

HOWDEN, W. E. "Methodology for the Generation of Program Test Data." *IEEE Transactions on Computers*, C-24, no. 5 (1975), 554–60.

HUANG, J. C. "An Approach to Program Testing." *Computing Surveys*, 7, no. 3 (September 1975), 113–28.

HUMPHREY, WATTS. *Managing For Innovation—Leading Technical People*. Englewood Cliffs, N.J.: Prentice Hall, 1987.

HUMPHREY, WATTS. "Characterizing the Software Process: A Maturity Model." *IEEE Software*, 5, no. 2 (1988), 73–79.

HUMPHREY, WATTS. *Managing the Software Process*. Reading, MA: Addison Wesley, 1989.

INGRAM, DOUGLAS. "Requirements Management Is Key to Software Quality." *CASE Outlook*, 1, no. 5 (1987), 1–17.

IVES, B., M. OLSON, and J. BAROUDI. "The Measurement of User Information Satisfaction." *Communications of the ACM*, 26, no. 10 (October 1983), 785–93.

ISHIKAWA, K. *What Is Total Quality Control?* Englewood Cliffs, N.J.: Prentice Hall, 1985.

JONES, C. L. "A Process Integrated Approach to Defect Prevention." *IBM Systems Journal*, 24, no. 2 (1985), 150–67.

JONES, T. Capers. "Building a Better Metric." *ComputerWorld Extra* (June 1988), 38–39.

JONES, T. Capers. "Measuring Programming Quality and Productivity." *IBM Systems Journal*, 17, no. 1 (1978), 39–63.

JONES, T. Capers. *Programming Productivity: Issues for the Eighties*, 2ed. Washington, D.C.: IEEE Computer Society Press, 1986.

JONES, T. Capers. *Programming Productivity*. New York: McGraw-Hill, 1986.

JOYCE, EDWARD. "Software Bugs: A Matter of Life and Liability." *Datamation*, 33, no. 10 (May 1987), 88–92.

JOYCE, EDWARD. "Is Error-Free Software Achievable?" *Datamation* (1989), 53–54.

JURAN, JOSEPH M., ed. *Quality Control Handbook, 4th ed.* New York: McGraw-Hill, 1988.

KAFURA, D., and S. HENRY. "Software Quality Metrics Based on Interconnectivity." *Journal of Systems and Software*, 2 (1981), 121–31.

KAFURA, D., and G. R. REDDY. "The Use of Software Complexity Metrics in Software Maintenance." *IEEE Transactions on Software Engineering*, 13, no. 3 (1987), 335–43.

KEARNEY, JOSEPH, ROBERT SEDLMEYER, WILLIAM THOMPSON, MICHAEL GRAY, and MICHAEL ADLER. "Software Complexity Measurement." *Communications of the ACM*, 29, no. 11 (1986), 1044–50.

KEARNEY, JULIA. "SORD Has a Better Idea." Source of publication unknown.

KEMMERER, R. "Testing Formal Specifications to Detect Design Errors." *IEEE Transactions on Software Engineering* (January 1985), 32–42.

KERNIGHAN, B. W., and P. J. PLAUGER. *The Elements of Programming Style*. New Jersey: Bell Telephone Laboratories, 1974.

KING, DAVID. *Current Practices in Software Development: A Guide to Successful Systems.* Englewood Cliffs, N.J.: Prentice Hall, 1984.

KING, JAMES C. "A New Approach to Program Testing." *SIGPLAN Notices,* 10, no. 6 (June 1975), 228–33.

KING, JAMES C. "Symbolic Execution and Program Testing." *Communications of the ACM,* 7, no. 19 (July 1976), 385–94.

KISHIDA, KOUICHI, MASANORI TERAMOTO, KOJI TORII, and YOSHIYORI URANO. "Quality-Assurance Technology in Japan." *IEEE Software,* 4, no. 5 (September 1987), 11–18.

KITCHENHAM, B.A. "Measures of Programming Complexity." *ICL Tech. J.,* 2, no. 3 (1981), 298–316.

KNIGHT, ROBERT. "CASE Paybacks Perceived, If Not Exactly Measured." *Software News,* 7, no. 2 (February 1987), 56–58.

KNUTSON, JEF. "Forgotten Types of Testing." *Software Maintenance News,* 7, no. 12 (December 1989), 8.

KOLENCE, KENNETH. *An Introduction to Software Physics.* New York: McGraw-Hill, 1985.

KRAMER, JOHN, PATRICIA OBERNDORF, JOHN LONG, CLYDE ROBY, MAX ROBINSON, JEFF CLOUSE, and JOHN CHLUDZINSKI. *CAIS Reader's Guide for DOD-STD-1838.* Alexandria, VA: Institute for Defense Analyses and Office of the Under Secretary of Defense for Acquisition (Research and Advanced Technology) Ada Joint Program Office, 1987.

LARSON, RODNEY R. *Test Plan and Test Case Inspection Specifications.* Kingston, N.Y.: IBM System Development Division, 1975. Note: TR-21.586.

LAUTERBACH, L., and W. RANDELL. "Six Test Techniques Compared: The Test Process and Product." Washington, D.C.: *Proceedings NSIA Fifth Annual National Joint Conference and Tutorial on Software Quality and Productivity,* 1989. Published by the National Security Industrial Association.

LEAVITT, DON. "An Approach to Measuring Productivity." *Software News,* 4, no. 8 (August 1984).

LEAVITT, DON. "Design Tools: The Real Starting Point." *Software News,* 6, no. 2 (February 1986), 57–59.

LEHDER, WILFRED, PAUL SMITH, and WEIDER YU. "Software Estimation Technology." *AT&T Technical Journal,* 67, no. 4 (1988), 10–18.

LEMPP, P., and R. LAUBER. "What Productivity Increases to Expect from a CASE Environment: Results of a User Survey." *Productivity: Progress, Prospects, and Payoff* (June 1988), 13–19.

LEVITT, T. *The Marketing Imagination.* New York: The Free Press, 1983.

LEW, K. S., T. S. DILLON, and K. E. FORWARD. *A Software Complexity Measure that Characterizes Module Interaction.* First Australian Software Engineering Conference. Software Engineering: Path to Computer Systems Reliability, 1986, Canberra, Australia.

LEWIS, T. G. *Software Engineering Analysis and Verification.* Reston, VA: Reston Publishing Co., Inc., 1982. Note: Includes some testing in a software engineering context.

LI, ELDON Y. *Structured Software Testing: An Introduction.* San Luis Obispo, CA: The Working Paper and Reprint Series; Center for Business and Economic Research, School of Business, California Polytechnic State University.

LI, ELDON Y. "Software Testing Techniques for the Information Systems Professional: A Curriculum Perspective." *Proceedings of the 9th International Conference on Information Systems* (1988), 119–28.

LI, ELDON Y. "Software Testing in a System Development Process: A Life Cycle Perspective." *Journal of Systems Management* (August 1990), 23–31.

LIENTZ and SWANSON. *Software Maintenance Management.* Reading, MA: Addison Wesley, 1980.

LIPAEV, V. V., B. A. POZIN, and I. N. STROGANOVA. "Complexity of Program Module Testing." *Programming and Computer Software*, 9, no. 6 (1983), 332–37.

LITECKY, CHARLES R., and GORDON B. DAVIS. "A Study of Errors, Error Proneness, and Error Diagnosis on COBOL." *Communications of the ACM*, 19, no. 1 (January 1976), 33–37.

LITECKY, CHARLES R. "An Expert System for COBOL Program Debugging." *DATA BASE* (Spring 1989), 1–6.

LITTLEWOOD, B. "Theories of Software Reliability: How Good Are They and How They Can Be Improved." *IEEE Transactions on Software Engineering*, SE-6, no. 5 (1980), 489–500.

LLEWELYN, A. I., and R. F. WICKENS. "The Testing of Computer Software." In *Software Engineering Concepts and Techniques*, eds. J. M. Buston, Peter Naur, and Brian Randell, New York: Petrocelli/Charter, 1976, 118–24.

LOWELL, JAY. *Programmer Productivity: Myths, Methods, and Murphy's Law.* New York: Wiley, 1983.

MAJKEIWCIZ, JANE. "A Test for SAA." *Datamation* (October 1989).

MARTIN, JAMES. *System Design From Provably Correct Constructs.* Englewood Cliffs, N.J.: Prentice Hall, 1985.

MARTIN, JAMES. *Recommended Diagramming Standards for Analysts and Programmers: A Basis for Automation.* Englewood Cliffs, N.J.: Prentice Hall, 1987.

MARTIN, JAMES, and CARMA MCCLURE. "The Latest Look in Programmer Productivity Tools." *Business Software Review* (May 1986).

MASON, HARDY, and IRWIN J. SITKIN. "Atena's Reusability Lab." *Software Maintenance News*, 7, no. 12 (December 1989), 10,12.

MAYS, R. G., C. L. JONES, G. J. HOLLOWAY, and D. P. STUDINSKI. "Experiences with Defect Prevention." *IBM Systems Journal*, 29, no. 1 (1990), 4–32.

MCCABE, THOMAS J. "A Complexity Measure." *IEEE Transactions on Software Engineering*, SE-2, no. 4 (1975), 308–20.

MCCABE, THOMAS J. *Structured Testing: A Testing Methodology Using The McCabe Complexity Metric.* NBS Special Publication, Contract NB82NAAR5518, 1982.

MCCABE, THOMAS J., ed. *Structured Testing.* Silver Spring, MD: IEEE Computer Society Press, 1983.

McCabe, Thomas J., and G. G. Schulmeyer. "System Testing Aided By Structured Analysis: A Practical Experience." *IEEE Transactions on Software Engineering*, SE-11, no. 9 (1985), 917–21.

McCabe, Thomas J., and Charles W. Butler. "Design Complexity Measurement and Testing." *Communications of the ACM*, 32, no. 12 (1989), 1415–25.

McClure, Carma. "A Model for Program Complexity Analysis." *Proceedings Third International Conference on Software Engineering* (May 1978), 149–57.

McClure, Carma. "*CASE Is Software Automation.*" Englewood Cliffs, N.J.: Prentice Hall, 1989.

Meredith, Dennis. "Planning Software Testing." In *The Handbook Of Systems Management: Development and Support*. Boston, MA: Auerbach, 1990.

Merlyn, Vaughan. *How to Select a CASE Tool*—Tutorial. Bellview, WA: CASE Research Corporation, September 1988.

Miller, E. F. *Methodology for Comprehensive Software Testing*. Santa Barbara, CA: General Research Corp., 1975.

Miller, Edward, ed. "Software Quality Assurance." *Computer*, 12, no. 8 (1979), 7–9.

Miller, E. F., Jr., and R. A. Melton. "Automated Generation of Test Cases Datasets." *SIGPLAN Notices*, 10, no. 6 (June 1975), 51–58.

Miller, E. F., Jr. "Program Testing: Art Meets Theory." *Computer*, 10, no. 7 (1977), 42–51.

Miller, Edward F., Jr., ed. "Program Testing." *Computer*; 11, no. 4 (April 1978), 10–12, 14–22, 25–32, 34–41, 44–60. Note: Includes papers by Miller, Fairley, Huang, DeMillo, Panzel, and Darrenger.

Miller, Edward F., Jr., and William E. Houden, eds. *Software Testing and Validation Techniques*. Los Angeles, CA: IEEE Computer Society Press, 1978. ISBN: 425 pp. Note: Reprints of papers on dynamic and static testing.

Miller, Edward F., Jr., ed. "Software Quality Assurance." *Computer*, 12, no. 8 (August 1979), 10–18, 20–24, 26–31, 33–36, 37–42, 43–50. Note: Includes papers by Geiger, Sorkowitz, Gannon, Holthouse, Bowen, and Buckley.

Miller, George. "The Magical Number Seven, Plus or Minus Two: Some Limits on Our Capacity to Process Information." *The Psychological Review*, 63, no. 2 (March 1956), 81–97.

Miller, Howard W. "Quality Software: The Future of Information Technology." *Journal of Systems Management* (1989), 8–14.

Mills, Harlan, D. "On the Statistical Validation of Computer Programs." In *Software Productivity*. Boston, MA: Little, Brown, 1983, pp. 71–81.

Mills, Harlan, Michael Dyer, and Richard Linger. "Cleanroom Software Engineering." *IEEE Software*, 4, no. 5 (September 1987), 19–25.

Mills, Harlan, and J. H. Poore. "Bringing Software Under Statistical Quality Control." *Quality Progress* (November 1988), 52–55.

Mills, Harlan. "Cleanroom Engineering: Engineering Software Under Statistical Control." *American Programmer*, 4, no. 5 (May 1991), 31–37.

MISRA, P. N. "Software Reliability Analysis." *IBM Systems Journal*, 22, no. 3 (1983), 262–70.

MOAWAD, R., and M. HASSAN. "Structural Approach Towards Software Reliability Evaluation." *Proc. COMPSAC 83*: IEEE 7th Int'l. Comp. Softw. & Appl. Conf., Chicago, 1983.

MOHANTY, S. N. "Entropy Metrics for Software Design Evaluation." *Journal of Systems & Software*, 2 (1981), 39–46.

MOHANTY, S. N. "Models and Measurements for Quality Assessment of Software." *ACM Computing Surveys*, 11, no. 3 (1979), 251–75.

MOHANTY, SIBA N. *On Software Verification and Validation*. McLean, VA: The MITRE Corp., 1981. Note: 52 pp. Describes IV & V.

MORRISON, JOHN. "A Wicked Problem—Software Testing in Large-Scale Systems." *American Programmer*, 4, no. 4 (April 1991), 3–10.

MOSLEY, DANIEL J. "Software Testing: A Process Metrics Approach." *System Development*, 11, no. 3 (March 1991), 5–9.

MOSLEY, DANIEL J., and BARRY KALMAN. "Future CASE: Information Technology Adoption Projections." Executive Briefing: CASE (January/February 1991), 1–2.

MOSLEY, DANIEL J. "Getting CASE Straight: Can You Use It Or Not?" *Chief Information Officer Journal*, 3, no. 2 (Fall 1990), 55–59.

MOSLEY, DANIEL J. *Basics of the New Application Development Platform*. Tutorial given at the ShowCASE V Conference; St. Louis, MO, September 17, 1990.

MOSLEY, DANIEL J. "Are We Ready for CASE?" *American Programmer*, 2, no. 3 (March 1989), 20–25.

MOSLEY, DANIEL J. *A Comparison of the White Box and Black Box Test Case Design Strategies*. Washington University in St. Louis, MO: The Center for the Study of Data Processing Working Paper Series, November 1988.

MOSLEY, DANIEL J. *A Data Structured Adaptation of McCabe's Structured Testing Methodology*. Washington University in St. Louis, MO: The Center for the Study of Data Processing Working Paper Series, 1987.

MUNOZ, CARLOS. "An Approach to Software Product Testing." *IEEE Transactions on Software Engineering*, 14, no. 11 (1988), 1589–96.

MURRAY, JOHN. "The Issue of Quality Assurance: Can We Afford Not to Do It Right the First Time?" *System Development*, 7, no. 1 (January 1987), 1–3.

MUSA, JOHN D. "A Theory of Software Reliability Prediction and Its Applications." *IEEE Transactions on Software Engineering*, SE-1, no. 3 (1975), 312–27.

MUSA, JOHN D. "The Measurement and Management of Software Reliability." *Proceedings of the IEEE*, 68, no. 9 (1980), 1131–43.

MUSA, JOHN, ANTHONY IANNINO, and KAZUHIRA OKUMOTO. *Software Reliability: Measurement, Prediction, Application*. New York: McGraw-Hill, 1987.

MUSA, JOHN D., and A. FRANK ACKERMAN. "Quantifying Software Validation: When to Stop Testing?" *IEEE Software* (May 1989), 19–27.

MYERS, GLENFORD J. "An Extension to the Cyclomatic Measure of Program Complexity." *ACM SIGPLAN Notices* (October 1977), 61–64.

MYERS, GLENFORD J. *Composite/Structured Design.* New York: Van Nostrand Reinhold, 1979.

MYERS, GLENFORD J. *The Art of Software Testing.* New York: Wiley-Interscience, 1979.

MYERS, GLENFORD J. *Software Reliability: Principles and Practices.* New York: Wiley-Interscience, 1976.

MYERS, WARE. "Can Software for the Strategic Defense Initiative Ever Be Error-Free?" *IEEE Computer,* 19, no. 11 (November 1986), 61–67.

MYERS, WARE. "Software Pivotal to Strategic Defense." *IEEE Computer,* 22, no. 1 (1989), 92–97.

MYNATT, B. T. "The Effect of Semantic Complexity on the Comprehension of Program Modules." *Int'l J. Man-Mach. Studies,* 21 (1984), 91–103.

NAKAJO, TAKESHI, KATSUHIKO SASABUCHI, and TADASHI AKLYAMA. "A Structured Approach to Software Defect Analysis." *Hewlett-Packard Journal* (April 1989), 50–56.

National Bureau of Standards FIPS Publication Series. *Guidelines for Life Cycle Validation, Verification and Testing of Computer Software.* Springfield, VA: National Bureau of Standards, June 1983.

NEAL, A., and R. SIMONS. "Playback: A Method of Evaluating the Usability of Software and Its Documentation." *IBM Systems Journal,* 23, no. 1 (1984), 82–96.

NECCO, CHARLES R., NANCY TSAI, and KREG W. HOLGESON. "Current Usage of CASE Software." *Journal of Systems Management,* 40, no. 5 (May 1989), 6–10.

NTAFOS, SIMESN C. "A Comparison of Some Structural Testing Strategies." *Software Engineering,* 14 (June 1988), 868–74.

OMAN, RAY C., and TYRONE B. AYERS. "Improving Data Quality." *Journal of Systems Management* (May 1988), 31–35.

ORR, KENNETH. *Structured Systems Development.* New York: Yourdon Press, 1977.

ORR, KENNETH. *Structured Requirements Definition.* Topeka, KA: Ken Orr Associates, Inc., 1982.

OTT, ELLIS, R., and EDWARD G. SCHILLING. *Process Quality Control, 2ed.* New York: McGraw-Hill, 1990.

OULD, M. A., and C. UNWIN. *Testing In Software Development.* Cambridge, UK: Cambridge University Press, 1986.

PARIKH, GIRISH. "Techniques of Measuring Programmer Productivity." *Data Management,* 23, no. 6 (June 1985), 18–22.

PARNAS, DAVID. "Software Aspects of Strategic Defense Systems." *American Scientist,* 73 (1985).

PERRONE, GIOVANNI. "CASE: The Passwords to Full Life Cycle." *Software Magazine,* 8, no. 13 (November 1988), 40–51.

PERRY, WILLIAM. *A Standard for Testing Application Software 1992.* Boston, MA: Auerbach, 1992.

PERRY, WILLIAM E. *A Structured Approach to Systems Testing, 2ed.* Wellesley, MA: QED Information Sciences, 1988.

PERRY, WILLIAM. *How To Test Software Packages: A Step-by-Step Guide to Assuring They Do What You Want.* New York: Wiley, 1986.

PFAU, LOREN. "Total Quality Management Gives Companies a Way to Enhance Position in a Global Marketplace." *Industrial Engineering* (April 1989), 17–18, 20–21.

PHILIPS, ROGER. "No-Test Software Is 'Unobtainable.' " *Software Magazine* (December 1988), 33–44.

PODGURSKI, A., and L. CLARKE. "A Formal Model of Program Dependencies and Its Implications for Software Testing, Debugging, and Maintenance." *IEEE Transactions on Software Engineering,* 16, no. 9 (September 1990), 965–79.

POLILLI, STEVE. "CASE Standards Advancing." *Software Magazine,* 8, no. 8 (June 1988), 24–27.

POOLE, BERNARD, and NOREEN PROKOP. "Miller's Magical Number: A Heuristic Applied to Software Engineering." *Information Executive* (1989), 12–13, 16, 68.

POPPER, K. R. *Conjectures and Refutation: The Growth of Scientific Knowledge.* New York: Harper & Row, 1968.

POSTON, ROBERT. "A Complete Toolkit for the Software Tester." *American Programmer,* 4, no. 4 (April 1991), 28–37.

POSTON, ROBERT. "The Power of Simple Software Testing Metrics." *The Letter T,* 1990. Programming Environments, Inc., Trenton Falls, N.J.

POTOSNAK, KATHLEEN. "Setting Objectives for Measurably Better Software." *IEEE Software* (March 1988), 89–90.

POWELL, P. B. *Software Validation, Verification, and Testing Technique and Tool Reference Guide.* Gaithersburg, MD: NBS Special Pub. 500–93, National Institute of Standards and Technology, 1982.

PRATHER, RONALD, and PAUL MYERS. "The Path Prefix Software Testing Strategy." *IEEE Transactions on Software Engineering,* SE-13, no. 7 (July 1987).

PRESSMAN, ROGER S. *Software Engineering: A Practitioner's Approach, 2ed.* New York: McGraw-Hill, 1987.

PRESSMAN, ROGER S. *Making Software Engineering Happen: A Guide to Instituting the Technology.* Englewood Cliffs, N.J.: Prentice Hall, 1988.

PRITCHARD, TERESA, and MICHELLE QUIGLEY. "The Information Specialist: A Malpractice Risk Analysis." *Online* (May 1989), 57–62.

RAMAMOORTHY, C. V., and S. F. HO. "Testing Large Software with Automated Software Evaluation Systems." *IEEE Transactions on Software Engineering,* SE-1, no. 1 (1975), 46–58.

RAPPS, S., and E. J. WEYUKER. "Data Flow Analysis Techniques for Test Data Selection." Proceedings of the Sixth International Conference on Software Engineering. Tokyo, Japan, 1982.

REYNOLDS, R. G. "Metrics to Measure the Complexity of Partial Programs." *Journal of Systems & Software,* 4 (1984), 75–91.

RICHARDSON, DANIEL R. "Regression Libraries Test Top-Down Development." *Infosystems*, 23, no. 2 (February 1976), 46–48. Note: A brief coverage of cause and effect graphing.

RINALDI, DAMIAN. "Software Developers Mired in Maintenance." *Software News*, 7, no. 11 (October 1987), 75–76.

RUBEY, RAYMOND J. "Quantitative Aspects of Software Validation." *SIGPLAN Notices*, 10, no. 6 (June 1975), 246–51.

RUBIN, CHARLES. "To Get Quality Code, Admit Bugs Are a Reality." *Software News*, 7, no. 11 (October 1987), 61–72.

RUBIN, HOWARD. *IS and Its Business Value: The Metrics Connection*. St. Louis, MO: ShowCASE Conference Tutorial, September 26, 1991.

RYAN, HUGH B. "Why CASE Is Not a Cure for Testing." *Journal of Information Systems Management* (Summer 1990), 63–66.

SAKTHIVEL, S., and MOHAN TANNIRU. "Information System Verification and Validation Using Petri Nets." *Journal of Management Information Systems*, 5, no. 3 (Winter 1988–89), 33–52.

SCHEFF, B. "Decision Table Structure as Input Format for Programming Automatic Test Equipment Systems." *Electronic Computers*, EC-14, no. 2 (April 1965), 248–50.

SCHERKENBACH, WILLIAM. *The Deming Route to Quality and Productivity*. Rockville, MD: Mercury Press/Fairchild Publications, 1986.

SCHNEIDER, G. M., R. L. SEDLMEYER, and J. KEARNEY. "On the Complexity of Measuring Software Complexity." *AFIPS Conf. Proc.*, 33 (1981), 317–22.

SCOTT, TONY, and DENNIS FARLEY. "Slashing Software Maintenance Costs." *Business Software Review* (March 1988), 35–43.

SELBY, R. W., V. R. BASILI, and F. T. BAKER. "Cleanroom Software Development: An Empirical Evaluation." *IEEE Transactions on Software Engineering*, SE-13, no. 9 (1987), 1027–37.

SEVIORA, RUDOLPH. "Knowledge-Based Program Debugging Systems." *IEEE Software*, 4, no. 3 (May 1987), 20–32.

SHARON, WILLIAM D. *The CASE Locator For Software Testing Tools*. Oregon City, Oregon: CASE Associates, Inc., 1990.

SHATTUCK, BILL, and DAVID BAYER. *A Market Introduction to Computer-Aided Software Engineering (CASE)*. San Francisco, CA: Montgomery Securities, 600 Montgomery St., 1987.

SHEN, V. Y., T. YU, S. THEBAUT, and L. PAULSEN. "Identifying Error-Prone Software—An Empirical Study." *IEEE Transactions on Software Engineering*, 11, no. 4 (1985), 317–24.

SHOOMAN, M. L. *Software Engineering: Design, Reliability, and Management*. New York: McGraw-Hill, 1983.

SILVER, BILL. "Symbols of Quality." *Software Quality World*, Guided Tour issue, 1989.

Software Quality Engineering. *Testing Tools Reference Guide: A Catalog of Software Quality Support Tools*. Jacksonville, FL: Software Quality Engineering, 1991. Note: This guide is updated yearly; See also reference for Durant, Jerry.

STAHL, BOB. "The Ins and Outs of Software Testing." *COMPUTERWORLD* (October 24, 1988), 87–92.

STEVENS, WAYNE, GLENFORD MYERS, and LARRY CONSTANTINE. "Structured Design." *IBM Systems Journal*, 13, no. 2 (1974).

SCHULMEYER, G. GORDON, and JAMES I. McMANUS. *Handbook of Software Quality Assurance*. New York: Van Nostrand Reinhold, 1987.

SUPNIK, R. M. *Debugging Under Simulation*. Englewood Cliffs, N.J.: Prentice Hall, 1971: pp. 118–36. Note: In Rustin Randall, ed. *Debugging Techniques in Large Systems*.

SYMONS, CHARLES. "Function Point Analysis: Difficulties and Improvements." *IEEE Transactions on Software Engineering*, 14, no. 1 (January 1988), 2–11.

TAGUCHI, G. *Introduction to Quality Engineering*. Tokyo: Asian Productivity Organization, 1986.

TANENBAUM, ANDREW S. "In Defense of Program Testing or Correctness Proofs Considered Harmful." *SIGPLAN Notices*, 11, no. 5 (May 1976), 64–68.

TICE, GEORGE. "Preventing Most-Probable Error in Testing." *IEEE Software* (March 1988), 86–88.

TRAVTECH, Inc. *TRAVTECH User Survey: Testing Practices Summary*. TRAVTECH, INC., One Tower Square, Hartford, CT.

TROY, D. A., and S. H. ZWEBEN. "Measuring the Quality of Structured Designs." *Journal of Systems & Software*, 2 (1981), 113–20.

VAN TASSEL, DENNIE. *Program Style, Design, Efficiency, Debugging and Testing*. Englewood Cliffs, N.J.: Prentice Hall, 1978. Note: 2nd edition.

VINCENT, JAMES, ALBERT WATERS, and JOHN SINCLAIR. *Software Quality Assurance Volume I: Practice and Implementation*. Englewood Cliffs, N.J.: Prentice Hall, 1988.

VINCENT, JAMES, ALBERT WATERS, and JOHN SINCLAIR. *Software Quality Assurance Volume II: A Program Guide*. Englewood Cliffs, N.J.: Prentice Hall, 1988.

VOAS, J., L. MORREL, and K. MILLER. "Predicting Where Faults Can Hide from Testing." *IEEE Software*, 8, no. 2 (March 1991), 41–48.

WALDSTEIN, NANCY S. *The Walk-Thru: A Method of Specification, Design and Code Review*. Poughkeepsie, N.Y.: IBM System Development Division, 1974. Note: TR-00–2536.

WALLACE, DOLORES R., and ROGER U. FUJII. "Software Verification and Validation: An Overview." *IEEE Software* (May 1989), 10–17.

WALLACE, DOLORES R., and R. U. FUJII. *Software Verification and Validation: Its Role in Computer Assurance and Its Relationship with Software Project-Management Standards*. Gaitherburg, MD: NIST Special Pub., National Institute of Standards and Technology, 1989.

WARD, WILLIAM T. "Software Defect Prevention Using McCabes Complexity Metric." *Hewlett-Packard Journal* (April 1989), 64–68.

WARNER, C. D., JR. *Evaluation of Program Testing. Report TR-00.1173*. IBM Data Systems Division Development Laboratories; Poughkeepsie, NY, 1964.

WARNIER, J. D. *Logical Construction Of Programs*. New York: Van Nostrand Reinhold, 1976.

WEINBERG, GERALD. *The Psychology of Computer Programming.* New York: Van Nostrand Reinhold, 1971.

WEINBERG, GERALD, and DANIEL FREEDMAN. *Handbook of Walkthroughs and Inspections.* Boston, MA: Little, Brown, 1982.

WESTLEY, ANNE, ed. *Software Testing.* Berkshire, UK: Infotech, 1979; ISBN: 286 pp. Note: Eighteen papers on testing.

WEYUKER, ELAINE J. "On Testing Non-Testable Programs." *Computer Journal,* 25, no. 4 (November 1982), 465–70. Note: What is right?

WEYUKER, ELAINE J. "The Evaluation of Program-Based Software Test Data Adequacy Criteria." *Communications of the ACM* (June 1988).

WEYUKER, ELAINE J. "An Empirical Study of Data Flow Testing." *Proceedings of the Second Annual Workshop on Software Testing, Analysis, and Verification.* Banff, Canada, 1988.

WEYUKER, ELAINE J., and TOM J. OSTRAND. "Theories of Program Testing and the Applications of Revealing Subdomains." *Software Engineering,* SE-6, no. 3 (May 1980), 236–46. Note: Domain testing.

WHITE, L. J., and E. I. COHEN. "A Domain Strategy for Computer Program Testing." *Software Engineering,* SE-6, no. 3 (May 1980), 247–57. Note: Domain testing.

WOODFIELD, S. N., D. W. EMBLEY, AND D. T. SCOTT. "Can Programmers Reuse Software?" *IEEE Software,* 4, no. 4 (1987), 52–59.

WOODFIELD, S. N., V. Y. SHEN, and H. E. DUNSMORE. "A Study of Several Metrics for Programming Effort." *Journal of Systems & Software,* 2 (1981), 97–103.

WOODWARD, M. R., et al. "Experience with Path Analysis and Testing of Programs." *Software Engineering,* SE-6, no. 3 (May 1980), pp. 278–85.

XI-AN, ZHU, and MELVIN A. BREUER. "A Knowledge-Based System for Selecting Test Methodologies." *IEEE Design and Test of Computers,* 5, no. 5 (October 1988), 44–59.

YEH, R. T., ed. *Current Trends in Programming Methodology, Volume 11, Program Validation.* Englewood Cliffs, N.J.: Prentice Hall, 1977.

YIN, B. H., and J. W. WINCHESTER. "The Establishment and Use of Measures to Evaluate the Quality of Software Designs." *Proc. Software Quality Assurance Workshop* (1978), 45–52.

YOURDON, EDWARD, and LARRY CONSTANTINE. *Structured Design: Fundamentals of Computer Program and Systems Design.* Englewood Cliffs, N.J.: Prentice Hall, 1979.

YOURDON, EDWARD. "The Decline and Fall of the American Programmer." *American Programmer,* 1, no. 1 (March 1988), 1–8.

YOURDON, EDWARD. "The Decline and Fall of the American Programmer, part 3." *American Programmer,* 1, no. 3 (May 1988), 1–2.

YOURDON, EDWARD. "The Decline and Fall Continues." *American Programmer,* 1, no. 6 (August 1988), 1–3.

YOURDON, EDWARD. *Structured Walk-Throughs, 4ed.* New Jersey: Yourdon Press Computing Series, Prentice Hall, 1989.

ZUALKERMAN, I., W. TSAI, and D. VOLOVIK. "Expert Systems and Software Engineering: Ready for Marriage?" *IEEE Expert,* 1, no. 4 (Winter 1986), 24–31.

Appendix B:

Journals, Magazines, and Newsletters That Are Software Testing Resources

JOURNALS, MAGAZINES, AND NEWSLETTERS THAT ARE SOFTWARE TESTING RESOURCES

This is a noncomprehensive list of publications that periodically include articles on software testing. It is compiled from past, and current, personal usage of these journals, magazines, and newsletters as sources for consulting, training, and academic purposes. The majority are available in the School of Technology and Information Management (STIM) Library located in Room 230 Prince Hall on the campus of Washington University in St. Louis, Missouri. The library is open to the public and its use is encouraged.

STIM Library has over 400 subscriptions to information systems and data processing periodicals focusing on management information systems and computer-integrated manufacturing, and over 5,000 volumes in related areas. The library has substantial holdings in the specific areas of computer-aided software engineering and artificial intelligence.

The facility uses state of the art CD ROM *Computer Select*, a data base of over 140 computer-related journals, hardware and software information and company profiles, available via Local Area Network. Retrieved information can be printed or downloaded electronically to patrons' disks. This system also has access to *Current Contents* online, a keyword-searchable data base providing bibliographic access to several thousand recently published technology journals. The network also allows access to other private and public libraries. The services offered include research consultation, referrals to other collections, telephone reference work, and other miscellaneous services.

Anyone wishing to use the library may do so simply by contacting the Librarian at 314-935-5366. Many of the services that are available do not require physical proximity with the library to use. The results of the various services can be mailed, express mailed, or faxed throughout the world. The STIM Library is not for profit and any charges associated with services are only to cover the direct costs incurred.

ACM Computer Surveys. Association for Computing Machinery, 11 West 42 Street, New York, NY 10036.

ACM Software Engineering Notes. Association for Computing Machinery, 11 West 42nd Street, New York, NY 10036.

ACM Transactions on Software Engineering and Methodology. Association for Computing Machinery, 11 West 42nd Street, New York, NY 10036.

American Programmer, Inc., 161 West 86th Street, New York, NY 10024-3411.

AT&T Technical Journal. AT&T Bell Laboratories, Circulation Group, Room 1B-413, 101 J. F. Kennedy Pkwy., Short Hills, NJ 07078-0905.

Business Software Review. P.O. Box 40946, Indianapolis, IN 46240.

Communications of the ACM. Association for Computing Machinery, 11 West 42 Street, New York, NY 10036.

Computer. IEEE Computer Society, 10662 Los Vaqueros Circle, P.O. Box 3014, Los Alamitos, CA 90720-1264.

Computer Journal. Cambridge University Press, 32 East 57th Street, New York, NY 10022.

Computer Language. Miller Freeman Publications, 600 Harrison Street, San Francisco, CA 94107.

Computer Weekly. Reed Business Publishing, Ltd., Quadrant House, The Quadrant, Sutton, Surrey SM2 5AS, England.

Computing Canada. Plesman Publishing, Ltd., 2005 Sheppard Ave. E., Suite 400, Willowdale, ONT M2J 5B1, Canada.

Datamation. A Cahners-Ziff Publishing Associates, P.O. Box 17162, Denver, CO 80217.

Digital Review. 44 Cook St., Denver, CO 80206-5800.

Hewlett-Packard Journal. 3200 Hillview Ave., Palo Alto, CA 94304.

IEEE Software Engineering Journal. Institution of Electrical Engineers and British Computer Society, Michael Faraday House, Six Hills Way, Sevenage, Herts SG1 2ay, UK.

IEEE Transactions on Software Engineering. Institute of Electrical and Electronics Engineers, 345 East 47th Street, New York, NY 10017.

IBM Systems Journal. International Business Machines Corp., Armonk, NY 10504.

InfoWorld. 1060 Marsh Rd., Menlo Park, CA 94025.

ITEA Journal of Test and Evaluation. International Test and Evaluation Association, 4400 Fair Lakes Court, Fairfax, VA 22033.

Journal of Information Systems Management. Auerbach Publishers, 210 South Street, Boston, MA 02111.

Journal of Management Information Systems. M. E. Sharpe, Inc., 80 Business Park Dr., Armonk, NY 10504.

Journal of Object-Oriented Programming. SIGS Publications, Inc., 588 Broadway, Suite 604, New York, NY 10012.

Journal of Systems and Software. Elsevier Science Publishing Co., 52 Vanderbilt Ave., New York, NY 10017.

Journal of Systems Management. ASM, 1433 West Bagley Rd., P.O. Box 38370, Cleveland, OH 44138.

PC Week. P.O. Box 1770, Riverton, NJ 08077-7370.

Software Engineering: Tools, Techniques, Practice. Auerbach Publishers, One Penn Plaza, New York, NY 10119.

Software Magazine (formerly *Software News*). 1900 West Park Dr., Westborough Office Park, MA 01581.

Software Maintenance News. 56 Bay St., Suite 400, Staten Island, New York, NY 10301.

Software—Practice and Experience. John Wiley & Sons, Ltd., Baffins Lane, Chichester, Sussex, po 19 lud, UK.

Software Quality World. ProQual, P.O. Box 337, Medfield, MA 02052.

Software World. A. P. Publications, Ltd., 351 City Road, London, EC 1U 1LR.

System Development. Applied Computer Research, Inc., P.O. Box 82266, Phoenix, AZ 85071-2266.

Testing Techniques Newsletter. Software Research, Inc. 625 Third Street, San Francisco, CA 94107-1441.

The Center for the Study of Data Processing Working Paper Series. CSDP, Campus Box 1141, Washington University, One Brookings Dr., St. Louis, MO 63130.

The Journal of the Quality Assurance Institute. Quality Assurance Institute, 7575 Dr. Philips Blvd., Suite 350, Orlando, FL 32819.

The Letter T. Programming Environments, Inc., 4043 State Highway 33, Tinton Falls, NJ 07753.

The Outlook. McCabe & Associates, 5501 Twin Knolls Rd., Suite 111, Columbia, MD 21045.

Appendix C:

The Hardware Tracking System Test Plan

TEST PLAN

Hardware Tracking System

Revail McCall, Perry Pinkley, Annie R. Purnell,
Kim Slater, Dave Zumbro

Contents

1. *INTRODUCTION*

1.1. System Description

    1.1.1. System Components
    1.1.2. System Environment

1.2. Testing Objectives

1.3. Testing Methods

1.4. Supporting Documents

2. OVERALL PLAN

2.1. Schedule

2.2. Budget

2.3. Test Plans

>   *2.3.1. Test Case Specifications*
>   *2.3.2. Test Run Binder*
>   *2.3.3. Discrepancy Reports*

2.4. Criteria

>   *2.4.1. Entry Criteria*
>   *2.4.2. Exit Criteria*

3. TESTING REQUIREMENTS

3.1. Hardware

3.2. Software

3.3. Testing Personnel

4. PROCEDURE CONTROL

4.1. Test Initiation

4.2. Test Failure

4.3. Risk and Contingencies

4.4. Change Control

4.5. Test Execution

4.6. Document Control

5. UNIT TEST PLAN—EQUIPMENT TABLE MAINTENANCE MODULE—HT0010

5.1. Objectives

5.2. Method

5.3. BASIS test analysis

5.4. Milestone

5.5. Requirements

5.6. Criteria

5.7. Resulting Test Materials

5.8. Execution Control

APPENDIX A. HARDWARE TRACKING SYSTEM MODULES

Figure 1.   Main Menu Module

Figure 2.   Maintenance Module

Figure 3.   Interactive Menu Module

Figure 4.   Batch Report Menu Module

APPENDIX B. DATABASE STRUCTURE AND ELEMENTS

Figure 5.   Data Base Structure

Figure 6.   Data Base Elements

APPENDIX C. TESTING SCHEDULE

Figure 7.   Testing Schedule for Module HT0010

APPENDIX D. TEST CASE DOCUMENTS

APPENDIX E. WALK-THROUGH REPORT

APPENDIX F. CHANGE CONTROL FORM

APPENDIX G. DECISION TABLES

Figure 8.   HT0010 Decision Table—Screen HT00101

Figure 9.   HT0010 Decision Table—Screen HT00102

APPENDIX H. CONTROL FLOW GRAPHS

Figure 10.   Control Flow Graph—Module HT0010—Screen HT00101

Figure 11.   Control Flow Graph—Module HT0010—Screen HT00102

APPENDIX I. TEST SCRIPT FOR UNIT TEST—HT0010

APPENDIX J. TEST CASE CONDUCT RESULTS

APPENDIX K. HTS SPECIFICATIONS FOR MODULE— HT0010

APPENDIX L. HTS SOURCE LISTING FOR MODULE— HT0010

1. INTRODUCTION

1.1. System Description

The *Hardware Tracking System* (HTS) is an on-line, menu driven system developed in COBOL, utilizing IBM's SQL/DS relational database product and ISPF Dialog Manager, and is operated in an IBM environment for all Forrest Ford Consultants, Inc (FFCI) offices. Refer to appendix A, figures 1–4, for a module hierarchy chart depicting the organization of the system. The HTS tracks hardware and allows flexibility of the following functions:

- entering new equipment
- changing existing equipment
- deleting inactive equipment
- viewing information
- printing reports

1.1.1. System Components. The components involved are module hierarchy chart, SQL/DS relational database, dialog manager, and COBOL table maintenance and reporting modules.
Information found in these tables are as follows:

- Equipment table: provides information about equipment purchase and location.
- Failure table: provides information about the tracking of equipment problem.
- Service contract table: provides information about the service contract and point-of-contact.
- Contractor's table: provides information about the contractor.
- Software table: provides information about the software license and point-of-contact.

For more detailed information, see figures 5 and 6 in appendix B.

1.1.2. System Environment.   This system is designed to be a single user system for an office complex of 50 people. All problems will be reported to the corporate system coordinator who will detect resolution and dispatch service calls as needed. Batch reports will be run on a weekly basis while on-line reports will be run when required. Development, system testing, and production/implementation will be generated at the same site.

1.2. Testing Objectives

The testing objectives of the HTS test plan are to ensure:

- Each test case will detect as many errors as possible early in the development process.
- Regression testing will be used to restore quality after the debugging of discovered errors.
- All user and system specifications are met.
- The correct, as well as incorrect, responses have been tested. The cause of the incorrect response(s) will be debugged and any resolution documented.
- The system is always responding with current or updated information.
- The system responds in a timely manner.

1.3. Testing Methods

The methods used during the various levels of testing are:

Testing Level	Testing Method
Documentation	Walk-through
	Inspection
Unit	Walk-through
	Inspection
	Decision Table
	Basis Analysis
System	Objectives/Requirements Test

1.4. Supporting Documents

All attachments used to support this project are illustrated in the appendices.

2. OVERALL PLAN

2.1. Schedule

The testing process is scheduled to begin August 6, 1990 and is estimated to take seven days for completion. The layout of the schedule is detailed in appendix C.

2.2. Budget

The overall development time is expected to be 600 man-hours, with approximately 27% (or 160 man-hours) allocated to testing. Using Forrest Ford's standard billing rate of $40.00 per hour, the cost estimate for testing is $6,400.00. Supplies and/or any other materials are expected to come from in-house facilities and are not included in this cost estimate.

2.3. Test Plans

The Hardware Tracking System Test Plan consists of two types of test plans: a unit test plan for each HTS unit (module), and a HTS system test plan. A Unit Test Plan will be written for each of the following units:[1]
Table Maintenance Module

- The Table Maintenance Menu
- The Equipment Table Maintenance Menu
- The Service Contract Table Maintenance Menu
- The Contractors Table Maintenance Menu
- The Failure Table Maintenance Menu
- The Software Table Maintenance Menu

The Interactive Display Module

- The Interactive Display Menu
- The Interactive Display Equipment List By Type Program
- The Interactive Display Software By Type Program
- The Interactive Display Failure by Serial Number Program
- The Interactive Display Equipment List By Assignment Program
- The Interactive Display Software Assigned By Serial Number

---

[1] However for the purposes of this term project only module HT0010 has been included and unit tested.

- The Interactive Display Failure By Date and Time Program
- The Interactive Display Convert Service Contracts Program
- The Interactive Display Service Contracts By Contractor Program
- The Interactive Display Service Contracts By Expiration Date Program

The Batch Reports Module

- The Batch Reports Menu
- The Batch Reports Equipment List By Type Program
- The Batch Reports Software By Type Program
- The Batch Reports Failure by Serial Number Program
- The Batch Reports Equipment List By Assignment Program
- The Batch Reports Software Assigned By Serial Number
- The Batch Reports Failure By Date and Time Program
- The Batch Reports Convert Service Contracts Program
- The Batch Reports Service Contracts By Contractor Program
- The Batch Reports Service Contracts By Expiration Date Program

The System Test Plan tests the integration of all HTS units.[1]

2.3.1. Test Case Specifications.   The test cases for both unit and system level testing have been created using white box testing methods. Various testing techniques have been used to derive a set of test cases that will test a selected subset of all input and output conditions, and independent paths. A Test Case Description form will be completed for each test case. See appendix D for an example of the Test Case Description form and other test case documents. Test cases will be reviewed by members of the test team not involved with the creation of that test case.

Test case input and expected output will be selected by the test team and made available as part of the test execution script.

2.3.2. Test Run Binder.   A test run binder will be maintained throughout the test execution process. This binder will contain all test plans, test case results, discrepancy reports, regression test results, corrective action procedures, and any additional testing activities or documentation generated by this test plan.

---

[1] Again for the purposes of this term project no system test is included—only module HT0010.

2.3.3. Discrepancy Reports.   Whenever a test case execution results in unexpected output, a Discrepancy Report form must be completed. This form will detail the actual input and output, the expected output, and the discrepancy. An example of this form is in appendix D. These forms will be used in determining regression testing.

2.4. Criteria

2.4.1. Entry Criteria.   Test execution will begin after the following criteria are met.

- Completion of a code walk-through for that module.
- Code completion for that module.
- Test cases developed and approved for that module.
- Unit Test Plan developed and approved for that module.
- System Test execution can begin after the individual units to be integrated are successfully unit tested.

2.4.2. Exit Criteria.   Test execution can be terminated when all tests conducts fail to generate any additional errors.

3. TESTING REQUIREMENTS

3.1. Hardware

IBM 9370 CPU (initially running as a single user machine) with 4 × 855 MB disk storage drives, accessed using IBM 3178 compatible terminals. Batch reporting will be accomplished using an IBM 3812 page printer. This equipment is currently installed and operational, and is available on an as needed basis.

3.2. Software

IBM's VM/CMS operating system will be used to run the testing environment which will include IBM's SQL/DS relational database product, ISPF Dialog Manager, and COBOL programming language. All software is currently installed and operational on the target testing environment.

3.3. Testing Personnel

Mike DeWoskin and Susan Ammerman, programmers acting also as test specialists, will comprise the testing team. Bob Putnam, the project leader, will act as the test team leader.

4. PROCEDURE CONTROL

This section provides some guidelines and considerations for those individuals involved in testing of the HTS. Consideration is given to guidelines and/or activities that must be adhered to during test initiation, execution, and failure, formal change control, and document control. All tests activities will be conducted by a test specialist.

4.1. Test Initiation

Prior to commencement of testing the HTS, the test specialist must ensure:

- First and foremost, that there has been the successful completion of a comprehensive Test Readiness Review (TRR). The objective of this review is to ensure that everything is in order for testing and, in so far as possible, that the test will succeed. All changes to the design, code and test should be reviewed. The meeting will include a test technical overview presentation, review of the test documentation status, and identification of test limitation, if any.
- In addition, any open discrepancy report(s) and their impact(s) should have been resolved.
- Any code revisions have been incorporated in the baseline document.
- That requirement/specifications are "frozen" (subject to formal change control).
- A clean compile of the program (or module) that has been accepted at a walk-through and are available and ready for testing, i.e., the programmer must be able to demonstrate (before passing to the test specialist) that:
    1. The test cases created by the programmer have been executed;
    2. The expected results of those test cases have been successfully achieved.
- That scripts (step-by-step of testing conduct) are complete and ready for execution.
- Data for data base has been initialized with representative and operational values and loaded into the test data base identical to the real data base.
- That the hardware/software test resources (e.g., mainframe time) have been scheduled.
- All needed hardware and software support required to run the tests, in accordance with the test schedule, are available.
- Sufficient disk space is provided to permit execution of test cases.

4.2. Test Failure

Some problems are so severe that testing cannot be reasonably continued until they are resolved. If an abnormal termination occurs or the results are not as expected during the test, a Discrepancy Report (DR) will be generated and will be graded as follows:

Priority A — major defect or deficiency in design software or hardware impacting all operations.

Priority B — restricts specific further testing in a given test case. This defect also impacts the next level of testing and requires a fix. Any DRs will require rerun (regression) of the test after all identified discrepancies have been resolved.

Priority C — testing can continue but with limitations.

Priority D — fix before transition to operational status. Any DRs will be resolved prior to the start of the next level of testing.

Whenever errors are identified and corrected, regression testing will be conducted to verify that the hardware and/or software has been corrected. Revisions to system code resulting from change control sometime requires modification to test cases and test data prior to regression testing. This involves re-testing the modified area, beginning with program testing stage by stage up to the current stage, using the same test cases as previously used.

Regression testing will be performed in groups rather than individually in order to avoid redundant test for multiple changes or correction which re-tested a single area of the system.

Regression testing will be the responsibility of the same individuals as originally assigned to the initial test.

Regression test will prove:

1. The modification identified and corrected was made correctly.
2. Any changes made did not create another error in the area of the modification.

4.3. Risk and Contingencies

System testing is difficult, time consuming and the risks of not meeting deadlines is high. In the event of unforeseen problems that may impact schedules, the following contingencies will be initiated.

- If the test uncovers more errors than expected, then a full time person will be assigned to perform debugging.
- If it is difficult to obtain sufficient computer time during the day-time, then testing will be scheduled at night.
- If an end user or other person who is assigned to the test team is not available on a full time basis, then another individual who can also be part of the test team will be identified.

4.4. Change Control

As software evolves during the development cycle, it assumes various forms and each form will be controlled to achieve and keep an understanding of the software objectives among all personnel. Changes to baseline documents must first be communicated to the programmer via the Change Control form (see appendix F). The programmer investigates the proposed change(s). If the recommendation is accepted, then it must be submitted to the Project Leader for approval. If the change is rejected by the programmer, the current baseline document remains unchanged and the change is marked as closed.

The investigator may put the change into either of the first 2 of the following three change control categories:

Level III—Informal change control—Changes which correct errors in computer program or documentation and which do not affect the "function" of a baseline are informal changes. The individual software engineer is free to change code until it passes unit test. The unit test is then ready for integration with other units and informal change control shifts to the group software engineer who is responsible for compatible change control within the existing baseline. During informal change control, the coder should, however, keep good documentation making sure it is current or up to date with his code. Some changes may affect other functional groups and changes should be controlled by the change control committee even though there is no baseline change.

Level II—When baseline changes are necessary during development, the change control committee still controls the changes but the customer's concurrence is also required.

Level I—Customer directed change.

4.5. Test Execution

Prior to execution of test cases, obtain a pre-dump of the data bases. After completion of the test conduct, obtain a post-dump to make sure the input produces the expected output. Also during execution the test specialist will obtain a screen print of all screens during the test conduct to be used during data analysis.

4.6. Document Control

Walk-throughs will be used to review and sign off all documentation produced, as well as results during the test.

Because of the importance of maintaining test cases, data and plans, these items must be kept and maintained over the lifetime of the system in the Test Run Binder. Test documentation will be updated along with other documentation each time a change is made to the software. This simplifies the maintenance programmer's task when changes must be made and tested.

5. UNIT TEST PLAN—EQUIPMENT TABLE MAINTENANCE MODULE—HT0010

5.1. Objectives

This is a program level test of the Equipment Table Maintenance module. For clarity and definition, a single COBOL program is declared to be a unit. As all tests for this system will be at the program level, the procedures should not be radically different from the other units that are to be tested. The equipment table maintenance program has two screens (HT00101 and HT00102) to add, change and delete equipment from the driver table. The tests will exercise the program's fault tolerance, the valid/invalid codes returned, and the edit checking of each field as follows:

The serial number can only be entered on the first screen, HT00101. It should be a protected required field on subsequent screens. Duplicate serial numbers are not allowed. Valid first screen options are

A for an add,
C for an change,
D for a delete, and
PF3 to exit.

If an add is requested, the serial number cannot previously exist on the equipment table. Conversely, a change or delete must specify a serial number that has previously been "added" before it can be changed. If the serial number and option combination are validated, the second screen (HT00102) is presented with all of the row fields represented for validation. Verify that the serial number is a protected field on this screen and that the following edits apply:

TYPE	—Required field. Describes the piece of equipment being logged. Must not be spaces.
BRANCH	—Required field. Identifies the Forrest Ford branch where the equipment is located. Must not be spaces.
DEPARTMENT	—Optional field. Identifies departmental responsibility for the equipment. No validation.
LOCATION	—Optional field. Physical location of the equipment. No validation.
VENDOR	—Required field. Identifies the sales institution to be referenced when there are problems with the equipment. Must not be spaces.
MANUFACTURER	—Optional field. Identifies the carrier of the warranty for the equipment. No validation.
PURCHASE DATE	—Optional field. Must be a valid date if entered.
COST	—Optional field. Must be numeric with 2 implied decimals if entered.
CONTRACT NUMBER	—Optional. Must match a contract number on the service contract table.

5.2. Method

The validation of the data fields on both screens will be tested according to the previous field requirements as well as the following:

- Every error encountered should display an appropriate error message.
- After a function is completed, all fields should be blanked out to avoid data carryover to the next record.

Test case generation will be derived from a variety of methods including basis and decision table tests. The resulting test cases are described based on their diagrams. Redundant test cases will be eliminated.

5.3. BASIS Test Analysis

See appendices G and H for the decision tables and basis test diagrams.

5.4. Milestone

This program module is the cornerstone to the system functioning as specified. As such it should be tested as soon as possible after the contractor and service contract modules are tested. They will supply input validation for this module and should be in place first.

Testing of this program should take no more than 4 hours with documented results being returned in less than 8 hours. Error correction will be completed within 1 day and regression testing will begin the following day.

5.5. Requirements

Testing hardware for this module is the same as for system implementation.

Program modules will be cleanly compiled and menu systems will be in place and tested prior to execution of program modules. Test case data will be entered online into the appropriate fields by the tester as this is primarily an online system.

Test case analysis and development is being done by Perry Pinkley.

Test case review will be done by Revail McCall, Annie Purnell, Kim Slater, and Dave Zumbro.

Testing will be done by Mike DeWoskin and Susan Ammerman.

Results will be recorded by the development team leader Bob Putnam.

5.6. Criteria

A walk-through of the program code must be completed by the testing team prior to physical execution of the test cases in order to eliminate some obvious trouble spots.

Program modules will be locked down prior to testing to ensure only authorized changes are allowed in after testing.

The test plan must be approved prior to execution.

Testing will be exited only when all test cases generate a negative response (i.e., show no additional errors).

5.7. Resulting Test Materials

Test results will be recorded with screen print images of the test execution and hand recorded test control documents. See appendix J.

5.8. Execution Control

Test initiation is to be done by following the script provided in appendix I.

Deviations from the test procedures are to be authorized by the team leader and full documentation of such deviations will be required.

No variance of response from the expected results is to be ignored.

APPENDIX A. HARDWARE TRACKING SYSTEM MODULES

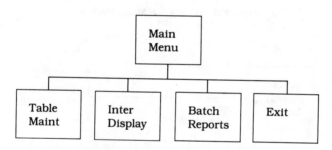

Figure 1   Main Menu Module

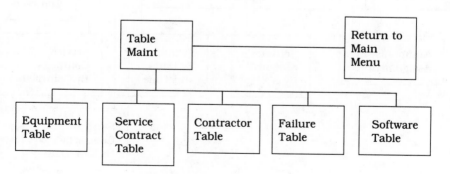

Figure 2   Maintenance Module

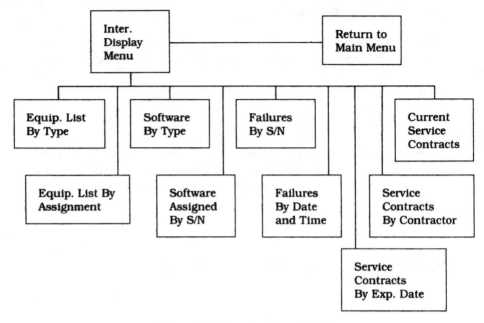

Figure 3   Interactive Menu Module

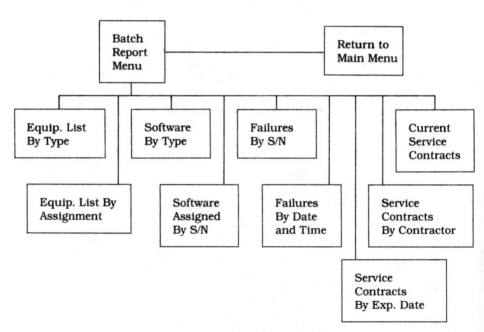

Figure 4   Batch Report Menu Module

APPENDIX B. DATABASE STRUCTURE AND ELEMENTS

EQUIP
Equipment
purchase and
location
information

FAIL
Equipment
problem
tracking
information

SERCONT
Service
Contract and
contract
information

CONTRACTOR
Hardware
Contractor
name and
address

SOFTWARE
Software
license and
contract
information

Figure 5   Database Structure

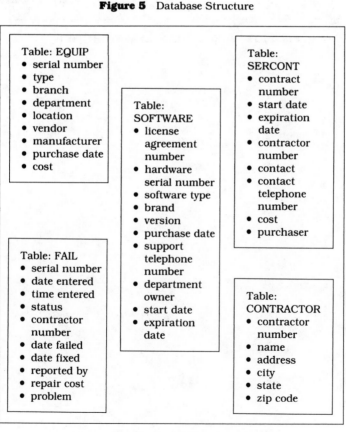

Table: EQUIP
• serial number
• type
• branch
• department
• location
• vendor
• manufacturer
• purchase date
• cost

Table:
SOFTWARE
• license
  agreement
  number
• hardware
  serial number
• software type
• brand
• version
• purchase date
• support
  telephone
  number
• department
  owner
• start date
• expiration
  date

Table:
SERCONT
• contract
  number
• start date
• expiration
  date
• contractor
  number
• contact
• contact
  telephone
  number
• cost
• purchaser

Table: FAIL
• serial number
• date entered
• time entered
• status
• contractor
  number
• date failed
• date fixed
• reported by
• repair cost
• problem

Table:
CONTRACTOR
• contractor
  number
• name
• address
• city
• state
• zip code

Figure 6   Database Elements

APPENDIX C. TESTING SCHEDULE

DAY	1	2	3	4	5	6	7
	2 4 6 8	2 4 6 8	2 4 6 8	2 4 6 8	2 4 6 8	2 4 6 8	2 4 6 8
Table Maintenance Module Unit Test	▬▬						
Interactive Display Module Unit Test			▬▬▬				
Hardware Tracking System Test					▬▬▬		
HTS System Test							▬

Figure 7   Testing Schedule for Module HT0010

APPENDIX D. TEST CASE DOCUMENTS

Test Case Description

Test Case Description No.: _____

Date: _____

Program Name: _____

Testing State: _____

Test Number: _____

Test Case Prepared by: _____

Test Administrator: _____

Discrepancy Report Number(s) (if any): _____

Expected Results:

Actual Results:

Test Case Results

Test Case No.: _____

Date: _____

Program Name: _____

Module Under Test: _____

Testing Level: _____

Difference between actual and expected output:

Discrepancy Report

Discrepancy Report Number: _____

Date: _____

Priority: _____

Program Name: _____

Testing Level: _____

Module Under Test: _____

Discrepancy:

APPENDIX E. WALK-THROUGH REPORT

Walk-through Report No.: _____

Coordinator: _____Project: _____

Segment for Review: _____

Coordinator's Checklist:

   1. Confirm with developer that material is ready and stable _____

   2. Issue invitations, assign responsibilities, distribute materials

Date: _____ Time: _____ Duration: _____

Place: _____

Responsibilities	Participants	Can Attend	Received Materials
_____	_____	____	____
_____	_____	____	____
_____	_____	____	____
_____	_____	____	____
_____	_____	____	____

Agenda:

_____1. All participants agree to follow the same set of rules.

_____2. New segment: walk-through of material.

_____   Old segment: item-by-item check off of previous action list.

_____3. Creation of new action list.

_____4. Group decision.

_____5. Deliver copy of this form to project management.

Decision: _____Accept product as is

_____Revise—no further walk-through

_____Revise and schedule another walk-through

Signatures _____   _____

_____   _____

_____   _____

_____   _____

_____   _____

APPENDIX F. CHANGE CONTROL FORM

Change Control No.: _____ Date Issued: _____ Page No.: _____

Date Assigned: _____

Program Changed: Title: _____

Identification no.: _____

Rev.: _____

Discrepancy Report Number(s) Incorporated: _____

_____

Description of Change(s):

Source Code Change(s):

Document Change(s):

Change(s) Prepared by: _____ Date: _____

        Approved by: _____ Date: _____

Change(s) Tested by: _____ Date: _____

        Approved by: _____ Date: _____

Software Library Updated by: _____ Date: _____

APPENDIX G. DECISION TABLES

Hardware Tracking System							
Module HT0010 Decision Table—Screen HT00101							
Serial Number	Non-Blank						Blank
SQL Code	Zero			100		Other	
Option	C	D	~2	~3	A	~4	~8
Error Msg			X	X		X	X
Change	X						
Add					X		
Delete		X					

Figure 8   HT0010 Decision Table—Screen HT00101

Hardware Tracking System					
Screen HT00102—Second screen Validation Tests					
Serial Number	Blank	Not Blank			
Type		Blank	Not Blank		
Branch			Blank	Not Blank	
Vendor	~4	~3	~2	Blank	Not Blank
Error Msg	X	X	X	X	
Update					X

Figure 9   HT0010 Decision Table—Screen HT00102

APPENDIX H. CONTROL FLOW GRAPHS

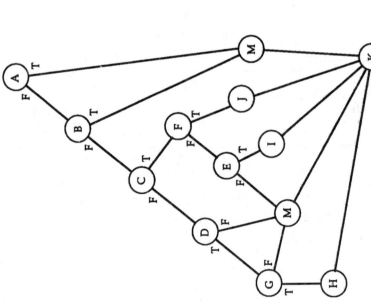

A = Serial Number Blank
B = Option Blank
C = SQL rc = 0
D = SQL rc = 100
E = Option = "C"
F = Option = "D"
G = Option = "A"
H = Second Screen – Perform "Add" operations
I = Second Screen – Perform "Change" operations
J = Second Screen – Perform "Delete" operations

K = Exit
M = Error Message

Module Complexity

7 Regions
13 Nodes
19 Edges

$$C = E - N + 2 = 8$$

or

$$C = R + 1 = 8$$

Basis Paths

1. ABCDGHK
2. ABCDGMK
3. ABCDMK
4. ABCFEMK
5. ABCFEIK
6. ABCFJK
7. ABMK
8. AMK

Figure 10 Control Flow Graph—Module HT0010—Screen HT00101

A = Serial Number blank
B = Type blank
C = Brand blank
D = Vendor blank
G = Update database

M = Error Message
K = Exit

Basis Paths

1. ABCDGK
2. ABCDGMK
3. ABCDMK
4. ABCMK
5. ABMK
6. AMK

Module Complexity

4 Regions
7 Nodes
10 Edges
$C = R + 1 = 5$
$C = E - N + 2 = 5$

Test Cases are:

S/N OPTION TYPE BRANCH VENDOR

1. ƀƀƀƀƀƀ A CPU STL IBM
2. SN-001 ƀ CPU STL IBM
3. SN-001 A CPU STL IBM
4. SN-002 C CPU STL IBM
5. SN-002 D CPU STL IBM
6. SN-001 A CPU STL IBM
7. SN-001 C CPU STL IBM
8. SN-001 D CPU STL IBM
9. SN-001 A ƀƀƀƀ STL IBM
10. SN-001 A CPU ƀƀƀ IBM
11. SN-001 A CPU STL ƀƀƀ

ƀ represents a blank or space

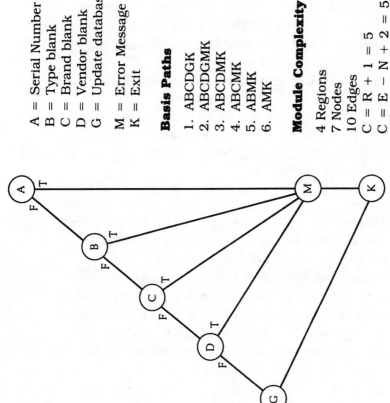

Figure 11 Control Flow Graph—Module HT0010—Screen HT00102

271

APPENDIX I. TEST SCRIPT FOR UNIT TEST—HT0010

1. Logon to IBM 9370 VM/CMS system using:
   - Id: CORPSYS
   - Password: CORPSYS
2. Initiate system by keying 'HTRACK' and depressing Enter.
3. The HTMAIN Menu should be displayed on your screen.
4. Key in a '1' and depress Enter.
5. The HTMENU1 Table Maintenance Screen should be displayed.
6. Enter a '1' and depress Enter.
7. The screen HT00101 Hardware Table Maintenance should be displayed.
8. Depress tab and enter the letter 'a' and depress Enter.
9. The message 'ENTER REQUIRED FIELD' should be displayed.
10. The cursor should be positioned on the Serial Number field.
11. Key in 'sn-001,' depress tab, key in a space and depress Enter.
12. The message 'ENTER REQUIRED FIELD' should be displayed.
13. The cursor should be positioned on the Option field.
14. Key in 'a' and depress Enter.
15. The screen HT00102 Hardware Tracking Maintenance should be displayed.
16. Key in 'cpu,' depress tab, key in 'stl' and depress tab.
17. Depress tab again, key in 'ibm' and depress Enter.
18. The message 'INSERT WAS SUCCESSFUL' and the HT00101 screen should be displayed.
19. Depress tab, key in 'sn-002,' depress tab, key in 'c' and depress Enter.
20. The message 'RECORD NOT FOUND' should be displayed.
21. The cursor should be located on the Serial Number field.
22. Depress tab, key in 'd' and depress Enter.
23. The message 'RECORD NOT FOUND' should be displayed.
24. The cursor should be positioned on the Serial Number field.
25. Key in 'sn-001,' depress tab, key in 'a' and depress Enter.
26. The message 'RECORD FOUND' should be displayed.
27. The cursor should be positioned on the Serial Number field.
28. Depress tab, key in 'c' and depress Enter.
29. The screen HT00102 should be displayed with the Serial Number protected and the cursor positioned on the Hardware Type field.
30. Depress Enter.

31. The screen HT00101 should be displayed with the message 'UP-DATE SUCCESSFUL' showing.

32. Depress tab, depress tab, key in 'd' and depress Enter.

33. Screen HT00102 should be displayed with the message 'CONFIRM DELETE' showing.

34. Depress Enter.

35. The screen HT00101 should be displayed with the message 'DELETE WAS SUCCESSFUL' showing.

36. Depress tab, depress tab, Key in 'a' and depress Enter.

37. The screen HT00102 should be displayed.

38. Depress tab, key in 'stl,' depress tab, depress tab, key in 'ibm' and depress Enter.

39. The message 'ENTER REQUIRED FIELD' should be displayed.

40. The cursor should be positioned on the Type field.

41. Key in 'cpu,' depress tab, key in 'bbb' and depress Enter.

42. The message 'ENTER REQUIRED FIELD' should be displayed.

43. The cursor should be positioned on the Branch field.

44. Key in 'stl,' depress tab, depress tab, key in 'bbb' and depress Enter.

45. The message 'ENTER REQUIRED FIELD' should be displayed.

46. The cursor should be positioned on the Vendor field.

47. Depress PF3.

48. The screen HT00101 should be displayed.

49. Depress PF3.

50. The screen HTMENU1 should be displayed.

51. Depress PF3.

52. The screen HTMAIN Hold should be displayed.

53. Depress PF3.

54. The VM screen should be displayed showing a 'READY.'

55. Key in 'logoff' and depress Enter.

56. 'Press Enter Or Clear Key To Continue' should be displayed.

57. Depress Enter.

58. Session is now terminated.

APPENDIX J. TEST CASE CONDUCT RESULTS

VIRTUAL MACHINE/SYSTEM PRODUCT

```
VV      VV   MM       MM                    SSSSSSS   PPPPPPP
VV      VV   MMM     MMM            //    // SS    SS  PP    PP
VV     VV    MMMM   MMMM           //    //  SS         PP    PP
 VV   VV     MM MM MM MM          //    //   SSSSSSS   PPPPPPP
  VV VV      MM  MMM  MM         //    //      SS      PP
   VVV       MM   M   MM        //    //       SS   SS PP
    V        MM       MM       //    //        SSSSSSS PP
                              //    //

(CD03)
```

```
LOGON CORPSYS
FILES: 001 RDR, 037 PRT, NO PUN
LOGON AT 14:36:36 CST SATURDAY 07/21/90
19E replaces Y (19E)
Y (19E) R/O
VM/SP REL 5 10/13/89 10:45
Shared Y-STAT not available
X (31A) R/O
CP SET PF13 RETRIEVE
CP LINK SQLDBA 195 195 rr
ACCESS 195 Q
```

```
Q (195) R/O
ACCESS 291 B
B (291) R/O
Ready; T=0.44/0.66 14:36:41

-------------------

HTMAIN          FORREST FORD CORPORATE SYSTEMS     DATE: 90/07/21
                   HARDWARE TRACKING SYSTEM        TIME: 14:37

COMMAND ==>           MAIN SELECTION MENU


                 1   TABLE MAINTENANCE MENU

                 2   INTERACTIVE DISPLAY MENU

                 3   BATCH REPORTING MENU


                 ENTER OPTION   OR   PF3 TO END
```

```
HTMAIN              FORREST FORD CORPORATE SYSTEMS         DATE: 90/07/21
                    HARDWARE TRACKING SYSTEM               TIME: 14:37

COMMAND ==> 1

                    MAIN SELECTION MENU

                    1  TABLE MAINTENANCE MENU

                    2  INTERACTIVE DISPLAY MENU

                    3  BATCH REPORTING MENU

                    ENTER OPTION  OR  PF3  TO  END
```

```
HTMENU1             FORREST FORD CORPORATE SYSTEMS         DATE: 90/07/21
                    HARDWARE TRACKING SYSTEM               TIME: 14:37

COMMAND ==> 1

                    TABLE MAINTENANCE

                    1  HARDWARE TABLE MAINTENANCE

                    2  SERVICE CONTRACT TABLE MAINTENANCE

                    3  CONTRACTOR TABLE MAINTENANCE
```

```
    4   FAILURE TABLE MAINTENANCE

    5   SOFTWARE TABLE MAINTENANCE

    6   HARDWARE FAILURE TYPE


ENTER OPTION   OR   PF3 TO END


------------------------

HT00101        FORREST FORD CORPORATE SYSTEMS        ENTER REQUIRED FIELD
                   HARDWARE TRACKING SYSTEM              TIME: 14:38

COMMAND ==>


          HARDWARE TABLE MAINTENANCE
                                      -----------

HARDWARE SERIAL NUMBER    -----------

          ENTER OPTION  A

                         A-   ADD
                         C-   CHANGE
                         D-   DELETE



                   PF3-TO EXIT
```

```
------------
HT00101          FORREST FORD CORPORATE SYSTEMS          ENTER REQUIRED FIELD
                    HARDWARE TRACKING SYSTEM                  TIME: 14:38

COMMAND ==>

                 HARDWARE TABLE MAINTENANCE

     HARDWARE SERIAL NUMBER      SN-001_____

              ENTER OPTION  _

                           A-  ADD
                           C-  CHANGE
                           D-  DELETE


                 PF3-TO EXIT
```

```
------------
HT00101          FORREST FORD CORPORATE SYSTEMS          ENTER REQUIRED FIELD
                    HARDWARE TRACKING SYSTEM                  TIME: 14:38

COMMAND ==>

                 HARDWARE TABLE MAINTENANCE

     HARDWARE SERIAL NUMBER      SN-001_____
```

```
ENTER OPTION  A

              A -    ADD
              C -    CHANGE
              D -    DELETE


              PF3-TO EXIT


----------------------------------------------

HT00102        FORREST FORD CORPORATE SYSTEMS      DATE: 90/07/21
                  HARDWARE TRACKING SYSTEM            TIME: 14:38

COMMAND ==>


           HARDWARE TABLE MAINTENANCE



SERIAL NUMBER: SN-001----------


HARDWARE TYPE: ----------           LOCATION:  ----------
BRANCH: ---    DEPARTMENT: ----------
VENDOR: ----------  MANUFACTURER: ----------
PURCHASE DATE: ----------   COST: ----------
CONTRACT NUMBER: ----------


              PF3-TO EXIT
```

279

```
------------------------
HT00102        FORREST FORD CORPORATE SYSTEMS        DATE: 90/07/21
                  HARDWARE TRACKING SYSTEM              TIME: 14:38

COMMAND ==>


                    HARDWARE TABLE MAINTENANCE


SERIAL NUMBER:  SN-001_____


HARDWARE TYPE:  cpu_____
BRANCH: stl     DEPARTMENT:_____         LOCATION: _____
VENDOR: ibm____   MANUFACTURER:_____   _____
PURCHASE DATE: _____   COST: _____
CONTRACT NUMBER: _____


                        PF3-TO EXIT
```

```
------------------------
HT00101        FORREST FORD CORPORATE SYSTEMS        INSERT WAS SUCCESSFUL
                  HARDWARE TRACKING SYSTEM              TIME: 14:38

COMMAND ==>


                    HARDWARE TABLE MAINTENANCE


            HARDWARE SERIAL NUMBER      SN-001_____
```

ENTER OPTION A

    A- ADD
    C- CHANGE
    D- DELETE

        PF3-TO EXIT

HT00101   FORREST FORD CORPORATE SYSTEMS   INSERT WAS SUCCESSFUL
                 HARDWARE TRACKING SYSTEM   TIME: 14:38

COMMAND ==>

     HARDWARE TABLE MAINTENANCE

HARDWARE SERIAL NUMBER   SN-002_____

     ENTER OPTION C

         A- ADD
         C- CHANGE
         D- DELETE

            PF3-TO EXIT

```
------------
HT00101              FORREST FORD CORPORATE SYSTEMS         RECORD NOT FOUND
                          HARDWARE TRACKING SYSTEM              TIME: 14:38
COMMAND ==>


              HARDWARE TABLE MAINTENANCE


        HARDWARE SERIAL NUMBER      SN-002_____

               ENTER OPTION  C

                              A-  ADD
                              C-  CHANGE
                              D-  DELETE


                         PF3-TO EXIT
```

```
------------
HT00101              FORREST FORD CORPORATE SYSTEMS         RECORD NOT FOUND
                          HARDWARE TRACKING SYSTEM              TIME: 14:38
COMMAND ==>


              HARDWARE TABLE MAINTENANCE


        HARDWARE SERIAL NUMBER      SN-002_____
```

ENTER OPTION D

     A- ADD
     C- CHANGE
     D- DELETE

PF3-TO EXIT

- - - - - - - - - - - - -

HT00101   FORREST FORD CORPORATE SYSTEMS   RECORD NOT FOUND
               HARDWARE TRACKING SYSTEM   TIME: 14:38

COMMAND ==>

HARDWARE TABLE MAINTENANCE

HARDWARE SERIAL NUMBER   SN-002_____

ENTER OPTION D

     A- ADD
     C- CHANGE
     D- DELETE

PF3-TO EXIT

```
------------------
HT00101           FORREST FORD CORPORATE SYSTEMS        RECORD NOT FOUND
                     HARDWARE TRACKING SYSTEM              TIME: 14:38
COMMAND ==>

            HARDWARE TABLE MAINTENANCE

       HARDWARE SERIAL NUMBER     SN-001_____

            ENTER OPTION  A

                        A-  ADD
                        C-  CHANGE
                        D-  DELETE


                     PF3-TO EXIT
```

```
------------------
HT00101           FORREST FORD CORPORATE SYSTEMS        RECORD FOUND
                     HARDWARE TRACKING SYSTEM              TIME: 14:38
COMMAND ==>

            HARDWARE TABLE MAINTENANCE

       HARDWARE SERIAL NUMBER     SN-001_____
```

ENTER OPTION C

    A- ADD
    C- CHANGE
    D- DELETE

PF3-TO EXIT

HT00102   FORREST FORD CORPORATE SYSTEMS   DATE: 90/07/21
                     HARDWARE TRACKING SYSTEM   TIME: 14:38

COMMAND ==>

HARDWARE TABLE MAINTENANCE

SERIAL NUMBER: SN-001_____

HARDWARE TYPE: CPU_____   LOCATION: _____
BRANCH: STL   DEPARTMENT: _____ MANUFACTURER: _____
VENDOR: IBM_____   MANUFACTURER: _____
PURCHASE DATE: 0001-01-01   COST: _____
CONTRACT NUMBER: _____

PF3-TO EXIT

```
---------------
HT00101          FORREST FORD CORPORATE SYSTEMS          UPDATE SUCCESSFUL
                    HARDWARE TRACKING SYSTEM                TIME: 14:38
COMMAND ==>

              HARDWARE TABLE MAINTENANCE

HARDWARE SERIAL NUMBER     SN-001--------

          ENTER OPTION   C

                    A-  ADD
                    C-  CHANGE
                    D-  DELETE


                   PF3-TO EXIT
```

```
---------------
HT00101          FORREST FORD CORPORATE SYSTEMS          UPDATE SUCCESSFUL
                    HARDWARE TRACKING SYSTEM                TIME: 14:38
COMMAND ==>

              HARDWARE TABLE MAINTENANCE

HARDWARE SERIAL NUMBER     SN-001--------
```

```
ENTER OPTION  D

              A-  ADD
              C-  CHANGE
              D-  DELETE


              PF3-TO EXIT
```

```
-----------
HT00102           FORREST FORD CORPORATE SYSTEMS        CONFIRM DELETE
                       HARDWARE TRACKING SYSTEM             TIME: 14:38

COMMAND ==>


                   HARDWARE TABLE MAINTENANCE


SERIAL NUMBER:  SN-001_____


HARDWARE TYPE:  CPU____
BRANCH:  STL    DEPARTMENT:  _____             LOCATION:  _____
VENDOR:  IBM____    MANUFACTURER:  _____
PURCHASE DATE:  0001-01-01    COST:  _____
CONTRACT NUMBER:  _____


              PF3-TO EXIT
```

```
--------------
HT00101                    FORREST FORD CORPORATE SYSTEMS          DELETE WAS SUCCESSFUL
                               HARDWARE TRACKING SYSTEM                 TIME: 14:38
COMMAND ==>


                   HARDWARE TABLE MAINTENANCE


                   HARDWARE SERIAL NUMBER      SN-001_____


                   ENTER OPTION  D


                                 A-   ADD
                                 C-   CHANGE
                                 D-   DELETE



                                 PF3-TO EXIT




--------------
HT00102                    FORREST FORD CORPORATE SYSTEMS          DATE: 90/07/21
                               HARDWARE TRACKING SYSTEM                 TIME: 14:38
COMMAND ==>


                   HARDWARE TABLE MAINTENANCE



SERIAL NUMBER:  SN-001_____
```

```
HARDWARE TYPE:  ------
BRANCH:  ---   DEPARTMENT: ----------   LOCATION: ----------
VENDOR:  ---   MANUFACTURER: ----------
PURCHASE DATE: ----------   COST: ----------
CONTRACT NUMBER: ----------

                        PF3-TO EXIT


HT00102        FORREST FORD CORPORATE SYSTEMS        DATE: 90/07/21
               HARDWARE TRACKING SYSTEM              TIME: 14:38

COMMAND ==>


                  HARDWARE TABLE MAINTENANCE


SERIAL NUMBER: SN-001----------

HARDWARE TYPE: ----------
BRANCH:  stl   DEPARTMENT: ----------   LOCATION: ----------
VENDOR:  ibm__ MANUFACTURER: ----------
PURCHASE DATE: ----------   COST: ----------
CONTRACT NUMBER: ----------

                        PF3-TO EXIT
```

```
------------------
HT00102          FORREST FORD CORPORATE SYSTEMS        ENTER REQUIRED FIELD
                     HARDWARE TRACKING SYSTEM               TIME: 14:38
COMMAND ==>

                     HARDWARE TABLE MAINTENANCE


SERIAL NUMBER:  SN-001----------

HARDWARE TYPE:  --------
BRANCH:  STL      DEPARTMENT: --------        LOCATION:  -----------
VENDOR:  IBM----  MANUFACTURER: --------
PURCHASE DATE: --------     COST:  --------
CONTRACT NUMBER:  -----------

                      PF3-TO EXIT
```

```
------------------
HT00102          FORREST FORD CORPORATE SYSTEMS        ENTER REQUIRED FIELD
                     HARDWARE TRACKING SYSTEM               TIME: 14:38
COMMAND ==>

                     HARDWARE TABLE MAINTENANCE


SERIAL NUMBER:  SN-001----------
```

```
HARDWARE TYPE: cpu_____          LOCATION: _____
BRANCH:  __    DEPARTMENT: _____
VENDOR:  IBM_____  MANUFACTURER:_____
PURCHASE DATE: _____      COST: _____
CONTRACT NUMBER: _____


                        PF3-TO EXIT
- - - - - - - - - - - - - - - - - -
HT00102       FORREST FORD CORPORATE SYSTEMS       ENTER REQUIRED FIELD
                   HARDWARE TRACKING SYSTEM              TIME: 14:38

COMMAND ==>

                   HARDWARE TABLE MAINTENANCE


SERIAL NUMBER: SN-001_____

HARDWARE TYPE: CPU_____          LOCATION: _____
BRANCH:  __    DEPARTMENT: _____
VENDOR:  IBM_____  MANUFACTURER:_____
PURCHASE DATE: _____      COST: _____
CONTRACT NUMBER: _____


                        PF3-TO EXIT
```

```
------------------------
HT00102        FORREST FORD CORPORATE SYSTEMS        ENTER REQUIRED FIELD
               HARDWARE TRACKING SYSTEM              TIME: 14:38
COMMAND ==>

               HARDWARE TABLE MAINTENANCE

SERIAL NUMBER: SN-001----------

HARDWARE TYPE: CPU----------                LOCATION: ----------
BRANCH: stl    DEPARTMENT: ----------
VENDOR: -----  MANUFACTURER: ----------  ----------
PURCHASE DATE: ----------  COST: ----------
CONTRACT NUMBER: ----------

                       PF3-TO EXIT
```

```
------------------------
HT00102        FORREST FORD CORPORATE SYSTEMS        ENTER REQUIRED FIELD
               HARDWARE TRACKING SYSTEM              TIME: 14:38
COMMAND ==>

               HARDWARE TABLE MAINTENANCE

SERIAL NUMBER: SN-001----------
```

```
HARDWARE TYPE: CPU_____                          LOCATION: _____
BRANCH: STL   DEPARTMENT: _____
VENDOR: _____    MANUFACTURER: _____
PURCHASE DATE: _____    COST: _____
CONTRACT NUMBER: _____


                            PF3-TO EXIT


HT00101        FORREST FORD CORPORATE SYSTEMS        DATE: 90/07/21
                  HARDWARE TRACKING SYSTEM                TIME: 14:38

COMMAND ==>

                   HARDWARE TABLE MAINTENANCE


HARDWARE SERIAL NUMBER    SN-001_____

          ENTER OPTION   A

                          A-  ADD
                          C-  CHANGE
                          D-  DELETE


                            PF3-TO EXIT
```

```
--------------
HTMENU1          FORREST FORD CORPORATE SYSTEMS       DATE: 90/07/21
                    HARDWARE TRACKING SYSTEM          TIME: 14:42
COMMAND ==>

                         TABLE MAINTENANCE

              1   HARDWARE TABLE MAINTENANCE

              2   SERVICE CONTRACT TABLE MAINTENANCE

              3   CONTRACTOR TABLE MAINTENANCE

              4   FAILURE TABLE MAINTENANCE

              5   SOFTWARE TABLE MAINTENANCE

              6   HARDWARE FAILURE TYPE


              ENTER OPTION   OR   PF3 TO END
```

```
-----------------
HTMAIN                    FORREST FORD CORPORATE SYSTEMS         DATE: 90/07/21
                              HARDWARE TRACKING SYSTEM           TIME: 14:42

COMMAND ==>

                          MAIN SELECTION MENU

                      1   TABLE MAINTENANCE MENU

                      2   INTERACTIVE DISPLAY MENU

                      3   BATCH REPORTING MENU


                      ENTER OPTION  OR  PF3 TO END


-----------------
Ready; T=10.88/15.01 14:42:28
Ready; T=0.01/0.02 14:42:28
```

APPENDIX K. HTS SPECIFICATIONS FOR MODULE—HT0010

FILE: HT0010 SPECS   VM/SP CONVERSATIONAL MONITOR SYSTEM

SYSTEM: HARDWARE TRACKING   DATE: 06/22/90   00010000
                                                                       00011000
                                                                       00020000
PROGRAM: HT0010   00021000
                                                                       00030000
PREPARED BY: BOB PUTNAM   00040000
                                                                       00050000
SUBJECT: PROGRAM SPECIFICATIONS   00060000
                                                                       00070000
                                                                       00090001
PROGRAM DESCRIPTION: 00091001

    PROGRAM HT0010 IS AN ONLINE COBOL, SQL/DS PROGRAM THAT WILL RUN UNDER DIALOG   00100002
MANAGER IN A VM ENVIRONMENT. THE PURPOSE OF THIS PROGRAM IS TO MAINTAIN AND   00110000
DISPLAY THE INFORMATION RESIDING ON THE HARDWARE SQL TABLE WITHIN THE HARDWARE   00120000
TRACKING SYSTEM. THIS PROGRAM WILL ALLOW THE USER TO ADD, UPDATE, AND DISPLAY THE 00130001
INFORMATION BY SELECTING THE APPROPRIATE OPTION ON THE HARDWARE OPTION SCREEN.   00140001
                                                                                    00150001
    THERE ARE TWO SCREENS THAT WILL NEED TO BE PROCESSED WITHIN THIS APPLICATION.   00150103
THE FIRST SCREEN, THE HARDWARE MAINTENANCE OPTION SCREEN, WILL CONTAIN TWO FIELDS   00151003
THAT HAVE TO BE ENTERED. THESE TWO FIELDS WILL BE THE INDEX INTO THE HARDWARE   00152003
TRACKING SQL/DS TABLE AND THE PARTICULAR OPTION THE USER WISHES TO PERFORM. THE   00153004
AVAILABLE OPTIONS WILL BE ADD, CHANGE, AND DELETE. THE SECOND SCREEN, THE HARDWARE 00160004
MAINTENANCE DETAIL SCREEN, WILL CONTAIN ALL OF THE ENTITIES ON THE HARDWARE TABLE   00161004
AND WILL ALLOW THE USER TO ADD OR CHANGE THE HARDWARE INFORMATION.   00162011
                                                                                    00163011
                                                                                    00170011

DETAILED SPECIFICATIONS:

HOW TO FORMAT SCREENS:

THE OPTION SCREEN WILL HAVE TO HAVE THE DATE AND TIME MOVED TO THE CORRESPONDING
FIELDS ON THE MAP. THERE ARE NO OTHER FIELDS THAT WILL HAVE TO BE MOVED TO THE MAP
PRIOR TO DISPLAYING THE OPTION SCREEN.

1) IF THE MAINTENANCE TO THE HARDWARE TABLE WAS "SUCCESSFUL" THE APPROPRIATE
   ERROR MESSAGE IS TO BE DISPLAYED WHEN RETURNING TO THE HARDWARE OPTION
   SCREEN(SEE MESSAGES).

2) IF THE MAINTENANCE TO THE HARDWARE TABLE WAS "UNSUCCESSFUL" THE APPROPRIATE
   ERROR MESSAGE IS TO BE DISPLAYED WHEN RETURNING TO THE HARDWARE OPTION
   SCREEN(SEE MESSAGES).

THE HARDWARE MAINTENANCE SCREEN WILL HAVE TO BE FORMATTED DIFFERENTLY DEPENDING
ON THE OPTION SELECTED ON THE HARDWARE MAINTENANCE OPTION SCREEN.

1) IF OPTION "A" (ADD) WAS SELECTED ON THE HARDWARE OPTION SCREEN THE ONLY FIELD
   THAT WILL BE MOVED TO THE MAP IS THE HARDWARE SERIAL NUMBER.

00170111
00170208
00170311
00170411
00170511
00171004
00180003
00181007
00182008
00190002
00200007
00200108
00201004
00210004
00220004
00230004
00240004
00241008
00242006
00243006
00245006
00246008
00247008
00248008
00249008
00250004
00260004
00270004
00271004
00320008
00330008

297

2) IF OPTION "C" (CHANGE) OR "D" (DELETE) WAS SELECTED ALL OF THE ENTITIES FROM THE HARDWARE TABLE ARE TO BE MOVED TO THEIR CORRESPONDING FIELD ON THE HARDWARE MAINTENANCE SCREEN.

3) IF THE OPTION SELECTED IS A "D" (DELETE) A DELETE CONFIRMATION MESSAGE IS TO BE DISPLAYED (SEE MESSAGES).

4) THE HARDWARE SERIAL NUMBER IS TO BE PROTECTED IN ALL MODES.

5) THE DATE AND TIME MUST ALSO BE MOVED TO THE SCREEN.

HOW TO PROCESS SCREENS:

1) ENTER AND PF3 ARE THE ONLY OPTIONS THE USER MAY PRESS, ANY OTHER PF KEY THAT IS PRESSED IS CONSIDERED TO BE IN ERROR. IF THE USER DOES PRESS ANY OTHER PF KEY AN ERROR MESSAGE IS TO BE DISPLAYED (SEE MESSAGES).

THE HARDWARE OPTION SCREEN WILL BE PROCESSED IN THE FOLLOWING MANNER WHEN THE USER PRESSES ENTER:

```
00340008
00350006
00350108
00350208
00350308
00350408
00351008
00352006
00353006
00360008
00370006
00370111
00370208
00370311
00370408
00370511
00371006
00380007
00390006
00391008
00392008
00400006
00410006
00420008
00430006
00431006
00431108
00431208
00432007
00433007
00435108
```

1) PF3 WILL BYPASS ALL EDITING AND END THIS APPLICATION.

2) ANY FIELD THAT IS FOUND TO BE IN ERROR THE SCREEN IS TO BE REDISPLAYED WITH THE CURSOR PLACED ON THE FIELD FOUND TO BE IN ERROR.

3) IF THE USER HAS PRESSED ENTER:

A) THE USER MUST ENTER DATA INTO THE HARDWARE SERIAL NUMBER. IF NOT, THIS IS AN ERROR AND THE CORRESPONDING ERROR MESSAGE IS TO BE DISPLAYED (SEE MESSAGES).

B) THE USER MUST SELECT ONE OF THE AVAILABLE OPTIONS. IF THE OPTION FIELD IS BLANK OR THE USER SELECTED AN OPTION OTHER THAN A, C, D AN ERROR MESSAGE IS TO BE DISPLAYED (SEE MESSAGES).

C) PRIOR TO DISPLAYING THE HARDWARE MAINTENANCE DETAIL SCREEN THE HARDWARE SQL/DS TABLE MUST BE ACCESSED SUCCESSFULLY WITH THE INDEX ENTERED ON THE HARDWARE MAINTENANCE OPTION SCREEN.

1) THE TABLE ACCESS IS SUCCESSFUL IF THE SQLCODE IS A ZERO AND THE OPTION SELECTED WAS EITHER A "C" (CHANGE), OR "D" (DELETE). IF OPTION "A" (ADD) WAS SELECTED AND THE SQLCODE IS A ZERO THIS IS AN ERROR DUE TO THE FACT THAT THE USER IS ATTEMPTING TO ADD A ROW TO THE HARDWARE TABLE THAT ALREADY EXISTS SO THE APPROPRIATE MESSAGE IS TO BE DISPLAYED ON THE OPTION SCREEN (SEE MESSAGES).

2) IF THE SQLCODE IS A +100 AND THE USER CHOSE OPTION "A" (ADD) THIS IS ACCEPTABLE. IF THE SQLCODE IS A +100 AND THE USER CHOSE OPTION "C" (CHANGE) OR "D" (DELETE) THIS IS AN ERROR DUE TO THE FACT THAT THE USER IS ATTEMPTING TO CHANGE OR DELETE A ROW THAT DOES NOT CURRENTLY EXIST ON

THE HARDWARE TABLE.

D) IF ALL OF THE VALIDATING WAS SUCCESSFUL THE HARDWARE DETAIL SCREEN IS TO BE
   DISPLAYED.

THE HARDWARE MAINTENANCE SCREEN WILL BE PROCESSED IN THE FOLLOWING MANNER:

1) PF3 WILL BYPASS ALL EDITING AND END THIS APPLICATION.

2) IF THE USER HAS PRESSED ENTER:

A) ALL FIELDS ARE TO BE EDITED, EXCEPT FOR HARDWARE SERIAL NUMBER. EDITING IS
   TO BE DONE IN THE ADD AND UPDATE MODES ONLY. EDITING WILL NOT BE NECESSARY
   IN THE DELETE MODE. ONCE AN ERROR IS ENCOUNTERED THE SCREEN IS TO BE
   DISPLAYED WITH THE CORRESPONDING ERROR MESSAGE AND THE CURSOR PLACED ON
   THAT FIELD (SEE SCREEN FIELD EDITS).

NOTE: IN THE ADD MODE, ALL FOREIGN KEYS MUST BE CHECKED TO INSURE THAT THAT
ROW EXISTS ON THE TABLE THAT IT IS A PRIMARY KEY. IF THE ROW EXISTS THE USER
MAY ADD THAT ROW TO THE TABLE. IF THE ROW DOES NOT EXIST THE USER MAY NOT
ADD THAT ROW TO THE HARDWARE TABLE AND AN ERROR MESSAGE IS TO BE DISPLAYED
(SEE MESSAGES).

B) AFTER ALL OF THE FIELDS HAVE BEEN VALIDATED THE MAINTENANCE MAY BE
   PERFORMED ON THE HARDWARE TABLE.

300

00438308
00438408
00438508
00438608
00438711
00438811
00438911
00439011
00439111
00439207
00439307
00439408
00439507
00439607
00439707
00439807
00439908
00440007
00450007
00460007
00470007
00480007
00481007
00490006
00491006
00492007
00493007
00494007
00495007
00496006
00500007

C) THE SQLCODE MUST BE VALIDATED AFTER EACH ACCESS OF THE HARDWARE SQL/DS   00510011
   TABLE. IF THE SQLCODE IS OTHER THAN ZERO THIS IS CONSIDERED TO BE AN ERROR   00520006
                                                                                   00520108
   AND MOVE THE CORRESPONDING MESSAGE TO THE MESSAGE LINE AND PLACE THE CURSOR   00520208
   ON THE OPTION SCREEN COMMAND LINE.   00520308
                                                                                   00520408
D) AFTER PERFORMING THE MAINTENANCE TO THE HARDWARE TABLE A MESSAGE WILL BE   00520508
   MOVED TO THE MESSAGE LINE INDICATING WHETHER THE MAINTENANCE TO THE SQL/DS   00520608
   HARDWARE TABLE WAS SUCCESSFUL OR IF AN ERROR WAS ENCOUNTERED. THIS   00520711
   APPLICATION WILL THEN DISPLAY THE HARDWARE OPTION SCREEN WITH THE MESSAGE.   00521011
                                                                                   00522011
                                                                                   00523011
                                                                                   00524011
                                                                                   00526011
                                                                                   00527011
                                                                                   00528011
                                                                                   00529011
                                                                                   00529111
HOW TO TRANSFER SCREENS: 00530001
                                                                                   00531008
                                                                                   00532008
                                                                                   00540007
1) PF3 - IF THE USER HAS PRESSED PF3 AND THE USER IS ON THE HARDWARE DETAIL SCREEN 00550007
   THIS APPLICATION IS TO DISPLAY THE HARDWARE OPTION SCREEN WITHOUT PERFORMING   00560007
   ANY MAINTENANCE ON THE SCREEN. PF3 IS TO ALLOW THE USER TO EXIT FROM THE   00570007
   DETAIL MAINTENANCE SCREEN. IF THE USER IS ON THE HARDWARE OPTION SCREEN AND   00580007
   PF3 THIS APPLICATION IS TO END.   00590007
                                                                                   00600007
                                                                                   00610007
2) ENTER - IF ENTER HAS BEEN PRESSED AND THE USER IS ON THE HARDWARE DETAIL SCREEN 00620007

```
THIS APPLICATION IS TO DISPLAY THE HARDWARE OPTION SCREEN, IF EDITING WAS A      00630007
SUCCESS.  IF THE USER IS ON THE HARDWARE OPTION SCREEN THIS APPLICATION IS TO    00640007
DISPLAY THE HARDWARE MAINTENANCE SCREEN IF ALL OF THE VALIDATING WAS             00650007
SUCCESSFUL.                                                                     00660007
                                                                                00670007
                                                                                00671009
                                                                                00672009
                                                                                00673009
                                                                                00674009
SCREEN FIELD EDITS:                                                             00680009
                                                                                00690009
                                                                                00690109
                                                                                00691009
THE FOLLOWING EDITS PERTAIN TO THE HARDWARE OPTION SCREEN:                       00700009
                                                                                00700109
                                                                                00700209
1) HARDWARE SERIAL NO - FIELD IS REQUIRED AND MUST BE GREATER THAN SPACES.       00700310
                                                                                00700409
                                                                                00700509
2) OPTION - FIELD IS REQUIRED AND MUST BE A, C, OR D.                            00700610
                                                                                00700709
                                                                                00700809
                                                                                00700909
THE FOLLOWING EDITS PERTAIN TO THE HARDWARE MAINTENANCE SCREEN:                  00701009
                                                                                00702009
1) HARDWARE SERIAL NO - FIELD IS REQUIRED AND MUST BE GREATER THAN SPACES.       00710010
                                                                                00711009
                                                                                00720009
2) HARDWARE TYPE - FIELD IS REQUIRED AND MUST BE GREATER THAN SPACES.            00730010
                                                                                00740009
3) HARDWARE BRANCH - FIELD IS REQUIRED AND MUST BE GREATER THAN SPACES.          00750010
```

4) HARDWARE DEPARTMENT - FIELD NOT REQUIRED.

5) HARDWARE LOCATION - FIELD NOT REQUIRED.

6) HARDWARE VENDOR - FIELD IS REQUIRED AND MUST BE GREATER THAN SPACES.

7) HARDWARE MANUFACTURER - FIELD IS NOT REQUIRED.

8) HARDWARE PURCHASE DATE - FIELD IS REQUIRED AND MUST BE A VALID DATE.

9) HARDWARE COST - FIELD NOT REQUIRED BUT MUST BE NUMERIC WITH TWO DECIMAL POSITIONS IF USER ENTERS DATA INTO THIS FIELD.

10) HARDWARE CONTRACT NUMBER - FIELD IS REQUIRED. ALSO, IF A ROW IS BEING ADDED OR IF THIS FIELD IS CHANGED THE SERVICE CONTRACT TABLE MUST BE ACCESSED TO INSURE A ROW EXISTS FOR THAT SERVICE CONTRACT NUMBER. IF A ROW EXISTS THE USER MAY INSERT OR UPDATE THE ROW IN THE HARDWARE TABLE. IF THE ROW DOES NOT EXIST THE USER MAY NOT ADD OR UPDATE THAT ROW IN THE HARDWARE TABLE.

```
00760009
00770010
00780009
00790010
00810009
00820010
00830009
00840010
00850009
00860010
00870009
00880010
00881010
00890010
00891010
00900010
00910010
00911009
00912009
00913009
00914010
00915010
00916010
00917010
00920009
```

FILE: HT00   MESSAGE*   VM/SP CONVERSATIONAL MONITOR SYSTEM

HT001 '   ' .ALARM=NO
'
HT001A 'RECORD FOUND   ' .ALARM=YES

303

```
'RECORD IS ALREADY ON TABLE          ' .ALARM=YES
HT001B 'RECORD NOT FOUND              ' .ALARM=YES
'SEARCH VALUE IS NOT ON FILE          ' .ALARM=YES
HT001C 'CONFIRM DELETE                ' .ALARM=YES
'PRESS ENTER TO CONTINUE DELETE FUNCTION, PF3 TO CANCEL
HT001D 'DELETE WAS SUCCESSFUL         ' .ALARM=YES
'ENTRY WAS DELETED FROM SQL TABLE
HT001E 'RECORD NOT UPDATED            ' .ALARM=YES
'ENTRY WAS NOT UPDATED IN THE SQL TABLE
HT001F 'RECORD NOT DELETED            ' .ALARM=YES
'RECORD INFORMATION WAS NOT DELETED -NOTIFY SYSTEMS
HT001G             'ENTER REQUIRED FIELD          ' .ALARM=YES
'ENTER REQUIRED FIELD AT THE CURSOR POSITION
HT001H 'UPDATE SUCCESSFUL             ' .ALARM=YES
'ENTRY WAS UPDATED IN THE SQL TABLE
HT001I 'MUST BE NUMBER > ZERO         ' .ALARM=YES
'THIS FIELD MUST BE NUMERIC AND GREATER THAN ZERO
HT001J '1 DECIMAL PLACE ALLOWED       ' .ALARM=YES
'PLEASE ENTER NUMBER WITH ONLY ONE DECIMAL PLACE
HT001K 'NO. ENTERED > 9999.99         ' .ALARM=YES
'ENTER COST WITH MAXIMUM OF 5 WHOLE NUMBERS & 2 DECIMAL POS
HT001L 'NO. ENTERED > 9999999.99' .ALARM=YES
'ENTER COST WITH MAXIMUM OF 7 WHOLE NUMBERS & 2 DECIMAL POS
HT001M 'INVALID VALUE                 ' .ALARM=YES
'ENTER AN ACCEPTED VALUE - A C D        ' .ALARM=YES
HT001N 'MUST BE NUMERIC               ' .ALARM=YES
'ENTER NUMERIC CHARACTERS (0-9) IN THE FORMAT XXX-XXX-XXXX
HT001O 'INSERT WAS SUCCESSFUL         ' .ALARM=YES
'ENTRY WAS INSERTED INTO SQL TABLE
HT001P 'INVALID CONTRACTOR            ' .ALARM=YES
'CONTRACTOR DOES NOT RESIDE IN THE CONTRACTOR TABLE - TRY AGAIN.
```

```
HT002G 'RECORD IN USE                                          ' .ALARM=YES
       'SOMEONE ELSE HAS READ THIS RECORD - TRY LATER
HT003A 'INVALID DATE FORMAT                    ' .ALARM=YES
       'ENTER 8 NUMERIC CHARACTERS IN THE FORMAT CCYY-MM-DD
HT003B 'INVALID CENTURY                        ' .ALARM=YES
       'CENTURY MUST BE 19 WHEN YEAR IS GREATER THAN 89
HT003C 'INVALID CENTURY                        ' .ALARM=YES
       'CENTURY MUST BE 20 WHEN YEAR IS LESS THAN 90
HT003D 'INVALID MONTH                          ' .ALARM=YES
       'MONTH MUST BE 1 TO 12
HT003E 'INVALID DAY                            ' .ALARM=YES
       'DAY MUST BE 1 TO 29 FOR MONTH 2 IN A LEAP YEAR
HT003F 'INVALID DAY                            ' .ALARM=YES
       'DAY MUST BE 1 TO 28 FOR MONTH 2 IN A NON-LEAP YEAR
HT003G 'INVALID DAY                            ' .ALARM=YES
       'DAY MUST BE 1 TO 30 FOR THE GIVEN MONTH
HT003H 'INVALID DAY                            ' .ALARM=YES
       'DAY MUST BE 1 TO 31 FOR THE GIVEN MONTH
HT003I 'START DATE > EXP DATE                  ' .ALARM=YES
       'START DATE MUST BE LESS THAN OR EQUAL TO EXPIRATION DATE
```

FILE: EQUIPTAB TABLES A1   VM/SP CONVERSATIONAL MONITOR SYSTEM

NAME: BOB PUTNAM   TABLE: HARDWARE TABLE

SYSTEM: HARDWARE TRACKING SYSTEM

DATE: 05/29/90

DESCRIPTION: THE HARDWARE TABLE WILL RETAIN ALL OF THE INFORMATION PERTAINING TO ALL OF THE HARDWARE. THE HARDWARE INFORMATION SHALL BE RETAINED FOR ALL OF THE FORREST FORD CONSULTANTS, INC. BRANCHES.

```
KEYS                                                 FORMAT
1 2 3
- - -          ENTITIES                              - - - - - -
               - - - - - - - -
X : :          HARDWARE SERIAL NUMBER      --        X(15)
: X:           HARDWARE TYPE               --        X(10)
: X:X          HARDWARE BRANCH             --        X(03)
: X:X          HARDWARE DEPARTMENT         --        X(10)
: X:X          HARDWARE LOCATION           --        X(10)
: : :          HARDWARE VENDOR             --        X(10)
: : :          HARDWARE MANUF              --        X(10)
: : :          HARDWARE PURCH DATE         --        DATE
: : :          HARDWARE COST               --        S9(07)V9(02)
: : :          HARDWARE CONTRACT NUMBER    --        X(15)
```

```
00010003
00020003
00030003
00040003
00050003
00060003
00070003
00080008
00090005
00100004
00110004
00120004
00130005
00140005
00150005
00160007
00170007
00180009
00190009
00200009
00210007
00220007
00230007
00240007
00250007
```

```
)ATTR DEFAULT(@+$)
 @ TYPE(OUTPUT) INTENS(HIGH) SKIP(ON)
 + TYPE(TEXT) INTENS(LOW) SKIP(ON)
 $ TYPE(INPUT) INTENS(HIGH) PAD(_) CAPS(ON)
 ⌐ TYPE(INPUT) INTENS(LOW) CAPS(ON)
 ¢ TYPE(INPUT) INTENS(NON) CAPS(ON)

 /*                                                            */
 /*  HARDWARE TRACKING SYSTEM                                  */
 /*  MAIN MENU                                                 */
 /*                                                            */

)BODY
+HT00101                 FORREST FORD CORPORATE SYSTEMS         DATE:@ZDATE  +
                            HARDWARE TRACKING SYSTEM            TIME:@ZTIME +

+COMMAND ==>⌐ZCMD

+              @SUBHEAD                           +


       @DESCR         +      $Z    +

                      ENTER OPTION $Z+

                               A-  ADD
                               C-  CHANGE
                               D-  DELETE
+
+
+
+
+
+
+
+
+
+
+
+
+
+
```

```
        PF3-TO EXIT

+
+
+
+
+
+
)INIT
.ZVARS = '(INDX OPT)'
&ZPF01 = HELP
&ZPF02 = ' '
&ZPF03 = END
&ZPF04 = ' '
&ZPF05 = ' '
&ZPF06 = ' '
&ZPF07 = UP
&ZPF08 = DOWN
&ZPF09 = ' '
&ZPF10 = ' '
&ZPF11 = ' '
&ZPF12 = ' '
&ZPF13 = HELP
&ZPF14 = ' '
&ZPF15 = END
&ZPF16 = ' '
&ZPF17 = ' '
&ZPF18 = ' '
&ZPF19 = UP
&ZPF20 = DOWN
&ZPF21 = ' '
&ZPF22 = ' '
&ZPF23 = ' '
```

```
  &ZPF24 = ' '
)PROC
  VER (&OPT,LIST,A,C,D)
  VPUT (INDX,OPT) SHARED
)END


FILE: HT00102  PANEL    *              VM/SP CONVERSATIONAL MONITOR SYSTEM

)ATTR DEFAULT(@+$)
  @ TYPE(OUTPUT) INTENS(HIGH) SKIP(ON)
  + TYPE(TEXT) INTENS(LOW) SKIP(ON)
  $ TYPE(INPUT) INTENS(HIGH) PAD(_) CAPS(ON)
  ⌐ TYPE(INPUT) INTENS(LOW) CAPS(ON)
  ¢ TYPE(INPUT) INTENS(NON) CAPS(ON)
  /*                                                    */
  /*  HARDWARE TRACKING SYSTEM                          */
  /*  MAIN MENU                                         */
  /*                                                    */
)BODY
 +HT00102      FORREST FORD CORPORATE SYSTEMS      DATE:@ZDATE    +
                  HARDWARE TRACKING SYSTEM         TIME:@ZTIME+
 +COMMAND ==>⌐ZCMD
 +              HARDWARE TABLE MAINTENANCE
 +
 +
 +
```

309

```
+SERIAL NUMBER: $SERNUM        +
+
+
+HARDWARE TYPE: $HARDTYPE  +                    LOCATION: $LOC
+BRANCH: $BRA+     DEPARTMENT: $DEPT       +
+VENDOR: $VENDOR     +    MANUFACTURER: $MANUF   +
+PURCHASE DATE: $PDATE    +          COST: $HARDCOST  +
+CONTRACT NUMBER: $CONNUM           +
+
+
+
+
+                              PF3-TO EXIT

)INIT
 &ZPF01 = HELP
 &ZPF02 = ' '
 &ZPF03 = END
 &ZPF04 = ' '
 &ZPF05 = ' '
 &ZPF06 = ' '
 &ZPF07 = UP
 &ZPF08 = DOWN
 &ZPF09 = ' '
 &ZPF10 = ' '
 &ZPF11 = ' '
 &ZPF12 = ' '
 &ZPF13 = HELP
 &ZPF14 = ' '
 &ZPF15 = END
```

```
&ZPF16 = ' '
&ZPF17 = ' '
&ZPF18 = ' '
&ZPF19 = UP
&ZPF20 = DOWN
&ZPF21 = ' '
&ZPF22 = ' '
&ZPF23 = ' '
&ZPF24 = ' '
IF (&OPT = 'D')
  .ATTR(SERNUM)    = 'TYPE(OUTPUT)'
  .ATTR(HARDTYPE)  = 'TYPE(OUTPUT)'
  .ATTR(BRA)       = 'TYPE(OUTPUT)'
  .ATTR(DEPT)      = 'TYPE(OUTPUT)'
  .ATTR(LOC)       = 'TYPE(OUTPUT)'
  .ATTR(VENDOR)    = 'TYPE(OUTPUT)'
  .ATTR(MANUF)     = 'TYPE(OUTPUT)'
  .ATTR(PDATE)     = 'TYPE(OUTPUT)'
  .ATTR(HARDCOST)  = 'TYPE(OUTPUT)'
  .ATTR(CONNUM)    = 'TYPE(OUTPUT)'
IF (&OPT = 'A')
  .ATTR(SERNUM)    = 'TYPE(INPUT)'
  .ATTR(HARDTYPE)  = 'TYPE(INPUT)'
  .ATTR(BRA)       = 'TYPE(INPUT)'
  .ATTR(DEPT)      = 'TYPE(INPUT)'
  .ATTR(LOC)       = 'TYPE(INPUT)'
  .ATTR(VENDOR)    = 'TYPE(INPUT)'
  .ATTR(MANUF)     = 'TYPE(INPUT)'
  .ATTR(PDATE)     = 'TYPE(INPUT)'
  .ATTR(HARDCOST)  = 'TYPE(INPUT)'
  .ATTR(CONNUM)    = 'TYPE(INPUT)'
```

311

```
IF (&OPT = 'C')
  .ATTR(SERNUM)     = 'TYPE(OUTPUT)'
  .ATTR(HARDTYPE)   = 'TYPE(INPUT)'
  .ATTR(BRA)        = 'TYPE(INPUT)'
  .ATTR(DEPT)       = 'TYPE(INPUT)'
  .ATTR(LOC)        = 'TYPE(INPUT)'
  .ATTR(VENDOR)     = 'TYPE(INPUT)'
  .ATTR(MANUF)      = 'TYPE(INPUT)'
  .ATTR(PDATE)      = 'TYPE(INPUT)'
  .ATTR(HARDCOST)   = 'TYPE(INPUT)'
  .ATTR(CONNUM)     = 'TYPE(INPUT)'
)REINIT
IF (&OPT = 'A')
IF (&ZDTMSG = ' ')
  &SERNUM   = ' '
  &HARDTYPE = ' '
  &BRA      = ' '
  &DEPT     = ' '
  &LOC      = ' '
  &VENDOR   = ' '
  &MANUF    = ' '
  &PDATE    = ' '
  &HARDCOST = ' '
  &CONNUM   = ' '
)PROC
)END
```

APPENDIX L. HTS SOURCE LISTING FOR MODULE— HT0010

```
FILE: HT0010  COBOL  A1

ID DIVISION.
PROGRAM-ID. 'HT-0010'.
*
AUTHOR. ROBERT PUTNAM
*
DATE-WRITTEN. JUNE 1990.
*
DATE-COMPILED.
*
*REMARKS. PROGRAM HT0010 -
*         MAINTENANCE PROGRAM FOR HARDWARE INFORMATION
EJECT
*
EJECT
ENVIRONMENT DIVISION.
*
CONFIGURATION SECTION.
*
SOURCE-COMPUTER. IBM-9370.
OBJECT-COMPUTER. IBM-9370.
*
INPUT-OUTPUT SECTION.
*
FILE-CONTROL.
*
```

313

```
      SKIP3
       DATA DIVISION.
       FILE SECTION.
      *
       EJECT
       WORKING-STORAGE SECTION.
       01  WORK-AREA.
           05  WORK-STORAGE-BEGIN      PIC X(26)   VALUE
               '****WORK-STORAGE-BEGIN****'.
           05  NAME-OF-PROGRAM         PIC X(08)   VALUE 'HT0010'.
           05  WHEN-COMPILED-HOLD      PIC X(20)   VALUE SPACES.
           05  WHEN-COMPILED-EDIT      PIC X(08)BBX(12) VALUE SPACE.
           05  CURRENT-PARAGRAPH       PIC X(03)   VALUE SPACE.
           05  FILLER                  PIC X(09)   VALUE 'RUN DATE:'.
           05  WS-RUN-DATE             PIC X(08).
           05  FILLER                  PIC X(09)   VALUE 'RUN TIME:'.
           05  WS-RUN-TIME             PIC X(05).
           05  GETLIST                 PIC X(10)
                                       VALUE '(INDX OPT)'.

      *    SWITCHES

       01  FILLER.
           05  CANCELLED-SW            PIC X(01)   VALUE 'N'.
               88  CANCELLED                       VALUE 'Y'.
           05  SUCCESSFUL-SW           PIC X(01)   VALUE 'N'.
               88  SUCCESSFUL                      VALUE 'Y'.
               88  NOT-SUCCESSFUL                  VALUE 'N'.
           05  REDISPLAY-SW            PIC X(01)   VALUE 'N'.
               88  REDISPLAY-ERROR                 VALUE 'Y'.
```

```cobol
               88  DO-NOT-REDISPLAY          VALUE 'Y'.
           05  SELECT-SW         PIC X(01)    VALUE 'N'.
               88  YES-SELECT                 VALUE 'Y'.
               88  NO-SELECT                  VALUE 'N'.
      *
      *    LITERALS
      *
           05  LIT-NO            PIC X(01)    VALUE 'N'.
           05  LIT-YES           PIC X(01)    VALUE 'Y'.
           05  LIT-C             PIC X(01)    VALUE 'C'.
           05  NUM-1             PIC S9(1)    COMP-3   VALUE +1.
           05  NUM-3             PIC S9(1)    COMP-3   VALUE +3.
      *
      *    COUNTERS AND NUMERIC WORK AREAS
      *
           05  SUB               PIC S9(3)    COMP-3   VALUE +0.
      *    SQL VARIABLES AND LITERALS
      *
           EJECT
               COPY ISPFPARM.
           EJECT
      *
      *    ERROR MESSAGES
      *
               COPY ISP00.
           SKIP3
               COPY HT00.
           SKIP3
               COPY SQL00.
           EJECT
               COPY WSGETSYS.
      *
```

```
****************************************************************
*  DIALOG MANAGER SYSTEM VARIABLES                             *
*                                                              *
   01  PSELECT-PANEL              PIC X(08)  VALUE 'HT00101'.
   01  PHARDW-PANEL               PIC X(08)  VALUE 'HT00102'.
*                                                              *
       COPY HT00101.
   SKIP3
       COPY HT00102.
   EJECT
*                                                              *
*  DECLARE SQL VARIABLES                                       *
*                                                              *
*******  SQL/DS STATEMENT:
*****EXEC SQL BEGIN DECLARE SECTION END-EXEC.
       COPY SQLINIT.
   SKIP3
*******  SQL/DS STATEMENT:
*****EXEC SQL INCLUDE HARDWARE END-EXEC.
****************************************************************00000100
                                                               00000110
*  HARDWARE TRACKING SYSTEM                                     00000120
*  CONTRACTOR NAME AND ADDRESS TABLE    LENGTH:                 00000130
*                                                               00000140
*  THIS IS THE AREA WHERE SQL TABLE DATA IS RETURNED           00000200
****************************************************************00000600
       HARDWARE                                                 00000700
   01  SERIALNO              PIC X(15) VALUE SPACES.            00001000
   01  HARDTYPE              PIC X(10) VALUE SPACES.            00001201
   01  BRANCH                PIC X(03) VALUE SPACES.            00001201
   01  DEPT                  PIC X(10) VALUE SPACES.
```

```
01  LOC                      PIC X(10) VALUE SPACES.                    00001202
01  VENDOR                   PIC X(10) VALUE SPACES.                    00001202
01  MANUF                    PIC X(10) VALUE SPACES.                    00001100
01  HPURDATE                 PIC X(10) VALUE SPACES.                    00001100
01  HARDCOST                 PIC S9(07)V9(02) COMP VALUE ZEROES.        00001100
01  SERVNO                   PIC X(15) VALUE SPACES.                    00001100


******** STRUCTURES FOR SQL/DATA SYSTEM IN-LINE CALLS
*****       BEGIN HERE:
01  SQL-BIND-FLAG            PIC S9(4) COMP VALUE +0.
    88 SQL-DONE-ONCE VALUE +1.
01  SQL-NULL                 PIC S9(9) COMP VALUE +0.
01  SQLTIE.
    02 FILLER OCCURS 12 TIMES PIC S9(9) COMP.
01  SQL-RDIEXT.
    02 SQL-RDIEXTEC          PIC X(8).
    02 FILLER                PIC S9(9) COMP.
    02 SQL-RDIEXTA OCCURS 9 TIMES PIC S9(9) COMP.
01  SQL-DA1-STRUCT1.
    02 SQL-DA-ID             PIC X(8) VALUE 'SQLDA   '.
    02 SQL-DA-BC             PIC S9(9) COMP VALUE +456.
    02 SQL-DA-N              PIC S9(4) COMP VALUE +10.
    02 SQL-DA-D              PIC S9(4) COMP VALUE +10.
    02 SQL-DATA-TYPE1        PIC S9(4) COMP VALUE +452.
    02 SQL-LEN1              PIC S9(4) COMP.
    02 SQL-DATA-PTR1         PIC X(4).
    02 SQL-INFO-PTR1         PIC X(4).
    02 SQL-NAME1             PIC X(32).
    02 SQL-DATA-TYPE2        PIC S9(4) COMP VALUE +452.
    02 SQL-LEN2              PIC S9(4) COMP.
```

317

```
02  SQL-DATA-PTR2      PIC X(4).
02  SQL-INFO-PTR2      PIC X(4).
02  SQL-NAME2          PIC X(32).
02  SQL-DATA-TYPE3     PIC S9(4) COMP VALUE +452.
02  SQL-LEN3           PIC S9(4) COMP.
02  SQL-DATA-PTR3      PIC X(4).
02  SQL-INFO-PTR3      PIC X(4).
02  SQL-NAME3          PIC X(32).
02  SQL-DATA-TYPE4     PIC S9(4) COMP VALUE +452.
02  SQL-LEN4           PIC S9(4) COMP.
02  SQL-DATA-PTR4      PIC X(4).
02  SQL-INFO-PTR4      PIC X(4).
02  SQL-NAME4          PIC X(32).
02  SQL-DATA-TYPE5     PIC S9(4) COMP VALUE +452.
02  SQL-LEN5           PIC S9(4) COMP.
02  SQL-DATA-PTR5      PIC X(4).
02  SQL-INFO-PTR5      PIC X(4).
02  SQL-NAME5          PIC X(32).
02  SQL-DATA-TYPE6     PIC S9(4) COMP VALUE +452.
02  SQL-LEN6           PIC S9(4) COMP.
02  SQL-DATA-PTR6      PIC X(4).
02  SQL-INFO-PTR6      PIC X(4).
02  SQL-NAME6          PIC X(32).
02  SQL-DATA-TYPE7     PIC S9(4) COMP VALUE +452.
02  SQL-LEN7           PIC S9(4) COMP.
02  SQL-DATA-PTR7      PIC X(4).
02  SQL-INFO-PTR7      PIC X(4).
02  SQL-NAME7          PIC X(32).
02  SQL-DATA-TYPE8     PIC S9(4) COMP VALUE +452.
02  SQL-LEN8           PIC S9(4) COMP.
02  SQL-DATA-PTR8      PIC X(4).
```

```
    02  SQL-INFO-PTR8           PIC X(4).
    02  SQL-NAME8               PIC X(32).
    02  SQL-DATA-TYPE9          PIC S9(4) COMP VALUE +496.
    02  SQL-LEN9                PIC S9(4) COMP.
    02  SQL-DATA-PTR9           PIC X(4).
    02  SQL-INFO-PTR9           PIC X(4).
    02  SQL-NAME9               PIC X(32).
    02  SQL-DATA-TYPE10         PIC S9(4) COMP VALUE +452.
    02  SQL-LEN10               PIC S9(4) COMP.
    02  SQL-DATA-PTR10          PIC X(4).
    02  SQL-INFO-PTR10          PIC X(4).
    02  SQL-NAME10              PIC X(32).
01  SQL-DA1-STRUCT2.
    02  SQL-DA-ID               PIC X(8) VALUE 'SQLDA   '.
    02  SQL-DA-BC               PIC S9(9) COMP VALUE +60.
    02  SQL-DA-N                PIC S9(4) COMP VALUE +1.
    02  SQL-DA-D                PIC S9(4) COMP VALUE +1.
    02  SQL-DATA-TYPE1          PIC S9(4) COMP VALUE +452.
    02  SQL-LEN1                PIC S9(4) COMP.
    02  SQL-DATA-PTR1           PIC X(4).
    02  SQL-INFO-PTR1           PIC X(4).
    02  SQL-NAME1               PIC X(32).
01  SQL-ADDR-RDIIN1             PIC S9(9) COMP.
01  SQL-RDIIN1.
    02  SQL-CALLTYPE            PIC S9(4) COMP VALUE +30.
    02  SQL-AUTHOR              PIC X(8) VALUE 'HT      '.
    02  SQL-PROG-NAME-LEN       PIC S9(4) COMP VALUE +6.
    02  SQL-PROG-NAME-VAL       PIC X(8) VALUE 'HT0010'.
    02  SQL-SECTION-NUM         PIC S9(4) COMP VALUE +1.
    02  SQL-CLASS-SECTION       PIC S9(4) COMP VALUE +0.
```

```
   02 SQL-CODEPTR          PIC X(4).
   02 SQL-VPARAMPTR        PIC X(4).
   02 SQL-AUXPARAMPTR      PIC X(4).
   02 SQL-TIE-PTR          PIC X(4).
   02 SQL-SPECIAL-CALL     PIC X(1) VALUE ' '.
   02 SQL-CALL-FLAG        PIC X(1) VALUE ' '.
   02 SQL-WAIT-FLAG        PIC X(1) VALUE ' '.
   02 SQL-RELEASE-FLAG     PIC X(1) VALUE ' '.
   02 SQL-VPARM-IND        PIC X(1) VALUE '0'.
   02 SQL-AUXPARM-IND      PIC X(1) VALUE 'I'.
   02 SQL-ERROR-FLAG       PIC X(1) VALUE ' '.
   02 SQL-DESCFLAG         PIC X(1) VALUE ' '.
   02 SQL-MAILBOX-LEN      PIC S9(9) COMP VALUE +687.
   02 SQL-RELEASNO         PIC X(1) VALUE '4'.
   02 SQL-CISL             PIC X(1).
   02 SQL-DATE             PIC X(1) VALUE ' '.
   02 SQL-TIME             PIC X(1) VALUE ' '.
   02 SQL-FEEDBACK         PIC X(4).
   02 SQL-RDIEXT-PTR       PIC X(4).
   02 SQL-EXTENSION        PIC X(4).
01 SQL-DA2-STRUCT2.
   02 SQL-DA-ID            PIC X(8) VALUE 'SQLDA '.
   02 SQL-DA-BC            PIC S9(9) COMP VALUE +456.
   02 SQL-DA-N             PIC S9(4) COMP VALUE +10.
   02 SQL-DA-D             PIC S9(4) COMP VALUE +10.
   02 SQL-DATA-TYPE1       PIC S9(4) COMP VALUE +452.
   02 SQL-LEN1             PIC S9(4) COMP.
   02 SQL-DATA-PTR1        PIC X(4).
   02 SQL-INFO-PTR1        PIC X(4).
   02 SQL-NAME1            PIC X(32).
   02 SQL-DATA-TYPE2       PIC S9(4) COMP VALUE +452.
```

```
02  SQL-LEN2             PIC S9(4) COMP.
02  SQL-DATA-PTR2        PIC X(4).
02  SQL-INFO-PTR2        PIC X(4).
02  SQL-NAME2            PIC X(32).
02  SQL-DATA-TYPE3       PIC S9(4) COMP VALUE +452.
02  SQL-LEN3             PIC S9(4) COMP.
02  SQL-DATA-PTR3        PIC X(4).
02  SQL-INFO-PTR3        PIC X(4).
02  SQL-NAME3            PIC X(32).
02  SQL-DATA-TYPE4       PIC S9(4) COMP VALUE +452.
02  SQL-LEN4             PIC S9(4) COMP.
02  SQL-DATA-PTR4        PIC X(4).
02  SQL-INFO-PTR4        PIC X(4).
02  SQL-NAME4            PIC X(32).
02  SQL-DATA-TYPE5       PIC S9(4) COMP VALUE +452.
02  SQL-LEN5             PIC S9(4) COMP.
02  SQL-DATA-PTR5        PIC X(4).
02  SQL-INFO-PTR5        PIC X(4).
02  SQL-NAME5            PIC X(32).
02  SQL-DATA-TYPE6       PIC S9(4) COMP VALUE +452.
02  SQL-LEN6             PIC S9(4) COMP.
02  SQL-DATA-PTR6        PIC X(4).
02  SQL-INFO-PTR6        PIC X(4).
02  SQL-NAME6            PIC X(32).
02  SQL-DATA-TYPE7       PIC S9(4) COMP VALUE +452.
02  SQL-LEN7             PIC S9(4) COMP.
02  SQL-DATA-PTR7        PIC X(4).
02  SQL-INFO-PTR7        PIC X(4).
02  SQL-NAME7            PIC X(32).
02  SQL-DATA-TYPE8       PIC S9(4) COMP VALUE +452.
02  SQL-LEN8             PIC S9(4) COMP.
```

```
02  SQL-DATA-PTR8         PIC X(4).
02  SQL-INFO-PTR8         PIC X(4).
02  SQL-NAME8             PIC X(32).
02  SQL-DATA-TYPE9        PIC S9(4) COMP VALUE +496.
02  SQL-LEN9              PIC S9(4) COMP.
02  SQL-DATA-PTR9         PIC X(4).
02  SQL-INFO-PTR9         PIC X(4).
02  SQL-NAME9             PIC X(32).
02  SQL-DATA-TYPE10       PIC S9(4) COMP VALUE +452.
02  SQL-LEN10             PIC S9(4) COMP.
02  SQL-DATA-PTR10        PIC X(4).
02  SQL-INFO-PTR10        PIC X(4).
02  SQL-NAME10            PIC X(32).
01  SQL-ADDR-RDIIN2       PIC S9(9) COMP.
01  SQL-RDIIN2.
02  SQL-CALLTYPE          PIC S9(4) COMP VALUE +30.
02  SQL-AUTHOR            PIC X(8) VALUE 'HT    '.
02  SQL-PROG-NAME-LEN     PIC S9(4) COMP VALUE +6.
02  SQL-PROG-NAME-VAL     PIC X(8) VALUE 'HT0010'.
02  SQL-SECTION-NUM       PIC S9(4) COMP VALUE +2.
02  SQL-CLASS-SECTION     PIC S9(4) COMP VALUE +0.
02  SQL-CODEPTR           PIC X(4).
02  SQL-VPARAMPTR         PIC X(4).
02  SQL-AUXPARAMPTR       PIC X(4).
02  SQL-TIE-PTR           PIC X(4).
02  SQL-SPECIAL-CALL      PIC X(1) VALUE ' '.
02  SQL-CALL-FLAG         PIC X(1) VALUE ' '.
02  SQL-WAIT-FLAG         PIC X(1) VALUE ' '.
02  SQL-RELEASE-FLAG      PIC X(1) VALUE ' '.
02  SQL-VPARM-IND         PIC X(1) VALUE 'I'.
02  SQL-AUXPARM-IND       PIC X(1) VALUE ' '.
```

```
    02  SQL-ERROR-FLAG       PIC X(1) VALUE ' '.
    02  SQL-DESCFLAG         PIC X(1) VALUE ' '.
    02  SQL-MAILBOX-LEN      PIC S9(9) COMP VALUE +709.
    02  SQL-RELEASNO         PIC X(1) VALUE '4'.
    02  SQL-CISL             PIC X(1).
    02  SQL-DATE             PIC X(1) VALUE ' '.
    02  SQL-TIME             PIC X(1) VALUE ' '.
    02  SQL-FEEDBACK         PIC X(4).
    02  SQL-RDIEXT-PTR       PIC X(4).
    02  SQL-EXTENSION        PIC X(4).
01  SQL-DA3-STRUCT2.
    02  SQL-DA-ID            PIC X(8) VALUE 'SQLDA   '.
    02  SQL-DA-BC            PIC S9(9) COMP VALUE +456.
    02  SQL-DA-N             PIC S9(4) COMP VALUE +10.
    02  SQL-DA-D             PIC S9(4) COMP VALUE +10.
    02  SQL-DATA-TYPE1       PIC S9(4) COMP VALUE +452.
    02  SQL-LEN1             PIC S9(4) COMP.
    02  SQL-DATA-PTR1        PIC X(4).
    02  SQL-INFO-PTR1        PIC X(4).
    02  SQL-NAME1            PIC X(32).
    02  SQL-DATA-TYPE2       PIC S9(4) COMP VALUE +452.
    02  SQL-LEN2             PIC S9(4) COMP.
    02  SQL-DATA-PTR2        PIC X(4).
    02  SQL-INFO-PTR2        PIC X(4).
    02  SQL-NAME2            PIC X(32).
    02  SQL-DATA-TYPE3       PIC S9(4) COMP VALUE +452.
    02  SQL-LEN3             PIC S9(4) COMP.
    02  SQL-DATA-PTR3        PIC X(4).
    02  SQL-INFO-PTR3        PIC X(4).
    02  SQL-NAME3            PIC X(32).
    02  SQL-DATA-TYPE4       PIC S9(4) COMP VALUE +452.
```

323

```
02  SQL-LEN4            PIC  S9(4)  COMP.
02  SQL-DATA-PTR4       PIC  X(4).
02  SQL-INFO-PTR4       PIC  X(4).
02  SQL-NAME4           PIC  X(32).
02  SQL-DATA-TYPE5      PIC  S9(4)  COMP  VALUE  +452.
02  SQL-LEN5            PIC  S9(4)  COMP.
02  SQL-DATA-PTR5       PIC  X(4).
02  SQL-INFO-PTR5       PIC  X(4).
02  SQL-NAME5           PIC  X(32).
02  SQL-DATA-TYPE6      PIC  S9(4)  COMP  VALUE  +452.
02  SQL-LEN6            PIC  S9(4)  COMP.
02  SQL-DATA-PTR6       PIC  X(4).
02  SQL-INFO-PTR6       PIC  X(4).
02  SQL-NAME6           PIC  X(32).
02  SQL-DATA-TYPE7      PIC  S9(4)  COMP  VALUE  +452.
02  SQL-LEN7            PIC  S9(4)  COMP.
02  SQL-DATA-PTR7       PIC  X(4).
02  SQL-INFO-PTR7       PIC  X(4).
02  SQL-NAME7           PIC  X(32).
02  SQL-DATA-TYPE8      PIC  S9(4)  COMP  VALUE  +496.
02  SQL-LEN8            PIC  S9(4)  COMP.
02  SQL-DATA-PTR8       PIC  X(4).
02  SQL-INFO-PTR8       PIC  X(4).
02  SQL-NAME8           PIC  X(32).
02  SQL-DATA-TYPE9      PIC  S9(4)  COMP  VALUE  +452.
02  SQL-LEN9            PIC  S9(4)  COMP.
02  SQL-DATA-PTR9       PIC  X(4).
02  SQL-INFO-PTR9       PIC  X(4).
02  SQL-NAME9           PIC  X(32).
02  SQL-DATA-TYPE10     PIC  S9(4)  COMP  VALUE  +452.
02  SQL-LEN10           PIC  S9(4)  COMP.
```

```
    02 SQL-DATA-PTR10        PIC X(4).
    02 SQL-INFO-PTR10        PIC X(4).
    02 SQL-NAME10            PIC X(32).
 01 SQL-ADDR-RDIIN3          PIC S9(9) COMP.
 01 SQL-RDIIN3.
    02 SQL-CALLTYPE          PIC S9(4) COMP VALUE +30.
    02 SQL-AUTHOR            PIC X(8) VALUE 'HT     '.
    02 SQL-PROG-NAME-LEN     PIC S9(4) COMP VALUE +6.
    02 SQL-PROG-NAME-VAL     PIC X(8) VALUE 'HT0010'.
    02 SQL-SECTION-NUM       PIC S9(4) COMP VALUE +3.
    02 SQL-CLASS-SECTION     PIC S9(4) COMP VALUE +0.
    02 SQL-CODEPTR           PIC X(4).
    02 SQL-VPARAMPTR         PIC X(4).
    02 SQL-AUXPARAMPTR       PIC X(4).
    02 SQL-TIE-PTR           PIC X(4).
    02 SQL-SPECIAL-CALL      PIC X(1) VALUE ' '.
    02 SQL-CALL-FLAG         PIC X(1) VALUE ' '.
    02 SQL-WAIT-FLAG         PIC X(1) VALUE ' '.
    02 SQL-RELEASE-FLAG      PIC X(1) VALUE ' '.
    02 SQL-VPARM-IND         PIC X(1) VALUE 'I'.
    02 SQL-AUXPARM-IND       PIC X(1) VALUE ' '.
    02 SQL-ERROR-FLAG        PIC X(1) VALUE ' '.
    02 SQL-DESCFLAG          PIC X(1) VALUE ' '.
    02 SQL-MAILBOX-LEN       PIC S9(9) COMP VALUE +709.
    02 SQL-RELEASNO          PIC X(1) VALUE '4'.
    02 SQL-CISL              PIC X(1).
    02 SQL-DATE              PIC X(1) VALUE ' '.
    02 SQL-TIME              PIC X(1) VALUE ' '.
    02 SQL-FEEDBACK          PIC X(4).
    02 SQL-RDIEXT-PTR        PIC X(4).
    02 SQL-EXTENSION         PIC X(4).
```

```
01  SQL-DA4-STRUCT2.
    02  SQL-DA-ID              PIC X(8)  VALUE 'SQLDA   '.
    02  SQL-DA-BC              PIC S9(9) COMP VALUE +60.
    02  SQL-DA-N               PIC S9(4) COMP VALUE +1.
    02  SQL-DA-D               PIC S9(4) COMP VALUE +1.
    02  SQL-DATA-TYPE1         PIC S9(4) COMP VALUE +452.
    02  SQL-LEN1               PIC S9(4) COMP.
    02  SQL-DATA-PTR1          PIC X(4).
    02  SQL-INFO-PTR1          PIC X(4).
    02  SQL-NAME1              PIC X(32).
01  SQL-ADDR-RDIIN4           PIC S9(9) COMP.
01  SQL-RDIIN4.
    02  SQL-CALLTYPE           PIC S9(4) COMP VALUE +30.
    02  SQL-AUTHOR             PIC X(8)  VALUE 'HT      '.
    02  SQL-PROG-NAME-LEN      PIC S9(4) COMP VALUE +6.
    02  SQL-PROG-NAME-VAL      PIC X(8)  VALUE 'HT0010'.
    02  SQL-SECTION-NUM        PIC S9(4) COMP VALUE +4.
    02  SQL-CLASS-SECTION      PIC S9(4) COMP VALUE +0.
    02  SQL-CODEPTR            PIC X(4).
    02  SQL-VPARAMPTR          PIC X(4).
    02  SQL-AUXPARAMPTR        PIC X(4).
    02  SQL-TIE-PTR            PIC X(4).
    02  SQL-SPECIAL-CALL       PIC X(1)  VALUE ' '.
    02  SQL-CALL-FLAG          PIC X(1)  VALUE ' '.
    02  SQL-WAIT-FLAG          PIC X(1)  VALUE ' '.
    02  SQL-RELEASE-FLAG       PIC X(1)  VALUE ' '.
    02  SQL-VPARM-IND          PIC X(1)  VALUE 'I'.
    02  SQL-AUXPARM-IND        PIC X(1)  VALUE ' '.
    02  SQL-ERROR-FLAG         PIC X(1)  VALUE ' '.
    02  SQL-DESCFLAG           PIC X(1)  VALUE ' '.
    02  SQL-MAILBOX-LEN        PIC S9(9) COMP VALUE +231.
```

```
       02  SQL-RELEASNO              PIC X(1) VALUE '4'.
       02  SQL-CISL                  PIC X(1).
       02  SQL-DATE                  PIC X(1) VALUE ' '.
       02  SQL-TIME                  PIC X(1) VALUE ' '.
       02  SQL-FEEDBACK              PIC X(4).
       02  SQL-RDIEXT-PTR            PIC X(4).
       02  SQL-EXTENSION             PIC X(4).
*****      END OF SQL/DATA SYSTEM DESCRIPTION ENTRIES
*****      THE PRECEDING COBOL SENTENCES WERE CREATED BY
*****      THE SQL/DATA SYSTEM PREPROCESSOR

********  SQL/DS STATEMENT:
*****EXEC SQL END DECLARE SECTION END-EXEC.
     SKIP1
********  SQL/DS STATEMENT:
*****EXEC SQL INCLUDE SQLCA END-EXEC.

*****  SQLCA STRUCTURE FOR SQL/DATA SYSTEM.
   01  SQLCA.
       05  SQLCAID                   PIC X(8) VALUE 'SQLCA   '.
       05  SQLCABC                   PIC S9(9) COMP VALUE +136.
       05  SQLCODE                   PIC S9(9) COMP.
       05  SQLERRM.
           49  SQLERRML              PIC S9(4) COMP.
           49  SQLERRMC              PIC X(70).
       05  SQLERRP                   PIC X(8).
       05  SQLERRD OCCURS 6 TIMES PIC S9(9) COMP.
       05  SQLWARN.
           10  SQLWARN0              PIC X(1).
           10  SQLWARN1              PIC X(1).
           10  SQLWARN2              PIC X(1).
```

327

```
        10  SQLWARN3              PIC X(1).
        10  SQLWARN4              PIC X(1).
        10  SQLWARN5              PIC X(1).
        10  SQLWARN6              PIC X(1).
        10  SQLWARN7              PIC X(1).
        10  SQLWARN8              PIC X(1).
        10  SQLWARN9              PIC X(1).
        10  SQLWARNA              PIC X(1).
     05  SQLEXT                   PIC X(5).

     SKIP3
 01  WORK-STORAGE-END             PIC X(24)
                 VALUE '****WORK-STORAGE-END****'.
     EJECT
 PROCEDURE DIVISION.

 ********  SQL/DATA SYSTEM DYNAMIC BINDING SENTENCES
 *****   BEGIN HERE:
     SQL-BIND.
         MOVE 1 TO SQL-BIND-FLAG.
         MOVE LOW-VALUES TO SQLTIE.
         MOVE LOW-VALUES TO SQL-RDIEXT.
         CALL 'ARIPADR1' USING SQL-DA1-STRUCT1
                 SQL-NULL
                 SQL-NULL
                 SQL-NULL
                 SQL-NULL
                 SQL-NULL
                 SQL-NULL
                 SQL-NULL
                 SQL-NULL
```

```cobol
                SQL-NULL
                SQL-NULL.
          CALL 'ARIPADR' USING SQL-DA1-STRUCT1
                SERIALNO
                HARDTYPE
                BRANCH
                DEPT
                LOC
                VENDOR
                MANUF
                HPURDATE
                HARDCOST
                SERVNO.
          MOVE +15 TO SQL-LEN1 IN SQL-DA1-STRUCT1.
          MOVE +10 TO SQL-LEN2 IN SQL-DA1-STRUCT1.
          MOVE +3 TO SQL-LEN3 IN SQL-DA1-STRUCT1.
          MOVE +10 TO SQL-LEN4 IN SQL-DA1-STRUCT1.
          MOVE +10 TO SQL-LEN5 IN SQL-DA1-STRUCT1.
          MOVE +10 TO SQL-LEN6 IN SQL-DA1-STRUCT1.
          MOVE +10 TO SQL-LEN7 IN SQL-DA1-STRUCT1.
          MOVE +10 TO SQL-LEN8 IN SQL-DA1-STRUCT1.
          MOVE +0 TO SQL-LEN9 IN SQL-DA1-STRUCT1.
          MOVE +15 TO SQL-LEN10 IN SQL-DA1-STRUCT1.
          CALL 'ARIPADR1' USING SQL-DA1-STRUCT2
                SQL-NULL.
          CALL 'ARIPADR' USING SQL-DA1-STRUCT2
                SERIALNO.
          MOVE +15 TO SQL-LEN1 IN SQL-DA1-STRUCT2.
          CALL 'ARIPADR2' USING SQL-ADDR-RDIIN1 SQL-RDIIN1.
          CALL 'ARIPADR2' USING SQL-CODEPTR IN
                SQL-RDIIN1 SQLCA.
```

```
       CALL 'ARIPADR2' USING SQL-TIE-PTR IN
             SQL-RDIIN1 SQLTIE.
       CALL 'ARIPADR2' USING SQL-RDIEXT-PTR IN
             SQL-RDIIN1 SQL-RDIEXT.
       CALL 'ARIPADR2' USING SQL-VPARAMPTR IN SQL-RDIIN1
             SQL-DA1-STRUCT1.
       CALL 'ARIPADR2' USING SQL-AUXPARAMPTR IN SQL-RDIIN1
             SQL-DA1-STRUCT2.
       MOVE LOW-VALUES TO SQL-EXTENSION IN SQL-RDIIN1.
       CALL 'ARIPADR1' USING SQL-DA2-STRUCT2
             SQL-NULL
             SQL-NULL
             SQL-NULL
             SQL-NULL
             SQL-NULL
             SQL-NULL
             SQL-NULL
             SQL-NULL
             SQL-NULL
             SQL-NULL.
       CALL 'ARIPADR' USING SQL-DA2-STRUCT2
             SERIALNO
             HARDTYPE
             BRANCH
             DEPT
             LOC
             VENDOR
             MANUF
             HPURDATE
             HARDCOST
             SERVNO.
```

```
MOVE +15 TO SQL-LEN1 IN SQL-DA2-STRUCT2.
MOVE +10 TO SQL-LEN2 IN SQL-DA2-STRUCT2.
MOVE +3 TO SQL-LEN3 IN SQL-DA2-STRUCT2.
MOVE +10 TO SQL-LEN4 IN SQL-DA2-STRUCT2.
MOVE +10 TO SQL-LEN5 IN SQL-DA2-STRUCT2.
MOVE +10 TO SQL-LEN6 IN SQL-DA2-STRUCT2.
MOVE +10 TO SQL-LEN7 IN SQL-DA2-STRUCT2.
MOVE +10 TO SQL-LEN8 IN SQL-DA2-STRUCT2.
MOVE +0 TO SQL-LEN9 IN SQL-DA2-STRUCT2.
MOVE +15 TO SQL-LEN10 IN SQL-DA2-STRUCT2.
CALL 'ARIPADR2' USING SQL-ADDR-RDIIN2 SQL-RDIIN2.
CALL 'ARIPADR2' USING SQL-CODEPTR IN
           SQL-RDIIN2 SQLCA.
CALL 'ARIPADR2' USING SQL-TIE-PTR IN
           SQL-RDIIN2 SQLTIE.
CALL 'ARIPADR2' USING SQL-RDIEXT-PTR IN
           SQL-RDIIN2 SQL-RDIEXT.
CALL'ARIPADR2' USING SQL-VPARAMPTR IN SQL-RDIIN2
           SQL-DA2-STRUCT2.
MOVE LOW-VALUES TO SQL-AUXPARAMPTR IN SQL-RDIIN2.
MOVE LOW-VALUES TO SQL-EXTENSION IN SQL-RDIIN2.
CALL 'ARIPADR1' USING SQL-DA3-STRUCT2
           SQL-NULL
           SQL-NULL
           SQL-NULL
           SQL-NULL
           SQL-NULL
           SQL-NULL
           SQL-NULL
           SQL-NULL
           SQL-NULL
```

331

```
        SQL-NULL.
CALL    'ARIPADR' USING SQL-DA3-STRUCT2
        HARDTYPE
        BRANCH
        DEPT
        LOC
        VENDOR
        MANUF
        HPURDATE
        HARDCOST
        SERVNO
        SERIALNO.
MOVE +10 TO SQL-LEN1 IN SQL-DA3-STRUCT2.
MOVE +3 TO SQL-LEN2 IN SQL-DA3-STRUCT2.
MOVE +10 TO SQL-LEN3 IN SQL-DA3-STRUCT2.
MOVE +10 TO SQL-LEN4 IN SQL-DA3-STRUCT2.
MOVE +10 TO SQL-LEN5 IN SQL-DA3-STRUCT2.
MOVE +10 TO SQL-LEN6 IN SQL-DA3-STRUCT2.
MOVE +10 TO SQL-LEN7 IN SQL-DA3-STRUCT2.
MOVE +0 TO SQL-LEN8 IN SQL-DA3-STRUCT2.
MOVE +15 TO SQL-LEN9 IN SQL-DA3-STRUCT2.
MOVE +15 TO SQL-LEN10 IN SQL-DA3-STRUCT2.
CALL    'ARIPADR2' USING SQL-ADDR-RDIIN3 SQL-RDIIN3.
CALL    'ARIPADR2' USING SQL-CODEPTR IN
        SQL-RDIIN3 SQLCA.
CALL    'ARIPADR2' USING SQL-TIE-PTR IN
        SQL-RDIIN3 SQLTIE.
CALL    'ARIPADR2' USING SQL-RDIEXT-PTR IN
        SQL-RDIIN3 SQL-RDIEXT.
CALL    'ARIPADR2' USING SQL-VPARAMPTR IN SQL-RDIIN3
        SQL-DA3-STRUCT2.
```

```
        MOVE LOW-VALUES TO SQL-AUXPARAMPTR IN SQL-RDIIN3.
        MOVE LOW-VALUES TO SQL-EXTENSION IN SQL-RDIIN3.
        CALL 'ARIPADR1' USING SQL-DA4-STRUCT2
            SQL-NULL.
        CALL 'ARIPADR' USING SQL-DA4-STRUCT2
            SERIALNO.
        MOVE +15 TO SQL-LEN1 IN SQL-DA4-STRUCT2.
        CALL 'ARIPADR2' USING SQL-ADDR-RDIIN4 SQL-RDIIN4.
        CALL 'ARIPADR2' USING SQL-CODEPTR IN
            SQL-RDIIN4 SQLCA.
        CALL 'ARIPADR2' USING SQL-TIE-PTR IN
            SQL-RDIIN4 SQLTIE.
        CALL 'ARIPADR2' USING SQL-RDIEXT-PTR IN
            SQL-RDIIN4 SQL-RDIEXT.
        CALL 'ARIPADR2' USING SQL-VPARAMPTR IN SQL-RDIIN4
            SQL-DA4-STRUCT2.
        MOVE LOW-VALUES TO SQL-AUXPARAMPTR IN SQL-RDIIN4.
        MOVE LOW-VALUES TO SQL-EXTENSION IN SQL-RDIIN4.
    END-SQL-BIND.
   *****    THE PRECEDING COBOL SENTENCES WERE CREATED BY
   ******** THE SQL/DATA SYSTEM PREPROCESSOR

050-MAINLINE.
***********************************************************************
*   CONTROLS THE PROCESSING OF THE PROGRAM.                           *
*                                                                     *
***********************************************************************

    PERFORM 100-HOUSEKEEPING THRU 100-EXIT.

    MOVE SPACES TO PSELECT-INDEX
                   PSELECT-OPT.
```

333

```
            MOVE PSELECT-VN-INDEX TO ISPF-CURSOR.

            PERFORM 200-PROCESS THRU 200-EXIT
                UNTIL CANCELLED.

            MOVE PSELECT-VN-INDEX TO ISPF-CURSOR.

            PERFORM 950-TERMINATION THRU 950-EXIT.

              GOBACK.
        050-EXIT. EXIT.
        EJECT
        100-HOUSEKEEPING.
       *****************************************************************************
       *     INITIALIZE FIELDS, VDEFINE DIALOG VARIABLES                          *
       *****************************************************************************

            MOVE '100-'                 TO  CURRENT-PARAGRAPH.
            MOVE LIT-C                   TO  SQL-ISL.

       *     STANDARD ROUTINE TO GET DATES AND TIMES AND USER IDS
       *
       *
            COPY GETSYS.
       *
            MOVE ZDATE                   TO  WS-RUN-DATE.
            MOVE ZTIME                   TO  WS-RUN-TIME.
            MOVE WHEN-COMPILED           TO  WHEN-COMPILED-HOLD.
            MOVE WHEN-COMPILED-HOLD      TO  WHEN-COMPILED-EDIT.
            MOVE MSG-HT001               TO  ISPF-MSG.

            PERFORM 110-GET-VARS THRU 110-EXIT
                VARYING SUB FROM 1 BY 1
       *
```

```cobol
                UNTIL SUB GREATER PSELECT-MAX.

        PERFORM 115-GET-VARS THRU 115-EXIT
            VARYING SUB FROM 1 BY 1
                UNTIL SUB GREATER PHARDW-MAX.

            MOVE '    HARDWARE TABLE MAINTENANCE    ' TO PSELECT-SUBHEAD.

            MOVE ' HARDWARE SERIAL NUMBER ' TO PSELECT-DESCR.

        100-EXIT. EXIT.

        110-GET-VARS.
       ****************************************************************
       **  CALL ISPF TO ESTABLISH VARIABLE ADDRESSABILITY            **
       **                                                            **
       ****************************************************************

            CALL 'ISPLINK' USING ISPF-VDEFINE
                            PSELECT-VARIABLE-NAME (SUB)
                            PSELECT-VARIABLE-VALUE (SUB)
                            ISPF-CHAR
                            PSELECT-VARIABLE-SIZE (SUB).

            IF RETURN-CODE EQUAL ZEROES
                NEXT SENTENCE
            ELSE
                MOVE RETURN-CODE        TO SAVECC
                MOVE MSG-ISP001P        TO ISPF-MSG
                MOVE LIT-YES            TO CANCELLED-SW
                MOVE 99                 TO SUB.
```

335

```
110-EXIT. EXIT.
EJECT
115-GET-VARS.
****************************************************************************
**   CALL ISPF TO ESTABLISH VARIABLE ADDRESSABILITY                    *  *
****************************************************************************
     CALL 'ISPLINK' USING ISPF-VDEFINE
                          PHARDW-VARIABLE-NAME (SUB)
                          PHARDW-VARIABLE-VALUE (SUB)
                          ISPF-CHAR
                          PHARDW-VARIABLE-SIZE (SUB).

     IF RETURN-CODE EQUAL ZEROES
         NEXT SENTENCE
     ELSE
         MOVE RETURN-CODE      TO SAVECC
         MOVE MSG-ISP001P      TO ISPF-MSG
         MOVE LIT-YES          TO CANCELLED-SW
         MOVE 99               TO SUB.

115-EXIT. EXIT.
EJECT
200-PROCESS.
****************************************************************************
* DISPLAY HT00101 FOR HARDWARE SERIAL NUMBER ENTRY AND OPTION
*    FOR ADD, CHANGE, OR DELETE
****************************************************************************
     CALL 'ISPLINK' USING ISPF-DISPLAY
                          PSELECT-PANEL
```

```
                    ISPF-MSG
                    ISPF-CURSOR.

    IF RETURN-CODE EQUAL ZERO
        MOVE MSG-HT001        TO ISPF-MSG
        MOVE SPACE            TO ISPF-CURSOR
        PERFORM 210-EDIT-FIRST-SCREEN THRU 210-EXIT
    ELSE
    IF RETURN-CODE EQUAL 8
        MOVE MSG-HT001        TO ISPF-MSG
        MOVE SPACE            TO ISPF-CURSOR
        MOVE 'Y'              TO CANCELLED-SW
    ELSE
        MOVE RETURN-CODE      TO SAVECC
        MOVE MSG-ISP001       TO ISPF-MSG
        MOVE 'Y'              TO CANCELLED-SW.

200-EXIT. EXIT.

*   PSELECT-INDEX IS THE INDEX INTO THE PARTICULAR TABLE WE
*   ARE PERFORMING MAINTENANCE ON.
*
210-EDIT-FIRST-SCREEN.

    IF PSELECT-INDEX = SPACES
        MOVE MSG-HT001G  TO ISPF-MSG
        MOVE PSELECT-VN-INDEX TO ISPF-CURSOR
        GO TO 210-EXIT.
```

337

```
        IF PSELECT-OPT = SPACES
            MOVE MSG-HT001G     TO ISPF-MSG
            MOVE PSELECT-VN-OPT TO ISPF-CURSOR
            GO TO 210-EXIT.

        MOVE PSELECT-INDEX TO SERIALNO.

*******  SQL/DS STATEMENT:
*****EXEC SQL
*****      SELECT SERIALNO, HARDTYPE, BRANCH, DEPT,
*****             LOC, VENDOR, MANUF, HPURDATE, HARDCOST,
*****             SERVNO
*****      INTO :SERIALNO, :HARDTYPE, :BRANCH, :DEPT,
*****           :LOC, :VENDOR, :MANUF, :HPURDATE, :HARDCOST,
*****           :SERVNO
*****      FROM HT.HARDWARE
*****      WHERE SERIALNO = :SERIALNO
*****END-EXEC.
      PERFORM SQL-BIND UNTIL SQL-DONE-ONCE
      MOVE ZERO TO SQL-RDIEXTA(1)
      MOVE SQL-ISL TO SQL-CISL IN SQL-RDIIN1
      CALL 'ARIPRDI' USING SQL-ADDR-RDIIN1.
*****     THE PRECEDING COBOL SENTENCES WERE CREATED BY THE
*******  SQL/DATA SYSTEM PREPROCESSOR


        IF SQLCODE = ZEROS
            IF PSELECT-OPT = 'C'
                MOVE PHARDW-VN-HARDTYPE TO ISPF-CURSOR
```

338

```
        PERFORM 215-MOVE-SQL-DIALOG THRU 215-EXIT
        PERFORM 230-CHANGE-ROW THRU 230-EXIT
        MOVE 'N'                TO CANCELLED-SW
    ELSE

    IF PSELECT-OPT = 'D'
        MOVE SPACES             TO ISPF-CURSOR
        PERFORM 215-MOVE-SQL-DIALOG THRU 215-EXIT
        PERFORM 240-DELETE-ROW THRU 240-EXIT
        MOVE 'N'                TO CANCELLED-SW
    ELSE

    IF PSELECT-OPT = 'A'
        MOVE MSG-HT001A      TO ISPF-MSG
        MOVE PSELECT-VN-INDEX TO ISPF-CURSOR
    ELSE

        MOVE MSG-HT001M      TO ISPF-MSG
        MOVE PSELECT-VN-OPT TO ISPF-CURSOR

ELSE
    IF SQLCODE = 100
        IF PSELECT-OPT = 'A'
            MOVE PSELECT-INDEX TO PHARDW-SERNUM
            MOVE SPACES     TO PHARDW-HARDTYPE
                               PHARDW-BRA
                               PHARDW-DEPT
                               PHARDW-LOC
                               PHARDW-VENDOR
                               PHARDW-MANUF
                               PHARDW-HPURDATE
                               PHARDW-CONNUM
            MOVE ZEROES    TO PHARDW-HARDCOST
            MOVE PHARDW-VN-SERNUM  TO ISPF-CURSOR
```

339

```
              PERFORM 220-ADD-ROW THRU 220-EXIT
                 UNTIL CANCELLED
              MOVE 'N'                   TO CANCELLED-SW
              MOVE PSELECT-VN-INDEX TO ISPF-CURSOR
           ELSE
              IF PSELECT-OPT = 'C' OR 'D'
                 MOVE MSG-HT001B    TO ISPF-MSG
                 MOVE PSELECT-VN-INDEX TO ISPF-CURSOR
              ELSE
                 MOVE MSG-HT001M    TO ISPF-MSG
                 MOVE PSELECT-VN-OPT TO ISPF-CURSOR
           ELSE
              MOVE SQLCODE TO SAVECC
              MOVE MSG-SQL002A  TO ISPF-MSG
              MOVE PSELECT-VN-INDEX TO ISPF-CURSOR.

       210-EXIT. EXIT.

       215-MOVE-SQL-DIALOG.

           MOVE SERIALNO        TO    PHARDW-SERNUM.
           MOVE HARDTYPE        TO    PHARDW-HARDTYPE.
           MOVE BRANCH          TO    PHARDW-BRA.
           MOVE DEPT            TO    PHARDW-DEPT.
           MOVE LOC             TO    PHARDW-LOC.
           MOVE VENDOR          TO    PHARDW-VENDOR.
           MOVE MANUF           TO    PHARDW-MANUF.
           MOVE HPURDATE        TO    PHARDW-HPURDATE.
           MOVE HARDCOST        TO    PHARDW-HARDCOST.
           MOVE SERVNO          TO    PHARDW-CONNUM.
```

```
215-EXIT.  EXIT.
EJECT

220-ADD-ROW.

    MOVE 'N'                        TO SUCCESSFUL-SW
                                       CANCELLED-SW.

    CALL 'ISPLINK' USING ISPF-DISPLAY
                         PHARDW-PANEL
                         ISPF-MSG
                         ISPF-CURSOR.

    IF RETURN-CODE EQUAL ZERO
        MOVE MSG-HT001              TO ISPF-MSG
        MOVE PHARDW-VN-SERNUM       TO ISPF-CURSOR
        PERFORM 300-EDIT-SECOND-SCREEN THRU 300-EXIT
    ELSE
    IF RETURN-CODE EQUAL 8
        MOVE MSG-HT001              TO ISPF-MSG
        MOVE SPACE                  TO ISPF-CURSOR
        MOVE 'Y'                    TO CANCELLED-SW
    ELSE
        MOVE RETURN-CODE            TO SAVECC
        MOVE MSG-ISP001             TO ISPF-MSG
        MOVE 'Y'                    TO CANCELLED-SW.

    IF SUCCESSFUL
        PERFORM 315-MOVE-DIALOG-SQL THRU 315-EXIT
        PERFORM 320-ADD-TABLE THRU 320-EXIT
        MOVE SPACE                  TO ISPF-CURSOR
```

341

```
        MOVE 'Y'                    TO CANCELLED-SW.
* PUT SUCCESSFUL ADD MESSAGE HERE.

220-EXIT. EXIT.

230-CHANGE-ROW.

    MOVE 'N'                    TO SUCCESSFUL-SW
                                   CANCELLED-SW.

    CALL 'ISPLINK' USING ISPF-DISPLAY
                         PHARDW-PANEL
                         ISPF-MSG
                         ISPF-CURSOR.

    IF RETURN-CODE EQUAL ZERO
        MOVE MSG-HT001          TO ISPF-MSG
        MOVE SPACE              TO ISPF-CURSOR
        PERFORM 300-EDIT-SECOND-SCREEN THRU 300-EXIT
    ELSE
    IF RETURN-CODE EQUAL 8
        MOVE MSG-HT001          TO ISPF-MSG
        MOVE SPACE              TO ISPF-CURSOR
        MOVE 'Y'                TO CANCELLED-SW
    ELSE
        MOVE RETURN-CODE        TO SAVECC
        MOVE MSG-ISP001         TO ISPF-MSG
        MOVE 'Y'                TO CANCELLED-SW.

    IF SUCCESSFUL
        PERFORM 315-MOVE-DIALOG-SQL THRU 315-EXIT
        PERFORM 330-CHANGE-TABLE THRU 330-EXIT.
```

342

```
230-EXIT. EXIT.

240-DELETE-ROW.

    MOVE 'N'                TO SUCCESSFUL-SW
                               CANCELLED-SW.

    MOVE MSG-HT001C         TO ISPF-MSG.

    CALL 'ISPLINK' USING ISPF-DISPLAY
                         PHARDW-PANEL
                         ISPF-MSG
                         ISPF-CURSOR.

    IF RETURN-CODE EQUAL  ZERO
        MOVE MSG-HT001         TO ISPF-MSG
        MOVE SPACE             TO ISPF-CURSOR
        PERFORM 340-DELETE-RECORD THRU 340-EXIT
    ELSE
    IF RETURN-CODE EQUAL  8
        MOVE MSG-HT001         TO ISPF-MSG
        MOVE SPACE             TO ISPF-CURSOR
        MOVE 'Y'               TO CANCELLED-SW
    ELSE
        MOVE RETURN-CODE       TO SAVECC
        MOVE MSG-ISP001        TO ISPF-MSG
        MOVE 'Y'               TO CANCELLED-SW.

240-EXIT. EXIT.
```

```
300-EDIT-SECOND-SCREEN.

    IF  PHARDW-SERNUM = SPACES
        MOVE MSG-HT001G             TO ISPF-MSG
        MOVE PHARDW-VN-SERNUM       TO ISPF-CURSOR
        GO TO 300-EXIT.

    IF  PHARDW-HARDTYPE = SPACES
        MOVE MSG-HT001G             TO ISPF-MSG
        MOVE PHARDW-VN-HARDTYPE     TO ISPF-CURSOR
        GO TO 300-EXIT.

    IF  PHARDW-BRA = SPACES
        MOVE MSG-HT001G             TO ISPF-MSG
        MOVE PHARDW-VN-BRA          TO ISPF-CURSOR
        GO TO 300-EXIT.

    IF  PHARDW-VENDOR = SPACES
        MOVE MSG-HT001G             TO ISPF-MSG
        MOVE PHARDW-VN-VENDOR       TO ISPF-CURSOR
        GO TO 300-EXIT.

    IF  PHARDW-HPURDATE = SPACES
        MOVE MSG-HT001G             TO ISPF-MSG
        MOVE PHARDW-VN-HPURDATE     TO ISPF-CURSOR
        GO TO 300-EXIT.

    IF  PHARDW-CONNUM = SPACES
        MOVE MSG-HT001G             TO ISPF-MSG
        MOVE PHARDW-VN-CONNUM       TO ISPF-CURSOR
        GO TO 300-EXIT.
```

```
    MOVE 'Y'                    TO SUCCESSFUL-SW.

300-EXIT. EXIT.

315-MOVE-DIALOG-SQL.

    MOVE PHARDW-SERNUM          TO SERIALNO.
    MOVE PHARDW-HARDTYPE        TO HARDTYPE.
    MOVE PHARDW-BRA             TO BRANCH.
    MOVE PHARDW-DEPT            TO DEPT.
    MOVE PHARDW-LOC             TO LOC.
    MOVE PHARDW-VENDOR          TO VENDOR.
    MOVE PHARDW-MANUF           TO MANUF.
    MOVE PHARDW-HPURDATE        TO HPURDATE.
    MOVE PHARDW-HARDCOST        TO HARDCOST.
    MOVE PHARDW-CONNUM          TO SERVNO.

315-EXIT. EXIT.

320-ADD-TABLE.

******* SQL/DS STATEMENT:
*****EXEC SQL
*****    INSERT INTO HT.HARDWARE
*****        (SERIALNO, HARDTYPE, BRANCH, DEPT,
*****         LOC, VENDOR, MANUF, HPURDATE, HARDCOST,
*****         SERVNO)
*****    VALUES (:SERIALNO, :HARDTYPE, :BRANCH, :DEPT,
*****         :LOC, :VENDOR, :MANUF, :HPURDATE, :HARDCOST,
*****         :SERVNO)
*****END-EXEC.
```

345

```
        PERFORM SQL-BIND UNTIL SQL-DONE-ONCE
        MOVE ZERO TO SQL-RDIEXTA(1)
        MOVE SQL-ISL TO SQL-CISL IN SQL-RDIIN2
        CALL 'ARIPRDI' USING SQL-ADDR-RDIIN2.
*****     THE PRECEDING COBOL SENTENCES WERE CREATED BY THE
*******   SQL/DATA SYSTEM PREPROCESSOR

      IF SQLCODE = ZEROS                       TO ISPF-MSG
          MOVE MSG-HT001
      ELSE
          MOVE SQLCODE                         TO SAVECC
          MOVE MSG-SQL001S                     TO ISPF-MSG.


  320-EXIT. EXIT.

  330-CHANGE-TABLE.

*******   SQL/DS STATEMENT:
*****EXEC SQL
*****     UPDATE HT.HARDWARE
*****         SET HARDTYPE  = :HARDTYPE,
*****             BRANCH    = :BRANCH,
*****             DEPT      = :DEPT,
*****             LOC       = :LOC,
*****             VENDOR    = :VENDOR,
*****             MANUF     = :MANUF,
*****             HPURDATE  = :HPURDATE,
*****             HARDCOST  = :HARDCOST,
*****             SERVNO    = :SERVNO
```

```
*****          WHERE SERIALNO = :SERIALNO
*****    END-EXEC.
         PERFORM SQL-BIND UNTIL SQL-DONE-ONCE
         MOVE ZERO TO SQL-RDIEXTA(1)
         MOVE SQL-ISL TO SQL-CISL IN SQL-RDIIN3
         CALL 'ARIPRDI' USING SQL-ADDR-RDIIN3.
*****    THE PRECEDING COBOL SENTENCES WERE CREATED BY THE
******** SQL/DATA SYSTEM PREPROCESSOR


         IF SQLCODE = ZEROS
             MOVE MSG-HT001H            TO ISPF-MSG
         ELSE
             MOVE SQLCODE               TO SAVECC
             MOVE MSG-SQL002B           TO ISPF-MSG.


     330-EXIT. EXIT.

     340-DELETE-RECORD.

******** SQL/DS STATEMENT:
******EXEC SQL
*****    DELETE FROM HT.HARDWARE
*****         WHERE SERIALNO = :SERIALNO
*****    END-EXEC.
         PERFORM SQL-BIND UNTIL SQL-DONE-ONCE
         MOVE ZERO TO SQL-RDIEXTA (1)
         MOVE SQL-ISL TO SQL-CISL IN SQL-RDIIN4
         CALL 'ARIPRDI' USING SQL-ADDR-RDIIN4.
*****    THE PRECEDING COBOL SENTENCES WERE CREATED BY THE
******** SQL/DATA SYSTEM PREPROCESSOR
```

```
           IF SQLCODE = ZEROS
               MOVE MSG-HT001D              TO ISPF-MSG
           ELSE
               MOVE SQLCODE                 TO SAVECC
               MOVE MSG-SQL001E             TO ISPF-MSG.

       340-EXIT. EXIT.

       950-TERMINATION.
      ******************************************************************
      *    THIS ROUTINE WILL CLOSE ALL FILES AND CHECK FOR GOOD EOJ.   *
      ******************************************************************

           CALL 'ISPLINK' USING ISPF-SETMSG
                                ISPF-MSG.

           IF NOT CANCELLED
               MOVE ZERO                    TO RETURN-CODE
           ELSE
               MOVE 500                     TO RETURN-CODE.
       950-EXIT. EXIT.
```

Index

DJM&A
Daniel J. Mosley & Associates
10431 Savannah
Frontenac, MO 63131
314-567-0774

Daniel J. Mosley completed his undergraduate work at the University of Missouri-Columbia where he graduated with honors in Psychology in 1973. He received an MS(Research) in Psychology from Saint Louis University in 1977, and completed the requirements for his doctorate degree with the exception of the dissertation.

He was formerly an information systems professional in the publishing, broadcasting, and construction industries and has extensive experience developing and maintaining commercial software applications. His expertise includes Software and System Engineering life cycle Methods, Techniques, and Tools; Business Process Redesign, Information Engineering and Computer Aided Software/Systems Engineering (CASE) technology; Continuous Software Process Improvement, Statistical Quality Control; Software Metrics; the Psychology of Organizational Change Management. He is a noted national lecturer in his areas of expertise.

He held a joint appointment from 1985 to 1992 in the Center for the Study of Data Processing as a Senior Technical Associate and as a faculty member of The School of Technology and Information Management in the School of Engineering and Applied Sciences at Washington University. He taught Professional Development seminars for the Center and taught in both the undergraduate and graduate academic programs. He also directed the Information Engineering area of concentration in the Master of Information Management degree program. He is currently an adjunct faculty member in the MIS Department of the School of Business at Southern Illinois University in Edwardville, IL.

He is a member of Phi Chi, Phi Beta Kappa, Sigma XI, The Data Processing Management Association (DPMA), and a past chair-person and current member of the St. Louis chapter of the Quality Assurance Institute. He is an active participant in the Information Engineering Users Group, and the St. Louis CASE Users Group. He served as the Faculty Advisor for the Washington University Student DPMA Chapter for two years.

He is a contributor to industry publications such as *American Programmer*, *Chief Information Officer Journal*, and *Executive Report: CASE*; is a reviewer for *IEEE Software magazine* and for Prentice-

Hall, Inc. College Technical + Reference Publications; was an organizer, chairperson, and speaker for the ShowCASE Conference Series. He is a frequent presenter at other national and international industry conferences. He is listed in the 1989–90 edition of *Who's Who In The Midwest*, the second edition of *International Leaders In Achievement*, and in the *Washington University Faculty Experts Handbook*.

He is currently Principal of DJM&A Consulting and Training. His firm differentiates itself because of its emphasis in the areas of *Business Process Redesign, Enterprise-level Information Engineering, Software Engineering, Quality Engineering and Computer-Aided Software Engineering (CASE)*. The company's specialty is consulting, and continuing education and training in these areas.

In addition, DJM&A is affiliated with Microcomputer Consulting and Training (MCT) of St. Louis and currently offers PC based training through MCT resources. The MCT affiliation offers significant advantages because the company has physical classroom facilities located in downtown St. Louis (the LaClede Gas Building) that can be conveniently utilized for training purposes. Thus, DJM&A in combination with MCT offers on-site training as well as off-site. The facility is equipped with state of the art 386 level PC workstations and can accommodate 20 attendees for hands-on training, two people per workstation. DJM&A and MCT instructors are available for training which is customized to an individual company's needs. DJM&A and MCT instructors are all highly qualified experts in PC-related training, as well as, mainframe-based training. Computer Aided Software Engineering (CASE) training will be available at the MCT facility in the near future.

DJM&A and MCT also offer consulting in all of the previously mentioned categories. DJM&A and MCT back their offerings (both consulting and training) with a thirty day money back guarantee. If a firm is not satisfied they do not pay! DJM&A and MCT also guarantee the level of quality provided. All personnel are required to be familiar with and implement the Data Processing Management Association (DPMA) Standards of Professional Conduct when representing DJM&A.

Questions regarding DJM&A or MCT and their services, should be directed to Daniel J. Mosley at 314-567-0774. For purposes of timely document exchange, Fax's can be sent to 314-432-6608. Full descriptions of services and references are available upon request. DJM&A and MCT can mail, Fax or send consulting information and seminar descriptions in five and one quarter or three and one half diskettes for Microsoft Word if desired.